SAAB CARS

The Complete Story

SAAB CARS

The Complete Story

LANCE COLE

THE CROWOOD PRESS

First published in 2012 by
The Crowood Press Ltd
Ramsbury, Marlborough
Wiltshire SN8 2HR

www.crowood.com

This impression 2016

British Library Cataloguing-in-Publication Data
A catalogue record for this book is available from the British Library.

ISBN 978 1 84797 398 6

Frontispiece: The Spirit of Saab: Modern branding with the original style captured by the official Saab 'frog' paint sample used by Saab dealers, which became a 'must have' Saab enthusiasts' accessory. (Robin Morley/Lance Cole)
Main cover photo: Chris Hull's Saab 93 makes the most of the sun at the Swedish Car Day 2010.

Typeset by Shane O'Dwyer, Swindon, Wiltshire

Printed and bound in India by Replika Press Pvt. Ltd.

DEDICATION

For my children, **EMILY** and **JACK**, as always.

And for all the people of **SAAB**.

ACKNOWLEDGEMENTS

I HAVE RECEIVED KIND help from a number of people during the research for this book. Many have been generous with their time and memories. Saab and the Saab Museum must take pride of place for their enthusiasm, great kindness and various permissions. My thanks to the following significant research contributors:

Saab Museum, Saab staff, veterans and others: Peter Backström; Bjorn Envall; Per-Borj Elg; Gunnel Eckberg; the late Robert Sinclair; Siggvard and Peter Johansson and Tage Flodén; Chris Partington; the Saab Veterans Club and archives; the Automotive Historical Society of Sweden; the Wallenberg Foundation.

Saab dealers, clubs, individuals and groups include Saab Great Britain; Saab Australia; Saab Club of America; Vintage Saab Racing Group USA; The Whitequay Group – Saab Newbury/Reading/Southampton and Graham Caddy; The Saab Owners Club UK/Mike Philpott/Richard Elliot/Ellie Wilson; Saab Owners Club France; Saab Club Uruguay; Swedish Day UK Robin Morley and Alex Rankin; Etienne Morsa; Alain Rosset; Joel Durand; Jean Francois Bouvard; Steve Wade 'Swade' Trollhättan/Saabs United/InsideSaab.com; Drew. Bedelph; Chris Day; Alan Sutcliffe; Dave Dallimore; Gary Stottler; Stefan Vaapa; Henk Ossendrijver; Bruce Turk; Dimitri Baumgartner; Martin Lyons; Jerry Peck.

Media include Steve Cropley; Hilton Holloway; Ian Fraser; Mark McCourt; Richard Gunn; Erin Baker and Paul Hudson *The Daily Telegraph Motoring Section*; Imprints; *Autocar*; *Classic & Sports Car*; *Classic Cars*; *Hemmings Auto News*; *Classic Car Weekly*; *Saab Driver*; *Saab Missions*.

The majority of commissioned photographs in this book were taken by the author; other lead contributors include Robin Morley for various Saab events and 9-3 and 9-5 photos, and Jean François Bouvard for Saab 900 classic in France photos and Cabotine. Joel Durand supplied shots of his French Sonett. The photo of Bob Sinclair was taken by Mark J. McCourt for *Sports & Exotic Car*.

Other photographs were kindly supplied under normal editorial rights permission by Saab Auto AB/Swedish Auto N.V. from 1979–2011.

CONTENTS

FOREWORD

WHEN I FIRST STARTED as a motoring journalist in 1993, I was far too junior to be allowed to drive any of the new test cars that were delivered to the magazine. One weekend, however, one of the senior journalists lent me his long-term test car, a 1990 Saab 900 LPT.

I did not know much about Saab or this, seemingly, old-fashioned car. But I can still remember that Sunday afternoon trip from central London into West Sussex. Perhaps my training as a product designer helped, but the more time I spent in the 900, the more it revealed the unique thinking and intelligence that went into virtually every aspect of its conception.

From 1995 I made innumerable overseas press trips and was always struck by the amazing number of Saabs (especially 9000s) in the long-term car park at Heathrow Airport. But then, Saab knew its loyal buyers were inveterate travellers who appreciated a car's ability to soak up long distances while leaving the driver unstressed. It took time to appreciate the deep-seated qualities of a Saab, but once you did, you were usually hooked for life.

After that first encounter with a 900 I took a great interest in Saab and its fortunes. Over the last two decades I have had the privilege of a front row seat as Saab struggled to find its feet first under GM-Wallenberg ownership and then under sole GM rule.

From the UK press launch of the final-edition 9000, through test drives of the extraordinary 'tilting' variable-compression engine to the Monaco launch of the controversial 9-3 Viggen and a secret unveiling of the 2003 9-3, Saab was always a deeply fascinating company on which to report.

Sadly, I was also witness to the slow decline of the company in the 2000s. There were highlights such as unveiling of the stunning Aero-X concept. But there were also head-scratching times, such as the launch of the truck-based, and short-lived, Saab 9-7X SUV.

However, it was the 2005 cancellation of the first 9-5 replacement – as result of the termination of the short lived partnership between GM and Fiat Auto – that marked the point when Saab entered its terminal stage. Although work on the next 9-5 got underway immediately, the new flagship car arrived in the wake of the global credit crunch and GM's bankruptcy forced the American giant to put Saab up for sale.

For a while, it looked as if Saab would be able to reinvent itself as a tiny independent. In 2010 I spent a fascinating evening in Trollhättan talking to Kjell ac Bergström, Saab's engineering genius-in-chief, about the clever Phoenix platform that would underpin a new generation of cars. A few months later we were back at Trollhättan to watch BMW director Iain Robertson announce a deal to supply BMW engines for the Phoenix-based cars.

It is also not widely known that GM exploited Saab's engineering genius to the full during the last decade. Trollhättan engineered the 'Premium Platform', which ended up under the Alfa 159 and made significant contribution to GM's global 'Epsilon' platform. It also developed GM's clever Adaptive 4×4 transmission and the torque-steer quelling Q2 mechanical differential. Arguably, Saab was at its best as an engineering think tank, whose numerous safety and emissions innovations had a huge influence on the wider industry.

With Saab now seemingly a permanent resident in the auto industry scrap yard, I commend Lance Cole for the huge effort in finally putting together a comprehensive history of how Saab was born and laying out in fascinating detail the depth of intelligence that went into building the company. Too little has been written about Saab and this book finally fills in the answers. It will be of interest to a far wider audience than just dedicated Saabisti.

I was lucky that my lasting memory of Saab will be a summer's evening cross-country drive from Trollhättan to Gothenburg, in a pre-production version of the 9-5 Aero. That remarkable car, with its refined V6 engine, superb four-wheel drive system and adaptive damping was, for my money, by far the finest Saab ever produced. It was a cruel twist of fate that it arrived too late to help avert Saab's decline into bankruptcy.

Hilton Holloway

Saab – Ethos, Place and Perception

Far out in the Pacific Ocean, nearly a thousand miles from land and moored upon the edges of the Coral and Tasman Seas, there is a small island called Norfolk Island. There are not many cars on Norfolk Island, and those vehicles that are there, arrive as deck cargo on small ships. Here, as far from industrial suburbia as you can get, way out in the blue wilds of the Pacific, two of the vehicles on Norfolk Island are Swedish cars. They are both Saabs. The reader might well ask why the somewhat unusual product of a small European car maker should be

wanted in such a location? Surely a Jeep or Land Rover would be expected, but why a sleek, curvy Saab?

The maker of those two Norfolk Island cars, Svenska Aeroplan Aktiebolaget (S.A.A.B.), generically known via various incarnations as Saab, is a small company from a small country, yet is a car manufacturer of global fame.

In the beginning there was Saab, in the end there was not, or not as we had known it. In between those events, from Tokyo to Boston and all points in between, Saab's cars have got everywhere, even the Australian outback, even on a Pacific Island. Now long separated from the Saab aircraft company, Saab and its cars represent a particular strand of automotive thinking

Björn Envall, father of the Saab 900 and the man who shaped Saab in the modern era.

new model year saw revisions to specifications and fittings, sometimes in a confusing and random manner.

In Sweden, the motoring media and the enthusiasts of the car-buying public had a phrase for Saab's habit of constantly updating in-production cars over a long model life span: 'Blir ni Trollhättan aldrig nodja?' – meaning: 'You in Trollhättan, aren't you ever satisfied?', or 'Can't you leave things alone?'. Saab was always changing something, yet in its first fifty years it only produced five new models of car.

The essence of the Saab enthusiasm stems from the fact that the Saab car seems to be a mix of engineering passion, clever design, a certain style, and handling and performance *par excellence*. Old Saabs even seem to have a distinct smell, a vintage aura and a sense of occasion that touches the senses – that vital element of a great car. There is a 'Saabness' apparent – an aspect of the brand that must reflect the fact that Saab's cars have never been fashion statements, nor have they ever been a response to focus groups or marketing 'spin'. Saabs are Saabs and not just consumer goods honed by accountants to be the cheapest, weakest, least durable product: built-in obsolescence was not a Saab trait. Perhaps therein lay the root of a sales and cash flow conundrum?

and have been tagged 'iconic', that much over-used term, which fails to properly encapsulate the ethos of Saab.

When in 2010 Saab was first faced with extinction, groups of Saab owners and enthusiasts literally took to the streets in mass protest across dozens of cities and countries around the world to save a much loved brand that somehow had engendered a degree of affection and loyalty far beyond the norm, or the size of the company's profile. In 2009, German academic research by Rüdiger Hossiep of Ruhr University Bochum found that Saab owners' perceptions and emotions about their cars were different from those normally to be expected. The 'Save Saab' campaigners (including the author) achieved international media coverage and major headlines on broadcast news. Theirs was the first global, internet-led automotive pressure movement, and without their efforts Saab might well have died at that moment. The Saab owners and enthusiasts and the internet helped save Saab, for Saab had gone viral in the digital age. This was not an insignificant achievement for a minnow of a car company on a world stage dominated by automotive sharks.

Irrespective of Saab's sporadic survival saga, its eventual filing for bankruptcy, and the possibilities of reincarnation in another form, the Saab story is one of great design and huge enthusiasm. The Saab story as a car maker may be over as we knew it, but the spirit of Saab, the audacity to do something different as an ethos, will never die. It seems that one explanation for the plethora of model variants and specification changes to Saab's cars stems from the fact that having designed and delivered its car to the marketplace, Saab's engineers, inveterate 'tinkerers' or 'fettlers', could not stop fiddling with their products. Each

Resisting Convention

Saabs were different, and it wasn't just marketing hype: Saab's cars really were designed and constructed in a different way from normal cars – Saab's designers actually *thought* differently. They did not respond to fashion or to passing public whims: the thought of 'customer clinics' informing design direction, or 'celebrity'-inspired styling, would have caused horror at Saab. Saab 900 owner Richard Gunn of the British *Classic Car Weekly* once wrote of Saab, 'Some cars pander to fashion, and date very quickly as a result. Saabs just seem to exist without compromise. The world adapts to them, not the other way around.'

Mark McCourt, editor with *Hemmings, Sports and Exotic Car* in the USA, is a dedicated Saabist and Saab commentator who believes that 'People who seek out Saab do so because it speaks to them on a personal level, it reflects something that they see in themselves – perhaps an individual streak, a defiant "differentness"', a clever and untypical way of approaching the same old issue.'

These two quotes neatly encapsulate the Saab spirit or 'Saab – andan, en del har den'.

In the context of the now, Saab's ethos can be explained in similar context to that of the Apple brand and Steve Jobs' thinking – setting a niche fashion via form and function, and not being a response to, or a victim of, mainstream thinking or fashion.

Saab, its engineer Gunnar Ljungström and its first designer Sixten Sason designed for the future – true future vision, insofar as they created shapes and details that did not date, and made ideas that would come into their own. Today the design enthusiast might draw a parallel with the thinking and sculptural technique of the design works of several car stylists. Ex-Ferrari designer Jason Castriota created the PhoeniX for Saab, a shape that was not a retro-pastiche nor an anodyne aero weapon, but instead a fresh face, a new sculpture of Saab design language that had elements of a past, but a vision of a future. The very different and controversial works of Chris Bangle at BMW did a similar thing in a different context by creating, not following fashion. Beauty, and the opinion of it, may lie in the eye of the beholder, but true 'design' runs deep, it comes into its own era, as the designs of Sixten Sason at Saab did, and as the works of true design always have.

In aviation, the talented designer Bert Rutan carved a similar design philosophy niche, and many military and civil pilots own Saabs. Architects have also been cited as Saab owners, and we can only speculate as to whether Frank Lloyd Wright would have felt an empathy with the Saab ethos.

In a broader perspective, the actor Peter Ustinov was a Saab owner, and Jay Leno, the American TV-show host, owns an old Saab 96 V4 and a two-stroke. Few people know that Kurt Vonnegut, the visionary and author, once sold Saabs as a Cape Cod Saab dealer. In the TV series *Seinfeld*, Jerry drove a Saab 9-3. In the film *Silence Becomes You*, an old 1960s Saab 95 was the starring car alongside Alicia Silverstone. Charlie Sheen encountered a Saab 9-5 in the film *The Arrival*.

In *Tripping*, the singer Robbie Williams seemed rather taken with a Saab – an ancient 95. In an older, 1970s dimension, Ernie Wise the comedian owned a Saab 99 GLE at the height of his fame with Rolls Royce and Jensen Interceptor owner Eric Morecambe. But Morecombe trumped his comedy partner by purchasing a red Saab 900 Turbo, and his wife drove a Saab 96 V4. Raymond Baxter, the World War II Spitfire pilot and subsequently a high priest of broadcasting, drove a succession of Saabs. James May, the writer of automotive philosophy and *Top Gear* presenter with a penchant for design details, is also a Saab fan. Stephen Bayley, design writer and former Design Museum luminary, is also a Saab and Sixten Sason admirer. The poet John Betjeman liked Saabs, and his friend and broadcast biographer, the BBC producer Jonathan Stedall, owned a blue 900 four-door. Stephen Fry the actor is a more recent Saab owner, and a blue 9-3 Turbo convertible was the star of the BBC's *New Tricks* series.

For the Discovery Channel's *Chop Shop*, Bangladesh's answer to Bertone, the designer Leepu Awlia chopped up a classic Saab 900 Turbo to create an incredible Saab 'gangster' car for *Spandau Ballet* singer-turned-actor Martin Kemp. The resulting one-off styling special looked like something from outer space, in true Saab tradition. Back in Britain, 1980s cricket star Ian Botham was also a Saab owner. The British town of Brighton, a centre of media, arts and culture, is full of Saabs ancient and modern. In France – itself a land of great design awareness – Saabs are as popular in Paris as they are in remote rural locations. So *even* the French took Saab to their hearts. The Dutch, Germans, Italians and Americans also adore their Saabs.

Saab 92 prototype UrSaab,
a flying saucer of a car.

Some of the staff at the world's oldest car magazine, *Autocar*, are rather partial to the Saabness of things, as are the staff at *CAR* magazine, and at *Octane* magazine journalist John Simister runs a white Saab 96. Numerous celebrities and royalty – including Queen Beatrix of the Netherlands – owned Saabs, but so too do many farmers, shopkeepers, policemen, vicars and academics. And there has to be a reason why the locals of Brixton, South London, love their Saabs. Music business and airline boss, Sir Richard Branson, drove a 9-5 Biopower.

Tennis star Bjorn Borg drove a 900 Turbo, and the great Formula 1 World Champion, Alan Jones, not only drove a 900 Turbo back home in Australia, he also raced in the one make Saab 900 competition series. Naturally ABBA, the Swedish singers, drove Saabs – they even advertised Saab on an album cover in 1980. Back in Britain, all sorts of Saab enthusiasts raced in the 900-series races, Haymill the Saab dealer sponsoring Chris Day to campaign in his 900 two-door.

Despite a few erroneous perceptions that have gathered down the years, Saab and the love of Saab cars is not a social science pigeonhole of the intellectual.

Swedish royalty, led by Prince Bertil, have also privately owned numerous Saabs as their personal cars – yet the Saab enthusiasm is not a class 'thing', it crosses cultural and social boundaries. On the US East Coast, the Saab was seen as an intellectual choice, yet to a Scottish farmer, a Saab was a workhorse car whose back seat could be folded down and sheep loaded in. In East Africa, the Saab brand is well known, and in South Africa, far out in the back of beyond, there is a Saab owner named Daniel Haakuri who drives his red turbocharged 9-5 five hundred miles to get it serviced, and five

ABOVE: **Saab Aero X, the ultimate modern face of Saab.**

LEFT: **Saab, maker of aircraft and cars: modern Saabs under a Viggen fighter.**

Saab 96 in classic red and containing two dedicated Saabists. Saab Great Britain was crucial to the brand's success. John Smerdon and Roy Clements were key to Saab GB's advancement.

hundred miles home. Daniel has also spotted Saabs in Sierra Leone, perhaps the most bizarre of the Saab sightings.

So Saab has appealed across all boundaries and many prejudices: Saab's cars transcend perceived thinking.

An often forgotten factor in the Saab story is the sheer depth of the company's scientific research, not just into aerodynamics and safety design, but also into engine management, cylinder head and combustion refinements, and gearbox design. The innovations of Saab are a testimony to its thinking.

Where or how did Saab's original journey start? The answer has to be on a sunny day in southern Sweden, where Saab's curves were created amid the bright shiny colours and shapes of the landscape, despite the bipolar Swedish weather and its effect on the Scandinavian psyche. Volvos – boxy and boring for some years, but great cars now – must have stemmed from a season of deep thinking amid the straight-lined days of a Swedish winter. In the beginning, the differences between the two companies were massive: Saabs were cheaper, small, sporty, curvaceous front-drive fun, while Volvos were rear-driven, American-inspired cars with conventional rear-driven characteristics. Jan Willsgaard's Volvo 144 design had a certain style, but it was huge. Saab also won the Monte Carlo rally with their little car: rallying was a big theme for Saab and Erik Carlsson.

Volvos of the 1960s were stylish in their own way, but by the 1970s had become 'Swedish bricks' as square-rigged galleons of cars, festooned with straight lines, chrome, big bumpers, and all the dynamics of a supertanker at sea. That would change of course, and Volvo's commitment to safety and good design from the start should not be forgotten; but Saab, from its early days, produced its curved, responsive cars that handled well, and which had a better chance of steering

around danger, as well as surviving it. Saab's long list of design and engineering innovation is often forgotten.

Strangely, while Saab became seen as a premium brand in America, Britain and in other markets, at home the Swedes never really perceived the earlier Saabs as upper class, and to this day there is some domestic Swedish reluctance to see Saab as a Swedish equivalent to Audi, BMW or Mercedes; this speaks volumes for Saab's small car origins, and of Saab forgetting that foundation for its brand.

Therein lies the clue to one aspect of Saab's downfall – the trend to go upmarket and abandon the concept of the small family car with sporting style and performance became a critical issue. There was an imbalance to Saab. But this is not to say that Saab's larger cars of the 1980s and later were without merit. After all, who was it that brought turbocharged, mass market performance *and* reliability to the market for the first time?

The answer was Saab with the 99 Turbo and latterly with the 900 range, a car that was an essential motoring icon of the late 1980s in many countries. The idea of turbocharging was soon copied by many, including the Japanese auto industry. The later Saab 9000 and 9-5 models built on such traits. In America, Saab was correct to go upmarket, but that was an American context of its time, not a panacea for a global car market grounded in Sweden.

The Ethos of Saab

Saab is a different sort of car, let alone a different type of Swedish car. For Saab is a somewhat unsung hero of design and engineering innovation. Saab used front-wheel drive and aerodynamic body shapes years before the Mini, Volkswagen, Ford or

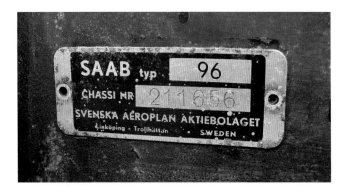

Saab-Svenska Aeroplan Aktiebolaget, as stamped.

Volvo embraced such ideas. While Volvos became boxy rear-wheel-drive behemoths, Saabs were small, nimble and rally proven. They were also different to the executive barges that Mercedes, BMW, Rover, Chrysler, Ford and so on were churning out in the 1970s and 1980s. Even the aerodynamic advance of the Citroën DS was years *after* the teardrop design of the Saab 92. And the so-called front-drive 'revolution' of the Mini was a decade after Saab's transverse-engined 92 went on sale.

The little Saab may not have been the first front-driven car, but it was the first to gather together all the features that it did, in a smaller car.

As the front-driven, aerodynamically shaped, flat-floored first Saab car was born, in Britain Issigonis was designing cast-iron dinosaurs of cars such as the Morris Minor 1000 with its pre-war styling and engineering. And even the French, Germans and Italians were persisting with rear-engined, thin-skinned contraptions of traditional and dated design – though at least these had some form of rear-engined technicality to them. Saab car design was ahead of the world, but hardly anyone knew nor cared. At that time, Saab was closer to the ethos of Porsche than it was to the fashion of Ford or Fiat.

In the Science Museum in London there is a permanent exhibit of what are suggested as the most influential and significant examples of European car design trends of the post-war era. Five historically and socially significant cars are piled up in a vertical tower, one on top of each other: those cars are the Austin Mini, the Citroën 2CV, the Volkswagen Beetle, the Ford Cortina and the Saab 93.

If the ethos of Saab's engineering came from its aeronautical roots, the men of Saab's 'Aeroplan' factory, the shape or style of Saab came from Sixten Sason the designer. The roots of his influences and styling preferences stemmed directly from his time in Paris and the French streamlining movement in the mid-1930s, and his tours in Germany and Italy at the height of the Art Deco years. The knowledge comes straight from early aviation and the pioneers of aerodynamics.

Saab's aviation department also honed the art of improving on existing designs that it had bought under licence, even Hawker airframes, and de Havilland and Rolls-Royce jet engines were modified and improved to Saab's way of thinking. And it was Saab who designed the J21 and J21R twin tail-boom fighter aircraft in 1939, long before others tried the same configuration.

Yet the weight of industrial might in central Europe and America was soon to smother the innovations of the advanced thinking of Sweden's small band of brothers at Saab.

Revolutionary

How could a lithe little Saab car reflecting a unique aeronautical psychology be accepted by the might of known industrial practice? It was a bit like the difference between a Supermarine Spitfire and a Hawker Hurricane: the Spitfire was honed to a finite degree of new thinking and against the 'perceived wisdom' fashion of the time that lay behind the evolution of ancient thinking that was the Hurricane, while the Hurricane grew from the traditions of its direct ancestors – biplanes; thus the Spitfire was a new idea. The analogy is a good one, for while Volvo's cars evolved from traditional pre-war designs, the new thoughts of the men from Saab – who had no previous legacy to draw upon or be constrained by in design terms when building their first car – really were revolutionary. Saab was the thinking of the new, struggling against the thinking of the established old. The results were bound to be different.

Perceived wisdom, with all its constraints and conceits, ruled the mass market while the men of the tiny little company that was Saab were left to tinker with their teardrop-shaped oddity and its smoky two-stroke engine. Yet they were not swept aside, in fact they prospered.

Saab had unique design motifs and hallmarks: it was a true innovator, bringing airflow management, safety and engine technology as well as other new ideas. It is often forgotten that Saab made an alloy and glassfibre composite car years before Colin Chapman created one for Lotus. And at Saab the aircraft maker, aerodynamics had been a real art before the first Saab took to the roads in 1949. The aviation link was not hype: Saab really was a 'Svensk bil med flygkvalitet' – a Swedish car with aircraft quality – created by aircraft people: perhaps we should call them the 'Aeroplan' men.

As early as 1949, Saab's car had the strongest windscreen pillars in the business and the most torsionally rigid cabin 'cell' you could then build, and this was before Mercedes Benz had developed further such thoughts. By the 1970s Saab had given us side-impact door beams, reinforced roofs with built-in roll-over bars, box-section sills, padded interiors, headlamp washers – all decades before the main-stream car manufacturers

'GAS'. Gunnar A. Sjögren, the author, artist-designer who joined Saab in Linköping in 1959. He followed the Saab design office to Nyköping.

As such, the first Saab, called the 92 and created by a small team of men (whose names included Svante Holm, Gunnar Ljungström, Sixten Sason, Rolf Mellde and a dozen or so others, named herein), was not a post-war copy of American car designs as many European automobiles were, but instead a unique teardrop shape. It was a front-drive car with a small, transverse, two-stroke engine, a reinforced cabin, and an amazing style and design that marked out the little Saab as something very different indeed.

In some contexts perhaps the Saab 92 was a Scandinavian Citroën or Fiat, only one that was more developed, more resistant to rust, had better safety, and with advanced thinking years before someone like Alec Issigonis got all the PR headlines for his much lauded Mini. The original Mini was unable to meet even basic US safety legislation, and was arguably one of the most structurally unsafe cars ever made, with its hollow doors and side panels, exposed fuel filler, narrow gauge sills, short low front, thin bulkhead and a metal flange across the cabin at leg height: it was a safety expert's nightmare. Such failings, highlighted early on in the Mini's 1960s lifetime by accident expert Dr Murray McKay of Birmingham University, failed to dent the Mini's longevity or success, despite its death toll.

By the 1970s Saab was building the Sonett glassfibre and steel-bodied two-seat sports cars alongside its 93–96 range and then a new mid-sized saloon, the 99. Saab was also building cars in Uruguay, Denmark, Belgium and the Netherlands. An internal separation from the over-arching aircraft business gave rise to a change of name and the christening of Saab Auto AB. By 1969 a merger with Sweden's long established heavy truck, car and engineering marque, Scania-Vabis, had created Saab–Scania AB. In that year Saab also began building cars at Uusikaupunki in Finland, in a joint venture with Valmet OY.

decided safety was fashionable. The early Saabs of the 1950s (fitted with standard seat belts) were safe, and they remained so and met all legislation through to the end of their production runs. Saab's safety knowledge (along with that at Volvo and Mercedes) shamed other car makers, especially certain European and American manufacturers. Ironically, when a Saab performed badly in European crash tests in the 1990s, it was a Saab based on GM underpinnings: the mistake has never been repeated.

Saab had originally made aircraft, and latterly, everything from airliners to the sharpest jet fighters such as the legendary Draken (Dragon), Gripen and Viggen, which sold to air forces worldwide. But after the dark days of World War II, the Svenska Aeroplan Aktiebolaget came up with the idea for a small, strong car that would be ideally suited to Scandinavia's winter climate and hostile post-war roads and driving conditions.

Jean Francois Bouvard and his son Tim – Saabists start young. The Saab 96 Cabotine and her owner and son.

Sixten Sason used his artistic abilities to present a really smooth and futuristic vision of Saab beauty in this painting of the Saab 92.

Saab, Scania and Vabis

Scania and Vabis were two of northern Europe's longest established engineering companies, and they brought to Saab a reinforcement of values, tradition and psychology. Saab had therefore not been diluted, but had grown.

Scania and Vabis, originally two separate engineering concerns, had merged in 1911. Founded in 1891, the Vaganfabriksaktiebolagat I Södertälje, or Vabis, stemmed directly from the work in the 1830s of entrepeneur David Eckenburg. Vabis was created in Sodertalje by a group of partners and a bank, and had an engineer named Gustaf Erikson who designed and built the Erikson car for Vabis in 1897. Vabis had started its engineering journey making railway rolling stock, but the first Vabis-production motor vehicle was a light truck produced in late 1903, powered by a V-twin configured engine.

By 1911, Vabis had merged with the company known as Scania, which had produced bicycles as early as 1900, and would design its first bus in 1910. Scania, which took its name from the town of Skane, started life as a company named Maskinfabriks Aktiebolaget via a British connection stemming from its work in building a British-designed bicycle or velocipede in a factory at Malmo in 1899–1900.

The two entities merged, and Scania-Vabis thrived as one, building tanks, diesel engines, buses, trucks and aircraft engines for over fifty years. In 1948, Scania-Vabis was also the general agent for Volkswagen in Sweden. In 1969 the intricate and long established automotive histories became the core of Saab-Scania. On 8 June 1969, Saab formerly changed its name to SAAB–SCANIA AB and divided itself into divisions, principally those of automotive, aerospace, electronics and industrial. By November 1970 Saab had built its 500,000th car, but it would be 1976 before the 1,000,000th Saab rolled off the production line.

Latterly Saab would change its nameplate and the badge that went on to every car, to a new 'Saab Scania' logo featuring the ancient symbol of the griffin. The new logo, designed by Carl Frederik Reutersward, echoed the griffin badge that had first appeared on a Scania vehicle in 1901. Saab would later disentangle its various arms and the auto division and become part of General Motors, whose British car company Vauxhall also used the symbol of the griffin in its badge, a coincidence not then considered.

Time of Change

By the 1980s the Saab 96, derived from the 92, had gone, yet the 99 model range had begat the larger 900, which sold nearly a million examples for Saab. In America, Saab's inspired and talented US chief, Bob Sinclair – a former Volkswagen salesman, Volvo employee, and a true gentleman of automotive adventure – created a golden period when Saab's monthly sales figures just kept on rising month after month, year on year. Sinclair also pushed Saab into building more luxurious versions of its cars, and pursued the convertible model that became a style icon. Sinclair's decision to make Saab a 'premium' choice was correct for *his* marketplace in North America.

ABOVE: **Classic American specification 99 EMS and 99 Turbo pair seen at speed. Note how the round headlamps alter the 99's design graphic.**

RIGHT: **The original top team at Saab seen in later years.** *Left to right:* **Svante Holm, Tryggve Holm, Gunnar Ljungström, Sixten Sason and Rolf Mellde.**

Robert Sinclair, 'petrol head' and the man who took **Saab** in the **USA** to its ultimate brand status, seen at the wheel of a **Saab 94 Super Sonett**.
McCOURT/HEMMINGS

Despite its success, Saab in Europe found itself without its earlier 'bread and butter' small car model, a crucial weakness, more so than in America. In 1985, lacking the time and the funds to build a totally new small car, Saab took the front of the old 99 and the back of the new 900 range and welded the two together into a car called the Saab 90. This car was the auto industry's weirdest and most deliberate 'cut and shut' ever seen. The Saabisti loved it, but no one else did: who would ever think of welding two different cars together to make a new model?

This strangely effective economy measure was soon forgotten, but some say it marks the end of Saab's stability at a time when solidity and safety came second to fuel economy and the passing fashions of shiny, flimsy modernity. In the main, car buyers cared about mpg, stereos, fog lamps, alloy wheels, vinyl roofs and spoilers: thoughts of how good the seats of a car were after a long drive, or how strong the roofs and doors of their cars were, was not the marketing conditioned mindset of the time.

When the Saab 99 first entered the market place it was up against cars of the 1960s, cars like the last of the Triumph Herald or the newer 1500 saloon, or others such as rear-engined VW products, and various Fiats and Peugeots. Yet while they went out of production, the 99 in revised versions soldiered on into the 1970s and onwards into the 1980s. The Saab, with its heavy-gauge construction, forensically tuned aerodynamics, rustproofing, orthopaedic seats and advanced ideas, was up against the chromatic-hued fashion of the likes of the later Ford Cortina, Renault 12, Vauxhall Viva and a new wave of lightweight cars from the oriental gargoyle school of design: Datsun 120 versus Saab 99? Toyota Cressida versus Saab 900? The market place really was made this way, but Saab rose above it, at its hidden peril.

Perversely it was in America, in a market place of cars with gross scale, acres of thin steel, chrome trim, yards of vinyl and sports stripes, that Saab's individualism seemed to stand out and appeal to a certain type of car buyer. Amongst the Fords, Chryslers and GM cars of the 1980s, the 'weirdness' of the Saab range and of the 900 convertible actually worked as a positive anti-fashion statement, and buyers flocked to Saab, while all around them the cars of the American dream came and rapidly went. But Saab's US sales growth masked a more deep-seated malaise.

Perhaps only the British, with their oddities such as the Austin Maxi, Allegro, Triumph Herald and Dolomite, and ancient behemoths that were the dying days of the once great Rover car company, ranked as bucking the mainstream trend, in a manner that led to their downfall. British Leyland became the laughing stock of the world, where 'BL' even managed to shatter Jaguar's crown and ruin the last chance the British car industry really had – the modern, safe, stunning futurism of the David Bache-designed (yet appallingly manufactured) Rover SD1, the car that leaked, flaked and regularly faltered.

Under BL, MG was murdered and Morris committed the sin of the Marina, a sort of faux Cortina minus proper front suspension and thrown together with all the skill a sometimes inept BL management and an often defeatist, politically embittered workforce, could cobble together, just as they did with Rover's SD1. Then there were devices such as the Austin Princess, the Ambassador and the Maestro, which are perhaps best not discussed – as with the Triumph Acclaim. And what of those shiny 1980s Fiats and Alfas? They looked great but rusted away during a lunch hour, and broke down, over and over again. And the French – they did their own thing in their own way as usual, and to occasional great delight, as long as you stayed near a garage. But the flimsy Citroën BX, the rusty Renault 14, the thrown together Peugeot 305, and various other horrors of build quality and a lack thereof, along with the cast of the aforementioned cars, were the landscape of cars circa 1970–89; meanwhile the likes of BMW, Mercedes, Volvo and VW carved their names and brands into the records of quality design and production values.

Hovering above them all was the future threat of Nissan, Honda, Toyota and Mazda, not to mention Suzuki, Subaru, Hyundai and the once wretched cars of Kia – now transformed by intelligent design. It would take years, but the old quasi-religious, perhaps even tribal certainties of Europe and American car making and practice would be swept away in a new order.

Alongside these events, the small failings of Saab seemed of little worry. Saabs still sold on their values, but trouble lay ahead. Saab failed to see that what it needed was a rival to the VW Golf, the car that saved Volkswagen from the quagmire of its own navel-gazing design period, and protected VW and the German economy from the march of Japan.

'Saabism'

For Saab, there then came a big car called the 9000, a project jointly developed by Saab and Fiat to provide them with shared costs on a larger saloon. The 9000, based on a Guigario design concept but with lots of Saab input, had a great deal of 'Saabism' added to it by Björn Envall in design terms, and Olle Granlund in engineering ideas: it was a great car and much underestimated. It was with the 9000 that Saab's advertising created the term 'Saabism'. But the economic crisis of the late 1980s left Saab in a weakened state – and it was not just the economic crisis that had caused the problem.

For the management of what was now called Saab Automobile AB – so deft at dovetailing with its designers and engineers as one big happy family in a most non-hierarchical and typically liberal Swedish manner – had, it seemed, lost its way. Basically, Saab had ignored its roots and failed to produce a complete model range – even Volvo had created a new small car range in the ghastly but strong 300 series.

However technically advanced its cars were, by 1990 Saab only made big expensive cars, and had failed to build a new small car range that reflected its roots or was tuned to the consumers of the age. It simply did not produce enough cars in numbers or models to create sustainable profits. Also its cars were old, with the longest model cycles in the industry – only the original Mini, the VW Beetle and the Citroën 2CV had stayed in production longer than the Saab 92–96, 99 and 900. Meanwhile the likes of Honda, Toyota and even Volkswagen were offering their customers new model ranges every four or five years.

Despite the success of the Turbo years at Saab from 1978 onwards, which at their height saw four out of every five Saab 99s or 900 ordered as a Turbo variant, these cars failed to build the financial barriers that Saab would need. It took Saab from 1978 to 1983 to sell 100,000 Turbo cars, while Mitsubishi, who followed Saab's Turbo lead and bolted a small turbocharger to nearly every car in its 1980s range, churned out cars by the millions. The Turbo years at Saab, reflecting the work of Bengt Gadefelt and Per Gillbrand, and the drive of Sten Wenlo, to name just a few of the players, were perhaps the defining era of Saab engineering, yet even the excellence of the turbo product did not save Saab from the tumult in store.

European Saab owners come in all shapes and sizes.

Difficult Decisions

Saab – held in affection, admired for its technical innovations and steadfast refusal to bend to the whims of fashion in the manner of the aerodynamic, yet agriculturally engineered paradox that was a prime example, the Ford Sierra – found itself up a backstreet with no way out. It was an accident perhaps, but it happened long before GM owned Saab, and it proves that not everything that happened to Saab was GM's fault: whatever the failings of GM's later stewardship of Saab, the fact was that from the late 1980s onwards, Saab was in trouble. This was largely because it was making a declining number of large, ageing cars in a narrow market sector from a high cost base, even if the 9000 was a temporary highlight. Saab did what Saab did, the Saab way, and for all the right engineering reasons, it failed to embrace the new way of doing things in a global automotive bubble where the likes of Kia, Hyundai or Fiat could now churn out great cars, cheaply, with just enough 'design' in them to touch the buyer's emotions.

In 2012, commenting in their academic paper about the death of Saab, automotive academics Matthias Hollweg of the University of Cambridge Judge Business School and Nick Oliver of the University of Edinburgh Business School seemed to independently concur with this author's views about Saab's own psychological problems. They opined that Saab's way of holding onto its independence was a factor in the company's demise. Could Saab be accused of a reluctance to embrace or integrate with GM, perhaps an internal resistance to another corporate and design psychology? The thoughts of Hollweg and Oliver on Saab's demise illustrate such possibility. Hard as it is to say, but as early as the late 1980s, the Saab 'cocoon' could not and did not endure – and it was the world's loss.

But it was Saab's cleverness, its intelligent innovations from safety design to turbocharged power, that brought it to the attention of the biggest name in car making. Despite its corporate structural problems, Saab had value within its intellectual property. The Saab mindset, that planet Saab 'cocoon', had given birth to brilliance.

But the Saab situation was to become an essential and enduring paradox. In the mid-1970s Saab only made the 96 V4 and the early, non-turbo 99, so it lacked a big car in its range that would earn more and sell to a wider market sector, reducing its costs. Back then Saab needed a big car, but having created a bigger car in the 900 and then the 9000, it then abandoned its small car range and put itself into the reverse position of only making big cars and of needing a small car range. Mistakenly, Saab seemed to make itself believe that if the 900 was its big car offering, the 99 (and 90) was its small car offering, which they were not and never had been. The focus on becoming a prestige brand had exposed the failure by Saab to create a new range of small cars, a 96 or 92 replacement. And what did becoming a premium brand have to do with Saab's key marketing brand pillar – rallying?

The petrol crisis of the mid-1970s and the Swedish economic crisis of the 1980s only served to underline how Saab had moved from one risky extreme to another, and could not rely on its small domestic market. The model range was now polarized in an opposite direction to that which it had been, therefore it had no breadth and Saab made fewer than 100,000 cars a year from a very high cost base. If it had been able to offer the late 1970s a small economy car, just as it had offered the 92 and 93 to the 1950s, it would have prospered – but just as that need grew, Saab went upmarket without attending to its original customer base.

The passing fads of 1970s fashion were not pandered to by Saab and its ethos, and this was quite understandable: after all, Saab and its cars were deeper than that. But therein lay the contradiction, because chrome-edged fashion sold: people wanted shiny, disposable cars. In the 1970s, few car buyers really cared about a Saab-like depth of design integrity and longevity, and if they did, they bought a Mercedes or a Rolls Royce. Saab's ideals were, it seemed, in the wrong market territory. It was easy to see how Saab's management were tempted to do something different for what appeared to be sound business reasons – but abandoning their original small car market can only be called an error.

General Motors

By the late 1980s, Saab had gone through a series of distinct periods or commercial phases, but it remained weakened by its tactic of putting all its eggs in one basket and relying heavily on American, British and Dutch markets served by a single ageing car range. The 1985 Saab 9000 was a great car, but it was but a stop-gap – a good and effective treatment, but not a cure. The combination of all these facets constitutes what happened to Saab – the issues as to *why* Saab was for sale or seeking a partner by 1990: it is why on 15 December 1989, General Motors (GM), the leviathan of Detroit, announced the first of its two investment moves into what by 15 March 1990 would become Saab Automobile AB, part owned by GM and no longer part of an aerospace company. The latter would end up in the hands of British Aerospace and a range of partners.

There was a *reason* why Saab was for sale in 1989–90 and it was *not* GM's fault. Saab's own men, the people who understood the Saab spirit, had actually stumbled into circumstantial error. They might say that this is easy to see with hindsight, but the fact is that they chose to realign Saab upmarket in a global context, without continuing with a basic small car range. Imagine the rewards if Saab had reinvented the 96 as a late 1970s Swedish version of the VW Golf or AlfaSud; failure to do this cost Saab dear, and such a scenario supports the suggestion of a strategic error for a European context by Saab.

By 1990, in its naive innocence, Saab had thought that investment from GM would allow it to develop the cars it needed and to address its own failings. But little did it know the machinations of the family it had married into. GM did indeed put money into Saab, but somehow, something went awry. Turning basic Opels/ Vauxhalls into rally-inspired Saabs was a tough call that would eat money, and if GM's new prestige beacon was to be just that, why was it so slow to react to opportunity and market forces? And why did GM sell its new prestige brand from the same showrooms as its more humble offerings? After all, Toyota did not share its showrooms with Lexus, nor VW with Audi.

Because the previously dominant Saab shareholding family, the renowned Wallenberg family of bankers, had always saved Saab, and had also had a long-term friendship with Italy's leading Agnelli family, in the 1980s it had been easy for Saab to link up with the Agnelli-owned Fiat company. This not only led to the co-produced Saab 9000, it also saw Fiat-Lancias sold in Sweden via Saab's dealers, who had a new medium-sized car to sell, the Saab-Lancia 600. But this was nothing more than the re-badged and dramatically unaerodynamic (Cd 0.46) Lancia Delta – it was hardly a real Saab. When the first Saab crisis came, most industry observers thought that Fiat would buy Saab, even if the much touted Saab–Volvo merger of 1977 had never happened (a previous suggested liaison in 1963 was also avoided). These events were Saab's lifelines, but they only masked or delayed reality.

Yet it was GM that bought shares in Saab from under Fiat's bumper in 1990, and by mid-decade had absorbed Saab totally. Before long Saab had a new model range, but the cars were based on those GM Opel/Vauxhall underpinnings, and it showed: underneath the pretty Saab curves lay the mundane world of the Vectra and Calibre ranges. Thus Saab's new cars were old and mediocre before they were born, and the motoring press didn't help: the key Saab elements – wonderful handling, communicative steering and brakes, all like those found on a Porsche, a true sense of design occasion, and an unbreakable feel to the fittings – were diluted. Saab was seen as slipping, and the media said so.

Some observers thought that Saab under GM would work: after all, Saab came under the control of GM's European arm of Opel of Germany, and despite memories of World War II, the European mindset should have helped. But Opel had in fact been owned by GM for many decades, and was therefore immersed in GM culture and marketing lore, which included highlights such as the pretty Opel coupés, the Manta and the Senator. GM's 1980s European design director, Gordon Brown,

was a master of airflow and styling panache: through him, GM had style, and his accidental death in 1983 was a major blow to the company's course.

Saab had also worked with the Germans in the 1920s and 1930s, producing its own versions of licence-built German aircraft and also absorbing engine ideas from German firms such as DKW until Sweden decided to build things for itself. Saab also latterly worked with the British car company, Standard Triumph, and had previous links with Hawker, De Havilland and Rolls-Royce: so to say that there was a certain international history between Saab, Opel, GM and others, was an accurate observation.

In typically paradoxical Saab fashion, the company spent the late 1990s developing its GM-based cars into better vehicles: thus as the first GM car, the new 900 became the much better 93. And whatever the one-sided opinions of the GM-haters amongst some of the Saabists, the fact is that GM *did* put money into Saab – but there were other factors at play within both GM and Saab.

But just as in the pharmaceutical industry, the car buyers were the guinea pigs for the product tweaks and design updates that 'post-marketing surveillance' (complaints) would bring about around the new GM version of the 900 model brand. British Leyland, Fiat and Citroën had all tried similarly disastrous ideas, as 'badge engineering', and all had ended up in crisis.

The 1994 replacement for the classic Saab 900 was a GM-based car, the 'new Generation 900', and it evolved into a more focused car, one that was ostensibly more of a Saab; it was re-christened the '9-3'. Then came the large, safe, stylish Saab 9-5, which although based on GM underpinnings, proved to be a great car and was in the main accepted as a Saab as it had character and its own style. In the end, under GM, it became Saab's top model and stayed in production for twelve years – though once again fell into that old Saab trap of a long model cycle that got left standing as the world moved on, with all but the most loyal of customers moving with it.

Amid a host of reasons, GM failed to enact for Saab the obvious, reasonable technique of a plan such as VW's shared-platform idea, which had proved could work so well. This was to use a universal floorplan, engine and structure to create a range of individually skinned cars based on one set of cost-effective underpinnings, without offending the loyal customers of each brand. But instead of enacting its own version of this idea, GM managed to come up with the strange theme of creating a stand-alone new 900, yet basing it on a collection of parts from an old GM parts bin. Then, with GM investing money into creating badge-engineered GM Saab-Subarus, the die was surely cast: was this irrational take on the shared platform concept, the perfect example of how GM, once a leading icon of design, disintegrated at the hands of many?

Badge Engineering

Could a four-wheel drive, horizontally opposed-engined Japanese car that guzzled fuel in all its model variants and which came from the opposite end of the design scale to Saab, become an overnight Saab? Of course not, and it defies logic to think that intelligent men persuaded themselves to invest millions in believing it could. And this was without the fact of the GM Chevrolet Blazer, an old lump of a wallowing 4x4, being turned into a Saab named '97x'. Such a beast, only sold in America, was the antithesis of all that was Saab and its appeal. The Saab-Subaru 92x was not much better either, even if the Subaru version was a great car.

Was this marketing spin and fashion response gone berserk? It was, in the opinions of some Saabists, a multi-million dollar madness for which only GM can be cited.

With a dearth of new models, no small car range, and with even its big cars based on old underpinings, Saab was in trouble, and thanks to GM's marketing mistakes, even Saab's loyal band of followers were buying other types of car – mostly VWs or the re-born Volvos, it seems. The ultimate General Motors, genetically modified, 'GM' non-Saab was perhaps that four-wheel-drive soft-roader, the Saab 97x, upon which millions of dollars were squandered.

GM (or perhaps its accountants) had failed to carve out a Saabness, a future for Saab, despite all the opportunties it had over two decades of confusion. There *were* Saab fans inside GM who wanted to create something new for GM and Saab, but they were eclipsed despite GM wanting the lure of Saab's prestige branding on the world's (if not Sweden's) stage. The Saab brand *had* been diluted, so for Saab, under GM, the 'mojo' was lost; it had taken GM twenty years to not understand what Saab meant, and perhaps in its defence, GM might rationally argue that Saab was locked into its own psychology.

Perhaps in their habit of being unable to leave standard parts well alone, as happened in the Fiat-Saab Type 4 debacle over the Saab 9000, Saab revealed a psychology that would later infuriate the management of GM. Saab simply could not leave things alone, it had to tweak things to Saab standard, at a cost of time, money and more. Admirable though this obsession for quality engineering was, it was financially unsustainable for a company making fewer than 100,000 cars a year.

Risky as it is to defend GM amongst Saab enthusiasts, perhaps in the interests of balance we should consider just how difficult it must have been for non-Saabists such as GM's management to grasp or understand why the Saab men changed so much of the GM parts-bin hand-me-downs. After all, had those parts not been perfectly suitable across a range of average cars and their buyers, notably in the demanding German market place? Why did the Swedes have to be so difficult, and at such

cost? This was often a GM question of Saab, and it revealed a lack of understanding as to what it, GM, had taken on. Saab's *modus operandi* was not called 'the Saab Way' for nothing.

The answer, as any Saab enthusiast would say, is because of the ethos and spirit of Saab to produce the finest engineering, engineering that had its roots in aviation-quality standards. Saab's engineers were forensic, obsessive, and touched with genius. That is why Saab was different.

And therein lay both the essential success and downfall of Saab in a different, accountancy-driven world of global marketing spin and disposable cars. In a nutshell, these are the reasons why Saab could not apply its original ethos in a modern, pared-down, accountant's world. The admirable Saab was probably doomed for decades, and there were not enough Saab enthusiasts to make the ethos viable any longer. The world had moved on – much to its loss.

The Last Chance Saloon

Ironically, just as the proverbial wheels were about to fall off the Saab brand, GM-Saab had finally readied a decent new GM Saab, one which Saab's men had been allowed to influence as far as was possible: in 2009 it was waiting in the wings as the new 9-5 – and it really was Saab's last chance saloon. Based on the GM Insignia model, the new 9-5 was Saabsied, lengthened and modified to the point where it had that aura of Saab. It also included a stunning new estate car or wagon in the range, one that had huge sales potential, at last.... There was even a Saab 94x ready, a more modern compact 4x4 that was late to the game, and also behind its competitors, the class-leading Volvo XC60 and the BMW X3 – though it was effective nonetheless. But GM wanted rid of Saab, dead or alive.

Over the course of the years 2009 to 2012 Saab struggled to survive, suitors came and went, the new 9-5 model was born, died, and was re-born in a saga worthy of the story of Viking longboats and the Scandinavian gods. Various people tried to save Saab, even the Swedish company of Christian von Koenigsegg, not to mention rumours of interest from F1's Mr Ecclestone. In the end, a Dutchman named Victor Roberto Muller (of Spyker cars fame) seized Saab by the scruff of the neck to pull yet another proverbial rabbit out the hat and see it survive for yet another season. En route, the production lines stopped and started, the company teetered upon a knife edge, and yet Saab's buyers and Saab's global fame endured.

In the end, Muller's experiment with Saab (which included the creation of a brilliant but distinctly premature motor show concept car, the 'PhoeniX' design study) came to an unexpected epilogue via bankruptcy petitions, and Chinese investments amid the man's remarkable ability to pull dozens of

New Saab 9-5, Saab's 'last chance' saloon.

Geneva 2011 PhoeniX with designer Castriota and Saab leaders Muller and Jonsson.

metaphorical financial rabbits out of many hats. In a final twist to the plot, GM – still a latent sleeping partner at Saab as part of the original sale deal – refused to sanction Chinese ownership for Saab, arguing that GM's intellectual property was at stake and could not go to China.

Over Christmas 2011, Saab the car maker as we had known it finally died as a brand entity. In 2012, attempts to secure or revive aspects of the business were to be expected. Did an MG/Rover-style reincarnation await? Would India step in and secure a massive automotive leap from the remains of Saab? Would Russia finally get in on the act? Could China still purchase the remains of Saab and create a massive leap forward for its emerging car industry? There was even a Turkish bidder for Saab's remains. Such were the latent possibilities of the ashes of Saab.

Whatever his critics might say, whatever any rights or wrongs, no one can accuse Muller of not loving Saab or of not working very hard indeed to save its skin. It is possible that in his non-stop globe-trotting efforts, Muller drove himself to the physical and emotional cliff face for Saab. But was Muller a corporate raider, an asset stripper, out to offer Saab as a stalking horse to a new world of car making for a country like Russia or latterly China, which had an outmoded car industry but which could take on the world, given the right leverage? Or was Muller a genuine petrol-head, intent on being the saviour of Saab and making it work in Sweden, whoever owned it? Opinions remain divided, but the man's record of actually being in the factory and creating change, speak volumes for his commitment, even if he does have a penchant for Lancias.

Similar Herculean efforts can be framed for Saab's people and by Jan Ake Jonnson, 'JAK', the acting CEO who kept Saab alive in what can only be termed the long wilderness months of 2008 to 2010. The loyalty of Saab's workforce should not go unmentioned, for they stayed put, despite the pressures on their lives and families.

Above or beyond such events and Saab's ultimate fate was the fact that Saab in its former glory was different; some people called their cars quirky, but the Saab enthusiasts – the Saabists – hated that tag. Saab made sporty little jewels of cars, and even when they did spread with age in the 1980s and 1990s into premium brand territory, they remained somehow different, and reached all quadrants of the globe. In Solvang California, and in both Vail and Aspen, Colorado, at one stage in the 1990s both the locals and the sheriff's department drove Saabs – an odd piece of social science in a land far removed from Scandinavia. In fact the Vail Police Department ran Saabs for over twenty-five years, finding the Swedish cars' snow traction far superior to rear-wheel-drive domestic products.

Ralph Millet and Robert Sinclair

Across America, from New England to Oregon, Saabs excelled and Robert Sinclair was the man who made it happen in the 1970s and 1980s, after Ralph Millet had started the story of Saab in America back in the 1950s. More recently for Saab USA, the late Jan Willem Vester was a well known and much admired stalwart of the Swedish brand in America. In the 1980s, Saab advertising men O'Reilly and Hopkinson worked with Sinclair and Sten Helling to frame Saab USA's golden years, calling the new 900s of 1979 the 'Command Performance Cars'. Len Lonnegran was Saab USA's PR man from the 1960s until the 1980s and helped frame the brand.

Sinclair's utter Saabness also saw him create and secure the 900 cabriolet, but few know that it was Sinclair who was the man behind a Saab motorcycle. A motorbike fanatic, Sinclair commissioned the building of a 'SAABSA' bike. This strange 1975-built device featured a two-stroke Saab 841cc engine mounted into a BSA Rocket III frame, topped off with a Morris Minor radiator tucked up under the front frame head. Details saw a Triumph primary case, clutch and transmission mated to a Vincent primary chain and sprockets. The motorcycle bore Saab badges, and Sinclair – then president of Saab America – rode it to work on a daily basis. The little Saab triple-cylinder engine with all its revved-up personality seemed ideal for a motorbike, even if its c.g. might have been a touch high for a motorcycle. Sinclair also owned a Ferrari 308, and he and his wife latterly lived the good life in Santa Barbara, California. Sadly the visionary Bob Sinclair, true Saabist and one of the greatest 'petrol heads' of all time, died from cancer, and the world lost his wisdom and vision long before it should have.

An example of the global fondness for Saab is provided in Tasmania, because that far-off island perched at the base of the world is packed with Saabs – and the reader could legitimately ask why this is so. The answer has to lie in the spirit of Saab. One Tasmanian, Drew Bedelph, has a collection of over twenty Saabs. Tasmania was also where the Saab enthusiast Steven Wade started his internet journey for Saab, with his Trollhättan Saab and Saabs United websites. These took him all the way to working for Saab in Trollhättan and becoming a social media corporate salary man at InsideSaab.com – thereby crossing the difficult divide from maverick amateur commentator to company representative with a claim to remaining an enthusiast observer.

To some, this was an intriguing challenge and a new hybrid role for a new media age; to others it was an attempt at corporate PR by the back door that was not beyond questioning. But whatever the issues, Wade, like all Saabists, was emotionally involved with the beloved brand, and he was a dedicated Saabist, even moving to Trollhättan, where in late 2011 the experiment ended with the demise of Saab. And Wade's old SaabsUnited.com was now owned by Swedish pilot Tim Rokka, and became perhaps even more important as the last rock of Saabism, an ethereal electronic home for a beloved brand that some believed was just temporarily in limbo.

A Museum to be Proud of

The spirit of Saab also created the wonderful Saab museum in Trollhättan, with a record of exhibits, publications and events that took people closer to the heart of Saab. Through the enthusiasm and care of people such as Per-Borje Elg and Peter Backström, to name but two, Saab's museum played a major role in preserving the Saab record. In 2012 the museum's existence was threatened as part of the bankruptcy proceedings, and the risk of its precious cargo being sold off across the world was real. Of great significance, the Wallenberg family, Saab's original backers, stepped in and with cash and clout formed part of a local group and saved the museum. The Wallenberg Trust, and Saab driver and racer Peter Wallenberg Jr, acted to save Swedish heritage – which was more than you could say of the Swedish government. The separate SAAB AB – the old remains of the original company from which the car business was long separated – also made a contribution to the saving of the museum. Sadly, GM's American-based Saab heritage collection was sold off.

The Wallenberg role in saving the museum came about through the intervention of Saab fanatic and photo-journalist Claes Johansson at *Klassiker* magazine. With the museum contents sale deadline due, and the threat of losing the museum cars to global break-up, the situation was desperate, so Johansson wrote to Peter Wallenberg on the afternoon of 18 January 2012 – just before Wallenberg was due to get married. Johansson, who had never met Peter Wallenberg, made a direct plea for the family to intervene and save the contents of the jewel in Sweden's industrial design heritage. Peter Wallenberg moved fast, as did the Trollhättan local council. Within hours, the plan to save the very essence of Saabism came to fruition.

Saabism was not only captured by the museum: in Gunnar Sjögren and Rony Lutz, Saab employed artist-designers who charted Saab cars from an in-house perspective by producing wonderful sketches, drawings, graphics and design themes. Few car companies made room for such artistic prowess on the payroll. Again, this was the spirit of Saab and the Saab way of doing things.

A Truly World Famous Company

Beyond Trollhättan, as far away as Africa, Argentina and in the Australian outback, Saab cars can be found, for the little Swedish company is truly world famous – far beyond the isolation of Sweden's geographic location. It seems that for many years the world forgot about the Swedes, a race of intelligent people of artistic depth who are also immensely practical. They also make

Sixten Sason's 1938 future vision seen in a view of his wing-influenced design motifs.

great rally drivers, learning the craft at an early age. In this blend, the Swedes make superb engineers and designers. For Saab, the Swedish demographic, the social science of Sweden, is a core ingredient in its DNA.

Contained in these pages is the basis of the amazing story of Saab's near seven decades of car making, one that may yet end in a reincarnation; whatever happens, this is the unique tale of the spirit of Saab cars and their survival, against and beyond all the parameters and constraints of perceived wisdom, and the quickly dating trends of shallow fashion. Like Citroën, that other marque of aerodynamic design distinction, Saab's individualism rose and fell, as did its bank balance. Despite all this, Saab and its ethos endured. The Saab men and women, the people of Saab's legend, ensured this.

This book charts the full story of Saab cars, and is the first to do so in the level of design and engineering detail presented in this text. Saab's corporate history is briefly explained in its relevance to its products, but this is not a company biography, it is a book about Saab cars, their design and those who created them. Saab is long overdue the credit for its ethos and innovation.

If the reader will allow the author a personal indulgence, as the owner of Saabs old and new, a 99 Mk1 and a classic 900 Gli, as a Sonett obsessive (for which the treatment must be glassfibre), and as the author of a previous Saab book and many Saab-related articles in print and online, as a dedicated Saabist it is therefore a privilege to chart a record of engineering design and innovation like no other.

To this writer, the design of the Saab 92, a veritable flying saucer of a car, or perhaps a flying wing with wheels, represents probably one of the greatest moments in car design and industrial design of the modern era. The shape ranks alongside those of the Supermarine Spitfire, the Rutan flying wing, the Jaguar E Type, Citroën DS, Corvette, Porsche 911, the IWC watch, the Vickers VC10 and the Concorde: an ultimate expression of the art of timeless design. The Saab 92 is a true inspiration, a blend of art and engineering expressed as an ethos of form. The later Saab 99 and 900 also evoke emotions and have proved timeless in their statement of design and elegance. These Saabs, 92 to 96, 99 and 900, represent something different. More recent Saabs have continued the theme, with the Saab 9000 being an unsung hero of Saab design, and the 9-5 being so characterful. In particular Björn Envall, Aribert Vahlenbreeder, Ralph Jonsson, Simon Padian, Anders Gustafsson, Tony Catignani, Ola Granlund, Cynthia Charwick, Bryan Nesbitt, Maria Thunberg, Aina Nilsson, Alex Daniels and Erik Rokke are some of the vital contributing designers to the Saabness of things.

In the last months of Saab 2010–2011, its GM-based cars were taken to a new level, that certain Saabness was more evident, and Jason Castriota's Saab PhoeniX was a massive if premature design statement of the moment and beyond. The stunning elegance of the new 9-5 estate wagon found approval worldwide, and the failure of Saab and Muller to get the car on to the road and into the dealerships cost it much needed cash flow. In 2012, Saab's cars were once again on the cusp of being brilliant and 'wanted'. The tragedy of Saab's death, as these cars and a new 9-3 hatchback were readied, was indeed a cruel irony.

Saab's oldest advertising strapline used to tell us: 'Go Swift Go Safe Go Saab', which was quaint but true. In modern times, Saab sold itself with 'Saab – move your mind'.

This book is the history of how Saab cars did just that.

LANCE COLE
Kintbury, Berkshire

SAAB – THE CARS

1947 92.001 (not mass produced)
1949 92
1955 93
1956 94 Sonett Super Sport 1 (not mass produced)
1960 95
1960 96
1966 Sonett II
1967 96 V4 / 95 V4
1967 Sonett V4
1969 99
1970 Sonett III
1978 99 Turbo
1979 900
1985 9000
1985 90
1986 900 Convertible
1994 900 Mk 2
1997 9-5
1998 9-3
2002 9-3 Mk 2
2003–2011 Revisions to 9-5 and 9-3
2010 New 9-5 saloon: wagon (not produced)
2011 94x

Note: The Saab-Subaru 92x and Saab-Chevrolet 97x were produced for the USA only.

TROLLHÄTTAN

Part of the Falls at Trollhättan.

OF WATER AND
WALLENBERGS

TROLLHÄTTAN

OF WATER AND WALLENBERGS

ORIGINALLY SAAB WAS AN aeroplane builder born of an engineering tradition in a town with its own DNA of engineering and design lineage, a place named Trollhättan. The town grew at a point where the bubbling waters of an inland lake and a series of waterways spooled up and spewed out over local geological formations as the land dropped down and away towards the sea. It was an ideal site for hydro-electric power generation, and thanks to water, an ancient settlement became a modern metropolis.

Trollhättan was an industrial town, and remains so today, yet one that was prettier than Birmingham, Detroit or Wolfsburg, and with fewer murders. Close to Lake Varnen and the Gota Alv river, and the quayside of the Gota canal now lined with cafés, Trollhättan's roots lay in hydro-power, turbines, railway tracks, locomotives, marine diesel engines and then in an emerging aircraft industry. It became a centre of engineering, design and thinking, perhaps not in an academic sense, but definitely in a mechanically creative sense. The clever Swedes could turn their hands to the opportunities that arrived or that they created. Trollhättan also had a relationship with the British early on, for the Gota Canal that crossed Sweden was constructed using British, Thomas Telford expertise and steam-driven dredges. Trollhättan's 30m-high waterfalls and water power were the key to its development.

In the early 1900s a prominent local Trollhättan family named Wallenberg, with interests in engineering and banking, came to the fore; at this time, local light and heavy engineering companies were joining forces, to build a Swedish network of industrial power. Thus a trained and talented workforce developed artisan skills across steel, wood, hydro-electric and other technologies: from turbines to trains and saw blades, engineering ruled.

The Wallenberg family owned a bank named Stockholms Enskilda Bank, founded in 1853 by A. O. Wallenberg. His descendant, K. Wallenberg, was Sweden's Foreign Minister from 1914 to late 1917 as World War I raged. The Wallenbergs also owned a shipping line, which came under the control of Marcus Wallenberg Snr, who also secured the Swedish rights to the diesel engines of Rudolph Diesel. Two of the family achieved domestic and international headlines: Marcus Wallenberg's son Marcus (and in turn, his own son Marc, continuing the Saab involvement), who steered Saab, and Raoul Wallenberg, the Swedish diplomat. In 1944, at the age of thirty-four, Raoul was head of the Swedish Legation in Hungary, and in this position was able to rescue hundreds of thousands of Jews by issuing exit visas for America from Budapest. Hungary was the last portal from which escape was possible from German rule. When that route was blocked, Raoul Wallenberg secured 10,000 Jews in the Swedish diplomatic compound and across the city. But with the entry of the Russian army into Budapest,

Raoul was arrested by the Soviet Red Army chief, Marshal Rodion Malinovski, on false charges of espionage, and disappeared.

Raoul Wallenberg's fate remains an enigma. Sightings of him in 1947 in Moscow's infamous Lubjanka prison led the Russians to admit that they had him, though soon after they claimed he died of a heart attack. But in 2011, papers discovered in Russia revealed an intelligence services file on Raoul Wallenberg, the existence of which had previously been denied for decades by the KGB and its successor the FSB. Strong evidence exists that Wallenberg was alive into the 1980s, held incommunicado by the Soviet Union for decades until his death, but no amount of pressure by Sweden or by campaigners secured the truth about Raoul Wallenberg from Russia.

In October 1943, 7,500 Jews escaped across the narrow channel from the Nazi invasion of Denmark using small fishing boats, an exodus that is almost unknown. On their arrival, it was the Wallenbergs who helped transport and shelter these refugees from tyranny.

The Wallenbergs, famous and influential as bankers, industrialists and diplomats, were the power behind Trollhättan's and Saab's advancement. No story of Saab can ignore this one family's contribution.

Design was also important to Sweden and to Trollhättan, not just engineering design, but design work in wood, metal and other materials. The effects of nature, of wood and water, and the importance of the Swedish sky and light quality, were to become key ingredients in a Scandinavian treatment of design – much of which mirrors the influences of Trollhättan and of Saab, and what Saab and its people thought and practised. The Swedish design 'school' was obvious early on and is part of the essence of Saab. Safety – a respect for environmental safety and personal safety – were also underlying social traits as a subconscious creed of the Swedes. Sweden and Saab had a very strong social science.

From the 1920s and through the 1930s, and with the looming threat of war, the local companies eventually came together, and with help and production orders from the Swedish government, created a Swedish aircraft industry – with the backing and integrity of the Wallenbergs underpinning it. The names of the companies reflected the heritage of Trollhättan and nearby Linköping, and the Bofors company had a major role in creating Saab – but the founding father of the roots of what became the industry that created Saab has to have been Dr Enoch Leonard Thulin. Thulin's factory works dated back to 1914, and through various incarnations of Enoch Thulin Aeroplanfabrik (AETA), employed up to 1,000 staff.

From this foundation came Svenska Aero AB in 1921, absorbed in 1932 by another major player – the Svenska Jarnvagsverkstaderna or Swedish Railway Works (ASJA). Also key players were Gotaverken, Nydqvist and Holm (Nohab),

RIGHT: **The control of water at Trollhättan.**

BELOW: **An early Scania truck circa 1903.**

Svenska Aero, Flygindustri, Stora Kopparberg and SKF, with BOFORS the major armaments manufacturers.

FOREIGN INFLUENCES

The licence-based building of British, French and German aircraft, and engine designs by the Swedes, laid the foundations of their own industry and their own designs. Bristol, Bleriot, Heinkel, Junkers and Le Rhone all had links with Sweden's new aviation industry from 1914 to the 1930s. Indeed the Germans, banned from having an air force after the Versailles Treaty of World War I, seem to have made the most of developing not just glider design and flying in Germany, but also motor-powered

flight through their Swedish associations with Svenska Aero in the 1920s and AB Flygindustri up to 1935. There were strong links between Junkers of Dessau, notably in the JU 88-derived Saab B3, and Saab. Indeed, when Supermarine Spitfire aerodynamicist Beverley Shenstone was studying at Junkers from 1929 to 1930, a Swedish national was present at Dessau doing likewise.

Saab also built licensed versions of the American NA-14 and the British Hawker Hart. In Saab's early aircraft there were also hints of Italian influence from Caprioni aircraft themes and a touch of Dornier design language. Perhaps Saab's first real own-brand aircraft was the Saab 17; it betrayed American design influences, but was built to Swedish-German standards. British aero-engines were also often seen in the Swedish-German creations, and both De Havilland and Hawker supplied airframes under licence.

As early as 1921, a company called Svenska Automobil Fabriken, or SAF, imported American 'Continental' brand car engines and components in an early attempt to build a car – an open tourer of 'sit up and beg' style. Twenty-five were made, but few sold. This was a little known early attempt at a Swedish-made car, but like the first Swedish aircraft, it was not home grown. Even so, the Swedes were early to grasp the concept of joint collaboration with other companies from other nations.

The Swedish government of the time, headed by Premier Per-Albin Hanson, realized that the situation had to be rationalized, and that a Swedish aircraft industry, not a foreign-influenced ad hoc design bureau, needed to be established. The Air Force had to be involved as well. By 1937, through a series of meetings and government moves, the merger of all the players and the involvement of Bofors and Nohab, and the amalgamation of talents and factories within the sector, created the Swedish aviation company or works (known in Swedish as A.B.). The new company bought land at Maloga village north of Trollhättan's central district.

Thus was born the Svenska Aeroplan Aktie Bolaget (AB) – the 'S.A.A.B.' The legacy of a government holding company known as AB Forenade Flygverkstader (AFF), which had been part of the early structure under an Austrian chief designer (Alfred Gassner), was also present.

Gunnar Dellner headed the new Saab group; the chairman was Torsten Nothin, a former Cabinet minister. Thrown into the mix were the remains of the railway engineering company, which had become an aviation company, with Wallenberg Stockholm Enskilda Bank as backing – the Svenska Jarnvags-verkstaderna Aeroplanvdelning, or ASJA.

The date on which we could say that Saab was truly delivered was 2 April 1937. It had share capital of SKr 4 million. Marcus Wallenberg (1899–1982) was the banking brains, and the new company was staffed not just by Swedes, but also by American, British and German engineers. So there have always been British engineers at Saab, right from the start. In 1939 this complex, multi-layered and hierarchical set-up was streamlined and clarified under Wenner-Gren and then with Ragnar Wahgren; Sven Otterback was his deputy. Soon Svante and Tryggve Holm would be essential elements in the management of Saab. Saab's first factory was quickly constructed at Tunhemsangarma, just north of Trollhättan and close to the River Alv, where flying boats could be operated. Aircraft production started in 1938.

At first there were about eighty factory floor employees, many of them coming from the nearby Uddevalla Workshop Apprentice training school. Other engineering schools in Lysekil and Mölndal provided willing apprentices from local families in the Dalsland and Värmland areas. Claes Sparre was the company's first engineering manager, and Bertil Sjögren the first factory manager.

THE ART OF AERONAUTICS

As war loomed, the rush was on to update and expand Swedish aeronautical design and the numbers of its own aircraft it could produce. Saab was closely linked to Swedish defence policy, and was staffed and supported by highly experienced and very influential figures. These factors and this impetus, and the need for home-grown Swedish design, must surely be cited as the turning point, the very birth of the Saab ethos. Here began the Saab psychology, and the stepping stone to a post-war world of cars as well as aircraft.

Saab and neutral Sweden excelled in design, creating early ejection seats, bomb sights, high speed hydrofoil boat hull designs, modified engines and a host of aircraft – including swept wing research, a delta wing idea, and rocket power design proposals. There were designs for prop and jet fighters, modified de Havilland jet engines, modified Boeing B-17s, and the Saab 21 fighter – a 'twin-boom' fuselage-shaped aircraft that predated a design trend.

In its aircraft, notably the model J21, which began as a prop-powered fighter and developed into a jet-powered variant of great ingenuity, Saab set a trend for its defining ingredient, that

The elegant Saab 90 'Scandia' airliner of the late 1940s, a sort of mini DC-3. It was used in Brazil up to 1969. Note the advanced wing fillet aerodynamics.

Saab's own wind tunnel, useful for a car maker.

ethos. In the Saab 91 Safir of 1945 designed by A. J. Andersson, Saab had provided a level of design and build quality in a general purpose light aircraft that was far above competing products. The three-seater Safir, or 91, was exquisitely detailed with chamfered aerodynamics and an ergonomic cabin and facia design, and it contained advanced safety features. Whereas other single cabin light aircraft had no roll-over or upper fuselage protection to save the pilot and passengers if the aircraft flipped over on landing (a common accident in light aviation), the Safir boasted a stout internal roll bar and hoop. It also had a very strong overall structure, and was used by several air forces as a trainer.

The Safir handled like a dream – responsive and fast, so slippery that slowing it down was often a problem. To prove the point, Erik Carlsson drove a Saab and flew his own Safir with equal verve.

So the Safir, which sold 168 examples across several countries, was a true Saab, and it was launched just as Saab decided to create its first car. The Safir's qualities clearly influenced the thinking of the Saab ethos that framed the car that was to come next for Saab, and the key figure in the creation of the Saab car was Gunnar Ljungström who had been part of the Safir's design team. At the same time, the advanced aerodynamic shape of Tord Lidmalm's Saab Scandia 90 as Saab's first airliner was also being launched: 1945 was a heady year for Saab, and the company was alive with brain power, action and metal bashing. The wind tunnel was busy, too.

The Saab men and their then and later colleagues such as Bjorn Andreasson, Eric Bratt, Arthur Brasjo, Lars Brising, Ragnar Haardmark, Kurt Lalander, Tord Lidmalm, Hans Eric Loftkvist, Kurt Sjorgen, Frid Wanström, were the key thinkers in establishing and building the Saab design ethos in the 1940s and 1950s, and on into the 1960s.

Just as it was creating its first car, Saab turned the J21 – a prop aircraft with a Daimler Benz engine, originally designed in late 1939 (its twin-boom fuselage and shape similar to the later American World War II Lightning) – into a jet-powered device. Designed under Frid Wanström, the J21 pre-dated the twin-boom fashion also later used by de Havilland, but replacing the J21's prop-powered engine in 1946 with a British jet engine produced the famous J21R; this was the only prop aircraft in the world to achieve series production having been converted into a jet. Needless to say, the unique J21 featured heavily in Saab's advertising for its new car. Both were examples of Saab's skills, as were the 1949 Tunnan, and the later Draken, Lansen fighter jets, and the plethora of aviation ideas that culminated more recently in jet fighters, the 340 airliner, and the Viggen and the Gripen fighters (although some of the jets had developed versions of de Havilland, Rolls-Royce and even Volvo engines). Sixten Sason, Saab's car stylist, also worked on the J21 and supplied drawings.

These aeronautical products really were the essence of Saab, and back in the 1940s the men who designed them also created Saab's first car, which was not just 'born from jets' as a Saab marketing headline once ran, but from props, jets, rockets, wings, guns, locomotives, turbines and all manner of engineering tangents. The point is, however, that the men who designed aircraft, also designed Saab's car. As Saab was designing its

Saab 91 Safir, with prototype swept and slatted wing prior to its use on the J29 'Tunnan' jet.

first car, it was also designing the 29, 91 and 90 aircraft types. The aeronautical link was therefore not hyperbole, it was engineering reality.

When Saab's men sat down to create its car for the people of its own land and their needs, the thought of global sales domination was far from their minds, for the Swedes were not made that way. Yet Sweden already had a car maker, which by 1947 was well established – Volvo. But in even its post-war PV444 model, the Volvo was a large, rear-wheel-drive car of American styling and layout. It was a good car, but was also a time warp of a vehicle that reflected pre-war themes in the same way that most other cars did, despite the massive technological and scientific advantages brought to industrial design by war-time development.

Intriguingly, it was the development of aviation, or aeronautics that had raced in World War II, where powerplants, structures and aerodynamics were the new sciences – and Saab was, of course, part of that. So surely it was natural for Saab to build a car that encompassed such thinking. Saab was not

in the mindset of building pre-war aircraft and pre-war cars to ancient design parameters. Saab was unhindered, unblinkered by a previous psychology: Saab the car maker could start with a blank sheet of paper and a whole load of new ideas. Climate and conditions in Sweden may have been relevant to Saab's first car design, but they cannot have been the sole key arbiter, otherwise Volvo would have been building something far more appropriate for the very same conditions, surely?

Trollhättan, home of Saab, had now carved out a niche, it had survived the war as Sweden had in neutrality but with strong affinity to the British when links with British aviation and engineering had been established, links that would soon transfer to the British motor industry. Saab had also expanded, with new offices and factories in the region at Nyköping and Linköping.

In late 1944, Volvo, by now in its second decade of existence, was planning its post-war cars, so by late 1945, after the Saab board had decided to diversify and seek new business incomes, the idea of a car for Saab was an obvious step. Saab had in fact faced a crisis in 1945: aircraft orders were drying up as peace came, and a glut of cheap American and British aircraft were on the market. The workforce at Saab did not have enough to do. Saab needed to build something other than aircraft, be that boats, houses, trains or machinery.

A SAAB CAR?

After much consideration, in early 1945 Saab president Ragnar Wahgren informed his board that 'the company has examined the feasibility of making cars'. Interest was sparked, and by late 1945 Saab had allocated precious money to a car development project (in the added knowledge that any ensuing export sales could earn much needed foreign currency), and a small team of men was gathered together to consider the starting point. Saab and its leaders knew that the company would need to diversify to survive in the new emerging economies. Key to the car project was Swedish car dealer Gunnar V. Philipson – he signed a contract for 8,000 of the new cars, and invested 1.8 million Swedish Kronor (SKr) into the project in advance.

Under the thinking of Sven Otterback – the vice president of Saab the aircraft company – the chosen engineer who was to become the father of Saab's first car came to the fore: Gunnar Ljungström. Ljungström was working as a wing stress engineer at Saab and became the chief engineer for the new car. The new Trollhättan factory would be the place to build the car after its birth in the Linköping site.

In 1944, Ljungström was designing a torpedo launching variant of an existing Saab aircraft; this brought him into further contact with the needs of airflow and aerodynamic behaviour, which was a good precursor for his next assignment in 1945, the Saab car.

THE ORIGINAL DEVELOPMENT TEAM

The original team of men for 92.001 ' UrSaaben' or 'Experwagen' – car number one – were hand-picked designers, engineers, senior and junior apprentices and time-served artisan craftsmen. Their names, in addition to those of Ljungström, Sason and Mellde, were as follows:

Bertil Baerendz
'Bror' Bjuströrmer (project manager)
Tage Flodén (roof bodywork / toolmaker)
Hans 'Osquar' Gustavsson (front bodywork)
Erik Ekkers (bodywork)
Sven Frederikson
Hermansson
Svante Holm (project head)
Olof Landbü (test engineer)
Nils Lidro (plans proportions)
Olle Lindgren (engine)
Siggvard Lenngren
Hugo Moller (assembly)
Ellis Olsson
Tore Svenson (chassis)

To the best recall and research, seventy years on, these are the names of the men of the beginning of the Saab car project (any omissions or errors are entirely accidental).

Saab's wing profile car and J21 design.

'Aeroplan' Men

Working at Saab, head engineer Ljungström was the 'father' of the first Saab car, and it was he who brought in the lead body designer Sixten Sason, the celebrated 1930s stylist and designer; Sason had worked in Saab's aeronautical drawing offices and had been a pilot. Also to come on board in 1946 just after prototype development in the metal began, was Rolf Mellde, an engineer with rally-driving experience and another man of vision and tenacity who went on to create Saab's brand profile through rallying.

Further Key Players

Berth Olofsson, Arne Frick, Erik Johansson, Olle Lindkvist, Lars-Olav Olsson, Gunnar Svanstrom, and Gosta Svensson are also names that were key elements of Saab's car project's early days. Two of the 92.001 UrSaab/Experwagen testing team, Mr Nyberg and Mr Garbing, were killed with Mr Landby (Landbü) in a non-car related accident in 1948.

Hugo Moller was in charge of tool design on the project and would go on to become Saab's chief tooling engineer and

Very early factory scene 1949–50.

TROLLHÄTTAN PLANT 1945–48:
RECORD OF GENERAL FACTORY STAFF NAMES

The following list is a record of known, currently listed and retrievable names of general Saab employees associated with aircraft and early car production 1945–48 in the Trollhättan plant, and including transfers from Linköping factory. These are presented in addition to the above listed lead names, as a tribute to the workers of Saab Trolhättan factory. Any errors or omissions are entirely accidental and apologies are offered in case of unintended error, for which no liability can be accepted.

M. Ahlberg	G. Hubenette	B. Olow
A. Axell	Johansson	B. Pedersen
O. Brant	P. Jurander	R. Pettersen
Barkland	S. Kahrle	Rane
T. Bergstrom	Kristensson	A. Sandberg
T. Callmin	Kvanstrom	Soderberg
G. Dahlgren	S. Larsson	S. Simonsson
E. Ekeber	Lester	Svensson
B. Fagerstom	N. E. Lindell	A. Sweno
A. Feltner	Liljevall	Torner
G. Funqvist	B. Mellin	R. Warner
R. Hellberg	H. Morner	E. Wennerlund
O. Holm	G. Olsson	Wetterholm

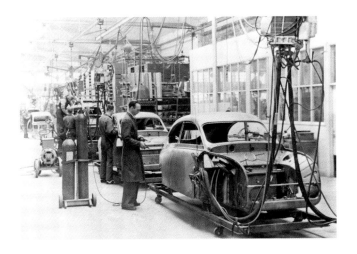

Ramping up production.

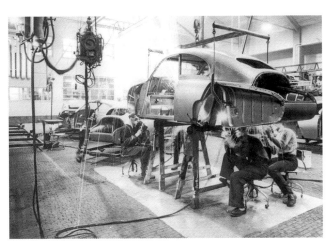

Hand built by craftsmen.

a patent holder. Svante Holm, the project leader, would (along with Tryggve Holm) become a senior Saab managerial figure. The Saab car team – to create car 'number one' as it was known – consisted of about fifteen to twenty men. Such men crafted the beginnings of a car that was the start of the Saab car story. But there was a team at Saab, and from the CEO down to the youngest worker, Saab was a family, and it is correct to record some of the names of the people who were the 'Aeroplan' men.

The mid-1940s Saab family, based at Linköping and Trollhättan, was headed by the CEO Gunnar Dellner. Lead players in the 1945 procurement were:

- Erik Rydberg: chief engineer of car production and production/tooling manager
- Claes Sparre: lead engineer
- Bertil Sjögren: senior planning manger
- Svante Simonsson: senior planning manager
- Gunnar Westlund: head foreman and field manager

DENMARK, GERMANY AND DKW

The starting point was to be a memory of a pre-war German car that had proved very popular in Sweden. This was the small, front-wheel drive, two-stroke DKW. DKW was a German company founded in 1928 by a man with a Scandinavian name, the Dane, Jorge-Skafte Rasmussen. Latterly DKW used American technology and built 6- and 8-cylinder engines for the Auto-Union group in Germany. It was Rasmussen who was instrumental in the joining of Horch, Audi-DKW and Wanderer AG into the Auto Union company; only Audi would re-emerge decades later. The cheaper pre-war DKW cars

were small and slow, but durable and very capable on slippery Swedish roads; DKW also made motorcycles and had already built an aerodynamic racing motorcycle. Surely Saab, the aircraft maker, could take the basic idea of such a car concept, apply aircraft design and engineering, and create something more modern but just as nimble? And what of DKW's foray into streamlined motorbikes? There lay food for thought.

Front-wheel drive had been briefly tried before in big cars – by Cord in America and by Citroën in France, as well as by the smaller DKW. But what of a transverse-engined, front-wheel-drive design for a small car family market, yet one with sporting handling and qualities all wrapped up in the safest body shell, and constructed boasting advanced aerodynamics on a scale never seen before? Did Saab actually know what they were about to dream up?

The Saab board might not have known what was coming, but the men on the ground, the engineers, had realized that they had to do something different to succeed. Just copying everyone else and creating a re-warmed pre-war car with leaf-spring or lever-arm suspension, bulbous, separate wing or fender panels and upright styling angles, enclosing a wheezing cast-iron lump of an engine sitting on a hefty chassis clothed in tin or even a part-wood or a canvas-clad body, was not going to tempt car buyers.

DKW's two-stroke thinking and legacy may have been the key influence on Saab's engine choice, but there were factors such as post-war shortages, a scarcity of machine tools and lack of raw materials, and the two-stroke had fewer moving parts. But if Saab could refine the two-stroke concept and fit such an engine in a car built to aircraft design standards, it might make its mark, or so thought the 'Aeroplan' men of Saab.

The Saab car was going to have to be radical and a fresh moment in design, not driven by ego, but by quality and safety

Now in his nineties, Tage Flodén (sometimes recorded as Flodan) was a young man in the mid-1940s. He was a toolmaker for Saab in the aircraft division, working on propellor aircarft and latterly on the J29 'Tunnan' jet fighter. But in 1945 he was seconded over to the Saab car project being run by Svante Holm and engineered by Gunnar Ljungström. Tage Flodén was a maternal line ancestor to the three generations of the Saab engineers of the Johansson family, Siggvard and Peter Johansson (of Haldex fame) being his direct descendants.

Because of Saab's need to secure funding for the car project, and the need to begin that project quickly in 1945 as aviation work slowed, Saab streamed aeronautical workers into the new car department faster than officialdom and government rubber-stamped approval could work. It is reputed that there was a degree of unofficial transference of government-funded aviation workers within Saab, actually working for the separate embryonic car project. Tage's grandson, Peter Johansson, takes up the story:

My grandfather Tage was a toolmaker, and he produced some parts for the first UrSaaben 92.001 and serial tools for the next series of Saab 92. He also worked on the J29 'Tunnan' aircraft. He claims that he drilled the first two-stroke engine (block) Saab produced for the 92. He mentioned that the casting was so hard that almost all the hardened steel drills had a tough time to machine the cylinder wall, and that he was forced to grind instead to get the proper dimensions and clearance.

Tage also confimed that he was employed by the aviation side, even though he transferred to the car side of Saab. Tage worked on UrSaab's body, as did Hans Osquar Gustavsson, each man being responsible for a part of the shell.

These men and their colleagues were the core of Saab, and the ethos of Saab stemmed from their creation of the 92.001 experimental, original Saab – the 'Experwagen' or 'UrSaaben'.

Marcus Wallenberg, the rock of Saab.

with all the details honed to provide something special. To the Swedish psyche, this was a natural process, to others beyond the Baltic, it was unconventional thinking. However, the problem with all this lateral thought was going to be keeping the design and manufacturing costs and the selling price down to reflect the gap in the market for a capable, new, cheap Swedish car.

Through such thinking, and the advancement of 200,000SKr as research funding, was born Saab's 'Project Small Car'. The idea was that the car could sell for around 3,900SKr, and Saab would have to sell 8,000 of them to recoup its money at the then known cost level. Soon 800,000SKr was allocated to build three prototypes. Meanwhile, given the employment situation and the 'national interest', Saab entered in talks with the Swedish government about seeking support for car production. By this time Saab had also discovered that the metal presses to build the car would need another 600,000SKr of investment. The costs were mounting, but there was a car to build. Saab the air-craft maker was to become Saab the car maker. The 'Aeroplan' men were to fly on the ground.

Wings were to give way to wheels – but slowly.

THE SAAB 92

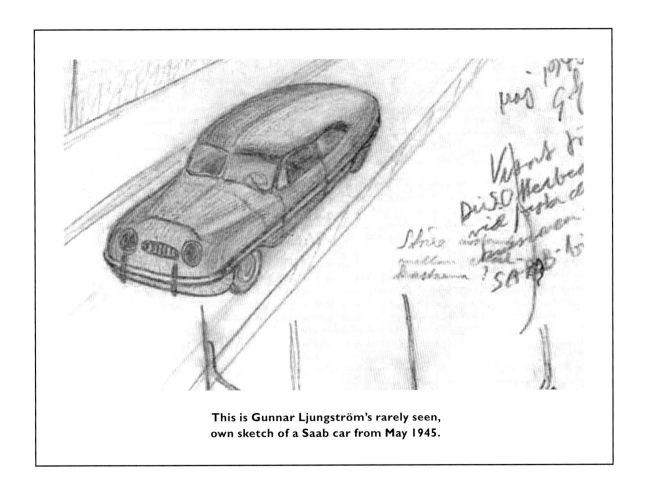

This is Gunnar Ljungström's rarely seen,
own sketch of a Saab car from May 1945.

VINGPROFIL – A
WING-SHAPED CAR

THE SAAB 92

VINGPROFIL – A WING-SHAPED CAR

GUNNAR LJUNGSTRÖM WAS the force behind the new car: he led the concept, but he was not the sole author and never pretended to be. At Saab, amid a band of brothers, the Saab car was a team effort: it was not the result of one man's thinking, but rather a collection of ideas that were honed and tailored into a new form and function: a new identity was to be created.

But what route should they follow? Should the car mimic Volkswagens, Fiats, Renaults and Tatras, rear-engined, rear-driven devices? What about Austin, Peugeot or Ford, with front engines driving the rear wheels and all clad in a dinosaur school of car design with running boards and upright windscreens? Remember this was 1945: American glitz, fins, chrome bezels and the carved and sculpted cars of the American General Motors styling schools had yet to be really born, or influence European design. Most cars had separate wings or fenders, and narrow slits of upright windscreens, while some still had canvas and wood in their bodyshells.

Perhaps only the VW Beetle marked a beginning to a styling departure: few people had ever seen what German aerodynamics experts had been thinking about for cars and aircraft in the 1930s and 1940s. Was this where Ferdinand Porsche gleaned his ideas – with a bit of help from others? Indeed, Ljungström admired Porsche's ethos, and he took a cue from it and VW – the teardrop shape, which Sixten Sason had focused on. But however often cited, Porsche was not the sole or major influence: France, Italy and even America were key influences in design terms.

The first basic design remit from a management decision was that the Saab car should be both faster and more economical than the DKW, and this could only be achieved through design – aerodynamic design. Less drag meant more speed and less fuel. It was a simple equation, and thus was set the foundation of the Saab car ethos. Unlike the Porsche and VW configurations, Saab and Ljungström chose a teardrop, but one that was front engined and front driven.

Here was the key, and the gateway to a design specification was unlocked. Perhaps the subconscious knowledge of just how popular the pre-war two-stroke German DKW had been in Sweden had played a role. The idea of a home-grown, updated version would certainly have appealed to one of Saab's backers – Philipson's the car dealers, for they had sold many DKWs. Suddenly, all thoughts and influences came together: Ljungström and the team had decided their own path, and seeded Saab with the ethos that came to mean so much: that of front drive in a slippery shape with some unique engineering ingredients.

Saab and Ljungström had to, in American parlance, 'bet the farm' regarding the choice of car design route they followed – and if they had got it wrong, Saab might well not have survived. It took guts, brain power and intuition for the Saab team to feel

A rare colour view of a 1940s Sixten Sason sketch. Elements of the 92 are obvious.

their way towards predicting the future. Like R. J. Mitchell and his design team in 1934 with the Spitfire, Saab defied convention and perceived thinking, and set a new design language: it was a massive reputational risk.

But the truth was that Saab had champagne taste and only beer money. The bunch of aircraft engineers and motoring enthusiasts who were the team wanted to forensically design a vehicle that was mathematically tuned to a high degree of efficiency. The 'Aeroplan' men had been used to aeronautical tolerances and the money to achieve them. Weights, thicknesses, resistances, load paths and performance were to be thought about and designed in just the same way that they would be for an aircraft or a rally or race car: that is, with the ultimate possible strength and least possible excess. It was a balancing act that no other car maker had really tackled outside motor racing, and as an ethos, it would cost time and money.

EXCELLENCE WAS EXPECTED

One of the earliest questions was, what should the advanced new concept be constructed from? Surely Saab, maker of aluminium alloy aircraft, could build its car from this strong but light metal and gain a massive advantage in terms of weight, performance and miles per gallon, not to mention rust resistance.

The reality was that Saab had made riveted aluminium aviation structures, but actually as a car body material aluminium would have been as complicated and expensive to weld as it is today, and Saab did not have the money or the experience. Glassfibre and plastics may have been an ideal aeronautical spin-off product from the war, but this was a technology in its infancy. Glassfibre-reinforced plastic body panels were time consuming to make and performed very poorly in a crash impact. Cash-strapped post-war Sweden was no place for a 1940s plastic test bed.

Despite the lure of alloy, one of the first decisions was to build the car in high quality, imported British steel as a stressed skin monocoque, yet using thicker steel and more reinforcement than any car had used up to that time (and well beyond it). The idea of a separate chassis with two battering-ram engine bearers extending forwards from under the car was thrown out, as was the idea of a built-up frame and skeleton. The car would have a fuselage – a one-piece monocoque structure with localized reinforcements where needed. It would have a soft nose and a hard cabin to protect its occupants.

The metal thickness used for the new Saab was over 20 per cent thicker than on any other contemporary car: the metal of the roof skinning was 1.11mm thick, the body side walls 0.87mm and the crucial, box-section steel sills were 1.59mm in thickness. In a unique, aircraft fuselage-inspired design, the main front roof supports and windscreen pillars featured extra steel inserts that ran down into the bulkhead.

The side rails or sills of the car were unique at the time, and remained so in the car industry until the Saab 99 copied their construction techniques. Most cars have thin gauge, pressed-steel sills that are welded up from several panels to create the sill, but these are easily deformed and can split open in an impact, and they also have seams that can rust. The Saab sills were thick box-section steel beams of immense strength with high levels of resistance to deformation. The middle of the car – the B pillars – were also box sectioned to form a roll-over hoop with unheard-of strength. The smoothed-in front wings or fenders featured large steel wheel arches with corner reinforcements to help absorb offset, driver or passenger side-only impacts.

There were no safety standards extant when Saab made its first car, but amazingly when they became law in later decades, the little Saab's ancient underpinnings sailed through such legislation. The cabin was tightly welded and filleted, and it had many aircraft-style rivets, too. There were no chassis rails, but instead a clever hull where experience was to prove that it did not split open in heavy impacts. In fact so strong was the 92 that when its offspring the 96 was crashed against a leading lightweight hatchback car of the 1980s, it was the ancient design of the Saab that performed best and suffered less structural intrusion into the cabin, and the floor and sills did not deform.

Thanks to Ljungström's previous role as a wing stress engineer at Saab, and the work of Olle Lindgren as stressman, and Erik Ekkers, the little Saab had a tough aircraft-style hull that resisted intrusion and could be dropped on its roof from a great height with minimal damage. The roof was made from one piece of metal, which was a unique feature at the time when most car roofs were made from a series of weak pressings welded together and then leaded smooth – and as such they were not rigid: by having a single piece of steel for the roof, the 92's torsional rigidity was increased.

The Saab's overall rigidity was very high, and load paths through the structure were carefully calculated, a rare move in late 1940s car design. Closely welded and properly undersealed, the body would stay stiff and strong through many Swedish winters. Just as in an aircraft, there were reinforcements around the cabin apertures. Only the rear-mounted fuel tank and front-hinged doors betrayed the thinking of its age, and these safety-related items were soon dealt with as knowledge advanced; the fuel tank was moved up to lie between the rear wheels, and the doors changed so they were forward-hinged.

Better safety was to be built in, but what shape would the car be? How would its drive train work, and what sort of character would it possess? These were the vital questions that hung in the cold winter air as 1945 turned into 1946 and a team of about a dozen men settled down to creating the first Saab car.

This is Sason's sketch number one, capturing what Ljungström wanted, yet in a new style for a new age.

Ljungström's mind was open, but he later stated that the idea for front drive came less from him and more from Sixten Sason, who pushed for the efficiencies of front drive. Driving the front wheels meant better traction, notably in snow and ice, with the engine's weight over the driven wheels. It also meant that weight was saved by not having a driveshaft running the length of the car to a rear differential. The floor could be flatter, the suspension easier to locate, and with the transverse engine alignment, more front cabin room could be found.

Front drive was safer, too, because there would be no rear-drive 'fishtailing' as power was delivered during turns or on slippery roads. The only real front-drive problem was where to put the gearbox – but Saab soon solved that.

The new car was to be a two-door, four-seater family vehicle with a large boot, with the capability to fold down the rear seats to create a small luggage deck whilst retaining two front seats. Not quite a van or an estate, this idea of a cargo or family area inside the saloon shape was to become a Saab trademark for decades. Saab also came up with the idea of giving the 92 removable seat cushions and a fold-down rear bench, thereby creating a small overnight or camping bed. It was an immensely practical and very Swedish thought that reflected the Swedes' need to make the most of summer and go camping in the country or by the sea.

Such were the details of design, but first came the key decision, what should the new car look like?

THE TEARDROP EXPLODES

With funding for a prototype and a development car to follow, Saab needed a shape, a form and a function. There were several ideas sketched up for the car's shape, and three of these were made into wooden and clay styling 'bucks' as small-scale models to help management decide which look to go for. A man named Bror Bjuströrmer, a figure in the Saab engineering group, has been cited as contributing to the initial schedule of design themes under Gunnar Ljungström's lead. Ljungström even sketched up his own idea for the car (see photo), a fast-back shape that was contemporary but unremarkable: it needed something else, and in a very self-aware move, Ljungström knew he needed help.

With two aircraft already in production, the factory was busy, and space for a new project was difficult to find. Thus it was in the Saab tooling department and their workshop that the new car began to be put together in the sketches and wooden models of 1946. But none of the proposals that Saab and its development team and management were considering was advanced enough, and a fresh look was needed. Enter the man with a sketch for a design that was truly innovative and aerodynamic. It came from an established name, a Saab employee, a pilot and a man well published and well known in Sweden. That man was Sixten Sason, formerly known as Sixten Andersson.

Tall and handsome, a debonair and charming Swede with a taste for Italian style, Sason had trained in sculpture in Paris and yet was a pilot as well as a technical thinker. He had been sketching aircraft and car designs from the 1930s, and was published in the motoring press. He worked for leading Swedish brand names, and would gain fame designing Hasselblad cameras such as the 1600F. He also designed the Electrolux vacuum cleaner, Husqvarna's iconic 1948 motorcycle the 'Silver Arrow', and a range of industrial design products including a moped for Monark of Sweden, and the cameras that men later took to the moon.

Sason lived and breathed airflow and styling; his ideas for a micro-car pre-dated the post-war German designs by over a

Sason's revisions were complete by late 1947: here we see the original sketch for the revised headlamp and bonnet.

A FROG OR A FLYING SAUCER?

People had various interpretations of the new car's shape: some Swedes said it was a 'green droplet', others thought it was like a bug or a frog. Whatever the correct metaphor, it was clear that the trends of the late 1920s and Art Deco motifs of the 1930s, allied to the thoughts of Paul Jaray, Jean Andreau, Gabriel Voisin and Hans Ledwinka, were also hinted at. A touch of American feeling was also present in the hints of coupé to the design.

Ferdinand Porsche's rear-driven, low-slung design theories may also have been of similar shape, but his own mass-market teardrop 356 coupé with teardrop styling, co-penned by Erwin Kommenda, was several years from its birth when Sason shaped the 92. And what role did the teardrop profile of the Cisitalia coupé and its Piero Dusio design play in the shaping of Porsche's first production car to bear his name, the little A-type coupé in 1948–49? And did such Latin-style influence permeate Sason's thoughts?

And what of Josef Ganz, the German-Hungarian who in the 1930s was also fascinated by car aerodynamics? Ganz rebodied contemporary cars and, say some, influenced Porsche, reputedly having some effect on his teardrop themes. From 1929 Ganz edited a car magazine and pursued his design themes for sleeker, more streamlined cars with better handling dynamics. His role in the 'Superior', a small car made by Standard in 1934, and in a car by Adler called the 'Makäifer' or 'May Beetle', may suggest he has a claim to have influenced the shape of the VW car project. Certainly the similarity of Porsche's 1938 VW 'Beetle' to the Standard Superior is evidenced to all but the most blinkered mind. But Ganz was part Jewish, and soon *persona non grata* in Nazi Germany. Eventually via a Swiss interlude he was driven into obscurity in Australia where he worked for Australian car makers, yet his design work was forgotten for decades.[1]

But the truth was that above all contemporary designs in 1945, Sason's singular work, *his* shape, his solo design style, was new and non-derivative – it was a design hallmark from the word go. Ljungström knew straightaway that it was the only choice, and he told the board so, advising that the shape would use much less fuel, be more stable, and permit higher speeds even if, as some felt, there was a touch of the 'frog' to its visual demeanour.

So where did Sason's 92 shape come from? Was it an aerofoil motif, or did its profile resemble a jet fighter's canopy? Was there something of a bridge-span or architectural motif in the sweep of the rear buttress? It was possible, as Sason liked bridges and even designed one. But what explained the unique stance of the new car's shape?

---

decade, and his 1930s designs included a people carrier and an aerodynamic, low-slung, steam-powered limousine. For Ljungström's new car, Sason walked in to the office and put down a sketch of a raked, stylish, fast-backed teardrop that had shades of French and pre-war Bohemian styling trends yet was styled with 'Vingprofilkordan' – a wing or aerofoil chord shape. However, the shape was Sason's own, resembling a sort of flying wing or flying saucer with wheels, or perhaps a smootheddown sleek tortoise! It was clearly influenced by nature and the wind. The slipstream and how to tame it was a vital element for Saab, even if the slipstream did have the rather unfortunate Swedish spelling of 'fartvind'.

Decades later, motoring writer and Saab author Eric Dymock likened the Saab's styling to a dish cover – maybe he was hinting at what later came to be called the 'jelly mould' school of car styling. Looked at from the viewpoint of hindsight, Sason's flying saucer with wheels was the first precursor of such styling language for the mass market – and didn't the Citroën DS take the idea one step further in the late 1950s? And could it be that the soft shapes of 1950s American General Motors' cars under the styling wand of Mr Earl aped the moulded shape and stance of the Saab 92?

CARROSSERIE, CARROZZERIA AND KAROSSEN

The design influences upon Sason were essentially French, German, and latterly Italian and American. In the early 1930s Sason had gone to Paris to study sculpture, and there he was thrown into the heady mix of the world of French streamlining. This was a movement that produced some amazing car designs *circa* 1936–39. The principal leaders of this trend were Giuseppe Figoni of the Figoni and Falaschi coachbuilding company, and Georges Paulin, a dentist who became a leading car stylist and whose talents touched not just French cars but also the 1939

Built up from a wooden base, filled, smoothed and blackened with polish, this is the original Saab 92.001 styling 'buck' for design presentation and approval.

Embiricos Bentley and the exquisite fastback form of the stunning 1950s Bentley Continental teardrop coupé.

Gabriel Voisin and his 'Aerodyne' cars might have paved the way, as had the Delahaye cars, but it was the smoother, sculpted, more integrated forms of Figoni and of Paulin that caused a sensation, not just in design, but in art and French fashion as a whole. Working separately, both men produced cars for the Talbot-Lago company, which signalled a new movement in design. In 1936–37, Figoni styled the elliptical, raked form of the Talbot T150 SS, and in 1939, the T150 C SS styled by Paulin took the look of the exotic, or even perhaps erotic, even further. Delahaye's Type 165 and various special body designs by Saoutchik, Le Tourneur et Marchand, alongside Panhards and the Peugeot aerodynamic cars such as Jean Andreau's 806, also made waves in the design sphere. But it was the curves and stance of the works of Figoni and Paulin that stunned the world then, and continue to do so today.

Amid these influences was Sixten Sason, based in Paris at the heart of this design revolution, and he cannot fail to have been awed by these huge, almost architectural cars. Aircraft were involved in the movement as well, with the French Dewotine company producing a streamlined, elliptically winged fighter aircraft not dissimilar to the Supermarine Spitfire – although without the Spitfire's advanced low drag, high stability wing, stemming from Beverley Shenstone's ground-breaking aerodynamics work and Alfred Faddy's vital structural input.

Paris and Beyond

Also studying the art of working in silver and then being fascinated by sculpture in Paris at the same time as Sason, was the Italian francophile Flaminio Bertoni (not to be confused with Nuccio Bertone), the man who went on to shape the Citroën DS.

After returning to Sweden from Paris, Sason poured out a series of advanced, elliptical, spatted, streamlined designs, which were published in the motoring press in Sweden and beyond. Sason's studio walls were covered in advanced cars and aircraft that all shared elliptical themes. Towards 1938 and beyond, he was further influenced by the German-led revolution in aerodynamic design.

Had Sason even seen the rare and almost unheard of Porsche-designed T61 racing car of 1940, with styling that suggested the top half of a VW Beetle moulded to a low-slung base unit that had echoes of Jaray and of French 1930s carrosserie? What of Porsche's 1939 Berlin to Rome racer, which was a precursor to the T61? But had Ferdinand Porsche seen Sason's advanced car design sketch published in 1938? This was a design for a true future-vision car with a sleek base unit featuring four enclosed wheel pods and a curved, dome-topped cabin. There were close similarities between Porsche's T61 and Sason's 1938 design sketch, and rare and expert knowledge of aerodynamics lay behind these similarities. The later 1960s 'Bluebird' world land record speed car was of similar body shape to that thought up by Ferdinand Porsche and Sixten Sason. This was the advance guard of automobile aerodynamics, and there were other names of great influence.

The Saab 92 was an amalgamation of ideas and themes that were manifested not as a pastiche, but as something genuinely new from the mind of a great designer.

Considering that the 92's basic underlying shape and structure remained in production from 1949 to January 1980, the integrity and the essential correctness of its timeless design can only be confirmed. Many observers feel that the Saab 92 shape was a demonstration of an absolute perfection of form in car design. It was a smaller car yet it looked like an exquisite piece of design jewellery: hyperbole may well be justified, not least because while the VW Beetle, Austin Mini, Citroën 2CV and Jaguar E Type have grabbed the design 'icon' headlines over the years, Sason's shape for Saab's first car has been somewhat ignored. The greatest car designs inspired by aerodynamics, the parabola and the ellipse, via the 1950s and 1960s design works of Flaminio Bertoni, Nuccio Bertone, Luigi Colani, Virgil Exner, Pietro Frua, Claus Luthe, Giovanni Michelotti, Robert Opron, Malcolm Sayer, Franco Scaglione, Giovanni Savonuzzi and Sergio Pininfarina, were yet to come; Chuck Jordan, Harley Earl, Bill Mitchell and Raymond Loewy were in evidence too – but the Saab was way ahead of everyone in 1946, in that no other production car had ever looked like that.

On the 92's debut, Britain's *Autocar* said that:

> Perhaps the most outstanding first impression is of the unusually smooth body shape of a type almost unknown on such a small car. The appearance is much that of a scaled-down, super sports two-four seater; it escapes the bulbous label, while retaining a touch of the exotic.

Motor magazine called the shape 'unorthodox', and crucially observed that such unorthodoxy 'sets the reviewer a task which is difficult because of the lack of normal standards for close comparison'. *Motor* called the 92 'ingenious', and noted the streamlined tail. The suggestion of it being a sports coupé in impression was again made.

In 2010, *Classic and Sports Car* magazine said of the 92:

> When launched, the 92 made almost every other European rival appear positively antediluvian … In addition

the 92's coachwork is some of the most elegant to be found on any post-war car…But to understand its impact, merely examine the result of Svenska Aeroplan Aktiebolaget's blueprint for a car built on aerodynamic aircraft principles. Then just consider that so many of its European rivals had engineering that dated back to the 1930s, or even 1920s.

Then and now, the shape of the Saab 92 was significant.

RULES OF THE AIR

Of particular note, the 'Exper-Vagen' or 'experimental wagon', prototype car 92.001 – or X9248 as it was coded in factory paperwork – had very highly swept windscreen pillars. The side panels were curved, and flowed into an aircraft-style rear fuselage that allowed the airflow to remain attached as it streamed down the back of the car. At the front, the first prototype had its headlamps faired in under a perspex fairing amid a low and wide style that looked like the leading edge of a wing aerofoil. The front wheels were also faired in under a somewhat bulbous wing or fender shroud line.

The car looked like a wing with wheels, and it was revolutionary. The sleek and sculpted prototype – the 92.001, now sometimes known as the 'UrSaab' (Original Saab) – was the 1940s equivalent of a concept car design, a one-off special, the sort of thing designers create for the Geneva or Turin motor shows to advertise what they can do. Rarely do such concept cars ever translate through to a production item as the 92 did: with only a few minor changes, Sason's flying wing fantasy of a car became a real car.

The 92 under test in the wind tunnel with tuft airflow markers. Note the minimal flow disturbance and attached rear airflow.

LEFT: **Sason was also known for under-the-skin design and his X-ray drawings. This Sason sketch shows off Ljungström's aviation structure work on the 92's skeleton.**

BELOW: **An early 'Sonett'-badged styling development of the 92.001 with the v-bonnet and faired-in square lamps framed by a revised grille treatment.**

To build the first wooden design prototype, created from a wooden base – a sort of table top in Swedish pine – the Saab team was given a space in the corner of the workshop. From that base unit, a team of six woodworkers built the mock-up, starting on 7 January 1946. As the wooden 'buck' took shape, Wahgren the company chief, his deputy Sven Otterback and Sixten Sason the stylist would come in and suggest changes to the work – asking for planing and sanding here and there to create the sleek, swept shape that would latterly become so famous. When the shape was finally formed and approved on 15 April 1946, after four months' work, it was painted and then waxed and polished by hand, by men with shoe polish and rag cloths. After that came the approval to construct the first car, in the metal.

That first styling 'buck' or development shape had been built from alder wood, with woodwork craftsmen from a small local firm called Motala assisting – but the next step, after approval of the shape, was to build a hand-beaten metal shell. This was created in May 1946 by artisan panel beaters over the wooden buck, reshaped with dried horse manure to achieve smooth compound curvatures and the correct resilience. The old firm of ASJ – railway engineers and carriage builders – helped with hand painting and lacquering the first 92.001 prototype body. The first metal prototype shaping was led by the hand by a man who was seventy years old – he was the craftsman with ancient skills who formed the first panels over the wooden buck and used manure to smooth the buck's curves for panel beating.

Stunning though the shape was, development work was needed at the front of the design. The 92.002 prototype was perhaps almost too futuristic. Bearing the registration plates of E14783/E1866, it had a broad, low, aerofoil-profiled front that

looked smooth but created a degree of excess cross-sectional drag (Cd.a) due to its large surface area, and the shrouded wheels had limited steering angle and soon fouled up their wheel-arch housings. Sason came up with a revised, more stylish podded headlamp and grille treatment, seen on car registration E14789 with its 'V'-pointed bonnet and two circular lamps, podded and inclined, on each side of the bonnet's V point. At one stage the V-shaped bonnet was fitted but the revised circular headlamps had not been thought of and the car retained its original faired-in square headlamps.

Sason also at this stage experimented with a wing-motif grille and bumper bar design, though sadly it was not deemed acceptable for production. A few rare photos and some archive film footage exist to prove these interim styling experiments that Sason undertook to modify the shape. Production prototype

No. 1 was completed on 1 May 1947, and the revised No. 2 less than one month later.

At one point Sason even fitted three headlamps in 'cyclops' style, though thankfully this was discarded. One 1948 proposal by Sason consisted of twin rectangular headlamps mounted high on a squared-off nose with a large chrome grille across the car: it looked very glitzy, very 1950s Americana, very ahead of its time, but it wasn't right for the little workhorse Saab. But it took another re-styling attempt to thin down the bulbous wing-section nose and create the higher, more upright frontal design that became the Saab 92 production tooled design after three prototypes – 92.001/02/03 – were constructed.

These changes took place prior to June 1947, when the shape was revealed to the Swedish press. The eventual production frontal design was less dramatic than Sason's earlier two proto-types, but it was more practical and had a lower cross-sectional drag figure. A bumper and a somewhat conventional grille aperture were added – so Sason's pre-space-age shape was being toned down a bit, although the revolutionary teardrop shell retained its purity of line and close relationship with the prototype. The early scale models of the Saab 92 for wind tunnel testing revealed a coefficient of drag (Cd) 0.32 at the Swedish aeronautical institute, and the full-size production car Cd was a stunning Cd 0.35 – far lower than the average drag figure for cars of the era, that being circa Cd 0.45–0.60.

The VW Beetle and Bad Airflow

Apart from the 1937 Lancia Tipo 97 'Aprilia' designed by Battista 'Pinin' Farina, the only other European mass-production car of the era to see a wind tunnel during design was the VW Beetle. According to Beverley Shenstone, the Supermarine Spitfire aerodynamicist who saw the Beetle prototype being wind-tunnel tested in Germany in 1938, Ferdinand Porsche's basic shape was a nightmare of drag-inducing eddies around its sunken window apertures, flat windscreen and protruding front and rear wings. Worse, despite the Beetle's sleek fast-back rear end, the rear styling failed either to keep its airflow attached down its rump, or to have a defined airflow-separation trigger point on its tail to control its wake vortex. A cloud of oscillating, ill-defined and drag-inducing turbulence spilled uncontrolled off the rump and sides of the ostensibly sleek Beetle. It evidenced that a curved teardrop shape was ruined if the fundamentals were wrong. Saab and Sason, meanwhile, got them correct.

Thus in comparison, the Saab, although initially styled by hand rather than wind tunnel, had an aerodynamic advantage that was real: it had at least 30 per cent less drag than the most aerodynamic car of the day, and 50 per cent less drag than a conventional car of the era. Early testing of a scale model in the Saab wind tunnel, with tufts attached to the body to indicate airflow, allowed Saab to refine the design elements. This reaped advantages in speed and economy. Gunnar Ljungström is reputed to have commented to those who were shocked by the shape: 'It does not matter if it has the look of a frog if it saves 100 litres of fuel a year.'

But the 92's aerodynamics were not just about reducing drag. As with all subsequent Saabs, the 92 was tuned to have good cross-wind stability, and the point at which the airflow separated – known as the critical separation point (C.S.P.) – was also finely tuned to reduce wake vortex 'base' drag behind the car, and to give lower levels of lift over the tail and under the car. By shaping the rear undertray, increasing ground clearance and tuning localized pressure, the airflow was encouraged to speed up and exhaust itself away from under the back of the car. This technique increased air pressure in the wake and so reduced drag and reduced lift. It was advanced design by anyone's standards in 1947, and stemmed directly from study of aircraft and missile stability.

The 92.001 and 92.002 design prototype bodies showing the developed rear window design.

In another rarely seen image, two of the original team of about fifteen men at work on the very first metal prototype; the older man is an artisan craftsman brought in by Ljungström.

Sason made the most of the benefits of the front drive configuration, one being the advantage of a flat floor by controlling vortices and pressure under the car, which according to later text book theory could reduce unwanted lift by 20 per cent. This early advanced thinking by Saab included adding underfloor shaping to tune the airflow's behaviour. No other contemporary production car was known to be designed this way.

The Saab car had to use flat glass in its side windows, so was short of inward curvature towards its top and roof, known as tumblehome; yet Sason was able to smooth and curve in the vital roof dome and rear end shapes to control the airflow, cheating it into thinking the sides were more curved than flat glass actually allowed.

SAAB AND THE SLIPSTREAM

Sason's intuitive scaling and sculpting reflected his knowledge of boundary layer and laminar airflow characteristics and the need to preserve localized airflow velocity, delaying airflow breakdown and decay over an aerofoil by creating ultra-smooth surface skinning, and this was vitally important to the design of the new car: Sason and Saab as aircraft designers knew that there are key rules to cheating the air and lowering drag, whether in aircraft or cars:

- The airflow over the front of the body should be free to flow sideways and not be channelled or forced under or over the shape. A rounded frontal planform is much better in this respect than a square-edge frontal design.
- Crucially, the rear of any fuselage or car body should decrease its cross-sectional area – its depth and width – towards its rear or trailing edge, and should do so, particularly for a car, at an angle that preserves airflow to a chosen point where it can be deliberately severed or separated. Premature separation of airflow must be avoided, but not at the expense of an overly long tail with variable separation points that might cause increased base drag and lift. The bobtail or 'Kamm' tail are key techniques in this respect, effectively 'chopping' the tail and securing a set, constant airflow separation regime.
- It is vital to tune the air pressure differential under the car to reduce base drag and induced lift, particularly at the rear.
- The angle and shape of the front windscreen is vital to preserving good aerodynamic qualities over the roof, sides and tail.
- Bumps, lumps, ridges and trigger points (excrescences) on the skin surfaces need to be avoided in order to avoid localized flow separation or airflow velocity slow-down and 'bubbling'. The boundary layer – that is, the sleeve of air passing closest to the body and subject to friction and interference effects – needs to be carefully considered and designed for.

These rules were the little known, yet crucial secret arbiters of car aerodynamics and of the Saab 92 shape, as was the consequent control of the form induced and interference drag coefficients. The Saab 92 reflected these rules to a degree greater than any production car at the time and for years afterwards, and it brought the standards of aircraft design and early streamlined racing car design to a mass market small car. Again, this is another fact for which the Saab has rarely received credit: Saab was doing for its first mainstream car what other car makers had not even thought of.

Sason's early vision included this longer-tailed theme.

When tested in the wind tunnel, the efficacy of the production 92's aerodynamic design was proven. It was not perfect, but the airflow stayed attached and the boundary layer was not upset by panel junctions, gutters or trims – all these had been reduced to smooth the flow of air. Unlike many contemporary designs and some modern cars, the 92 was a 'clean' car, meaning that it did not suffer from extreme airflow upset or a turbulent rear end that sucked up road spray on to the car.

ART DECO AND AERODYNAMICS

In the 1930s, a few designers had begun to apply streamlining rules to aircraft, cars and trains. The Supermarine Spitfire, the Douglas DC-3, the Lippisch Delta wings, the Horten brothers all-wing designs, the Auto-Union grand prix cars, the Mercedes silver arrow racing cars, Gresley's A4 Pacific streamlined locomotives, and the cars of Voisin, Figoni and Paulin were arguably some of the key Art Deco icons of industrial design. The clean, sweeping forms and ellipsoid shapes of the Art Deco era were a significant moment in design history, yet in the main, normal family cars were left behind by Art Deco as designers focused upon the expensive and the exotic, such as the shapes of the Bugatti Atalanté, the Cord 812, Peugeot 302 Darl Mart coupé, Talbot Teardrops, and the sheer style of the Alfa Romeo coupés of 1937–39.

The 1939–45 war focused research into aerial weapons and not car design. But apart from racing cars and the marketing-led moment that was the Chrysler Airflow, deep, academically funded scientific research into automotive aerodynamics was the 1930s preserve of Dr Wunibald Kamm and a few fellow scientists in Stuttgart's Research Institute for Vehicular Science and Engines. Beyond Germany, just a handful of names are obvious, notably that of Gabriel Voisin, the French aircraft designer and manufacturer who turned to making cars that made a massive aerodynamic design statement.

The American NACA research body in the 1930s was devouring original German research on aerodynamics and re-publishing the translated version as a series of NACA 'memorandums'. These papers were to become key research tools for American aircraft and car designers. Ironically, Kamm later went to America and did much work there, but it would be the late 1960s before Ford and GM funded the first major manufacturer studies and wind tunnel research in road vehicle aerodynamics. This was long after Saab, Citroën, NSU and Jaguar had paved the way – a route pioneered by British, French, German and other European researchers.

Although in the 1930s there were a few research papers that were mainly concerned with the effect of aerodynamics on car-handling characteristics, there really was little to go on for anyone wanting to design a truly aerodynamically efficient car. In England, W. E. Lay had written a paper entitled 'Is 50 miles per gallon possible with correct streamlining?' in the *Journal of the Society of Automotive Engineers* in 1932, and J. Andrade had written 'Wind tunnel tests and body design' in the same journal in 1931. In Britain, Frederick W. Lanchester had pioneered aerodynamic and elliptical study as early as 1896, and went on to build cars, but beyond these highlights, knowledge was rare and hard to find.

In Germany, W. Klemperer had published 'Investigations of the aerodynamic drag of automobiles' in *Zeitshrift fur Flugtechnik* 1922, and the names of W. Kamm, C. Schmid, O. G. Tietjens, F. Neesen and L. Prandtl were the few pre-World War II names with academically published automotive aerodynamics knowledge. This learning stemmed from aerodynamic and hydrodynamic works that reached as far back as the research of Nikolai Egorovich Zhukovskii – known in the West as Joukowski or Joukowsky, circa 1900. Prandtl, a high priest of early aviation design, had also looked at cars and boats for his flow studies.

In the 1920s and 1930s, Gabriel Voisin, Paul Jaray and Hans Ledwinka were the advance pathfinders for aerodynamics in car design. Prior to 1930, Jaray was perhaps the only one to pioneer thinking about aerodynamics as part of the whole design package. Sason was to do likewise in the mid-1930s. Such were the key ingredients, the roots of the Saab car.

The Stuttgart School

Northern Europe was the centre of aerodynamics study, and of note, Baron Reinhard von Koenig-Fachsenfeld was a German aristocrat who attended what became the Research Institute for Vehicular Science and Engines in Stuttgart (now part of Stuttgart University of Technology), and made an early study of road vehicle aerodynamics. Blessed with the resources to concentrate on this obscure new science, he came up with advanced aerodynamic car body detailing and shapes born of his love of fast racing cars. As a young man, von Koenig-Fachsenfeld had also worked for and become inspired by Zeppelin, where Paul Jaray had also been studying; latterly he worked for Mercedes Benz in the 1930s, influencing their racing cars.

In 1937, von Koenig-Fachsenfeld designed an advanced aerodynamic car body that was built as a one-off and fitted to a BMW 328 chassis. This was built by Wendler coachworks and became the the Wendler Stromline coupé. The shape encompassed much new smooth-skinned, 'teardrop' thinking in the mode of Jaray, yet had an overly long, pointed tail. But von Koenig-Fachensfeld worked with Kamm and both men recognized the advantages of the shorter, chopped or sliced tail. Now known as the Kamm tail, perhaps it ought to bear some reference to von Koenig-Fachsenfeld's name as well. The pair built a 'Kamm Coupé' body design based on a DKW chassis. Again the styling was 'teardrop', yet it incorporated new thinking – notably that of the curtailed rear. The front end was a blend of ellipsoid ideas with precursor shapes of the later E Type Jaguar, whereas the rear had overtones of later Porsches. The

drag coefficient was an amazing Cd 0.25. Baron von Koenig-Fachsenfeld had also designed a teardrop shrouded racing body for a DKW motorcycle – the same DKW company that Saab was taking close note of.

Herr Prof. Dr-Ing Wunibald Kamm of German, Stuttgart fame, was in fact Swiss-born, but became a scion of the Stuttgart Institute and its study of aerodynamics; his post-war years in America widened knowledge and appreciation of his work. But back in the late 1930s, the likes of Kamm, von Koenig-Fachsenfeld and a few others were ahead of mainstream thinking in automotive design. Perhaps they started by looking at aspects of detail design rather than Jaray's overall assessment of airflow, but Kamm and von Koenig-Fachsenfeld did significantly influence thinking at the time.

In the same period and in the spheres of auto-aero design, Sixten Sason, the pilot and aviation fanatic, was also turning out his advanced styling ideas for cars and aircraft; these were widely published in the Swedish and European motoring press. Of note, he designed the whole package, not just a detailed tweak: Sason was developing theories aligned with the German research leaders, and being multi-lingual he was also able to discuss and digest these new developments on a wide platform.

The young Sason travelled extensively in Europe in the late 1930s, notably in France, Germany and Italy, meeting top designers, visiting design houses and absorbing everything he could. In Paris he had been wowed by Voisin's shapes – even if they did have running boards and separate wing or fender panels: the 'gouette d'eau', or teardrop school of design, was evident, especially in Voisin's Aerodyne models and certainly in the cars of Figoni and of Paulin. All they needed was blending in, and smoothing down or modernizing to aircraft standards; the same could be said of Josef Ganz's ideas. Certainly, Sason's sketches of circa 1936 show hints of such revision and advance upon the bare bones of the ideas.

Saab 92 final production prototype.

The English aircraft maker, Bristol, also turned to making cars, and did so via close links with BMW and Frazer Nash. It was no surprise, then, that by the early 1950s Bristol was soon creating its own 'teardrop' shapes born from various strands of research, furthered in its own aeronautical design department. Bristol, like Saab, also had access to, and links with, German aeronautical developments. A further link came about via a connection with Alexander Lippisch and his flying wings, when Beverley Shenstone, the Supermarine aerodynamicist who had trained under Junkers and Lippisch amid the advanced art of glider, all-wing and delta-wing design in Germany in 1929–31, was posted to the Bristol company in 1940 to overview their design work for the Air Ministry.

By 1944, the Bristol aeroplane company was an advocate of swept-wing and all-wing design. Soon after, in the early 1950s, Bristol Cars began to create its curved aerodynamic car designs; this was not long after Malcolm Sayer, the great exponent of parabolic and elliptical forms, had started working for William Lyons at Jaguar. Few realize that Sayer learned his craft working at the Bristol Aeroplane Company in World War II – where the man who shaped the Spitfire's almost-ellipse of a wing, Beverley Shenstone, had also been present before his move to the top secret research facility at Wright Field, now known as Wright-Patterson AFB, Dayton, Ohio, USA. Curiously, it was at Wright Field that Alex Tremulis, the man who styled some of the 1950s most flying sauceresque and aeronautically inspired cars (as well as the Tucker) spent part of his war – sketching flying saucers

and advanced swept-wing or all-wing devices that had German design roots, and contributing to the legend of 'Hangar 18'.

The Italians were using air, boat, and car racing experience to develop their knowledge of streamlining, yet their focus often remained at the extremities of car design – large land-yacht-style grand cruisers and tiny little micro-cars.

Once again, the links between aviation, automobiles, the men that designed them and the advanced guard of Northern European aerodynamic design knowledge came together in a series of coincidences and events. One thing was for sure: if wings, fins and flying saucer styling comprised a post-war fashion, its roots lay in work by a handful of men from Paris, Stockholm, Stuttgart and London.

Combining the design elements of aircraft and cars was a rare process, and it was Saab – alone in the first place for a production car maker – which was to meld the two tangents of philosophy together successfully. Latterly in the 1950s, Fiat, which also manufactured aircraft, created air- and auto-influenced themes, but it was the pioneering aerodynamic studies in Germany and northern Europe between 1929 and 1944 that cannot be overlooked as key influences on advanced car and aeronautical design.

Saab, the aircraft maker with access to scientific research as well as that wind tunnel, was by 1944 unique in its combination of aerodynamics and automotive research knowledge. It was knowledge that Saab was the first to apply not only in a mass market car – but its *first* car.

Presenting the first car to the top men at Saab. Note the headlamp fairing and grille.

So Sason, and Saab, were ahead of mainstream practice: Sason's sculptor-trained hand was one of intuitive genius, yet he was not just about art: unusually for a creative, he had a scientific mind. Ljungström said of Sason that he was 'A genius; an engineer with the talents of an artist, or an artist with the temperament of an engineer ... the ideal partner to work with.'

THE DETAILS OF DESIGN

At the crucial rear of the car, the 92's curvy tail and rear deck angle preserved the airflow down to the rear base of the car. Some designers have argued that the tail is too long and that a more 'chopped' tail would have reduced drag further, but close analysis of woollen tuft and smoke flow results confirm that the 92 kept its flow attached down to its rear end. Sason *had* in fact, gently bobbed the tail according to the Kamm theories – it was *not* a long, torpedoesque stern even if it lacked a sharp razor-sliced rump. Only the danger of premature airflow separation triggered by a crudely moulded rear window trim strip could ruin the achievement, and that did not occur on the 92–93. In fact Sason used elliptical shapes to deliberately trigger a degree of airflow separation with minimal drag over the split rear windscreens and provide controlled aerodynamic behaviour. The production car, with its smoother one-piece rear windscreen, was even more finely tuned in terms of airflow down the rear rump of the car. The way in which the side panels curved inwards and joined under the rear windscreen was a design highlight – as was the brilliantly simple chromed rear bumper bar.

By achieving a 'fastback', Sason also reduced the wake behind the car and lowered induced lift through pressure differentials at the sides and underbody. The domed or upturned dish mould shape and very smooth skin surfacing also tuned the secondary vortex flows around and along the 92's body sides, tuning these reduced yaw effects in side slip and crosswind sensitivity. The 92 had low drag *and* stability. Only the roof gutter on the production 92 caused problems: Sason wanted it smoothed down as per prototype 92.001, but there was no other way of realistically securing the roof to the sides; a spot-welded flange and roof gutter was the manufacturing compromise. It did cause local flow disturbance, but to the smallest possible degree.

Why did the 92 have faired-in front wheels? Covered rear wheels were a 1930s streamlining norm, but hidden front wheels? The answer was that turbulence from the rotating front wheels and buffeting from the wheel arches could upset the airflow pattern down the side of the car and underneath it. Fairing in the front wheels reduced bubbles of flow separation and turbulence, and this is why 92.001 had completely faired-in front wheels – to lessen turbulence and drag. But a compromise had to be reached for a mass market car as the 92 had to run on real roads, often rural dirt roads, where racing circuit, low-drag styling was not appropriate.

Why did the 92 have such a sleek and curved form? What was the reason that the roof 'turret' was both domed and channelled into the sides in the way it was? Why was the passenger compartment so expertly blended into the overall reducing cross-sectional shape? Why did the shape taper to the rear? How and why was this car's surface skin so smooth?

The answers to these questions lay in Sason's knowledge that on a car or an aircraft, airflow slowed down as it passed along the body. As the airflow slowed down, it was more likely to degrade and break up into eddies of turbulence, causing drag and possible instability. By curving the sides of the car and the join between them and the roof, Sason tuned the airflow to retain its speed or even accelerate, and stay 'attached' longer. This not only lowered profile or form drag, it also created a cleaner, smoother aerodynamic behaviour around the back of the car. As a pilot and aerodynamic designer, Sason knew more than most car designers of the time. He knew that shape and smoothness were the key tuning tools for any shape, be it winged or wheeled. Crucially, Sason knew that wind-tunnel testing of small models of full-size items was fraught with risk.

Testing a model of a proposed car design in a wind tunnel did not produce the same results as full-scale testing of the actual product, because items or design features scaled down proportionally do not produce proportional results. The results become disproportionate due to scale effects. This means that reliable estimation of the effects of a design or styling feature assessed in a model cannot be ascertained and predicted for

Leaving the workshop is this very early 92.

the full-size item. In plain English, the resulting wind-tunnel-observed aerodynamic effects upon a small-scale model bore little resemblance to what would happen to a full-sized version of the same design.

Even the design of the wind tunnel itself could alter the results. Over-reliance on wind-tunnel results was to become a significant issue in the developing art of aerodynamic design and tuning. Only experienced aircraft designers knew this in the late 1930s, and Saab and Sason had grasped the problem early on.

The effects on drag of trim and items such as gutters, panel gaps, mirrors, door handles and window frames were impossible to assess cumulatively, and even more difficult to assess especially as their true behaviours and values changed when scaled down. Both the cross-sectional area of such items, and the smoothness of the overall skin, were vital elements in reducing both their actual shape-engendered, and interference effect, drags. Applying such thinking to a production car was a new art.

92.001 was an artist/aerodynamicists' prototype aimed at the best possible low drag shape, and although it was slightly altered for production, the key attributes of 'aero' styling were retained. It is significant that in the 1970s when the study of car aerodynamics really came to the fore, scientists, and notably A. J. Scibor-Rylski, tried to create the ideal minimum drag body shape for a car. The shape chosen was a mixing of parabolas and blended asymmetric half-ellipses, with a lower lobe shape that

was curved and tapered differently to the upper body. The shape, resembling a whale or shark, was built as a test model and subjected to fluid, smoke and computational analysis.

The results showed that the theories were correct, and overall drag and the problem of ground or road surface interference under the car were addressed, and the flow problems solved. What was startling was just how similar Sason's prototype 92.001 aerodynamic concept shape had been to this later experimental asymmetric shaped study of the 1970s. Despite the 92.001's touch of overly bulbous frontal width, the actual blend of part-ellipsoid shapes in front, profile and plan view was very obviously similar to the later scientifically proposed, theoretical minimum drag shape of Scibor-Rylski *et al.*

In fact, 92.001's fat, asymmetrically curved frontal lobe turned out to be not as bad as some had thought in the late 1940s, because the 1970s experiment revealed that despite the cross-sectional area issues, the somewhat bulbous lower body shape helped in reducing the road or ground surface interference drag problem, despite its fullness of shape. The transformations of body panels and shapes further down the 92's body also predate similar, later findings. Amazingly, Sason's 1945 shape for 92.001 was very close to the findings of the 1970s minimum drag research outcome. Despite some recent claims to the contrary[2], the Saab's Cd. 0.35 in production form (Cd 0.32 in prototype) was much lower than the

An early Saab 92 with the Saab-designed hydrofoil boat seen on the river behind it. Pure 1950s Saabism.

The 92.001, a veritable flying saucer of a car.

THE MAGICAL ELLIPSE

The study of the ellipse by British and German aerodynamicists in the 1920s set a trend. As far back as the 1890s, Frederick Lanchester was designing and building elliptically winged aircraft that had enhanced flight and glide ratios stemming from lower induced drag. The Swiss designer Karl Steiger-Kirchofer had in 1891 designed an amazing elliptical aircraft with futuristic streamlining and an ellipsoid T-type tail configuration. Steiger-Kirchofer also published his aerodynamic theories for moving vessels in his 1892 book *Vogelflug und Flugmaschine* (*Bird Flight and the Flying Machine*); and even earlier, in 1781, Karl Frederich Meerwin, a balloon pioneer, designed an elliptical low drag flying wing. The short jump from fluid flow to air flow around the ellipse was perhaps best grasped by Nikolai Zhukovskii.

These men and their studies were the foundations of streamlining, later to be manifested in 1930s aircraft and then in cars. For Saab the planemaker and car maker, the story and details of early aerodynamics and the role of wartime technological developments cannot go unmentioned, for without the history of aerodynamics, Saab, its aircraft and its first car would never have existed.

Just prior to World War II, Supermarine Spitfire genius R. J. Mitchell used elliptical shapes in his S.4 racing aircraft and on a 1929 flying boat design. In 1927, the Shorts-Bristow Crusader float plane designed by W. G. Carter of Glosters under the supervision of a Colonel W. A. Bristow for the Schneider Trophy contest, featured a broad-bladed, fully elliptical wing with a recessed trailing root edge (a feature later perhaps aped by the Heinkel 70 and specifically the Heinkel 111). The ellipse and its use in the 1925 Baumer Sausewind monoplane and its offspring the Heinkel 70, as well as in the Italian Piaggio Pegna P.C. 7 Schnieder trophy racer of 1929, proved the point of the ellipsoid benefits. These types developed the earlier foundations of new design principals.

By 1930 German glider design had gone elliptical, and the use of ellipsoid design in the 1934 British Supermarine Spitfire and American Lockheed P-38 Thunderbolt, as well as the Lockheed P-41 jet prototype of 1941 and other aircraft (such as the DC-3), had revealed much to designers. Elliptical planforms, parabolic profiles and specially shaped fillets that smoothed out the joins or transformations between wings and fuselages were factors that Saab, Sason and others could easily translate not just to aircraft but to cars. Sason 'got' the ellipse and it became a key theme in his designs.[3]

Sason's design sketchbook included numerous elliptically influenced shapes, his V-tailed, elliptically formed twin-engined airliner being particularly redolent of the advantages of the parabolic form. Lowering body drag, induced drag and interference drag were the key elliptical issues. Sason and Saab had access to all this knowledge, aided by being able to read early pre-war and then captured wartime technical and scientific reports written in German. To apply such a range of techniques to aircraft was one thing, to use them with a four seat, small family car – Saab's first car – was noteworthy: but it went uncredited to a wider audience.

1940s norm, in fact it was outstanding. Such a revelation should not go unnoticed in the annals of automotive design.

It was clear that the 1970s wind-tunnel experimental shape, and Sason's 1945 shape, both reflected to some extent the early works of Paul Jaray, other Frenchmen and German scientists. Jaray was particularly keen on swept and curved windscreen design, and the French and Germans had truly embraced the proven low drag advantages of elliptical or parabolic teardrop shaping. Curiously, except in the Spitfire aircraft, the later Hawker wing shapes and a few sailplane designs, the British were slow to embrace curves in car design – but Bristol, Jaguar and Bentley would change that.

A DEPTH OF DESIGN KNOWLEDGE

How did Sason know all this *and* how to solve the problems? The answer was in the totality of his experience as a sculptor, aerodynamic designer and pilot. He also had vision – future vision, an ability to predict what would evolve. Here was a designer who could think in 3D.

Sason had studied aerodynamic skin smoothness criteria. Similarly, German research into the ellipse, boundary layer and swept wing surfaces, notably by Alexander Lippisch, and Messerchmitt for whom Lippisch had worked, and also by Heinkel, Multhopp, Tank and others, was studied by Saab's aircraft designers in the pre-war and wartime years. One of Saab's immediate post-war aircraft, the J29 Tunnan, designed at the same time as the 92.001, made clear references to such research.

Building on his aerodynamics learning for the car, Sason wanted a highly curved windscreen on the new 92 in order to reduce pressure changes, turbulence and drag around the passenger compartment. The technology to build a cheap, mass production, curved, one-piece windscreen for a car did not exist. Highly curved one-piece moulded windscreens were then reserved to fast aircraft. So the 92 had to compromise with its highly raked, V-angled front windscreen and smoothed windscreen pillars and roof that were expertly faired in. Twenty years later, Sason applied his knowledge to the windscreen shape of the Saab 99. This shape – the most curved windscreen design ever used on a mass production car, which drastically reduced airflow separation and consequent pressure changes, buffeting and side panel turbulence – became a Saab design motif on the 99 and the 900.

The 92 had its unusually steeply reclined front windscreen angle in order to meet the basic rules of advanced low drag design – compare its windscreen rake with other cars of the era, and the 92's advance becomes more obvious. Decades later, research showed that there were two crucial factors needed to reduce pressure and drag caused by a car's front windscreen and its cabin turret. These were that the front windscreen's angle rake should be set close to an optimum 48 degrees, and that at the base and sides of the windscreen, good airflow to the side panels should be created by smooth, open panel angles. Incredibly, the designed-by-hand 92 approaches these parameters, yet was created decades before they were formally established.

In 1946, for 92.001, Sason created the unique windscreen rake angle and domed or blended cabin and roof joins in order

Saab 92.001, showing the bulbous frontal aspect.

to best apply low drag theories – these key elements were transferred through to the production 92 without change. On a normal car, airflow became unattached around the flat, upright windscreen and created a pressure bubble on the bonnet, as well as creating drag-inducing vortices down the sides and over the roof of the car, where with luck, the airflow might reattach. Sason's 92 design cured these problems, which until then had been accepted as the unsolvable norm, and took the car to the leading edge of aerodynamic efficiency – the airflow from the bonnet, over the windscreen and down the sides, top and back of the car was as close to the smoothest laminar flow condition that had ever been achieved. At the rear, the 92.001's two small elliptical rear windscreens created minimum drag around their shape.

The level of thought that went into the aerodynamics of Saab's first car was unprecedented – and there was more to tempt the engineering minded. For Sason had also made a close study of Werner von Braun's uniquely advanced rocket missiles, and had even sketched the details of a crashed Nazi V-1 rocket. It is reputed that he then travelled to Britain in the wartime bomb bay of the clandestine de Havilland Mosquito service to present his findings to British Intelligence and their Ministry of Aviation boffins (a group that included Beverley Shenstone, of Spitfire aerodynamics repute) in London.

Advanced aerodynamics and advanced German research – available to the Swedes during and after the war and quickly read by them in German – had a major impact on Saab's knowledge of airflow behaviour at high and low speeds. A key missile design-related discovery was to shape the rear or trailing edge of a body to change air pressure behind the body, and this in Sason's mind could be applied to a car, reducing both drag

and lift off the car. Achieving a venturi effect under the car also sucked it down on to the road – much safer than having it lift at high speeds.

Sculpted smoothness and its effect upon the aerodynamic boundary layer that lay close to the skin surface of a shape was the further vital ingredient, and Sason had discovered that missile aerodynamics and their effects on missile stability were vital factors in directional stability for any vehicle, whether air or road borne. By tuning the boundary layer, the centre of pressure and the rear wake pressure and 'base' drag, Sason and Saab created a car shape with both aerodynamic and dynamic stability. Treating the shape of a car as a wing and tuning the resultant characteristics was not new, but actually creating a wing-shaped car (minus the lifting action) was. Just as with 1930s gliders, the surface or skin smoothness was the key to drag reduction for the Saab car.

ABOVE: **Saab 92 of 1949 design in the MIRA wind tunnel, showing the excellent frontal airflow transition over the crucial windscreen angle.**

LEFT: **Reality: retaining its design purity, the Saab 92 prototype evolves into the metal.**

Sason was the key influence on the design language of the Saab 92, and after some tweaking to the prototype's front end, its shape became defined in May 1947. The stance of the shape and the strength of the Art Deco-themed rear C pillar and its grand sweep suggesting a buttress or maybe a fin, gave the car immense presence. The 92 had a strong 'down the road graphic', the term modern designers use to quantify the visual impact of a design. The 92 was a blend of Art Deco and modernism, and as such it predicted design trends. Within a few years a range of cars, notably the Bentley Continental fastback, Bristol 403, Porsche 356 and others, had deployed teardrop shapes, swooping C pillars and a blend of coupé styling elements. By late 1950, there was even a car that seemed to take Sason's shape, throw in some Volvo PV 544 themes and Americanize it with shades of Jaray and Kamm added in. This car was the 1950 Nash Airflyte super coupé. Soon, American design trends, framed by the likes of Earl, Jordan and Cole, had also embraced curved styling as the 1950s evolved.

Yet in terms of smooth saloon-coupé modernity, perhaps the late 1950s Citroën DS was the ultimate symbol of the design trend first set off by the 92. Certainly the 92 and the ID/DS seem to share a similar stance. Park a Citroën ID 19 and a Saab 92, or a DS and 92.001 beside each other, and the stylistic linkage is clear in terms of sculpture, angle, stance and domed form. The fact that their respective designers, Sixten Sason and Flaminio Bertoni, both studied sculpture in Paris at the same time provides an intriguing parallel.

The combination of Art Deco symbolism and the advanced modernism of aerodynamic thinking behind the shape that Sason came up with has rarely been credited, and has not been

ABOVE: **Under the bonnet of P92.001.**

LEFT: **The incredible interior: Art Deco-style seats with chromed rails; note the massive side walls and sill to the A-post structure.**

forensically analysed. Given the facts now revealed, one thing is more obvious, and that is, Sason's shape for the 92 was both an influence on others and a new design statement long before Citroën claimed the plaudits for causing something similar. Underneath that shape, there was more that was ahead of its time.

In Saab's 92, in Sixten Sason's amazing visionary design, the wing-shaped, boundary layer-tuned and truly aerodynamic production car had become reality. It was a moment in design history.

GUNNAR LJUNGSTRÖM: THE ENGINEER WITH INTELLIGENT VISION

Gunnar Ljungström, 'father' of the Saab car.

Gunnar Ljungström's father Frederik had been an engineer with patents held in agricultural engineering and marine and hydro-power inventions; he worked with his brother, Birger, on these schemes, and had designed a new type of gearbox mechanism, which his son Gunnar had tried to promote. After graduating in engineering in 1932, the young Ljungström spent a brief spell with the British company A. C. Wickam Ltd, and then, via periods at Nohab and Alfred Gassner, was absorbed into Saab in the late 1930s.

Just before that time, Gunnar Ljungström conceived an idea for a people carrier or minibus-type vehicle, but production plans came to nothing. At Saab, Ljungström trained under A. J. Andersson, and made his mark working on a solution to an aircraft engine cooling problem by designing a hydraulically actuated cooling system. But wings were Ljungström's thing at Saab – strength, weight and shape were all conflicting issues, and Gunnar Ljungström put his problem-solving talents to work in this area.

Ljungström was an engineer, a mechanics and structures man, but he also turned his mind to airflow requirements and car body shapes. Across a lifetime of thinking, Gunnar

Ljungström became not just an icon of engineering, but the senior figure behind the ethos of Saab. He went from working on wing design and studying not just load paths and structural issues, but also the effects of attaching underwing devices and bomb bay aerodynamics, straight to creating the chassis and hull of the first Saab car – which he fitted with a flat-bottomed undertray.

Gunnar Ljungström was the solid rock behind the development of engines and gearboxes at Saab, notably as the 92 developed through the 93 series into the 96 and 96V4. Gearboxes were a Ljungström passion, as was efficient combustion behaviour in the cylinder head.

Even up to the Saab 99, Ljungström was thinking in advanced terms of stresses, compression patterns and load paths, all worked out by hand long before other car makers used 'super computers' to do the same thing.

Can we look to Ljungström for the insistence on safety being built into the first Saab car? It seems we can, as he brought with him the idea of reinforcing any opening in the car's structure – in true aviation style. And it was Ljungström who went with front engine, front-wheel drive at a time when most others – including VW, Porsche, Fiat, Renault and Morris – were choosing rear engine or rear-wheel drive.

Gunnar Ljungström rose to be head of the Saab engineering department, and retired in the 1970s. He was showered with awards, notably a Fellowship of the Society of Automotive Engineers. This award, only ever given to a few of the world's finest engineers, cited the fact that Gunnar Ljungström had shown 'outstanding leadership in the development of a small, front-wheel drive car with superb aerodynamic qualities ... and for successful application of his early aeronautical experience to the car, in areas such as lightweight construction, aerodynamics, material properties and economics'. There was a gold medal from the Swedish Academy of Engineering Sciences. Gunnar Ljungström was truly the father of the Saab car, and a great man to whom much is owed.

SIXTEN SASON – THE DESIGNER WHO COULD SEE AIRFLOW AND THINK IN 3D

Sixten Andersson was born in 1912 at Skovde in Sweden; by 1939 he was a well known name within the narrow field of design and illustration – though his name had changed. Sixten had wanted a more unusual label, a name that would be more memorable than the ubiquitous Andersson, so he changed his last name to Sason, which in linguistic terms equated to 'spice'. But Sason was no flamboyant artist: he was also an engineer, a calm thinker who could work with men such as Ljungström and Mellde.

From an early fascination with flying, the then Sixten Andersson trained as a pilot in the Swedish Air Force, but in an aircraft crash his chest was penetrated by a wing strut, and he lost a lung and suffered significant impairment. Struck down by infection, he was in hospital for months. Yet within a few short years he had reinvented himself as an illustrator, and then as an industrial designer. He also studied to be a silversmith, and that passion may explain some of the exquisite detailing in his designs, be they cars, cleaners, cookers or cameras.

Sason went to Paris in the mid-1930s and trained in sculpture, at a time when Citroën's future designer, Flaminio Bertoni (latterly stylist of the Citroën DS), was also studying sculpture in the city. The moving sculptures – the automotive works of Voisin, Figoni and Paulin – were also dominating car design and the Art Deco movement. From Paris, Sason returned to Sweden by way of Italy and Germany, where he noted the advanced art of streamlining and the developments in aerodynamics. By 1939, two important things had happened in Sason's life: first, his designs and drawings were featured in the motoring press; and second, he started to work in the illustration department of the rapidly expanding aircraft maker that was Saab. Initially Sason specialized in producing x-ray-type see-through structural drawings of Saab aircraft and their components, but soon he would be studying aerodynamics and shaping Saab's first car.

Sason became a major name in Swedish design and in the world of global industrial design, famed for his ability to think in

Sixten Sason, designer with the mind of an engineer and the skill of a futurist.

three dimensions, or 'in the metal'. He designed the Saab 92, 93, 96 and 99. He also designed the Husqvarna Silver Arrow motorcycle in 1955, and the Hasselblad camera of 1948 and its later series. He shaped the first Electrolux Z70 vacuum cleaner, the Monark moped, and not only a Husqvarna chainsaw but also that manufacturer's waffle cooker – a stunning device that looked just like a spaceship or UFO. He also styled a range of cookers and fridges, designed the Zig-Zag sewing machine, and came up with a defining shape of electric hand-iron. His drawing board and studio were packed with sketches for boats as well as elliptically shaped flying machines of great futurism. Sason also designed a proposal for a suspension bridge at Oresund. All this work was product design and industrial design with a scale of function and perfection without excess. Sason's designs were mature, organic and original, and as such they are hallmarks in design.

In a drawing of 1941, Sason sketched out a rocket-powered fighter, delta-winged, all-wing or blended-wing in shape, with the capability for short take-off and landing: over seventy years later it still looks like an advanced stealth design. How much this 1941 design influenced Saab's later Erik Bratt-designed Draken jet fighter, itself a design icon, is a long argued point, but there are those, including Rolf Mellde, who have suggested some similarity – so maybe a link between the two is not as fantastical as some might argue.

Sason's archives, exhibited in the Vastergotland Museum in 2009, also show that in the 1930s he was designing micro-cars that pre-dated post-war German micro-cars by over a decade. Sason also drew people carriers, sports coupés and a radical steam-powered, aerodynamic limousine. He shaped the Catherina two-door styling proposal that introduced the targa-top roof design and had flying C pillar rear buttresses, both later used by other designers. The detail elements of Sason design were also stunning; for example, his Art Deco-style headrest design for the 96 and 99 was a singular sculptural statement of great originality in the world of the mundane art of car seat styling.

Continued overleaf

Continued from previous page

SIXTEN SASON – THE DESIGNER WHO COULD SEE AIRFLOW AND THINK IN 3D

Sixten Sason died in April 1967, aged just fifty-five, just as his last car, the Saab 99, was about to be launched. By then he had taken on (in 1961) the young Bjorn Envall, and he encouraged Envall to contribute to the 99 as his health failed.

Sason was a tall, elegant man with a penchant for Italian style. He was known for his long research trips around the design houses of northern Italy, where he was held in great affection, and for his love of fine food and wine. He was also a man of humour according to those who knew him. Sixten

Sason died early, but left a legacy of elegant and functional industrial design, his Husqvarna motorcycle and waffle cooker symbolizing his sheer blend of style and functional elements at their best. His work was the subject of a tribute in London at the Design Museum in the 1990s. But perhaps his flying saucer of a car, the Saab 92.001 and its production descendants – leading to the 99 – should qualify him as one of the great unsung figures in car styling and product design of the twentieth century.

This view of an early car in dark blue, still with shrouded front wheels, proves that not all the first Saab cars were green as is so often claimed. A few were blue.

A very early production interior – touches of the Bauhaus, perhaps.

ROLF MELLDE – ENGINEER AND DRIVING FORCE

Rolf Mellde was another icon of Saab – he joined the company in 1946 straight from army service, and the 92.001 prototype was under way when he arrived at Saab. Before that he had worked for a number of small engineering companies. Mellde had developed two main interests, these being engine design and rally driving. He had worked on the design of a two-stroke boat engine whilst working for a marine engineering company after he had graduated from the Stockholm Institute's technical school. At one stage he had sought backing for a small car he had designed. Through his passions, the ingredients for a Saab ethos came as much from Mellde as they did from others. Efficiency and handling

Rolf Mellde, key figure in the genesis of the ethos of Saab and the rally success story.

were his focus. Latterly, Mellde would seek the finances from senior Saab management to create engineering laboratories and rolling-road testing equipment.

With his concentration on rallying (and race circuit driving), Mellde's sheer energy and drive propelled Saab into creating its rally department and the international PR that flowed from those early 1950s beginnings. For Saab, rallying was what modern corporate-speak would call a 'brand pillar'. Whatever the cliché, the truth is that without Rolf Mellde, that would not have happened, for he was the character behind the idea and the profile. The driving characteristics of the cars can also, to some notable degree, be put down to the Mellde ethos.

Mellde risked his early mid-1950s middle management position to pursue the secret of the Sonett – the first composite two-seat Saab of 1955–56. It was Mellde who gambled much on making the car without formal approval. Similarly, it was Mellde who risked his career to challenge Saab boss Tryggve Holm in order to foresee and lay the foundations for the four-stroke engine at Saab, and to begin its study internally at Saab long before official sanction existed.

If anyone knew how good a two-stroke engine could be, it was Mellde; conversely, he also knew the limitations of the

type. By 1960, Mellde knew that Saab's engineering and design ethos was being hampered by its engine choice. But management was unlikely to be moved in its views. So Mellde, at some professional risk, set up a four-stroke engine development unit deep within Saab. It is reputed that he even hosted design meetings in his own home. He wrote a letter about the need for a better engine and sent it to Ljungström and Svante Simonson, then Saab's production chief.

Described by some as a strong character who could give orders and argue his corner, Mellde was a man of vision and tenacity. Whilst Erik Carlsson rightly gets the plaudits for his career, it should not be forgotten that as early as 1950 Mellde won the tough Rikspokalen rally in a Saab 92. Mellde, K. V. Svedberg, Great Mollander and Margaretha von Essen all drove Saabs in the 1950 Monte Carlo Rally, ensuring the start of the Saab rally legend in the 92's first year of full production. Mellde then won the 1953 Swedish Championship.

The tuning of engines, steering, brakes and suspension was Mellde's passion, and his early works before the great names of rallying came to Saab in the 1950s should not go unacknowledged – the 'feel' of the early cars stems from the team at Saab and from Mellde's work.

Would Saab have rallied or got to Le Mans without Mellde? It is unlikely. Would the 96, the V4 and the 99 have been what they were without Mellde? Without doubt they would not, for if there had been no 96, V4 and then no 99, Saab may well have died, and it was Mellde who pushed these vital projects along. Mellde may have been a late comer to the early days of the 92.001, but he became a key member of the founding team at Saab: he was technical director from 1962 to 1971. Amazingly to some, he left the company to pursue new engineering opportunities at Volvo in the 1980s; but his contribution to Saab was his longest running theme. Mellde was an inspirational part of the spirit of Saab.

BENEATH THE SLIPPERY SKIN

Under the car's skin lay the influence not just of Gunnar Ljungström and several others, but also of Rolf Mellde.

Mellde, who joined Saab in 1946, was a young man going places. Articulate, intelligent, an 'ace' rally driver with advanced car control skills on high-speed ice as well as tarmac, he had experience of setting up car engines, drive lines, suspension and steering. He was the man who set up Saab's racing or rallying department: he had been drawing engines since he was a boy. The early 92.001 and the three styling development cars had already been built when Mellde joined Saab fresh from the army. Yet he was instrumental in developing the car at late prototype stage. While we can credit the legend that is Erik Carlsson with influencing Saab's direct and responsive steering, braking, suspension performance and 'feel' it must, surely, be to Mellde that we look to as a promoter of what were to become the Saab handling traits and ultimately a Saab brand motif.

The decision to use an aluminium-headed, two-stroke 2-cylinder engine was both genius and ultimately in the long term a handicap – the leap in Saab 96 sales when it was re-engined with a V4 engine tends to confirm that. But that was two decades away, and first there came the 2-cylinder, transverse-aligned, oiled-up, two-stroke, 25hp Saab-designed engine, with 764cc in the production version.

Again the influence of the little DKW and its two-stroke engine was to be felt. These engines had done well in Sweden in pre-war years, and their oil mix did not freeze or wax up in the deep-frozen winter conditions. Swedish mechanics knew how to fettle the engines, even if a decoke was needed every few thousand miles. Light, with fewer moving parts, the two-stroke was simple, cheap and unburstable; it also revved

beautifully. Compared to a low compression, 4-cylinder, cast-iron lump, a Ford V8 or another side-valve antiquity, there was something nicely alternative about the valveless two-stroke, even if it did scream and smoke.

Gunnar Ljungström designed his own, improved version of the DKW two-stroke engine and the prototype engine – with its 'thermoisophonic', or thermal cooling system, built with help from Albinmotor AB.

Water-cooled, with a three-speed gearbox and with wonderfully responsive rack and pinion steering as opposed to the convention of the vaguer feel of the worm and roller type then in mainstream use, the mechanics of the 92 were as honed as the bodyshell. Of note, the engine was mounted well forwards in the under-bonnet void, which brought two major advantages: more weight was over the front driven wheels, and there was plenty of rearwards crush room in an impact, leaving space for the engine to move before it impacted the main bulkhead. The oil-to-petrol mix was set at 4 per cent. Unusually the engine had its own mounting cradle featuring a small leaf-spring component with rubber buffers that resisted torque shunt. This drastically cut vibration, which was vital with the 2-cylinder's characteristic 'thrum' and 'buzz' sound effects.

Rock Steady Suspension

The suspension was by torsion bars with independent rear mechanisms. Front suspension loads were transferred into the bulkhead and stiff central tub area, in a manner that aped wing-to-fuselage loads and stress path design. The mounting of the rear suspension arms was well inboard of the wheelbase, reducing weight and pendulum loads and effects on the car. Telescopic shock absorbers and good roll and rebound

OPPOSITE PAGE:
**The sensation of Saab:
a 92 screams along.**

THIS PAGE:
**The smooth coupé style of the
airflowed rear.**

rates produced a car with deft handling and the responses of something far more exotic, but a hard ride. It steered like a sports car, a small fighter aircraft or a sports glider, so it was direct, with minimal 'play' and little input needed: the car told you what it was about to do. In effect the 92 drove, steered and rode with the finesse of a real driver's car. Keeping the engine revs up and learning how to make quick gear changes soon became the key to fast progress in the little car.

To ensure reliability, Mellde even installed Saab's new design of two-stroke engines in old DKWs as development cars, and won a rally and was placed in others using these test 'mules'. Thanks largely to his work, the 92 was a fine driver's car, and steered and braked with wonderful feedback and accuracy. The prototypes also racked up thousands of kilometres of testing to ensure that the Saab-designed engine and components were fit for their purpose. Test drivers from Philipsons, the garage chain that was co-funding the 92, had to deal with a busy schedule, as the prototypes were driven night and day around the rough rural roads and tracks of the Östergötland county and the Norrköping Road. Bumpy roads and exhaust fumes were tiring for the drivers, but many worthwhile changes to the production car specification resulted from this long development period, overseen by Olof or Olle Landby (Landbü), the Saab 92 chief test driver/engineer. Landby was sadly drowned with two Saab test department colleagues (Mr Nyberg and Mr Garbing) in a non-car-related accident in September 1948.

Just one crankshaft failure marred the development of the engine; the car was tested in total for over 280,00km, day and night throughout 1946–47. With the engine and gearbox integral as one unit (different from the DKW design), and with clutch and input shaft aligned with the crankshaft, every rotat-

ing shaft was in parallel, thus reducing internal stress and vibration. The car's radiator was mounted behind the engine near the bulkhead, away from cold air coming though the grille. This was fine in winter, but gave rise to overheating in the summer due to a lack of engine bay airflow.

A column gearshift was used – a touch ponderous perhaps, but the standard of the day. A 'freewheel' clutch allowed the driver to disengage the gears and save fuel by coasting. There were other oddities such as no boot lid, so luggage had to be loaded via the main cabin doors. Amazingly, early versions of the 92 had no heater, which seemed especially mean for a Scandinavian car. The dashboard design was very spartan and simple, and the tubular-framed deckchair-type seats might have come out of a 2CV if it had not been for their thicker padding and design motifs, which in turn echoed 1930s Bugatti design architecture. Indeed, 92.001 had a French or Italian feel to its interior furnishings, with salmon grey buttoned cloth and angled seat squabs amid a sparse, simple room that was lightened by painted panels.

For aircraft men used to no expense spared in securing the ultimate in efficient design, creating a car on a minimal budget was a new regime. Yet this was a good thing, as Saab did indeed use second-hand parts to create 92.001; this included using a DKW fuel tank and various other parts-bin remnants – and no one can say where the steering wheel came from. Saab also purchased a second-hand Opel Kadett and a Hanomag as reference points.

Hans 'Osquar' Gustavsson was one of the team of men who created and built the 92.001. Gustavsson worked on creating the hand-formed body panels and frontal design, which required the help of several small engineering companies, all

THIS PAGE:
A rare sunroof-equipped 92.

OPPOSITE PAGE:
**Henk Ossendrijver's lovely old 92
in a western Australia setting.**

sworn to secrecy. The ASJ, Thorell and Northern Light companies supplied machined parts, panel beaters and casting skills, respectively. A lot of trial and error was involved in creating the world's first, mass production, standard class monocoque, safety-designed bodyshell – which is what the Saab 92 represented. Nobody else knew how to make a monocoque – except other aircraft makers. Saab's men made a visit to Nyokopings Automobilfabrik to see what they could learn from the company that had been building cars from imported knock-down or kit components. But all these cars had been chassis-based examples of the ancient art of coachbuilding, and nobody seemed to know how to build a stressed skin car body.

It was clear that Saab would have to think about wings and fuselages, about the design of hatches and doors in self-supporting hulls, and from there, create a wheeled hull or fuselage with suitably reinforced apertures and correct load paths through the structure: essentially, Saab was to build an aeroplane with wheels!

NEW CHALLENGES
IN A NEW ERA

Saab set itself a high target when it started car production at Trollhättan, for at the same time the company was launching a series of civil and military aircraft, and embarking on building its jet engine under licence from de Havilland of England. Saab cars and Saab aero engines (Flygmotor) were to assist each other in many ways.

There was a great deal of heavy engineering required, and forces of between 350 and 500 tons were required in the new pressing machines used to build the cars. Expert pressing and fabrication skills were also needed for the aircraft parts and

engines. Links with the British were to prove strong, and old friendships were to be very useful. Several aspects of the tooling machinery required for Saab to build the 92 and 93, and the 95 and 96 were sourced in Britain with Vauxhall in Luton, and through Vickers-Armstrongs, the aircraft and ship builders of Newcastle and Weybridge, who were providing expertise.

One question often asked is why Saab's production factory's main area was called the 'Winter Palace': the answer lay in the fact that the white paint on the ceiling began to flake and drop showers of paint flakes down on to the workforce below, in what looked like a snowfall – hence the nickname.

The early 92 bodies were transported around the production area on trolleys or carts, but as things grew and production ramped up in the 1950s, Saab created a proper convey-type car-body assembly line. Early 92 metal bodies were welded up inside a wooden frame and then gas welded.

There was close co-operation between the 92's design team and the tooling/build workers, and Sixten Sason was not just the creative mind one might expect of a designer: he also got closely involved with the build process, and had an understanding of the construction process. Ljungström and Mellde all worked closely with the 92's build team, and this eased the development problems. Such was the spirit at Saab, that it built the spirit *of* Saab.

TWO POT POWER
AND AMERICANA

For the engine, Sweden's war-time expertise at roller and ball bearings meant that creating a three-bearing crankshaft was easy for Saab. The production 92 weighed in at 885kg (1,775lb). It was no lightweight, but neither was it a cast-iron lump, and

it had low drag and that spiteful, perky engine to row it along. Going over 900kg would have put the 92 into another tax band in Sweden, so weight was crucial, though not at the expense of safety or rust resistance. Despite the weight, top speed was cited as 115km/h (65mph). However, fuel consumption was not as good as four-stroke small engines: even with its low drag shape, the Saab struggled to get to 7.06ltr/100km (40mpg), and oil had to be added to the two-stroke mix. Ljungström's design, allied to Mellde's tuning skills, did, however, produce a car that was fast through the gears, with overtaking speed performance from the two-stroke being particularly strong – well above class average, provided the engine was kept nicely revved up.

In late 1947 the Swedish motoring press were shown the first recognizable Saab 92 car – the 92.002. This was the car with the revised chromed grille and with two round headlamps set each side of a raised prow. It was a development of changes made to the original 92.001 registered as E 1866 and E14783, after which the aerofoil-shaped, faired-in front was altered to provide a V-angled bonnet with two podded headlamps set each side of the nose.

The debut happened not in Trollhättan but at Saab's Linköping base in the canteen on an expensive antique rug. The car's debut was attended by everyone, from Marcus Wallenburg down. Reaction to the 92 was both favourable and curious, and soon the first stages of production build-up were begun at Trollhättan. The car was to have a name, but as it was a follow-on from Saab's last product, the Saab 91 Safir aircraft, it seems that the car got stuck with just a number: 92. After further extensive testing involving the first five cars, the pre-production models in 1948, the first public view of Sweden's

Sleek Saab style for suburbia.

Production car with cut-away front-wheel arches and green paint.

LEFT: **Simply stylish, the 92 interior with early 'strip' speedometer.**

ABOVE: **The exquisite door handle detail, perhaps reflecting Sason's interest in silversmithing.**

new 'other' car was in April 1948 when 14,000 people turned up at the Grand Hotel in Stockholm to see the 92. Then in mid-June 1949 the 92 went on public show in its home town of Trollhättan. But the car was a basic specification variant, right down to having only one windscreen wiper and a very sparsely equipped dashboard.

Behind the scenes, Saab was spending millions of Krona on building the factory and the body-pressing equipment. The bill for the presses to form the body parts was 2,240,550SKr, and the total cost to get the Saab 92 into production line reality from design sketch to rolling cars was 4,577,062SKr. It was a massive amount of money at the time, and had begun with just 200,000SKr of development funding. The price of the car had risen, but here Saab had also been influenced by tax band levels and government regulations. The initial price per car was set to be 3,200SKr, but this rose to 3,900SKr and then to over 5,000SKr at the government's order.

British Steel

As Saab was buying British steel for the car, it approached a British company, Pressed Steel Ltd, to supply the body pressing equipment – but Pressed Steel Ltd turned Saab down. Svante Holm, the 92's lead project manager, then turned to America, and after a visit to the Budd steel fabrication works, secured the services of an American company named Heinz Manufacturing of Philadelphia; this company shipped over the giant body-pressing tools, weighing between 70 and 300 tons, to the Linköping factory where the early 92 work was done. When the move from the Linköping factory to the Trollhättan factory was made, the expensive new presses – Saab's biggest investment – were sent by canal barge, a journey that nearly ended in disaster as one of the vital, massive pressing machines nearly capsized its barge, and Saab's first venture into car production came close to sinking before it was built. Three Heinz company employees travelled to Sweden to oversee the setting up of the giant presses: William Meyers, Joe Slobojan and Edward Tipper.

Saab built three body presses, and their operation was overseen by lead production engineer Nils-Gustav Nilsson. All went well after the initial near-disaster on the canal barge, but in 1954, as production was really ramping up, the press that was producing the 92's roof malfunctioned, and lengthy and major repairs to the machine were needed. In the interim Saab had to fabricate major panels from other locations and presses.

As early as 1952, Saab began considering 92 production outside Trollhättan, and beyond Sweden itself. Enquiries were flooding in for the car from all over the world, notably from North and South America. At one stage Philipson's, the garage chain that had backed the 92's development, considered setting up their own production plant near Stockholm. Within a few years, Saab would be building cars in South America.

A Saab 92B, as good as new, perhaps better. How many other 1950s cars looked like this!

The Saab 92 was a Swedish-designed car with international style, with French, Italian and German engineering influences, a German-derived engine, American-sourced trim items and a body made from British steel that was pressed in American machinery. The little Saab was a polyglot product.

By late 1949, Saab had settled on a production specification for 1950 for a better trimmed, de luxe variant – with a heater, engine thermometer, ashtray, sun visors and clock, and with bigger bumpers and painted wheel rims. The biggest external difference was that the grille was now chromium plated and not the body paint colour. Twenty pre-production 92s were made: two were the base model and eighteen were the higher specification cars. Philipson, the dealer who had invested in the car, wanted the de luxe version to be the sole model to introduce the Saab car brand, and at a price of 6,750Skr – almost double Saab's price estimate of 1944.

Legend has it that all Saab's early cars were painted green – a particular shade of left-over wartime green paint – but in fact several of the early base model cars were painted in a very smart navy blue (see photo). In December 1949, the Trollhättan factory was ready for proper series production. It is known that a least one car was produced prior to the Christmas break on 12 December, but real rolling production started in the first week of January 1950: on 16 January 1950, Saab delivered the first three of the series production cars for customers. Only one month after production started, the cars of chassis numbers

7 and 8 were entered in the Monte Carlo rally, driven by Rolf Mellde/K. V. Svedberg, and Greta Mollander/Margareta von Essen. They finished in fifty-fifth and sixty-ninth places, respectively. Better results were to come, but few recall that as early as December 1949, a very early pre-production Saab 92 won its first rally at the Circuit of Ostergotland, driven by K. V. Svedberg.

Saab managed to make up to four cars a day, and produced a total of 700 cars in the first full year. In 1951, chassis numbers ran from no. 701 to 1,469. For 1952, new VDO instruments were fitted, replacing American, Stewart Warner fittings. For 1953, several modifications were made – a rear window that was 53 per cent bigger, a repositioned fuel tank and filler, and a proper external boot access.

It was in 1953 that such a modified 92B series was first cited, but it wasn't until the 1954 model year that the B label was publicly launched, after 8,000 original 92s had been manufactured. Four new paint colours were added, and a new carburettor from Solex (the 32BI) boosted output to 28hp. Extra chrome trim mouldings on the wings, and the trademark plexiglass window-draught shields were fitted. The facia panel was also painted to match the chosen body colour, which smartened up the interior to a significant degree. More powerful Hella headlamps replaced the weak, sealed-beam American specification lights of the early cars. The easily broken, piano-wire starter-handle cable was replaced with a more durable and rather organic rope! At this stage, the Saab car lacked a starting key. The inconvenient placing of the battery under the boot floor was also changed to an engine bay location.

The first Saab car was shipped to America in mid-1951, and more were to follow. From 1950, a Danish company, Nordic Diesel Auto AS of Copenhagen, began selling the 92. By early 1951, thirty cars had been imported, not least a 92 for Her Majesty Queen Ingrid of Denmark who, like the Swedish royal family, soon had a penchant for the little Saab. By 1953 Saab had exported forty-eight cars to Denmark from a total of 330 export cars, and had also exported some 92s to Morocco – a surprising destination for a winter-tuned car. In 1954, the running of Saab's Danish agency changed hands, and Leon Jorgensen became general agent until 1957.

For the 1955 model year an electric fuel pump was fitted; and in 1956, two new colours were added to the range, bringing the total to seven in the Saab palette. By late 1956, Saab's first car had sold a remarkable 20,128 examples, of which 14,828 were of the B specification. But the car had been developed only to a certain point, and after five years of life some significant updates could be envisaged. The pace of development across Europe's car makers was significant, and Saab had to move on: the 92 would need to grow up. Yet the basic ingredients had been set, because the little Saab was a joy to drive – responsive and tactile, it sent messages back to the driver through the steering and the suspension. The brakes and the steering had a communicative feel, and you knew what the car was doing, or about to do next: driving the Saab was an involving experience – and one that was about to get better.

By 1956, a revised Saab 92 – the 93 – was reality, and it wasn't just a facelift, but a heavily reworked, re-engineered car. Perhaps it was the real beginning of a wider fame for Saab's amazing little aero weapon of a car. But in the 92, Saab's unusual story had truly started, and the spirit of Saab, the ethos of its engineering excellence, had begun to roll.

ABOVE: **Under the bonnet: transverse front-wheel drive with two-stroke.**

BELOW: **Tech spec: Saab 92 X-ray view.**

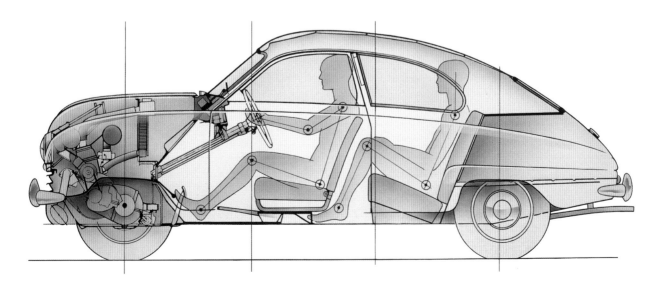

Production of 92 began 12 December 1949 after 1947 92.001 prototype

Engine

Type	Transversely mounted 2-cylinder 2-stroke valve-less engine. Water cooled with thermoisophonic circulation
Cylinder bore	80mm, stroke 76mm, volume 764cc
Compression ratio	6.6:1 25bhp (18kW) at 4,000rpm
Caburettor	Solex 32 AIC type. Mechanical fuel pump feed. 4% oil mixture by pre-mixing at tank

Transmission

Front-wheel drive. Single disc dry-plate clutch: Column change Speed gearbox and freewheel device. Synchromesh on top gears

Suspension and steering

Suspension	4-wheel independent springing with transverse torsion bars front and rear: hydraulic shock absorbers
Steering	Rack and pinion with 5.5m radius

Wheels and tyres

15-inch wheels

Brakes

Type	Hydraulic Lockheed system of drum brakes all-round. Handbrake activated on rear wheels

Electrics

6 volt system.

Bodyshell

Stressed skin monocoque with reinforcing beams in windscreen and door pillars. Box-section sills and reinforced front bulkhead. Cd 0.35 in production trim

Dimensions:

Wheelbase	2,470mm
Overall length	3,920mm
Overall width	1,620mm
Overall height	1,425mm
Unladen weight	765kg

Performance

Top speed	105km/h

Price in Sweden at launch

Skr. 6,550

The original Saab 92 advertisement, 1950.

**Stylish Saab 93: even the badges
were designed to be beautiful.**

POLISHING
THE JEWEL

THE 93 TO 96 V4

POLISHING THE JEWEL

WITH THE 92, SAAB had not just won its gamble, it had triumphed. Vast amounts of money had gone into making the aircraft company's first car. Thanks to intelligent innovation in engineering and design, the little car captured the minds of the motoring press and public alike. Demand was growing, and all of Saab's spare aeronautical production capacity was focused on the car part of the business. But post-war shortages were still limiting factors: Saab wanted top quality British steel and no compromises were to be made for the thick-skinned car. Saab needed 1,600 tonnes per year – a trifling amount, which, as Tryggve Holm often pointed out, America could churn out in a few hours.

Yet the 92 was not perfect, and there were things which could have been done better with more time and a bit more experience. Saab's men, restless and enthusiastic, did not sit on their laurels. Before 1955 was over, the thoughts that had been buzzing around the design team's heads for over a year were manifested in a developed version of the original car: the Saab 93. Gunnar Philipson, the garage chain owner, knew what his customers wanted to add to the 92, he told Saab, and the idea of the 92B and then the 93 was further reinforced.

First announced in December 1955, the early production 93 model cars were produced alongside the 'run out' 1956 model year 92B specification cars, which were still on sale at the end of 1956. For the revised car – a further honed and tweaked version of the 92B – Saab had been busy. All the things that buyers had noted and asked about were acted upon, and there was some added style thrown in. Launched on 1 December 1955, the 93 had been announced on paper in August during the summer break, in the traditional, quiet summer news period. The highlights of the new model were:

- New engine
- New gearbox
- Revised styling
- New suspension
- Better trim

The changes to the car were far more dramatic than had been expected by anyone; only the body really remained the same, and even that had undergone styling surgery. Underneath there was a new engine, though it was not a four-stroke engine as Saab could not afford to design its own, and Trygve Holm, the senior Saab director, seemed wedded to the concept of the two-stroke. There were, however, a new gearbox and major suspension changes – even the suspension load paths into the bodyshell were changed from the 92's set-up.

AN ITALIAN FRONT AND A GERMAN ENGINE

Externally there was a stylish new frontal 'face' to the car – an 'Italian' front styled by Sixten Sason after yet another hard driving charge southwards to the design houses and motor shows of northern Italy. Inspired by Turinese style, Sason drew up a new frontal aspect and grille design of Alfa Romeo or Lancia-inspired shape, flanked by chrome bars and twin headlamps that really gave the car a new presence, a much stronger image. It was not a copy, but a new look with hints of other influences. This was perhaps less organic in design terms than the 92's frontal design, but it gave the car a level of international elegance and sophistication that many admired. The addition of chrome strips over each wheel arch and more elaborate bumpers also added what today we would call 'bling', but in 1955 was a touch of brightness in post-war European austerity design. Sason, a fan of American themes, had added a bit of trans-Atlantic panache and Italian style.

That panache was somewhat diluted when Saab added the 'Klimator' winter heating device to its car – this included a radiator blind that ruined the style of the elegant grille, although it did allow warmth to be quickly generated for the engine and heater. The price of the 93 at launch was over 8,000Skr, largely due to a new tax regime and rising manufacturing costs.

Of great note was the fact that suddenly, Saab's car was no longer transverse-engined. Front-wheel-drive it remained, but lurking under the bonnet was a three-cylinder, longitudinally mounted engine. The question was, why? The answer lay in a riddle, because DKW, the company Saab had taken its cue from for the 92's engine design, had bounced back with a pretty little two-door car powered by an efficient and torquey three-cylinder engine.

A beautiful rendering of the 96 Italian front by Saab's own Gunnar A. Sjögren – 'GAS'.

Dr-Ing Hans Müller

Saab hit back with its own new, larger engine, but it would not lie across the engine bay. The basic design principle remained the same – the valveless two-stroke cycle with oil added to the combustive mix at 3 or 4 per cent. The engine was a design by Dr-Ing Hans Müller and was flexible and revvy, spinning and wailing up to 38bhp at 5,000rpm. Best of all, the torque figure exceeded the horsepower figure by creating 52lb/ft of torque at 2,700rpm. Mounted at a 30-degree inclined angle with a radiator providing water cooling placed at the bulkhead, the new alloy-headed, iron-block motor actually had less cubic capacity at 748cc than Saab's original 764cc engine, but more bhp and more torque.

Müller's engine was a development of ideas he had been working on for some time – it may even have had a pre-war basis with Heinkel lineage (not DKW, as so often erroneously cited). But he refined it, and added an anti-vibration shaft as well as carefully designed block construction to reduce harshness and vibration. Working with Ljungström, who designed the new ZF-built gearbox, and due to production capacity issues in Sweden, the first 3,000 engines were contract built in Stuttgart by Ernst Heinkel's company – once an aircraft maker. Saab's new engine factory in Volvo territory, Gothenburg, would soon produce the new engine. With its radiator mounted so unusually behind the engine at the bulkhead, a fan with a long drive shaft was needed to create engine-bay airflow into the radiator. Saab owners soon decided that this was an 'overhead fanshaft'. There was also a water pump and a thermostat for the first time.

Saab spent money on developing the suspension. The 93 now boasted coil springs, hydraulic telescopic dampers and some clever locating arms. At the rear, the torsion bar had gone, replaced by a cleverly located axle. The handling and ride quality in terms of spring and damper rates, and resulting roll and rebound characteristics, were transformed to a new level. A tighter turning circle with better 'feel' through the steering was also evident. Other major improvements included:

- Twelve-volt electrics
- Better heating and ventilation
- Tubeless tyres
- One-piece chrome bumpers
- New seats with foam rubber cushioning
- New gearbox design with clutchless shifting on first and second gears, and revised freewheel device
- Interior camping bed conversion kit, marketed as 'bedable'
- Interior cargo box liner for the rear seat
- Safety fuel tank between the rear wheels

The new gearbox had a short length, achieved by the gear drive through just two gearwheels on the main shaft. For the 1957 model year, the 93, with its very comfortable and strongly framed new front seats, was fitted with two-point safety belts as standard, a major innovation in the market place; three-point belts would soon follow. Also for 1957 came the Saxomat automatic clutch as an option: this Fichtel & Sachs device was an early form of mechanically controlled semi-automatic gearbox. Even though many cars of the 1950s were equipped with four-speed gearboxes, Saab stayed loyal to its tough three-speed gearbox. Somehow, with the engine's flexible torque and pulling ability, which now gave a top speed of 70mph (118km/h) and a 0–60mph time of just under 20 seconds, only having three gears was not the handicap that perception might have suggested. Overtaking performance and times through the gears were excellent, and the car could be stoked along with great verve even in a Swedish winter when Saab's aircraft-style carburettor heating was needed (this device could be deactivated for the summer).

If all these changes were not enough, Saab then tweaked the 93 even further for 1958, creating a 93B. Sason added more chrome, a one-piece front windscreen with bright trim, and a new windscreen wiper design and sweep pattern. The old-fashioned, external turn indicators on the door pillars were also deleted, and new indicator lamps fitted front and rear. From a mechanical standpoint, the oil-to-fuel ratio for the combustion chamber was reduced from 4 to 3 per cent. In the cabin, Saab raised the rear seat base – children had complained that they could not see out due to the low seat height. Clearly this was a car company that listened to its customers.

The only cloud on the horizon was neither the fault of Saab, its head of production Svante Simonson, nor of Ljungström, or of engine designer Müller – namely, the concept of any two-stroke, valveless, 3-cylinder engine exposed, in its combustion and cycle action, the internal engine surfaces to bore and liner wear, particularly if left standing or if badly lubricated. Engineer Josef Eklund was Saab's 'man on the spot' in Germany, who managed the development and production of the new engines in Stuttgart, and then back in Sweden. Eklund had joined Saab in November 1953 as a gearbox designer, and would rise to become leader of the engine development laboratory, a department that included fellow engine man Olle Lindkvist. Paul Broman was the department's foreman, and the 1950s team included Alvar Andersson, Arne Gustavsson, 'Lille Bengt' Törnquist, Bengt Ullström, Tore Jönsson and Olle Johansson (there were several generations of the various Johansson families at Saab), who became a test engineer and had a penchant for American V12 engines. Ake Järkvik also joined the engine laboratory team during this early era.[4]

LEFT: **Something special in Saab blue. This 93 has the Italian front but the front-opening doors. Rare and lovely, seen outside ANA in Trollhättan.**

BELOW: **Pure Saab, in Sweden.**

Saab also had to re-engineer parts of Müller's engine design due to excess pin and bearing wear, and Eklund became the two-stroke, 3-cylinder engine guru at Saab. There were problems to solve: the 3-cylinder engine's development had not been problem free, and the development of a new gearbox would require solutions to engineering challenges related to vibration, wear and noise. One example of this development period was how Eklund devised a clever internal oil feed for the gearbox via hollow shafts. New tooling and steel presses were needed as production expanded and the car was developed; Bengt Aker-lind was the plant production manger who oversaw these elements of the factory's expansion. Many cast housings or casings, such as that of the gearbox, were manufactured by German companies.

Despite the new 3-cylinder engine's behavioural foible (which was less likely to become apparent on engines used on a daily basis), the 93 was a massive success and sales figures shot through the roof: by 1958 over 13,969 were sold in one year, and Saab had sold its 50,000th car in 1958. That year alone 17,778 examples of the 93s were sold. In 1958 Torsten Noth-in, an original Saab chairman, retired, and was replaced by Erik Boheman as chairman. Royal patronage continued, with HRH Prince Bertil of Sweden ordering a 92 in 1951 and then a 93, and latterly a 93 750 Granturismo in yellow and blue. Meanwhile in the Netherlands, young Princess Beatrix bought herself a

smart, chrome-trimmed, blue-black, white wall-tyred, 93 split-screen model.

In Great Britain, an ex-RAF officer named Robert Moore (Saab's test pilot for the J29 Tunnan jet fighter in 1948) would be the founding figure of Saab in the country, a land destined to become one of Saab's biggest export markets, and in America

750 GRANTURISMO

In April 1958, Saab surprised the motoring press and the market by showing a sporty version of the 93B. This was a car with twin carburettors, 50bhp and a special tuning kit option to raise output to a heady 57bhp SAE, or a touch less at 55bhp when expressed as DIN. There were extra driving lights, sports stripes, and an interior with padded seats that could be adjusted to over a dozen settings. A classy, three-spoke alloy and wood-rimmed steering wheel looked the part, as did the fitting of a Haldex 'Speed Pilot' timing chronograph device on the dashboard. Two paired chrome stripes were added to each side of the car, making it look longer. Radial tyres – grippy but soft Pirelli Cinturatos – were fitted as standard; a switch to longer-lasting Dunlop SP tyres would be made. Before long, Saab was also offering the rather less crucial fitment of chromed hubcaps.

Just like the standard 93, the GT 750 needed to be stirred along: changing gear at high revs required a technique to be learned, as the unburstable little engine had to be kept revved up beyond 4,000rpm in order to keep its pace going. Once mastered, this high revving method of driving meant that the Saab could keep up with larger engined and much more powerful cars. The resulting sound and noise levels were best described as unique.

What caused this new model to appear? The answer lay in the fact that Saab had begun to build its profile in America and in Great Britain. The idea of the 750 and the later GT 750 Super was to raise the car's abilities alongside its marketing profile. Saab was learning. Furthermore by now, Saab had a massive profile in the world of rallying, Rolf

The smooth rear of the 93: this one is a Granturismo 750.

Granturismo bluebird.

Mellde had overseen that, and the name of a certain Erik Carlsson was becoming legend. The 750 Granturismo was a great way of marketing Saab and all it stood for.

Fastbacked, sleek and sexy in an intellectual kind of way, and not a fin or swage line in sight. A classic Saab advertising image from the 1950s.

ABOVE: **Super Coupé 93 in an upmarket setting.**

LEFT: **Sheer style: the US spec Saab looking like an expensive coupé.**

the aviation connection would continue via aeronautics engineer Ralph T. Millet. Millet originally had the idea of licence building Saab cars in America, but that vision did not materialize. Millet thought that a 4-cylinder engine would make the Saab an attractive proposition, not least against the VW Beetle and the rise of the small car theme in America. Millet was doubtful about the chances of the two-stroke-engined Saab, yet a meeting with Saab's Tryggve Holm in 1955 resulted in Millet agreeing to Holm's strong wish to send some two-stroke Saabs to America to test the market. Millet would soon hire Bob Sinclair, who by late 1958 was a Saab man, and he would go on to play a pivotal role in Saab's future.

In 1956, Saab shipped four 93s and an early example of its two-seater Sonett (see chapter 4) to America and booked floor space for a stand at the first International Automobile Show in New York. At the event, such was the expression of interest in the Saab 93 that within days Millet had decided to set up a company to import and sell Saabs in America.

Rallying was to be the key (see chapter 8). Rolf Mellde, winner of the 1952 Swedish rally championship in his 92, was despatched across the Atlantic to oversee a competition campaign that delivered strong results and huge publicity gains. Entering the Great American Mountain Rally in thick November snows on the eastern seaboard, a 93 driven by Bob Wehmann and Louis Braun won the three day rally. Mellde was sixth and another 93 was seventh. The 93s won their class and the team award. Thus the abilities of the 93 and the engineering within it were proven to an American public sceptical of small European cars. Saab as a brand in the United States of America was born.

Creating a car to reflect such achievements and to tap into the marketing vein opened up, was the idea behind the 750 Granturismo; 605 examples of this model were sold, of which 546 were exported to the newly opened American market. By this time Saab had taken control of imports, and set up Ralph Millet to head the company.

The 750 GT, as it became known, created to frame Saab's image, stormed to success in America, and off the back of its reputation sales of Saab 93s increased. Saab, quick to react, readied a revised version of the 93 for the dawn of a new decade. After minor trim and specification changes in the 1959 model year, the 1960 model year Saab 93F was announced on 7 October 1959 in the Hotel Palace, Stockholm. This car had front-hinged doors at last – hence the 'F' for 'Front' – and a smartened up interior with (one) headrest and new door-mounted arm-rests. There was even more exterior chrome, as rear wheel-arch splash guards. The cooling system capacity

ABOVE: **Saab Sport, iconic logo.**

LEFT: **The quintessential Saab interior.**

was increased. The ultimate version of the car was the 93F GT 750. 93F was a huge success, but it was perhaps an interim event in that it bought Saab time while behind the scenes it prepared the Saab 96 – a totally new car, not just a facelift.

The 93 GT 750 was perhaps a stop-gap, but it was reincarnated in 1960–62 in the new Saab 96 bodyshell with an 850cc engine: in America it was badged 'Monte Carlo', in Britain it was the 'Saab Sport'. But before the new body of the 96 came to the market, Saab pulled another surprise out of its toolkit: a Saab estate car, the Saab 95. First marketed in 1959, the estate model was the first real departure from the origins and skeleton of the 92.

Between 1955 and 1960, Saab built 52,731 examples of the 93/B at Trollhättan.

ESTATE OF THE ART

As Saab designed its updated and reshaped 93 – the 96 model, new for the 1960s – it encountered delays, yet several components were ready and waiting by late 1958. A new 841cc engine and a four-speed gearbox had been planned and tooled up. Front-hinged doors, designed for the 96, were brought prematurely to the 93 to keep it going until the truly revised 96 was ready. There were also other revised and improved items on the shelf of the Saab parts bin – so why not use them, was the thinking of Saab's design team.

Many Swedes and others had been asking for more carrying capacity, a bigger rear seat and a larger boot/trunk. The ability

Looking the other way, from the driver's seat: true Saabism from the inside out.

to carry cargo and people was vital in rural communities and to growing families. So Saab gathered together all its inventory of unused parts and also those new or revised mechanical items, Sixten Sason put his design skills to work, and very quickly Saab had a new model, a proper estate car or wagon with

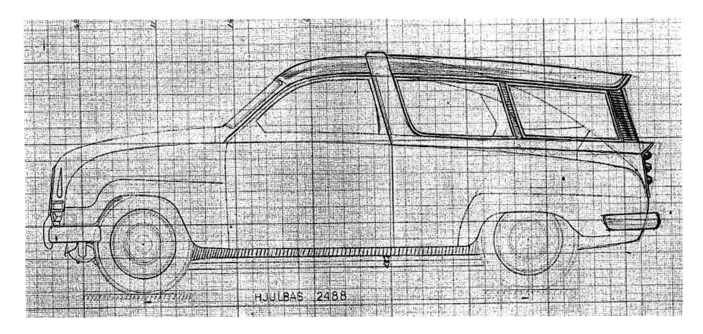

The Saab 95 design drawing.

family appeal and a seven-seater long before anyone else. It was also popular with farmers and tradesmen, spawning a rare, panelled van variant. Thus was born the Saab 95, the numbering system following on from the stillborn Saab 94, otherwise called the Sonett.

The 95 was announced in May 1959, yet did not enter production until late September of that year – as the 1960 model year car. Production start-up was slow, and by December fewer than 100 95s had been built. The early cars featured a two-tone paint scheme designed by Sason to make the most of the car's

long side panels and Kamm rear end. Again, as with other Sason themes, the car had a touch of the American styling trends, yet looked European at the same time; from the rear, some observers said it had hints of the Chevrolet Nomad. There were vestigial 'fins' off the rear wing line, and early prototypes carried chrome B and C pillar embellishments. This, and the two-tone paint scheme, were soon dropped and as a result the 95 assumed a less transatlantic look. The first pre-production cars also had the front-opening doors that Saab was eager to delete from the 93 and the upcoming 96. So what

ABOVE: **In a pose of its era, the prototype, two-tone 95 estate with steel trims on the roof pillars; it had an Italian-looking beauty to go with it.**

RIGHT: **Saab 96 and the Saabo Caravan.**

was the point in persisting with them for the 95, argued the planners, so by the time series production began, the 95 had front-hung doors, the 96's revised engine and an array of improved and refined trims and fittings.

The 95 could carry 500kg (1,100lb) of cargo payload – a significant amount for a small estate car, hence its appeal as a commercial or farm vehicle, and as a van, of which a few were made in Denmark. With its strong hull and reinforcements, the 95 was also a safe place for those in the rear seat. A rear-ward-facing seat suitable for two children was built in, with suitable box-section strengthening beams in the rear floor to protect the occupants of the seat. The longer roof and Kamm back with a sharp roof-top separation point for the airflow aided the aerodynamics of the more boxy shape. However, the rear window was in a turbulent void of air and Saab did not want to fit a rear wiper, so instead it designed a roof-mounted aerofoil wing or blade that redirected some of the airflow down on to the rear windscreen to effectively brush it clean with the power of the airflow's passage. This roof-top

device was the 'air wiper' and is now seen on many estate-type cars, but it was a Saab idea in 1960.

Saab's four-speed gearbox, designed for the 96, was used for the 95 first – so Erik Carlsson grabbed a 95 for the Monte Carlo rally of 1961, finishing fourth in an estate car. The Saab 95 became a fondly regarded member of many car-buying families in Europe and in the USA and Canada. It went out of production in February 1978, yet stocks remained on sale for some time, bringing the sales total to 110,527 across the course of its two decades of production.

ANA – AB Nyköpings Automobilfabrik

Saab also took a decision in the 1950s that would affect its early backer, Gunnar Philipson, and the sale of Saab cars in Sweden: it began to purchase an interest in a garage/dealer chain called AB Nyköpings Automobilfabrik, better known as ANA. Today, ANA is as much a part of the Saab legend as any key factor in the structure of Saab. ANA, like Saab, was born in 1937, when it began to build kits of imported Chrysler cars for the Swedish market. It also imported Skoda cars and had a distribution deal with Standard–Triumph, and it went on to sell Simca cars and Ferguson tractors. By 1960 it was selling Saab's cars through its national outlets and was part of Saab. In the same year, Saab Great Britain was also created.

RIGHT: **Swedish modernity, the longer-nosed V4 estate.**

BELOW: **Two generations of 95s separated by chrome and rubber bumpers. Note the difference in the side window corner radii. The later car has the 'air wiper' roof.**

The later 95's updated 1970s profile.

MELLDE'S 'MONSTER'

Rolf Mellde, always thinking ahead, had the 4-cylinder project to keep him busy in the late 1950s. Yet he also wanted to know if the concept of front-wheel drive could handle higher power – and there was also the possibility of attempting to get into the world record books for engines with smaller outputs: a speed record attempt might be made.

The problem of transferring power to the front wheels via short, high-revving drive shafts of equal or unequal length, and the resultant need to control torque, was not the only problem. A large engine meant more weight, and more weight over the front wheels, which would lead to a greater dynamic understeer effect. For any car that might be given a bigger engine, weight and the centre of gravity changes were vital issues. When it came to Mellde's special car – the one that became his 'Monster' – he tried to reduce the weight, even fitting a lightweight plastic bonnet held in place by leather straps.

Working with a few members of his engine team – which by now included Hugo Bock, Siggvard Gustafsson and Olle Johanssen (not to be confused with Siggvard Johanssen, who joined Saab and invented the Haldex clutch system) – and by making one man, Kjell Knutsson, his lead performance engineer (who was responsible for Erik Carlsson's rally car engines), in 1959 Mellde took a standard red 93 and began tinkering with the engine. Could he join two Saab 3-cylinder motors together? How would the gearbox accept its drive source? Some form of complex gear transfer mechanism was needed. Josef Eklund was in on the project, with a handful of others including Ingvar Andersson who worked with Kjell Knutsson. Eklund went on to lead Saab's engine and drive-train research, but it was Knutsson who was the key hands-on mechanical engineer behind the Monster.

Mellde's idea of joining two 3-cylinder engines together was in terms not of actual engine blocks, but of a shared power transfer mechanism. The two 3-cylinder units were to be coupled via a spiral-cut conical gear-connecting device, a form of inertia coupling. The combined output of the two engines would be 138bhp (103Kw), giving a weight ratio in a

ABOVE: **Mellde's Monster: the x2 triple cylinder with its ingenious power linkage to the fore. The bonnet or hood was plastic.**

BELOW: **The Monster – a transverse-linked engine.**

Saab 93 of 7.7kg per bhp. This engine, with its two 3-cylinder blocks mounted together, was placed transversely across the engine bay to become the world's first *de facto* transverse straight-six engine, even if it had two blocks! It also had two distributors, and that intriguing and complex gearbox and clutch amalgamation.

The issues of vibration, revolving torque forces, opposing engine torques and the complex engine bay mountings needed to tie down the structures were significant issues that would require internal Saab funding to solve. Sychronizing the two throttles was no easy task as they had to be closely matched, and the gearbox input shaft speeds would also need reducing to avoid over-revving and consequent destruction.

MELLDE'S 'MONSTER'

Test drivers of the converted red 93, known as the 'Monster', were Sven Olsson, Carl-Magnus Forest and Rolf Ebefors. The Monster was tested at Satenas airfield and achieved straight line speeds of up to 198km/h (123mph), with one reputed run of over 200km/h (124mph). Sadly neither of these runs – the fastest then ever achieved in an engine of such capacity – were calibrated or recorded according to the strict FIA world record rules, and transmission failure ended the mandatory record rulebook second or return run.

The Monster was further tested at the race circuit of Gellerasen in Karlskoga, where on the twists of the circuit, massive understeer and strong torque steer were evident. In the end it was the transfer of power from two engines into a single gearbox that proved the Monster's undoing – the gearbox transfer device broke and ended the experiment. None the less, Saab and its engine design team had learned a great deal about high power, front-drive applications. Saab had also built its first 6-cylinder-powered car, though it would be three decades before it did that again. But there was a postscript to the story when three decades later, Neo Brothers, the British Saab tuning company, rebuilt a 96 and put the turbocharged 2.3-litre engine and running gear from a Saab 9-3 under the bonnet.

SPECIFICATIONS SAAB 93 TECHNICAL SPECIFICATION

The Saab 93 was introduced on 1 December 1955 alongside a 92B run-out model

Body

Stressed skin monocoque two-door with reinforcements as per Saab 92; Cd 0.35

Engine

Type	Longitudinally mounted 2-stroke valveless engine
Cylinders	3
Cooling	Water-cooled with pump circulation
Bore and stroke	66mm×72.9mm
Capacity	748cc
Compression ratio	7.3:1
Carburettor	Solex 40 AI; electric fuel pump
Max. power	33bhp (24kW) @ 5,000rpm
Max. torque	7kgm (68Nm) @ 3,000rpm

Transmission

Type	Front-wheel drive; column shift three-speed gearbox with freewheel and synchromesh on the top two gears
Clutch	Single dry plate

Suspension and steering

Suspension	Coil springs and hydraulic shock absorbers front and rear with rigid rear axle; independent front suspension
Steering	Rack and pinion, 5.5m radius

Wheels

15in

Brakes

Hydraulic drum brakes all round

Electrics

12V with 33Ah battery capacity

Dimensions

Wheelbase	2,488mm (98in)
Length	4,010mm (158in)
Width	1,570mm (62in)
Height	1,470mm (58in)
Weight (net)	787kg (1,735lb)

Price in 1956

Skr7,500

Saab 93 looking somewhat Citroën **DS**-esque in stance. Sason's 'Italian' frontal restyle surely had shades of Gabriel Voisin's 1937 Aerosport coupé.

The art of aerodynamics, Saab style: the rare Swiss-French brochure.

THE 96 – DEVELOPING THE THEME

Once again the men of Saab had been busy, and in 1960 their work of constantly developing and refining was about to produce another heavily revised version of the original Saab car. Announced in late 1960 as a 1961 model, the Saab 96 was a thorough reworking of the ethos.

The under-the-skin panels and tooling remained unchanged in the main, but at the rear there was a new Sason-styled cabin and boot, with new internal structures and a larger fuel tank. A wrap-around rear windscreen, reshaped rear side windows and a 25cm (10in) increase in cabin width were all significant improvements. The rear window was 117 per cent larger. The aerodynamics were even better, with Sason taking the opportunity to better preserve the airflow around the rear end and down the tail into a Kamm-style spoiler at the boot/trunk lid, as a sharply edged horizontal fence. A pair of clever, low-drag air extractor vents on each rear 'C' pillar quickly removed stale or humid air from the cabin and assisted with vortex control and side wind stability.

The early 96 kept the Italian front, but by 1965 the 96 had a new, longer nose, which curved downwards in a clean arc of wing line. It was known 'in house' at Saab as 'Project Emilia'. There was even a vestigial under-bumper front spoiler to control air pressure under the car. It would be over a decade later that other production cars – even the aerodynamic Citroën GSA – would sprout the same techniques. The 96 was probably the most aerodynamic mass production car in the world in its era, in fact its Cd 0.35 shamed even 1960s supercars. One leading aerodynamicist went on to label the 96 as having the ideal shape for low drag in a standard car.

For 1961, under the front was a revised two-stroke engine, and before too long, a four-speed gearbox. The large engine capacity had an effect on speed, raising top speed to 125km/h (80mph) and greatly improving overtaking performance. In 1961 disc brakes, and then in 1963 Saab's diagonally split safety braking system were introduced. By 1963 Saab had sold 100,000 of the 96. For the model years 1961–64, Saab made annual tweaks to the specifications of the 96 and 95. This included in 1964 the launch of Saab's gearstick and ignition key locking mechanism, which prevented key withdrawal unless the gear lever was in reverse gear.

The Saab essence at Swedish Day, UK. Britain was a massive market for Saab. Saab GB expanded under John Smerdon and Christer Skogsborg. Brian Hatter joined Saab from BMW GB.

A stylish new instrument panel with round dials really spiced up the previous Saab interiors, but for the 1960s, the 'strip' or thermometer design of speedometer was substituted. A sunroof and the semi-automatic 'Saxomat' clutch using a three-speed gearbox remained options. For the 1965 model year, announced on 19 August 1964, the new engine horse-power and a revised cooling system were added, accommodated by the new, longer nose styling of the 1965 model year cars. In some countries, a 96 'Special' was marketed; these cars had the sports-tuned engine from the 'Monte Carlo' variant, yet minus all the trim items that the Monte Carlo 850 and its forebear the GT 750 had carried. One small but significant tooling change across the 1966 cars was the use of top-hung pedals; these replaced the floor-mounted lever-arm type pedals that had begun with the 92.

The five years of annual upgrades developed the 96, but Saab knew it had to comprehensively update it, because it was neither as economical as its rivals, nor as fast, and was still a somewhat smoky two-stroke. Saab had increased production, enlarged the factories at a cost of nearly Skr 50,000,000 and was approaching annual production of 50,000 cars. But behind the scenes, a battle – perhaps the subconscious battle for Saab's stability and security, its very survival – was taking place.

FOUR CYLINDERS OR BUST

Saab seemed welded to the idea of the two-stroke – or was it that Tryggve Holm, inspired Saab director, seemed determined that the small two-stroke engine in a small Saab was the sole Saab ethos? Later events were to prove that his fears of abandoning the small car idea were well founded; however, the subsequent record and opinions show that his reputed insistence on the two-stroke was an error in marketing terms.

Saab needed to join the four-stroke, 4-cylinder world if it was to survive, though a 4-cylinder engine did not necessarily have to mean the end of a small Saab. There were many people within Saab who were working hard to convince the management of the need for a new engine – Gunnar Ljungström and Rolf Mellde were two of these influential names.

The men of Saab were not wallflowers, and Rolf Mellde, by now Saab's engineering/technical director, was also a strong character who was more often than not utterly focused, targeted and correct in his opinions and actions. It was Mellde who started to look at a 4-cylinder engine, despite Holm's edict that it should not be countenanced. Mellde, with the knowledge of just a few colleagues, seems to have set up an unofficial engine research group. Kjell Knutsson and Ingvar Andersson were two of the test engineers who were part of this perhaps somewhat clandestine unit, and Paul Broman would come to be foreman

of the 'lab'. From 1962 onwards the Saab engineering men were quietly looking at creating a small 4-cylinder engine, not just for the 93's derivative the 96, but also for a completely new Saab. A capacity of around 1.2ltr was their target.

By 1965, Saab had been tweaking the 96's two-stroke to produce more power and less smoke for several years. The car was faster and had a triple carburettor. Under Josef Eklund's lead, the Saab engine laboratory carried out a series of advanced studies into cylinder head, bolt torque, piston behaviour and gasket design during the early developments to the 3-cylinder engine. These resulted in a novel approach to controlling the two-stroke, 3-cylinder engine's behaviour, creating a reliable cylinder head/gasket regime that neither warped, leaked nor failed. Further studies into piston behaviour saw Saab fit a plexiglass window into the side of an engine block to allow the team to observe piston and combustion behaviour by spectroscope, and to solve an early problem with an internal engine issue where the fuel feed failed and piston pins failed. Using chromium-plated piston rings and modified connecting rods solved the problems.

After all this earlier work, by 1965 Saab's main engine was the 850cc, 44bhp (SAE) 3-cylinder with a hydraulic clutch and a new fuel pump. But the effect of this further tweaking of the design was an unwanted increase in fuel consumption, to the point where a reputation for being a touch fuel-thirsty was being created: this was effectively the ultimate two-stroke engine, a new modified unit with triple carburettors and higher power, while oil mixture decreased from 3 to 1.5 per cent, which reduced the emissions. But with its liking for fuel, the car's sales figures fell in the important Swedish domestic market: total sales decreased from 48,500 to 37,000, a drop of over 10,000 in one year 1965–66, reflecting the poor mpg figures.

Rolf Mellde had been drawing engines and engineering components since he was a boy. He attended the Stockholm Institute, and after graduation worked on a number of projects for local firms. He spent two years working for a company producing two-stroke engines for boats; after that he did his army service, and then in 1946 found his way to Saab. If anyone knew how good a two-stroke engine could be, it was Mellde – conversely, he also knew the limitations of the type. By 1960, Mellde knew that Saab's engineering and design ethos was being hampered by its engine choice. But management, specifically Tryggve Holm, was unlikely to be moved in its views. So Mellde, at some professional risk, set up a four-stroke engine development unit deep within Saab. It is reputed that he even hosted design meetings in his own home. He wrote a letter about the need for a better engine, and sent it to Ljungström and Svante Simonson, then Saab's production chief.

Slowly the journey to a 4-cylinder engine began, and from here started the engine department's expansion that led ultimately to the turbo years of Saab. Key names of the engine development team under Mellde included Ingvar Andersson, Paul Broman, Josef Eklund, Per Gillbrand, Olle Granlund, Bertil Ilhage, Tore Jonsson, Kjell Knutsson, Olle Lindkvist, Lars Olov Olson, Dick Ohlsson, Bertil Pedersen, Lennart Rosen, Gosta Svensson and Bengt Tornqvist. Nils-Gunnar Svensson was hired by Mellde in 1965 to work on developing the two-stroke and, like others, became part of the development team.

Mellde's development team soon evaluated a range of engines from competing manufacturers; it also forged links with the British Ricardo company, a link that would be manifested in the engine of the Saab 99. But before that happened, there was the story of a Ford V4 engine that found its way into the Saab 96.

V4 FOR VICTORY

In the early 1940s, Sixten Sason drew up a design for a radically configured, steam-powered car. The obvious question was why? Odd as it may seem from today's perspective, by the 1950s there was a serious consideration of steam power as an energy source for cars. In 1940 Sason was an early supporter of the idea. In the USA, even Ford and GM were spending part of their research budgets on steam studies. Steam offered lots of torque, but it was a nightmare to engineer for it in a car, as the threat of explosion and the need for a pressure chamber were major engineering issues. Yet Saab still looked at steam as a motive power source.

This should have come as no surprise to anyone, because in the 1930s, the German names of Hugo Junkers and Alexander Lippisch had considered coal-fired, steam-driven power for aircraft. Lippisch had even drawn a delta wing that could be

powered by coal. But whether it were steam turbine or gas turbine, the smooth bands of resulting power leading to thrust were no use in the constantly changing requirements for revs and torque in a car.

Inside Saab's aircraft division, under its technical director Tore Gullstrand, the thought of powering an aircraft by steam was neither weird nor eccentric: it was simply the extension of an idea that had been around since the 1930s. So it seems that precious time and resources were spent inside Saab researching steam power. The men of the automotive division's engineering department were aghast. What they wanted was a nice, small, efficient, and above all tractable and perky four-stroke engine with which to go rallying, and to power a new Saab.

Ljungström was working on refining the two-stroke principle, and trying to cure its problem of needing lubrication within the piston and cylinder action. Although abandoned as a research idea, it had spawned thoughts of a V-angled two-stroke; in later years, the orbital cylinder cycle concept would make more of this research theme. But it was the research of the late 1950s that led Saab to look for a V4 engine. Before then, and in the light of the rotary cycle Wankel-engined NSU Ro 80, and also the knowledge that Mazda was researching the Wankel and that Citroën were also considering it (resulting in the later GS Birotor), Saab had to look at all the options, even the Wankel rotary concept – but thankfully rejected it.

The increasing significance of emissions regulations, notably in California, was also going to be a key 1960s driving force behind the need for a cleaner, leaner burning engine. The upshot was that Saab needed a new engine, and Mellde and Josef Eklund started looking. A series of engines from European car makers were tested, in the hope that Saab could buy in an off-the-shelf engine and save itself millions in development costs; thus

The 96 loked really good in white, especially with the Italian front styling.

engines from the Fiat group, VW, Opel, British companies and from Ford were all tested. The main contenders for consideration were the engines of the Lloyd Arabella at 748cc, the Morris 848cc unit, and a Lancia Appia four-stroke of 1098cc. But before all of these was the attraction of a small, V-angled engine from Ford.

Ford and a Borrowed Engine

After testing these engines for over 400 hours per engine, including assessing new all-alloy units, only one met Saab's requirements: Saab focused on the new German Ford V4 alloy unit, and purchased some of them for further evaluation. The Ford was smooth, strong, reliable and not so heavy as to upset the 96's balance, and Saab thought it could probably 'tweak' it to make it even better. One thing was for sure, if Saab were to compete not least on domestic soil against the new 4-cylinder Volvos, it needed a new engine, and quickly. Before long, by 1964, Olle Granlund and Per Gillbrand had jumped ship from Volvo to join Mellde at Saab (ironically, Mellde would later jump ship to join Volvo). Granlund and Gillbrand brought with them vital knowledge of engine design and turbo charging gained from working on truck and car engines, and reinforced the four-stroke 'gang' at Saab.

Mellde approached Ford to see if the V4 engine from Ford's 'Cardinal' project might be available for Saab. He had identified the 'over-square' 60-degree V4 with 1,498cc – a 1.5-litre – as being suitable for the 96. Note that because it was 1967, it was before Ford in Germany and Britain were joined under the Ford Europe umbrella, and so this V4 was the German Ford-built V4 and not the British-built Ford V4 engine so familiar to many British car buyers.

Mellde made a trip to America under the cover of attending a technical conference for the Society of Automotive Engineers – but Saab's top team had no idea what their man was up to. It seems that Ford had even been testing their new V4 engine in a Saab 96 two-stroke body as late as 1961. Apparently the Saab was deemed a good 'cover' story for what was then a very small engine for Ford in an American perspective – but one that would obviously have a use within Ford's international branches.

Ford gave the Saab deal a code name 'Daisy', whereas Saab called their end of the project 'Operation *Kajsa*'. After negotiations at the top of the Ford management structure in Detroit, and after some delays, the answer from Ford to Mellde's request for the engine was 'yes', and a five-year licensing agreement was suggested. Although the engine was to be seen in the Ford Corsair and the front-wheel-drive, German-made Taunus 12M and 15M, Saab would have its own version, Ford had agreed – but

the problem was that Saab's Tryggve Holm had not. The battle still raged.

Mellde now had to reveal what he had been up to, and how far his 'research', as he framed it, had got. He made a presentation to Holm's namesake, Svante Holm, and the Saab directors, but still Tryggve Holm said 'no'.

Could Tryggve Holm not see that Saab might falter if the four-stroke engine was rejected? It was at this point that Mellde risked all – even his career and professional reputation within Saab: somehow he had to win. For Mellde to challenge Holm, the boss, over Saab's adherence to the two-stroke would have had serious professional implications, so Mellde boxed clever and approached Marcus Wallenburg's son, Marc, and he in turn worked on his father. Wallenburg Senior was the number one shareholder in Saab, and when Wallenburg Senior advised Tryggve Holm to pursue a four-stroke future, the doors were opened. Rolf Mellde had won a battle that had far greater implications than many people realized. Mellde and his men really had saved Saab: they opened the doors to a new era, a new dimension, and Mellde deserves much credit for this.[5]

Mellde was a man with management power, so he set up a V4 development unit inside Saab. The car had to be lengthened a little in the front end, and he even sent Gillbrand to Italy to test the V4 engine and its 96 installation in secret. This was Saab funded, but how many people at the top of Saab knew? Gillbrand told everyone he was taking a leave of absence to manage the family paint supply shop! In fact he, his wife and young son ended up at 28 Via Sirmionie, on the corner of Via Giuseppe Gambotti in the town of Desenzano del Garda, Italy; here, behind the gates to a house rented from Giacomo Acerbi, and which had a secure garage, they experimented with the installation of a Ford V4 engine in a Saab 96.

Gillbrand was there for more than four months, tinkering with the engine and the car, driving thousands of miles around the local roads. Mellde drove another V4-engined 96 down to Italy and spent time with Gillbrand touring the local roads and adjusting the car. Long nights in the garage fettling the engine set-up must have made the locals wonder just what was wrong with the little Swedish car: Fiats did not need such daily servicing!

For the project to succeed secrecy was vital, and Saab had to ensure that its new suppliers did not let the cat out of the bag. If the public found out that the two-stroke 96 was doomed, Saab would be left with a lot of unsold cars. Less than a dozen people knew about the Saab V4 and its fitting to the 96, and that level of secrecy stayed that way for a year, even despite Mellde ordering several of the engines from Germany and having to send Saab staff to fetch them. Was it possible that Josef Eklund was kept in the dark for a bit – perhaps to avoid putting him in a difficult position? The names of the men who knew about the V4 secret project other than Mellde were

Svante Holm, Haakon Sörgården, Rune Ahlberg, Per Gillbrand, Kjell Knutsson and Lennart Rosen.[6]

The Ford V4 seemed well suited to the 96's temperament: it was an engine that revved easily, if noisily, and could be kept 'on the cam' – that is, spooled up and ready to deliver its torque. Saab softened the valve springs in their version of the engine, which further lowered vibration. In fact valves were to be the V4s only real issue – if not properly maintained, the valve stems could stretch and the valve seats fatigue, leading to poor sealing and lower compression. A rise in tappet noise was to be looked out for in hard-driven engines. The fitment of the correct type of oil filter was essential to ensure appropriate oil flow and return. As with all front-wheel-drive cars, gearbox noise would soon indicate an underlying issue. The V4 had no timing chain, and the camshaft's fragile fibrous gear wheel was an area that required later modification. Saab fitted heavy duty driveshafts that lasted for many miles – unlike certain other European FWD car manufacturers.

These issues were more use and maintenance related, rather than design problems, and thankfully, the early V4s were reliable – which was more than Saab's customers had experienced with the 92 and 93 engines in their early production forms. The robust V4 was ideal for the 96, and complemented its character. With its vibration control measures and proper engine mountings, the V4 could be tuned down to levels of smoothness approaching that of a straight-blocked, 4-cylinder engine. Meeting ever stricter emissions rules did, however, mean that Saab had to (latterly) lean off the fuel mixture, which weakened throttle–combustion response times.

Another issue relevant to all Saab's engines, from the two-stroke to the turbo 4-cylinder, was that of head gasket sealing and reliability. In the extreme arctic temperatures that were the Saab's natural environment, cylinder heads, engine block, liners and many metal components could behave at varying rates according to air temperature, the temperature of the component, and the operating temperatures around the engine and engine bay. An engine starting and running from extreme cold was likely to heat up at different rates in different parts of the engine, which could cause gasket failure, leakage and other problems. So thermodynamics really was an important science at Saab.

Eklund's Laboratory

During the development of the 3-cylinder engine for the 93 and 96 models, Josef Eklund's engine laboratory men had to carry out many experiments to assess and achieve the correct performance from such vital engine components. Simply over-tightening the cylinder-head bolts was not the Saab way,

Chris Partington's 96 two-stroke at the Save Saab rally 2010. Partington was technical director at Saab GB and a renowned tuner and rally manager.

nor the answer, and special experiments had to be made; one included using fluid dye and special gaskets to assess the performance of the engine bolts, block and cylinder-head gasket and their integrity. This led to the creation and use of a special cylinder-head bolt analysis where their torque/tension and tensile strengths could be calibrated and then added to an assessment of their angle of action. Using these techniques, the clamping or pulling forces on the cylinder head, block and gasket could all be calibrated to a degree previously unknown. Not only was this work by Saab highly advanced, it was a precursor to later studies in this field. The Saab team also studied piston temperatures and expansion rates within the cylinder to further refine the 3-cylinder engine's performance.

The larger 850cc Saab engine with twelve cylinder-head bolts stemmed from this early innovative experimental learning by Saab's engine laboratory, and so too did its record of not suffering from gasket or cylinder-head problems in normal use. When it came to altering the valve tensions and cylinder-head loads for the new V4, Mellde, Eklund and the team had a wealth of experience to draw on from their two-stroke days.

SAAB GB

In Great Britain, Saab's second most important export market after America, the 96 V4 was launched at a price of £801 (the two-stroke had been £742), and that rose to £1,350. The 96 was advertised under the 'Go Swift Go Safe Go Saab' strapline by Saab GB Ltd – which was no longer of 207 Regent Street, London, but now of 6 Wellcroft Road, Slough, Buckinghamshire.

A strange comparison of the 1967 market place was that the safe, sporty 96 V4 cost the same amount to buy in Britain as a Wolseley 1100. This bizarre comparison framed the landscape of cars at the time and also marked an improvement for Saab – who had been charging over £500 more for a 96 two-stroke Super Sport than the cost of a new Cortina 1600 GT, which outclassed the Saab in performance if not in strength. In Germany there were sporty Opels rather than elderly VWs to compete with, for at this time, GM's Opel was on a high: it was the default choice for the younger, more sports-oriented buyer, and some of its designs were at the leading edge of styling and aerodynamics.

Tuning

In 1972, Saab further enhanced their enthusiast buyer base by making a range of 'Sport' tuning kits available in Great Britain. These Carlsson-inspired, rally-specification kits included the option of a new crankshaft, which increased capacity to 1700cc, a Weber 40 DFI progressive twin-choke carburettor kit, and revised manifold and air cleaner specifications. Stronger valve springs were also returned to. Buyers could also choose a new, freer-flowing exhaust system, a sports steering wheel, a 'golfball'-type alloy wheel design, and even new decals.

Down at Saab GB, Chris Partington, who rose to be technical director, was the expert-in-chief, and his modified cars, including a 95 V4 estate that was used as a rally support car, really did fly. Specifying the full modification kit for a Saab 94 V4 would cost £299.93, a not insignificant sum. However, performance, response and handling were taken to new levels. The fitting of Koni shock absorbers and Pirelli Cinturauto CN36 tyres added the final elements of road-holding and suspension/tyre rebound finesse to the car's set-up.

The factory-produced modifications added nearly 24km/h (15mph) to the car's top speed, and reduced the 0–60mph

Saab 96 two-stroke driven by the Saab GB stalwart Chris Partington.

time to 11.5sec. A top speed of over 145km/h (90mph), perhaps even 160km/h (100mph) in still-air conditions, was achieved. The car's 0–130km/h (0–80mph) time was halved – to 23sec. For £300, British and other nations' Saab 96 V4 owners could transform their cars into something that could see off all but the most serious of sporting competitors. Perhaps the best part of the tuning works was that the engine lost neither torque nor smoothness – it did not become a breathless, clattering cauldron.

Further enhancements came from the 'Chilton tuning catalogue', which contained a series of improvements for private Saab owners. A milled cylinder head, stronger valves, machined camshaft and compression changes would all boost power. Chilton also reminded its clients that lowered ride height from shorter springs, wider tyres and sports dampers would lower the roll centres, lower the centre of gravity, provide a wider tyre footprint and improve the car's handling and ultimate breakaway point prior to a skid. The British in particular were as keen on tweaking their little Saabs as the Swedish.

The rally victories of the 1960s also helped create the Saab legend, and by 1971, when Saab won the RAC Rally as outright winner and team prize winner, the free publicity was worth millions. The results at the 1971 rally were as follows: Blomqvist/Hertz were the winners, Orrenius/Persson were third, Eklund/Andreasson sixth, and Utrianend/Lento tenth – and all driving 96s.

Spirit of Saab. 96 V4 rally spec with some expensive lighting.

To stop the new V4 with its greater power and heavier engine weight, Lockheed swing-caliper font disc brakes were fitted, along with the by then standard Saab dual-line split-diagonal safety braking system. The front of the 96 had to be redesigned to house the little V4 – new pressings for the inner wings, engine mounts and cross members were needed – effectively a new, longer nose, and new tooling, jigs and small presses were needed. These were sourced in great secrecy from Chausson of France and Vickers of England. Such was the pressure of time that a Saab team went to Vickers' plant in Newcastle and brought the new tooling presses home via a North Sea ferry to Gothenburg and then by road to the factory.

In August 1966, just after some especially chosen employees had been called in for extra-time working to convert a large batch of 96s to V4 engines, Saab made an earlier-than-usual announcement for the ensuing model year: it announced the 96 with V4 power. The reaction was huge.

With its 1498cc or 1.5-litre capacity (later pushed to 1.7), and pumping out 73bhp (SAE)/65BHP (DIN), it transformed the Saab. The vital 0–60mph (or 0–100km/h) time was under 15 seconds and top speed was well over 113km/h (70mph) and up to 150km/h (93mph). Fuel consumption when carefully driven could be 7ltr/100km (40mpg), and the magic metric fuel usage figure of less than 7ltr/100km was achieved, although an average figure of just over 9ltr/100km (30mpg) was more realistic. Overtaking performance in the vital 48–80km/h (30–50mph) sector was good with that sprint taking 11sec, a vast improvement on the two-stroke's 20sec time.

This was a major advance, but strangely, Saab kept the two-stroke version on the market, priced at just 560Skr less than the V4-powered model – yet 13,350Skr would buy a brand new 96 V4. Only hardened Saabists would still purchase the two-stroke, surely? But Saab kept the two-stroke on, even badging a special export version for the USA as the 'Shrike' and keeping the Monte Carlo 850 on sale. But soon Saab saw the light, and a V4 Monte Carlo appeared. For the 94 V4 a revised interior with full three-point seat belts was announced, as were the strange devices that were the detachable, Saab in-car waste-paper baskets – rubbish bins made of plastic that hung from the seats or cabin footwells.

In its haste, despite provision for in-car waste bins, Saab had not ordered enough new 'V4' badges for the new model. There is a story that Saab workers were sent out to Ford dealers to buy spare V4 badges, until some sticky labels were quickly ordered – but these did the car no favours, and soon the smart, chromed 'V4' badges appeared on the upper front wings/fenders; they looked incongruous here, however, and were soon re-sited lower down behind the front wheel arch.

The effects of the V4 on Swedish domestic sales and the world market were dramatic. Once word got out about the 96 V4's abilities, the sales figures rose steeply. An increase of over 40 per cent in sales simply from fitting a new engine to an existing car – and one that was far from being youthful – may be a unique record. As an example of the effect, in 1966 Saab sold 29,766 of the two-door 96 two-stroke and 7,243 of the estate version. In 1967 it sold 37,633 96 two-door models and 11,478 of the estate. During 1968, however, only twenty-eight two-stroke 96s were registered in Sweden. The two-stroke died at the end of 1968, after 320,000 had been produced.

TRIMMED FOR SUCCESS

Saab did not rest on its works, either, because from 1968 the 96 V4 was given a bigger (laminated) windscreen that was 7cm (3in) taller, a bigger rear windscreen that was 11cm (4in) deeper, a new safety steering wheel, revised instrument trims and a proper textile carpet that complemented the nylon or woollen weave set trim options – all major improvements. The 95 also got the taller windscreen aperture, which made looking up at traffic lights a lot easier for Saab drivers who had developed a bent neck technique to see upwards out of the old, narrow windscreen. The improvements kept on coming in the form of a 'De Luxe' variant that had side rubbing strips, opening rear side windows, and rather overworked, fussy chrome wheel rim embellisher rings. A V4 version of the US market 'Shrike' was also produced.

La Voiture Idéale

Across Europe and the world, Saab invested heavily in an advertising programme to promote the new car. Advertisements showed the handling and safety benefits, with headlines that read 'Saab 96: the plane-maker's contribution to safer driving' and 'Saab 95: for the professionals'. There were quotes from Stirling Moss, which, given that Erik Carlsson was married to Pat Moss, was an easy win for Saab. Safety played large in Saab's advertising, with one British advert quoting *Motor* magazine of 17 August 1968: 'The Swedes are precise and meticulous engineers with probably the strongest bias in Europe towards safety in both its primary and secondary forms.' In France, the 96 was advertised as the ideal car – '*La voiture idéale*'.

Saab's inveterate fettlers or tinkerers kept on fiddling with – or better stated, improving – the 96 V4's specifications. From 1969 through to 1974 a constant programme of upgrades took place. Of note, to echo his changes to the new 99, Bjorn Envall – now back at Saab after a period working in the design studio of Opel in Germany – gave the 96 rectangular headlamps (though the US versions had to have a round lamp due to legislation requirements). Also fitted were a more curved bumper design and a new grille. This was the first year that Saab fitted a collapsible steering column across all its cars. 1970–74 saw changes to dashboard colours and trims, and the production of cars at Saab's new Finnish factory at Uuskiaupunki, a joint Saab-Scania AB and OY Valmet company.

The 96 was getting bolder – brighter, stronger colours in blue, orange, yellow and brown echoed the fashion of the decade, and bigger indicator lenses made a bolder statement too. The amount of stainless steel brightwork 'chrome' trim on the car was reduced – notably the air-vent trim on the scuttle was deleted. Constant revisions in 1971–73 saw new side protection strips, bigger rear lamps, the innovation of an electrically heated driver's seat, halogen headlamps, and some rich new paint colours such as Toreador Red and Amber Yellow (though the less said about Sienna Brown, the better, perhaps).

For 1974, the Saab 96 V4 was given a more extensive makeover. This featured a new black plastic radiator grille with a Saab 99-style bright cross-bar trim, revised badging, inertia-reel seatbelts, better rustproofing, and colours that included Sunset Orange with a Manilla Brown interior trim. There were also bright blue and vivid green interiors to complement new exterior colours. Saab decided that these improvements warranted a trim motif – and so was born the 96 'L'. Often forgotten was that a special production 1.7-litre version of the engine also appeared in 1975, having first been part of a Saab tuning kit in late 1972. In 1976, Saab fitted the smart, black rubber, self-repairing cell construction bumpers to the 96 that had appeared on the 99. For 1977, the high-backed seats from the 99 were also fitted to the 96, and a clever full-width rear boot/trunk spoiler also improved the management of airflow off the car's tail.

Sason's restyling of the rear of the 93 to fashion the 96 created a defining look for the aeroweapon 96. Saab's advertising tapped into the chic 1960s feel of things in this classic shot.

Saab 96 'Cabotine'. Swedish-built and Saab style enhanced long before the 900 lost its top. The Cabotine is based on an original Sixten Sason idea for a softtop 92.

Cabotine, the one-off 96 conversion. Sheer style.

REVERSE ENGINEERING – THE SAAB 98 AND BEYOND

In 1975 Saab also had the idea of creating an updated 95 estate: something with cleaner lines and a more contemporary style was envisaged. Envall got busy, and the result was Project X14 (the code also suggested for the 99 estate) or the Saab 98, a three-door cross between an estate and a hatchback with a sloped rear end. Was this the Combi-Coupé principle applied in reverse to the old 96? The prototype building was assisted by Cogglia in Italy. Today it would be called a 'sportback', but it was sadly discarded. Perhaps the practical but less-than-

stylish brown paint scheme it was presented in at the time did not help its cause? Or was it that the 98 was that old Saab trick – reincarnating an existing design?

So it was that for the 1970s the 96 V4 soldiered on. In 1974, the 96 was given a restyled front grille and valance with a tall, upright, matt black central grille portion. For 1975 a 1.7-litre variant with alloy wheels, leather steering-wheel cover and a tachometer was marketed. It was fast and could be tuned up, too. On the Swedish market various domestic variants, or 'B' models with differing engine specifications, were offered in the late 1970s. Gradually Saab was narrowing the marketing and sales territories of the tough old car. By 1976, the Saab 99-style black 8km/h (5mph) 'parking-proof' bumpers had made it from the 99 and the Sonett on to the 96; they didn't help its aerodynamics, but they did modernize its look. Re-tooling the rear floor also allowed a revised floorpan that gave 5cm (2in) extra legroom, a belated and odd tooling change in a car so old.

From 1977 to 1980 Saab could not resist tweaking and altering the car, even in its dying days. In the end the engine produced nearly 70bhp (DIN), and the car came with a plethora of trim upgrades and items taken from the Saab 99 parts and trim shelf, including high-backed seats, wheels, mirrors and paint. For 1977, the 96 became the 'V4 Super' in its badging. A very effective

Saab 98. A still-born attempt to create a 1970s sportback estate from the 96. It was a good idea, but too little, too late.

V4 was Mellde's victory. The Ford V4 was German designed and built, not the British V4 of the same era.

black rubber rear 'lip' spoiler appeared across the bootlid in 1978, extending the previous chrome mid-panel lip spoiler handle. The Finnish, Valmet-built 96s were of outstanding quality and looked very smart in their late-1970s metallic paint hues.

In 1975 Great Britain also saw the 96 V4 Silver Jubilee edition Saab 96 of 300 specially trimmed cars designed to mark the anniversary of Saab GB. These cars were finished in Crystal Silver metallic with black-painted rear 'C' pillar vents, and fitted with a special design of side-body moulding. The interiors were a melange of orange and brown trim materials, best described as distinctive.

In this period, the Saab engineering department had to clean up the V4's exhaust emissions to meet new Swedish legislation, and the issue of catalytic converters for the Californian and US rules was also addressed.

As mentioned above, for 1977–78 the V4 became the 'V4 Super', and more enhancements were made to create a 'GL'-badged status. These included a power hike to 68bhp, more Saab 99 trim items, larger indicator lamps all round and a range of metallic colours, one of which was Cardinal Red, which became one of the few Saab paints to suffer from quality and corrosion problems across both the 96 and 99 ranges. The Saab 95 estate was withdrawn from production when the last 95 body was welded up on 28 February 1978, after over 110,000 Saab 95 estate cars had been produced since 1959.

By 1978, all 96s were being built in Finland, to a very high build quality standard. The cars of the 1979 and 1980 model years were given de-chroming and black-painted window frames – a small design detail, yet one that made a surprisingly large visual, graphic difference to the car. 'Minilite'-type alloy wheels and 'soccer ball' 99 EMS-style wheels were also fitted, and these created visual changes to the design as well.

A limited edition run of 150 special edition 96 V4s was seen on the British market in 1976, each with their own numbered dashboard plaque. These were the 'Souvenir' editions designed to mark the end of the RHD Saab 96 in Britain. They were little different from the standard 96L, and were all painted in the troublesome Cardinal Red paint, which so readily flaked and rusted. In Sweden the 96 could be had in Acacia Green, a paint colour taken from the 99 and 900 Turbo ranges.

In 1980, the 96's 'run-out' year, there was a special Swedish market edition of 300 cars produced in Aquamarine silver-blue metallic with colour-coded wheels and interior trim. But less than a thousand examples of the venerable thirty-year-old base design that was the 92–96 story were sold in Sweden in 1980.

In total, Saab sold 547,221 of the 96, and the 95 estate sold 110,527; the early cars saw 52,731 Saab 93s and 20,128 Saab 92s built and sold (not including prototype and pre-production examples).

Erik Carlsson – 'Mr Saab' – drove the last 96 out of the factory and into the Saab Museum. It was less the end of a love affair and more the end of a generation. Yet there was a twist in the tale of the 93 and 96, for way back in its youth the little Saab had been asked for by a people who lived at the bottom of the world, and Saab had also set up foreign manufacturing bases in Europe for the car.

EUROPEAN PRODUCTION PLANTS

In its life and times, there had been a focus on the essential Swedish character, as well as the 'Saabness' of the 92, 93 and 96. This was a Swedish car from Sweden, with Swedish values built in. Yet the 93 and the 96 were produced overseas, and one region that took the Saab to its heart was South America, which first noticed the little Saab 92 in 1947. But before the South American experiment happened, Saab expanded production amidst the rain of northern Europe's flat coastal low countries.

In Saab's export story, the plot takes a turn close to home, in Denmark. Saab had exported cars to Denmark very early in the life of the 92, with a handful sold from 1950 onwards. But from 1957–63, Saab was shipping semi knocked-down (SKD) cars the short distance by trailer, and then by special train wagons, to Denmark for final completion and assembly. These were essentially fully trimmed, painted, boxed 'kits' of cars that could be put together without the need for a massive factory infrastructure.

For the Danes, the attraction of building cars in-country would be 10 per cent lower purchase tax and cheaper labour rates, and the Saab car could be sold for a good 'local' price in Denmark. During the second half of 1957, after selling 29,711 Swedish-built cars in Denmark in the previous year alone, Saab changed its general agent in Denmark to a company named Automobil Forretningen ICI A/S, Copenhagen (Glostrup) – not to be confused with the British ICI chemical company. In fact Automobil Forretningen ICI Engines later changed its name to ISIS, after the Egyptian deity, and some in Saab refer to the Danish production as the ISIS Engine Company, rather than ICI cars.

By February 1958, after a pre-trial run of one car in December 1957, the first fully painted SKD car 'kits' were arriving on a regular schedule from Trollhättan, to be built up in Denmark. The only significant specification difference was the use of French Kleber tyres.

Twenty-one people were employed, and at the height of operations, fifteen cars a day could be produced. Only 140 cars were produced in the first year, due to a series of local tax and regulatory issues, but by 1959 Saab Denmark had made 740 cars. In 1962, the Glostrup plant produced 3,776 cars – mostly 96s, with some 95s. Advantageous tax rules in Denmark also helped create the Saab 95 van, because blanking out the windows of the estate car made it subject to less tax. So was born the rare 95 panel van, built exclusively in Denmark.

By 1963, Saab had sent more 'cars', albeit as kits, to Denmark than it had exported to America. Denmark was therefore Saab's nearest and biggest export market. At one stage in 1963, Danish-built Saabs were being sent back to Sweden

TOP: **The 'Paddan', or Toad: a wider, disguised prototype Saab 99 dressed up as a widened 96.**

ABOVE: **The Toad seen from the rear, where the extra width is very obvious. The public must have wondered what Saab was planning.**

for sale – a total of 995 entering the Swedish market place after storage near Skane in barns and greenhouses!

Yet the story ended abruptly, and certain changes meant that the advantages of reconstructing Saabs in Denmark disappeared overnight. These were tax changes for 1963, the rise of the European Free Trade Area (EFTA), and another new Saab factory in Mechelen, Belgium, where in a plant once used by Mercedes, locally welded complete knocked-down (CKD)

Saab cars were created. The last batch of 1,250 cars was sent to Glostrup between January and June 1963. In total between 1958 and 1963, Saab made nearly 10,000 SKD Saabs in Denmark (9,630 cars).

Making Saabs in Denmark ceased, just as making Citroëns in Britain at Slough, close to Saab GB's headquarters, would also end. Saab also had Belgian CKD agreements with Brondeel and IMA, its main Belgian plant being with IMA in Mechelen,

Belgium, where it made 276 of the 93 model and 2,348 of the 96 model. In the 1970s, the Belgian plant would go on to make the Saab–IMA manufacturing agreement for the Saab 99, with 1,500 as SKD and 23,321 as CKD, giving a total of 24,821 Belgian-built Saab 99s.

In 1962, Saab also entered into a two-year SKD agreement with Chrysler at their Rotterdam, Netherlands-based factory: 570 Saab 96s were locally produced for the important Dutch market.

In the American market, the 96 proved a huge hit and a great alternative to the VW Beetle. The sight of Saab 96s in the Manhattan traffic became a normal event. On the eastern seaboard in the USA with the cold winters and twisting rally tracks of roads, the 93 and the 96 created a legend.

Meanwhile, far away near the base of the earth, there was the unusual story of Saab building cars in South America.

SOUTH AMERICAN SAABS?

Saab had been selling aircraft in Brazil, notably the Saab Scandia 90 airliner (which went on to serve Brazilian civil aviation for nearly thirty years), so it was natural for the car division to open a sales franchise in that country. As early as 1950, Saab appointed a Swedish company, Janer AB, to act for it in Sao Paolo and Rio de Janerio. Saab was soon to ship six 92s to Brazil, where it would also undertake hot climate and rough road development of the car, and get some off the record, safari-style rallying practice.

Strict government import tariffs and currency regulations meant that importing more cars was to become impossible, as they would be priced out of the market. The only way to sell Saabs in Brazil would be to build them there. By 1952 Saab was talking to a Brazilian company, Vemag S.A., about using its light engineering and vehicle assembly plant in Sao Paulo to construct 92s from kits that would be shipped in crates across the South Atlantic. The two parties agreed that 1,000 Saabs could be built from 1953, rising to 5,000 per annum by 1958. In fact the agreement was confirmed in written letters of discussion on 1 October 1953.

Despite much planning and a basic draft agreement, the idea was stopped in its tracks by the detail and delays of trying to meet new government restrictions in Brazil, which were put into place just as the Saab deal was about to get going. The full contract – drawn up to the final stage – was never signed.

It seemed as though Saab car production in South America was not going to happen, but then Uruguay entered the field. As early as 5 May 1947 interested parties in Uruguay, upon hearing of Saab's intention to launch a car, had written to Saab asking if it could represent the company for the setting up of an import agency in Montevideo. This was just under a month before Saab announced its 92 prototype in June 1945.

Further approaches were made to Saab from various interested Uruguayan companies eager to sell cars. During a sales tour of Argentina with the new Saab Scandia airliner in 1949, Saab met with ten various representatives of these potential partners from Uruguay. Due to demand in Sweden and northern Europe, and shortages of raw materials in a post-war

The updated 96V4 interior for the later period in its life.

The orange lozenge – a Saab 96 'cabrio' retaining the roll hoop and its Saabness.

environment, the idea of selling or even building CKD Saabs in Uruguay came to nothing. But Saab did not forget how keen and how early into the fray the Uruguayans had been, and in 1952, ten Saab 92s were shipped to Uruguay and eighty to Peru, and several found their way down to Chile, Venezuela and Argentina, where, legend has it, a lost handful remain, awaiting their fate as 'barn finds'.

Automotora Boreal, Montevideo

A decade later, in 1963, Saab's export manager, Goran Hagstrom, entered talks with a Uruguayan company, Automotora Boreal of Montevideo. And this time it would happen: the story of the small Saab with the big heart was about to touch the people of Uruguay, who in turn would come to love 'their' Saabs.[7]

After discussions in 1963, Saab entered into an agreement with Automotora (who were already selling BMWs to a local market that included many Germans) for the Uruguayan company to build two-stroke Saab 96s from semi-knocked-down (SKD) kits – kits that would arrive ready painted with all major components boxed and crated ready for reassembly. In February 1964 the first SKD components, enough to construct twenty-three cars, arrived for assessment by the import control and tariff authorities; from that assessment were set the rates and costs for SKD Saabs in Uruguay, Saab's most-distant SKD/CKD market.

The key men in Saab's Swedo-Uruguayan operations were Brynolf Holmqvist and Goran Hagstrom for Saab, and Jose Arijon and Rene Irion for Automotora. Assembly of the SKD factory facility continued into June, and by December, 193

two-stroke 96s had been built and sold to eager customers. 1965 saw only fifty examples of the 96 sold, but twenty of the 95 estate from SKD kits were made in Uruguay and sold.

Automotora wanted to show what it could do, and Saab wanted to make the cars cheaper, and this could be done by moving to a completely knocked-down (CKD) production basis, where basic panels and items were shipped from Sweden, and Automotora then welded up the complete cars and painted and trimmed them. The possibility of reduced import taxes was also raised by the sourcing of some locally procured components. On 5 April 1966, the then Swedish ambassador Ake Jonsson attended a formal ceremony at the Automotora factory upon the occasion of the first truly locally built Saab car. This was the first time Saab had entered full CKD production outside Europe, and is an often overlooked chapter in Saab's history.

The build quality and paint finish of the local Uruguayan-built cars was very high: Saab's local men set high goals for quality, and Automotora was similarly minded. But late in 1966, government and policy issues in Uruguay caused a temporary halt in production. However, all turned out well, and by mid-1966 Automotora-Saab was churning out 96 V4s – much to the locals' delight.

This delight also manifested itself in the form of a highly active local Saab competition department and rally entries (see Chapter 8).

Further Uruguayan state intervention in tariff and policy agreements led to further halts in the production, but after political changes in 1967, and a visit to Sweden by Automotora's management, CKD production of 96 and 95 V4s continued. By 1969 Automotora wanted the new Saab 99, and pushed for

LOCAL SUPPLIES

Locally sourced items for the Uruguayan 99 programme included the following:

- Upholstery material
- Internal boot floor panel
- Battery
- Exhaust
- Doors and side window (locally pressed steel items)
- Rear window glass
- Paint – pigment, base and lacquer coat

a contractural agreement and CKD supply from Saab. But Saab was struggling with production capacity and supply demands, and the possibility of the Saab 99 starting a South American life was postponed. At the same time, Saab was embroiled in its merger with Scania, to create Saab-Scania in 1969.

By January 1970, however, the first two-door Saab 99 CKD crates were on their way to Uruguay. Automotora had agreed with Saab that much of the trim items and even the paint would be locally sourced by Automotora. So the Uruguayan Saab 99s were unique – not least because by 1969, Automotora was building CKD BMWs and selling Alfa Romeos in Uruguay. It was possible that Saab 99s might emerge from Automotora's factory wearing a coat of BMW or Alfa Romeo paint.

Between April and September 1970, seventy-five Saab 99 two-door cars were shipped as CKD kits for building and painting in Uruguay, a total that later reached 100. Records are

Saab 96 in Scandinavian blue. Note the rear deck spoiler to enhance the airflow separation point and to lower drag.

unclear as to whether all 100 CKD cars were built, but by the end of the year, politics and policy had intervened again. Sporadic local assembly of 1970 delivered kits is believed to have continued, but by the mid-1970s, Saab's high quality, Uruguayan manufacturing story was finally over, after nearly 500 cars of the 96, 96 V4, 95 and 99 models had been produced. Some of these cars remain on the road today in South America.

Uruguay has an active Saab club, with Alberto Domingo as president; it has hosted Erik Carlsson as a guest in recent years. In Argentina there is a strong classic car movement and a Saab club; also two very smart Argentinian Saab 92s, one in black and one in dark maroon, can be seen running in Buenos Aires.

Saab's total overseas production for the period 1957–78 in Denmark, Belgium, Holland and Uruguay from SKD/CKD kits (not including Finnish factory production figures) came to an impressive total of 38,123 cars. Although small in scale, perhaps the story of the South American Saab 93–96 once again captures the energy and internationalism of the small Swedish company and its little cars that ranged across the world. To this day, Saab has a dedicated following in parts of South America.

URUGUAYAN SAAB–AUTOMOTORA PRODUCTION FIGURES	
Saab 96 including two-stroke and V4 as SKD:	243
Saab 96 including V4 as CKD:	65
Production total:	**308**
Saab 95 including V4 as SKD:	20
Saab 95 including V4 as CKD:	50
Production total:	**70**
Saab 99 two-door as CKD:	100
ALL MODEL PRODUCTION TOTAL:	**478**

ABOVE: **American spec 96 with the round headlamps and grille design. Many prefer the round-lamped look.**

RIGHT: **A V4 prior to the rubber bumper variant. True beige Saabism.**

ABOVE: **Modified classics – a 96 in Subaru WRC blue paint and the orange 96 cabrio conversion.**

GLOBAL SAAB?

Despite the small numbers involved, with this South American achievement Saab had shown what it and its cars were capable of. The 93–96 ranges had made another international mark – and it may have made an even bigger one. During the 1960s and 1970s, Saab was keen to diversify overseas, and its parallel aircraft business was opening doors to foreign customers' home markets. Inside Saab, a special overseas unit studied possible markets and production locations for SKD, CKD or full factory production of the 96 and 99.

Of significance, Saab held serious discussions with Bulgarian authorities in 1966 about a possible East–West tie-up. In 1968 a working party explored possible CKD manufacture of 96s in Colombia. The chance of producing tough little Saabs for Africa was explored via Portuguese assistance in Angola, and then via the British in Kenya where there were numerous local SKD or CKD car factories, as there were in what was then Rhodesia. In the 1970s, two locations came close to seeing Saab car production: the first was in 1974 when Saab discussed and investigated setting up production in emerging Indonesia. Then in 1975, Saab had talks in Australia about local production, though these came to little.

New face for the 96 from 1974 – which took the car into the 1980s (just).

But in 1978 it was attempting to sell second-hand jet fighters to India. Would the Indians also be interested in a tough, strong little car called 96V4? The Indians demanded four doors, just as they had with certain British cars being built locally in CKD form, and Saab were quite happy to modify and create a four-door 96, even at this late stage in its model lifespan. But the deal to sell Saab Draken aircraft and Saab 94s sadly fell through.

At the end, in February 1980, when Saab killed off the 96, it also ended its relationship with Ford for the supply of engines. Therein lay a strange event linked to a future not yet cast: on 14 February 1980, Ford's top man in Europe wrote to Saab's chairman, Marcus Wallenberg, expressing warm affection for

Saab and for Ford's dealings with Saab over the supply of the Ford V4 engine. Above all, the letter from Ford's director clearly stated the wish and hope that at some stage in the future the two companies would co-operate again in a joint endeavour. The Ford man who wrote that letter in 1980 was a certain Robert Lutz.

Little did anyone know what the passage of three decades would bring in terms of the men who would so affect Saab's fate.

So ended the tale of the Saab 96, a car that traced its direct roots back to the 92.001 of Saab's car beginnings in 1947 and the start of Saab car production in 1949. Only the 2CV, VW

SPECIFICATIONS   SAAB 96 V4 (1969)

Saab 96 replaced Saab 93 F model in February 1960 using revised body and updated technical specification. Note, Saab 95 production specification introduced December 1959 with the bigger engine of the 96 two-stroke with 841cc. V4 engine introduced 1967

Body
Stressed skin monocoque with carry-over reinforcements from earlier shell; revised rear body with larger windscreen and wider rear cabin, improved aerodynamics

Engine

Type	Overhead valve engine built on licence from Ford Motor Company Taunus 15M German model; 3-bearing crankshaft
Cylinders	4 in 60-degree V angle, configuration longitudinally mounted
Cooling	Water
Bore and stroke	90mm×58.86mm
Capacity	1498cc
Compression ratio	9.0:1
Carburettor	Autolite C8 GH 9510g; cam-driven fuel pump
Max. power	73bhp (54kW)
Max. torque	12kgm (117Nm) @ 2,700rpm

Transmission

Type	Front-wheel drive; 4-speed full synchromesh gearbox with column shift and freewheel device
Clutch	Single dry plate

Suspension and steering

Suspension	Coil springs and hydraulic shock absorbers at front, rigid rear axle; 95 estate has lever-arm shock absorbers to rear
Steering	Rack and pinion with 5.3m radius

Wheels
15in 4J rims, radial tyre option of 155×15

Brakes
Diagonal-split safety system with front discs and rear drums

Electrics
12V 4Ah battery capacity

Dimensions

Wheelbase	2,498mm (98in)
Length	4,200mm (165in); Estate 4,300mm (169in)
Width	1,580mm (62in)
Height	1,480mm (58in); Estate 1,490mm (59in)
Weight	890kg (1,962lb); Estate 955kg (2,106lb)
Top speed	147km/h (91mph)

Price at 1968
Skr14,785;
ESTATE Skr16,560

Beetle and Mini could claim similar titles to longevity. For hundreds of thousands of families worldwide, the Saab 92–93 and the 96 were more than cars: they were part of the family, a characterful, truly iconic piece of twentieth-century industrial design, of which the nearly 700,000 Saab 96s and 95s signalled their half-a-million-made mark.

96s on the move. The Save Saab convoy with Erik Carlsson, in Britain in 2010.

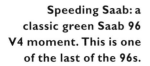

Speeding Saab: a classic green Saab 96 V4 moment. This is one of the last of the 96s.

SONETT

**The Saab 94 or Sonett I with the one-off
private derivative seen to the rear.**

LATERAL THINKING

SONETT | *LATERAL THINKING*

I N THE 1950S THE Saab factory was littered with lots of parts, a real feast for anyone who wanted to pick up a range of components and build a car. Surely it was inevitable that in a place populated by true petrol-heads, someone was going to collect everything from a spare engine to a suspension system and use these and a host of other parts to create something different. If anyone would, Rolf Mellde would, and he did.

Saab's strong but weighty 92 and 93 cars were a success in rallying, but too slow for circuit racing. VWs and Porsches were beating the teardrop-shaped Saabs on racing circuits and timed tarmac rally stages. Saab needed a lighter car, perhaps a racer to take it to success in the international arena. Mellde had drawn up such a car in his mind and on his drawing board. He just needed parts-bin components, and if not an official sanction, then quiet approval to see what he could do.

So began the Sonett saga; initially termed the Saab 94, Sonett was a story that would have a false start, yet be reincarnated in following years as something else entirely.

To think solely of the Saab Sonett as a late 1960s to 1970s glassfibre-bodied coupé that embodies a forgotten, sportier side of Saab is an error, for the Sonett actually started life in 1954 as one of the most revolutionary and advanced examples of post-war car design in terms of its construction rather than its styling. This was a true composite semi-monocoque construction, a uniquely made, open-topped two-seater that looked like a cross between an MG and an Alfa Romeo, or perhaps a Maserati. Yet it was many years before what was to become this stillborn wild child of a Scandinavian design group actually became the Saab Sonett as a production car.

In Swedish 'Sa natt' is derived from 'Sa natt den ar!' or 'How neat it is', which is what Mellde is supposed to have said when the first body for the car was finished and mounted on its chassis with a two-stroke engine: hence 'Sonett'. Some attribute this and even a sonnet or poem alliteration to Sason, but as Sason had wanted to call a car Sonett long before 1954, the origin is arguable. Whichever tale is correct, no other car has ever had the name. The Sonett's secret development team – who were building the first car off site, in a barn away from the factory – initially termed the car a 'hot-rod', for Mellde wanted to create a real racer.

Unlike its 1950s contemporaries, the original Sonett did not have a tubular steel chassis or fabricated body, nor did it have a floppy monocoque. Instead it boasted a unique body made from a blend of aluminium and plastic moulded panels weighing just under 100kg (220lb); these were bonded and joined together to form a stiff, aviation-style, part-stressed hull. Years later Colin Chapman created the original Lotus Élite's glassfibre unitary monocoque body (which itself was abandoned in favour of a chassis clothed in a weaker, one-piece glassfibre shell), and decades before a car maker made an aluminium production car.

AVIATION INFLUENCE

Again, aviation had played a role. In the late 1940s, the British had built a composite construction, moulded, plastic and resin aircraft known as the 'Aerolite Spitfire'. The Germans had built a similarly constructed Me 109 and the Americans and Canadians were also experimenting with one piece, polymer, resin and moulded chipboard aircraft construction. Saab itself has started to investigate the use of plastic-based, glass-reinforced fibre technology for aircraft parts. Ease of moulding meant that smooth, aerodynamic and curved structures were much simpler to make in the new material than they were in metal. But there were problems with load bearing, strength and crash protection using the new plastics technology. Could the

Saab Super Sonett at speed, as intended.

Saab Super Sonett I or Saab 94. Call it what you will, it was a world-beater.

lightness of resin and plastic be bonded to the lightness and strength of aluminium? If it could, a radical new answer, a solution to the problem, could be developed.

Mellde wanted to produce a metal and plastic tub with reinforcements placed strategically around the body. The original 748cc, 190km/h (120mph) Saab 94 – or Sonett I – was dreamed up by Rolf Mellde. Along with Mellde, the Saab team included Arne Frick, Lars-Olof Olsson who built the chassis and body, and Olle Lindqvist who modified and installed the engine. Gosta Svensson was the other person involved at this early stage. With them, Mellde created an alternative Saab to the firm's teardrop-shaped 92–93 range of steel-bodied family saloons. They cooked up the hot little car in a barn at Asaka, half an hour's drive from Trollhättan, mostly in their own time starting in January 1955. The car was essentially a spare-time project carried out in secret deep within Saab.

BACK TO FRONT?

With a tuned 748cc 3-cylinder engine that screamed its beat to high revs, a high 10:1 compression ratio and twin-choke combustion, coil springs and an ultra-stiff body tub to carry the suspension loads, the Sonett I had that essential 'rightness' in terms of a sports car. This was, in effect, a high-tech answer at a time when most so-called sports cars were based on 1930s and 1940s engines and chassis. Some had bodies in steel or the new-fangled plastic, but so weak and flimsy that doors would open in bends as the body structure twisted. Only the men at Jaguar, with aeronautics-trained Malcolm Sayer on hand, were even thinking in the same sphere of composite alloy chassis tubs and aerodynamics. The Sonett's engine was placed behind the front axle, aiding its weight distribution and race-car handling aspirations; several components and the drive train had to be reversed in order to make this configuration work.

In order to keep the two-stroke engine cool – the two-stroke cycle is more efficient when running cold – an elaborate engine cooling system was devised. This was controlled by two water pumps, twin thermostats and a high capacity header tank. Ignition timing was to be adjustable from the cockpit. Like its big brother the 93, the car had to be revved hard to get the best out of it and to avoid heat and oil build-up on the sparking plugs.

Saab management let the geniuses get on with it, without actually being officially involved – not that they really knew about Mellde's little secret. Yet ultimately, upon seeing the Sonett, Saab management whisked it off to become an official motor-show prototype of their new sports car: the ultra-light Sonett could do over 193km/h (120mph) from 57bhp.

Before that happened, the decision had been made to build a plastics and alloy-based semi-monocoque with an alloy tub or punt: was this the first true composite car, as opposed to simply draping flimsy glassfibre panels over a spaceframe or girder chassis? For this was the idea in the minds of Mellde and his men: this was the first use of aluminium as a sole construction basis. Pre-war racing cars had the chassis clothed in alloy panels, but the blend of aluminium as a tub and then combining it with a plastic skin in a monocoque was the stuff of science fiction to most people. But at Saab, the aircraft maker, was it anything other than might be expected?

Sonett I's total weight was 500kg or 1,100lb, the alloy base of the body weighed less than 100kg (220lb) – approximately 73kg (160lb) – and with a tuned-up engine, even if it and the gearbox were installed in reverse configuration, the car simply flew along in a buzzing, rasping, high-revving cacophony. The Sason-tweaked rear wing edges – small fins – gave excellent aerodynamic behaviour in terms of wake drag, separation point, and yaw angle/cross-wind stability, and they looked very professional, too. Sonett had a pert style and a pure 'roadster' character.

ARNE FRICK RECALLS A SECRET 'HOT' CAR

Sonett 1 was so secret that Mellde gave orders to his recruits that they were not to discuss the car with anyone. Arne Frick, one of the small team chosen from the workshops by Mellde, recalled in his Saab Veterans Club memoirs[8] that Mellde was insistent on secrecy for a project they came to call 'Hemlighteta' or 'Secret Hot', a play on a description of a 'hot' or tuned car. Frick was working under his foreman, Thage Gustavsson, when he got a request via Karl-Evert Eriksson who was 'in' on the secret project at the Saab engine laboratory, to see Mellde.

The outcome was that Frick was to join a development project off site. He went home, and all he could tell his wife was that he had a new temporary role on a project away from the factory. Frick drove off every day in his own recently purchased Saab 92. In fact this was a historic car in its own right, as it turned out be production car number seven, previously owned by none other than Gunnar Ljungström and then Sixten Sason. Eventually the car ended up in the Wallenberg's private collection.

From the factory for his first visit to the secret project 'Hot', Frick drove off in a two-car Saab convoy across the airfield and via Fors Stena, Bryggum and Mull Torp villages and on out towards a remote farming area near Aska. There they entered a nondescript barn. Inside were men working on plastic panels and moulds for a car chassis. These men were Erik Johansson, Sven Fredriksson and Elis Olsson.

It is often written that Rolf Mellde did not drive the Sonett 1 until 14 October 1955, but Frick insists that he and Erik Danielsson, who lived next door to the barn, knew that the first run was in June, in the summer sun. The secret prototype was run late at night without its body, but in the perpetual midnight sun of the Swedish summer, it was spotted, not least because the noise of its two-stroke engine wailing and screaming away at full revs must have been difficult to ignore. The country roads around Aska were 'buzzed' by a spitting viper of a rolling chassis that apparently looked like a rowing boat with wheels. The locals, it seems, kept the secret of the wild men in their barn and the monster that they wheeled out at night.

Sonett 1 was raced in 1956 and entered the Spring Trophy in Sodermanland, with Arne Frick the car's mechanic. He recounts that Saab's deputy service manager was Clas Magnus Backstrom, who gave them tickets for the Stockholm Motor Show. After the show, when Saab had decided to produce the Sonett 1 as five more prototypes, Arne Frick drove the prototype to Linköping so it could be measured and copied. To help with the laying up of the glassfibre, a Gothenburg-based firm, the curiously named SOAB (Svenska Oljeslageri AB) was brought in to work with the American-imported resins and fibres. This firm had begun to use glassfibre to build boats, so had some experience with the new material.

Frick also explains that in later years, in 1998, the well known Sonett enthusiast Klaus Muller-Ott got the remaining members of the Saab team together and revealed the story of what happened to one of the two 'Facett' versions of the Sonett. These cars were given two proper seats, a hard top, and more creature comforts for on-the-road use. One Facett had been heavily crashed and lay about unrepaired for years. According to Frick, his was the car that Muller-Ott had restored. Rolf Mellde was present to see the finished job.

TOP: **It's that blue theme again. Mellde's ideas, Sason's elements, and those smart and aerodynamic rear wing fences just simply worked.**

LEFT: **Simple, Saab, and so right: the prototype's interior. Notice the gear lever location, race-car style.**

Rear view of the so-called 'Facett', with shades of Triumph in the roof and Citroën in the rear lamps.

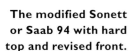

The modified Sonett or Saab 94 with hard top and revised front.

WHO SHAPED THE SONETT 1?

Who designed the style of the first Saab 94 or Sonett 1 – the open two-seater with a composite body? Perceived wisdom and published records say that it was Sixten Sason – but was it? Sason did indeed contribute to the shape of the Saab Sonett 1, but did he actually sculpt the body form? There are several who were there, whose recollections support a claim that the basic stylistic genesis of the Sonett 1's shape started with no less a figure than its progenitor, Rolf Mellde: Sason was involved and must have contributed, say the Saab veterans[9], but it seems

that Mellde had strong ideas on the lines of the car, and pushed them through.

In interviews and supported by co-workers, and the Saab veterans' archives, the memories of the Sonett team clearly state that Mellde shaped the Sonett's profile from the inspiration of the long, feminine, 'waisted' shape of a 1950s series Maserati. Mellde was also a fan of World War II fighters, and liked the scooped radiator inlet shape of the P-51 Mustang and its Meredith-effect design, which is said to have inspired his creation of the Sonett's under-nose air vent – although a similarly styled vent appeared under the nose of Saab's early development 92s. Sason at this time was working as a consultant on other projects for several Swedish companies – he was no longer deep within Saab. Mellde definitely brought Sason in to assess the secret car, but it seems possible that Mellde, a forthright and driven character, led on Sonett I in style as well as engineering.

It is said that it was Sason who built a small-scale styling model for the start Sonett's shape, but there is much evidence that while Sason did contribute to the car and built that early model, the clothing of the original composite underframe was penned by Mellde himself. However, Sason seems to have finessed the themes – but can we hold Mellde responsible for the engineering-style, flat sides, or was that due to problems with the infancy of glassfibre construction inhibiting both Mellde and/or Sason's hand? Perhaps we shall never know if one man dominated Sonett I's design, other than to say that these two strong characters had worked well together before and would do so again – so each can take credit.

ADDING LIGHTNESS

By late October 1955, after being road-tested in its bare bones, the fully clothed Sonett was ready for driving on public roads; however, it was kept secret until the Stockholm Motor Show of February 1956. The 57bhp car could hit 214km/h (133mph), but it was its style that dominated the subsequent headlines. The Sonett caused a sensation in the motoring press and was great PR for Saab on a global scale, yet the revolution of its *de facto* composite construction was lost on all but the technically enthusiastic.

In April the car made its debut at the 1956 New York Motor Show and earned more PR for the Saab brand. During 1956 it covered over 5,000km (3,000 miles) in testing. The car known as the Saab 94, the next number in Saab's in-house numerology, was soon dismissed as Sonett came closer to reality.

One car had been built, almost as a private affair, but now it was real, now it was once of the cleverest and prettiest sports cars of the 1950s, what should happen to it? And was the Sonett also to be a victim of Saab's strict adherence to two-stroke power? The American sports-car market, the Corvette-inspired marketing arena, loved the look of the Sonett, but the discovery of a sub-1000cc two-stroke engine under the bonnet soon killed off the mainstream buyers' enthusiasm, at least until they drove the little devil!

However, for the time being, Saab's management had bitten the bullet and funded the creation of a total of six Sonetts as development cars. In the end, however, the Sonett story was to falter.

By the end of 1956, the firm of ASJ in Linköping was asked to build the first few cars, and they in turn brought in a specialist commercial body-building company known as Karossverk-staderna of Katrineholm. Development took place, and in parts of the design metal replaced some aluminium in the development cars, and a four-speed gearbox would replace the stock Saab three-speed column-shift gearbox. By 1957, Saab was discussing how many Sonetts it could make with ASJ's help. Could they manufacture 2,000 a year?

Despite various plans and projections, and despite a great reception from press and public – including in America – Saab's exquisite little car never made it to production life. At one stage Jensen were to build the bodies in the UK, but the Jensen brothers seemed slow to respond, and did not travel to Sweden to pursue Saab's interest, so the Sonett stayed Swedish. And could a folding soft-top be designed to make the car more buyer friendly? Was a winter hard-top possible? Could Saab build the Sonett itself? All these questions and possibilities were within Sonett's grasp, even if its two-stroke engine was its possible future Achilles heel.

The Sonett was raced – Erik Carlsson drove the car to win in its debut at the Karlskoga races of 1957, and other Sonetts were driven by Harald Kronegard and Clas Backstrom. At one stage a Sonett was modified to single-seat, racing mono-posto specification with a fairing over the passenger seat area, and a specially moulded, one-off driver's windscreen and shroud. Sonett's last race was in September 1957 when, driven by Erik Lundgren, it won the Solvalla circuit race.

Despite all these good intentions, Saab never took hold of the Sonett I. Somehow, amid all the enthusiasm and the incredible achievement from a small team, only six Sonetts were made before the idea died. At the same time, international FIA car competition rules were changed, and tuned production saloons were allowed to form a racing group, wiping out the Sonett's justification. At the same time the more powerful Saab 93 GT 750 was launched, notably in America where it could quickly make the most of the enthusiasm generated by the Sonett and Ralph Millet's marketing and PR campaign.

So ended a revolutionary idea, one that if it had had the resources of a major motor manufacturer would surely have become an instant super car – a more advanced sort of Porsche with a hint of something else of Italian feel thrown in. Its legacy was to provide the 93 with a developed engine, and to sow the seeds for a future not yet cast. Clarification comes from knowing that the modified Facett car owned by Sorenson was latterly converted back to true Sonett I status as the 'green car' by the German Saab enthusiast Herr Muller Ott, and that today's apparent Facett-type Sonett is a rebuild (using the rumoured long-discarded parts) created by Rene Hirsch, the Swiss-based Saab enthusiast and tuner of Hirsch accessories fame.

The fate of the original six Sonetts is as follows: car No. I went to the Saab Museum; car No. 2 to Philipsons, the Saab sponsoring garage chain, and then to the USA; car No. 3 went

SPECIFICATIONS SAAB 94 SUPER SONETT I (1956)

Unveiled 16 March 1956. Six were built

Body
Two-seat open, glassfibre/plastics in composite with aluminium structure

Engine

Type	3-cylinder valveless
Cylinders	Longitudinally mounted with reverse layout installation
Cooling	Water-cooled with pumped circulation
Bore and stroke	66mm×72.9mm
Capacity	748cc
Compression ratio	10:1
Carburettor	Solex 40 AI type, electric fuel pump
Max power	57.5bhp (42kW) @ 5,000rpm
Max torque	9kgm (88Nm) @ 3,500rpm

Transmission

Type	Front-wheel drive; floor/sill-mounted shift three-speed gearbox with freewheel and synchromesh on top two gears. Four-speed box on later Sonett Is
Clutch	Single dry plate

Suspension and steering

Suspension	Coil springs and hydraulic shock absorbers on all four wheels with rigid rear axle. Independent front suspension
Steering	Rack and pinion, 5.5m radius

Wheels and tyres
15in

Brakes
Hydraulic brakes, all-round drums

Electrics
12V with 33Ah battery capacity

Dimensions

Wheelbase	2,210mm (87in)
Length	3,485mm (137in)
Width	1,420mm (56in)
Height	825mm (32in)
Weight (net)	500kg (1,103lb)

Top speed
160km/h (99mph), closed top claim of 200km/h (124mph)

---

to a private individual, as did No. 4, this person believed to be Sigvard Sorenson, who reputedly converted the car into the 'Facett' project featuring a hard top and restyled body and cabin. Car No. 5 went to Saab, and car No. 6 also found its way to the USA. Rumours of a 'spare' car built up from bits in the 1950s have always circulated, but remain a rumour.

From the ashes of the Saab 94, or the original Sonett, was to come a reincarnation: Sonett II. But the path to the birth of another attempt at a Saab sports car was fraught with delay and blind alleys.

MR KERN AND THE QUANTUM CARS

Over in America circa 1956–63, Saab's little marketing niche meant that the idea of a sports car from Saab was likely to be received with enthusiasm, if not exactly expected. Frustrated with the lack of a Saab sportster, one enterprising private citizen named Walter Kern, an academic and physicist who worked at the Massachusetts Institute of Technology (MIT), decided to build a Saab-based sports car of his own – while all around him his fellow Americans were lapping up Triumphs and MGBs based on wheezing, ancient underpinnings and soft steel.

In fact Kern's swoopy, 1962 fibreglass-bodied idea for a Saab two-seat sports car – perhaps even a true Saab Spyder – had its roots in his creation in 1959 of a steel and alloy panelled single-seat, Saab-powered private racing car, which he had designed and christened 'Quantum'. He made two such hand-finished circuit racers, but these, although not road cars, led him to what some term 'Quantum' and others cite as 'Quantum III' – the elegant, plastic-bodied Saab Spyder idea that had the support of Ralph Millet, the man who had started and owned Saab in America.

Kern made his first sketches for a Saab sports car on 7 January 1958. He drew a single-seat open racer with an 1,850mm (73in) wheelbase, 1,420mm (4ft 8in) track and an overall length of 2,690mm (106in). The drawings were clearly marked 'Saab Spyder'.

After creating two of these lightly clad cars, Kern took more stock Saab parts, engine and gearbox, wheels and numerous items and set them into a curved, fibreglass open-top body design; initially this featured the ungainly windscreen from the 96, but it was later replaced with a shallower, more sporty windscreen frame. Underneath the moulded body was a steel tube chassis designed by Kern using his employer's Super-Computer, something no car manufacturer had yet managed (though Ford would soon do so for the Cortina). The body was a smooth, curved amalgamation of themes, but it had an identity of its own. It also had definite shades of being a miniature Jaguar E-Type in the styling genre of the day. Kern's fibreglass Quantum or Saab Spyder proposal was built by Merrill & Company, and it is believed that the lead player in the construction of the body was a Henry Rudkin, who may have also contributed styling details to Kern's shape.

Ralph Millet's Saab USA took an interest in the Kern self-build project and exhibited the car on its 1962 New York Motor Show stand as an unofficial Saab named 'Quantum Saab'. Kern built at least one more development prototype, and his Quantum found its way to Trollhättan where Saab tested it and decided that it was not for them. But it was food for thought, and reinforced a marketing survey for the US market that indicated that American buyers wanted a two-seat, sporty Saab. If a privateer could do it, could Saab?

But there was a twist in the tale: Walter Kern had built the single-seat, Saab-powered club racer, and then his two-seat fibreglass-bodied sportster named 'Quantum', and these gave rise to further variations upon its theme. Using the Saab two-stroke engine and suspension components, a series of single-seat lightweight Saab-powered racing cars were built as private ventures. Through the 1960s, the Quantum-based cars, under confused nomenclature, were later raced in Sports Car Club of America (SCCA) category H (modified) class events, and in the Formula C category, sometimes cited as a later Formula S.

Some later Saabists refer to the cars as a range of Quantum series numbering 1 to 5, and much chronological confusion as to their status and timing exists. Walter Kern did not label his creations in such manner, but research suggests that the Quantum cars began with Mark 1 in 1959, a Mark 2 version in 1960, and the fibreglass two-seater Mark 3 and Sonett proposal in 1962. The same year saw a Mark 4 or Formula S single-seat racer, which was not a Walter Kern project. In 1965 a further variant of the Quantum car was created and has

subsequently become categorized as the Mark 5. Strangely it was clothed in a body from a British Ginetta car.[10]

From 1959, a series of Quantum-titled cars in various states of design used the Saab two-stroke engine in specially developed chassis units. The first 'Quantum 1' had a raw, steel-panelled racing body over its chassis and a 750cc engine; a second variant was built, and this led to the fibreglass sportster design that was also the better known two-seat Quantum that Ralph Millet placed on Saab's 1962 New York Motor Show stand. This is the car that may well have been a motivating factor in Saab's decision to reincarnate the Saab 94 Sonett as the 1960s Saab 97 Sonett range. Thus Saab turned down Mr Kern's design, but it did use his idea. The seeds of Sonett II and III were grown from a design that had been what Walter Kern thought Saab needed, as indeed it did.

Ultimately, the Quantum series took on a life of its own beyond Walter Kern, and a single-seat Saab-based racing car was created, which looked and drove like an overgrown kart racer. These two-stroke cars were clearly a step forwards from Saab's own Formula Junior car, but unlike the Junior, the little Quantum-derived racers were rear-engined and did not suffer from the understeer that so affected the Saab-built Formula Junior cars.

Walter Kern also formed a Quantum Motor Car Company to produce private racing kit cars. Ralph Millet, head of Saab's American sales company, soon snapped up Kern's idea and company as vital PR tools for the Saab brand. Up to fifty of these racing cars built from a kit of parts are believed to have been sold by Saab in America, and several are still to be seen on the vintage racing club scene in the USA.

From Formula Junior to the Quantum series, Saab has a long-forgotten racing heritage, which, while not as well known as the company's rallying exploits, still proves that there was a secret side to a sportier Saab.

Fifty years later, Kern's alloy-bodied, single-seat racer versions of the Quantum can still be seen on the private vintage racing scene in the USA, and the later single-seat cars are also still part of the vintage Saab scene.

If in Doubt, Procrastinate

The curvy fibreglass Quantum Saab, with its upright windscreen and tubular chassis, was not, however, the car for Saab or the market. Nevertheless, Mr Kern's car was a pathfinder, and in hindsight its influence was clearly stronger than some realized at the time. Rolf Mellde's Saab 94 or Sonett I might have been the original 1954 in-house precursor, but nothing came of it. Did it take Walter Kern to provide inspiration in 1962 for the later Saab Sonett range? We can surely suggest that without Kern and

Catherina looked better in profile, the awkward windscreen being less obvious. This was a 1960s design that framed Sason's future vision for the 1970s. This could have been Saab's supercar.

Catherina with the roof on, and seen from above – as Sason and Envall always ensured. We can see shades of later Jaguar, Toyota and American designs in this 1960s car design.

Ralph Millet, Sonett II, V4 and III might never have happened. Was Sonett II what Kern's idea became in another context? Of note, in later years Walter Kern took a keen interest in the Sonett story, and modified a Sonett III to electric power. He was also behind the rare turbocharged Sonett III.

Back in 1961, by coincidence, Sixten Sason was sketching up a new Saab sports car, assisted by the young Bjorn Envall. This resulted in another Saab 93/96-based prototype two-seater – the 'Catherina'. Built as a one-off by ASJ, the car, like the Quantum, was hamstrung in its style by the use of a flat wind-screen from a Saab 96. But Catherina had Sason's eye for the future within its design. This car had shades of the French and Italian trends, and in profile it had the look of something exot-ic from the Riviera. There was also a lift-out roof panel, which could be stored in a slip-bag in the boot; was this the birth of the targa-top, soon used by Porsche and VW? Many believe that Sason and Envall did indeed dream up the idea.

The car was presented to Saab's top team on 9 February 1964 in Linköping, in a dance hall. Then it was shown to the dealers and to the Swedish public at the Saab dealers' Spring Motor Show, and over 100,000 Swedes flocked to see Sason's smooth, long-limbed and elegant Catherina. The roof shape and swept rear buttresses had hints of Ferrari 275 LM, which as Malcolm Sayer would prove on the later Jaguar XJS, were aerodynamically sound. The Catherina's aerodynamics were, however, handicapped by the flat, upright windscreen: more work was needed.

If only the car had been fitted with the curved windscreen from the concurrent Saab 'Project Gudmund' – the 99 – and been sleeker and faster, then Saab's management might have ordered production. As it was, Catherina was a typical Saab-design concept, stillborn but full of future themes, yet it was eclipsed by the perceived wisdoms of the 96 Super Sport. But once again, Catherina, a sporty Saab, reminded Saab's directors

Sixten Sason's 'Catherina' proposal. Note the targa top and rear buttress C pillars. What a shame that the Saab 96 windscreen detracted from the design. Sason wanted a curved windscreen similar to the 99s.

that they were capable of a sports car. Catherina was elegant, despite its windscreen problem, and with minor design development it could have been a significant sports car design of the 1960s – but it was not to be. However, Sason's archive clearly shows a collection of sketches for a long-nosed, high-decked, Kamm-tailed two-door fastback coupé, which bears more than a passing resemblance to the Sonett III that was latterly shaped by Segio Cogglia and Gunnar Sjögren. So Sason's background influence upon the Sonett II and III should not be dismissed.

Saab had encouraged Sason to create Catherina, but was Saab also encouraging a rival design with a healthy bit of competition to see who could create Saab's first sports coupé? Several commentators have stated that this is the case, but the structure of events may be less definite, because essentially another privateer, if not quite as isolated from Saab as the Quantum's Mr Kern, had an idea.

MR KARLSTRÖM AND HIS SPORTSTER

Bjorn Karlström was a well known Swedish illustrator and designer. He left school in the mid-1930s and began to train as an aircraft mechanic, but a skill for illustrating aircraft led to commissions from magazines and by the 1940s he was embarking on a career as an illustrator and designer.

From comic strips to book covers, Karlström moved on to industrial design, and by the early 1960s had designed motor cycles and household products. By 1963, he had sketched his idea for a Saab sports coupé. By securing sponsorship from Malmo Flygindustri (MFI), a well known Swedish design and aeronautics supplier and a one-time subsidiary of Trellborgs Gummifabric AB, Karlström obtained the funding and resources to build a one-off sports car proposal based, as per the fashion,

on Saab 96 parts, only this time minus the constraints of the Saab 93's windscreen!

The result was a stunning modern shape that owed nothing to anyone and, despite a few undeveloped details, could have been a design project motor-show car from a major car maker. Certainly the clean shape and the lack of swage lines and embellishments put it ahead of the then current fashions: this was a shape for the late 1970s, but one drawn in the 1960s. With its deep side windows, glazed, rear wrap-around canopy and smooth panels, this was a shape definitely more suited to 1974, and not the year of 1964 when it was styled. Can we see, in Karlström's original thinking, hints of later era cars such as the Porsche 924 or TVR? Karlström's achievement has received little profile beyond the Saab cognoscenti, not least as it was absorbed into the styling of the Sonett II, which masked the purity of his basic thoughts.

Did Karlström start off entirely as a privateer, or was there a degree of support from Saab? The historical records sometimes disagree. One thing is for sure, he dreamed up a jewel, and he did it solo.

Karlström's career included work for major international media organizations, and he became a well known name in aircraft modelling. Like Sason, his career began with aircraft, and was recognized through the award of several medals, including a Paul Tissander award from the FAI. Perhaps his aviation background explains his ability to appreciate clean, smooth, integrated forms.

Karlström's design featured a lightweight boxed-steel subframe tub and chassis beneath some cleverly curved steel and plastic body panels, with that exotic, wraparound glass rear windscreen and chopped 'Kamm' tail, and in February 1965 it was ready for the media. Only the slightly angular front air intake and side windows needed a bit more design work, but in total, the little car, christened the MFI 13, was not just competent, it had a look of the future, despite one or two rough edges. It was paraded to the media at the Hedendula Conference Centre on 4 February 1965. Before long, within months, Karlström the privateer had become the author of the next Saab car – the Saab 97, or as it would become after an intense period of 'Saabification', the reborn, rebadged, Sonett II.

SONETT II

By late summer 1965 Saab's management had decided to build a sports car, known internally as the Saab 97 and soon to be a rechristened, reincarnated, as the 'Sonett'. But there was an impending design issue: by 1966 Sason was unwell (he died in early 1967) and anyway was finishing off the 99 with Envall, who was soon to go and work for Opel in Germany. Saab therefore lacked a design leader – and could it qualify for government funding to produce the MFI car by creating a new project for a new factory? There were many tangents to events.

The old firm of ASJ from Arlov near Malmo were brought back in, for Saab was going to make the car in fibreglass plastic resin, yet with a strong steel floorpan and under-structure using Saab 96 and 95 pressings. For extra safety a tubular steel roll-hoop would be placed inside the cabin, as the plastic body would have little natural crush resistance.

By January 1966 more early production cars had been built, one in steel to form the basis of the fibreglass mould – this was proving problematical, so a master copy was created, followed by two more, which were shown to the Swedish motoring press in January 1966. The new Saab Sonett, with two-stroke power, was ready for its main European launch at the Geneva Motor Show of March 1966. Twenty-five hand-built, early production cars were readied for the media and marketing and for the US launch in New York. However, the car was expensive to build, and the price of 20,000Skr was an issue. For Ralph Millet in the USA, the price of $3,500 was a major stumbling block. Despite this, and the retention of two-stroke power, the 1966 Saab Sonett II began to sell in increasing numbers,

The early 1966 model year Sonett was produced in a total of twenty-eight cars: these were the oval-grilled pilot production cars with the strange, mesh-covered grille intake resembling, according to one wag, a pre-war radio set's loudspeaker. The Saab-theming of Karlström's design had included making the car's front end more definitive; most controversially, the car was also given a more pronounced, moulded 'hip' line along its side from front to rear, reflecting the styling themes of the era; and the deep side windows were reduced in size.

Although it was a more integrated shape than Karlström's prototype, many feel that the production Sonett II looked older and more dated than the cleaner Karlström MFI 13 prototype

Sixten Sason wanted to style something modernist for Sonett and this sketch from the Västergtöland Museum Sason exhibition proves it.

upon which it was based. Karlström's futurism had taken a backward glance, and his design had been made more contemporary in its translation from prototype to a Sonett II – but it might just have been more advanced in its original form than Saab had realized. Was this the one time when Saab played safe and rejected a really futuristic shape for something more contemporary? Not everyone liked the Sonett's revised production styling, and the American media thought it was ugly.

Perhaps it is true to say that Karlström's styling was advanced but lacked integration, and that Saab in its attempt to integrate those elements produced a shape that became dated, fussy and a bit disjointed. Yet the overall form had charm, and a certain cheek, or pertness. Media claims of the day, that the car lacked a coherent wholeness, seem in retrospect a bit hard on the sweet little Sonett.

What was kept amid the restyling was the one-piece front bonnet/hood and wing/fender design, where the entire front of the car swings upwards in one piece in the manner of the Triumph Spitfire or the Jaguar E Type. In 1966, Saab made sixty of the new Sonetts, though ten were retained by the company for development projects.

These very early 1966 cars were seen in Saab publicity shots with the elaborate chrome wheel-trim embellisher rings from the 96. They were fussy in design and did not look the part. By 1967 the car had been properly productionalized, even if Karlström's 1963 idea of an opening glass hatch was abandoned, leaving the Sonett with woeful luggage access and a strange 'letterbox' boot/trunk access panel. Inside the cabin, a full-width dashboard of mahogany plywood with a light walnut finish was fitted (early pre-production cars used a metal panel).

LEFT: **Sonett III came later, but in this shot seems to have a hint of 'Catherina'.**

BELOW: **Saab Sonett 11 with Erik Carlsson at the wheel.**

Super Sonett racing in 1956.

The early production cars had a chrome-plated roll-over bar behind the seats, but this was later a factory-issue black.

The front of the car had a clean, curved leading edge with a thin and very neat rubbing strip across its prow; removing it made the car look even better, but left it with no low-speed parking bump protection. Another attempt at tidying up the front panel was also made with a revised rectangular grille air intake. The drag coefficient was Cd 0.35.

From 748cc and 57.5bhp origins, the Sonett's triple-cylinder power was upgraded to 847cc with Solex carburettors and 60bhp at 5,200rpm. With the two-stroke wailing away under the plastic front end and the cabin warming up, progress in the Sonett was never dull. With a total weight of 740kg (1,654lb) the car was a flyer: 0–100km/h (0–60mph) took just 12sec, and 160km/h (99mph) top speed was obtainable. However, for emissions-obsessed California, the special 803cc 'Shrike' engine from the 96, with its direct oil-injection, was used in California-bound Sonetts to bypass regulations related to cubic capacity and output. Other unusual design touches included moulded fibreglass one-piece seat pans – another design innovation long forgotten now.

Strangely, Saab had not produced a 'Sonett' badge for the car – and neither had it really thought about the cabin ventilation system: the cockpit got hot, especially with all that glass; so Saab used the idea of the rear C-pillar vents from the Saab 96, and suddenly the 1967 model year Sonett had ungainly 'elephant's ear' extractor vents on the B pillars. An air-intake vent was also moulded into the bonnet/hood. The Triumph-style chrome-plated bonnet/hood catches were replaced with competition-style rubber strops. The wooden dashboard panel was now fitted in place of a turned steel facia, and a host of Saab trim items added. The little car was starting to look rather 'busy'.

Saab used the 'Carlsson effect' by getting Erik to pose against the 1967 Sonnet, with his own Saab 91 Safir private aircraft in the background. But despite such illustrious advertising, only 258 examples of the original two-stroke Sonett II were ever sold. The idea had yet to really take off.

Sonett II 2-stroke showing off the rear canopy.

SPECIFICATIONS SONETT II (1966)

Prototype build and pre-series cars January–July 1966. Premiere Geneva Show March 1966. Production series September 1966

Body

Two-seat glassfibre shell mated to Saab 95/96 steel underbody with roll-over bar built in

Engine

Type	3-cylinder valveless
Cylinders	Longitudinally mounted
Cooling	Water-cooled with pumped circulation
Bore & stroke	66mm×72.9mm
Capacity	748cc
Compression ratio	10:1
Carburettor	Solex 40 AI type, electric fuel pump
Max. power	Rating 60bhp (43kW) @ 5,200rpm
Max. torque	9kgm (88Nm) @ 3,500rpm

Transmission

Type	Front-wheel drive, floor/sill-mounted shift three-speed gearbox with freewheel and synchromesh on top two gears. Four-speed box on later Sonett Is
Clutch	Single dry plate

Suspension and steering

Suspension	Coil springs and hydraulic shock absorbers on all four wheels with rigid rear axle. Independent front suspension
Steering	Rack and pinion, 5.5m radius

Wheels and tyres

15in

Brakes

Hydraulic brake discs to front, rear drums

Electrics

12V with 33Ah battery capacity

Dimensions

Wheelbase	2,160mm (85in)
Track	1,220mm (48in)
Height	1,116mm (44in)

Top speed

150.9km/h (94mph)

RIGHT: **Non-standard paint, perhaps, but very smart. Joel Durand's Sonett V4.**

BELOW: **Pure Sonett – but does it hint at TVR?**

THE SONETT V4

Some Saabists refer to the 'Sonett II V4', but this is in error: the Sonett II was two-stroked, whereas the addition of the V4 engine from the Saab 96 in 1967 required extensive alterations to the car. This was a new model, and not just a re-engined Sonett II. So the Sonett II became the Sonett V4; it really ought to have been Sonett III, but that would have subsequently given rise to a Sonnet V V4.

Changes to the stock V4 engine included harder valve springs and, along with a freer-flowing air filter mounted in a new position as a two-piece unit, these were significant performance changes, as was a two-piece exhaust system. The wheels were wider, and extra chassis supports were needed.

The 'new' V4 engine was 35kg (77lb) heavier than the two-stroke 3-cylinder that it replaced, but it ran at lower revs and had a more even torque band. In such a light car as the Sonett, this change in the weight ratio had more effect than it did in the heavier, steel-bodied 96. This meant that although the V4 was faster than a well stirred two-stroke, it was only just so. However, the Sonett V4 was quieter, cooler running and more economical, and, vitally, it did not need separate lubrication added to the mix. With more weight over the front wheels, the V4-engined Sonett felt less agile than the sporty little light-weight Sonett II and had lost a little of its point-and-squirt, race-car type agility and feedback. Even the front suspension had to be made heavier and the chassis revised. Despite this, it still had good responses, and Erik Carlsson and Pat Moss-Carlsson were to be seen rallying the Sonett; but it was not what it had been in two-stroke form.

In 1969, a Sonett V4 entered by Sture Nottorp with semi-official Saab backing and driven by Simo Lapinen was in third place in its class in that year's very icy Monte Carlo rally, when strange goings-on denied the Sonett its result. Some form of problem with an unmanned rally control post amid organizational dysfunction on the part of the rally organizers meant that the Sonett was not officially logged at one zone. Despite assurances that all would be well, the Sonett was belatedly disqualified and the French entrant placed above it.

Sason was now dead, and the long-nosed, high-tailed, two-door coupé design that had been on his drawing board was forgotten. With his death went any idea of a radical restyling for the V4. Sonett II would be re-incarnated instead, and as the Sonett V4, sales were slow.

The Sonett V4 also gained a black plastic-finished dashboard, and an unfortunate blister in the bonnet /hood to give the V4 extra room, and larger bumpers. There were also 'Sonett V4' badges, and a further cluttering of the pert little shape: the attaching of some large, square, black rubber, front bumper over-riders really upset the car's curved frontal aspect. The media,

especially the influential American motoring press, slated the car's looks – but even so, the little Saab had a happy band of followers, and despite the changes, the car still drove well.

Over 200 V4s were sold in late 1967 and 846 in 1968. For 1969's model year, when 509 Sonetts were sold, Saab's annual round of tweaking included new, high-backed seats with head-rests, and an unusual adjustable lumbar roll pad for each anatomically shaped backrest. There was even a lid for the glovebox – at last, after many complaints. The Sonett II had a sound-absorbing headlining, and side panels in the cabin with sound-deadening pads and thick door-card trims; but despite these measures the car was noisy and hot to travel in for long distance runs. The addition of a less absorbent vinyl, interior headlining and more vinyl cabin trim in later Sonetts only compounded the noise levels. But as the Sonett two-stroke and the Sonett V4 purists would say, what a noise!

Saab, through its long-standing advertising agency Tema of Gothenburg, had undertaken an extensive advertising campaign for the Sonett and the V4, and the strapline 'This is Sweden's idea of an expensive toy' was cleverly placed over a shot of a speeding Sonett, which, thanks to photographic effects, looked a touch longer and sleeker than it actually was.

In 1969, 509 Sonett V4s were sold, but in the background Saab were at it again – tinkering with the bits and pieces in their parts bin. Sonett III (or should that have been Sonett V?) was in the wings.

SONETT III AND BJORN ANDREASSON

In 1969 Saab had realized that the Sonett had become rather a stylistic mess, especially in V4 guise. A facelift was needed, and while they were at it, why not revise the car from front to rear? So Saab commissioned a revised Sonett. This Sonett III was a long-nosed coupé with overtones of Italian exotica – as penned by the Milanese designer Sergio Coggiola. Saab did, however, get its own in-house artist Gunnar A. Sjögren to style much of the new Sonett's plastic body details.

Inside Saab – or rather, inside Malmo Flyg Industri (MFI), by this time owned by Saab – was the Swedish aircraft designer Bjorn Andreasson. He had designed a range of small aircraft for MFI, and was working on translating one of these into the Saab MFI-17 Safari and its military version the 'Supporter'. Andreasson was also working with the Saab team creating the Saab Transporter, a twin-engined small airliner type, which became the highly successful Saab 340 airliner a decade later.

Before that happened Andreasson, also a car fanatic, proposed his idea for a new body shape for the Sonett. He, too, had kept the Sonett II's centre section and windscreen, but had

RIGHT: **The Sonett II dashboard with 1960s wood trim and a lovely Saab steering wheel.**

BELOW: **Stunning Sonett captured in an early Saab brochure.**

Bjorn Andreasson's Sonett III design sketch of 1968. Shades of Lamborghini Espada, perhaps.

SPECIFICATIONS   SONETT III

Body
Revised two-seat Sonett II glassfibre shell mated to Saab 95/96 steel underbody with roll-over bar built in, new front and rear sections. Cellular bumpers added later

Engine

Type	4-cylinder overhead valve engine built on licence from Ford Motor Company (FoMoCo) Taunus 15M German model
Cylinders	60-degree V-angle configuration longitudinally mounted
Cooling	Water-cooled
Bore & stroke	90mm×58.86mm
Capacity	1498cc
Compression ratio	9.0:1
Max. power	68bhp (54kW)
Max. torque	11kgm (117Nm) @ 2,700rpm

Transmission

Type	Front-wheel-drive with four-speed full synchromesh gearbox
Clutch	Single dry plate

Suspension and steering

Suspension	Coil springs and hydraulic shock absorbers on all four wheels with rigid rear axle. Independent front suspension
Steering	Rack and pinion, 5.5m radius

Wheels and tyres
15in

Brakes
Hydraulic brake discs to front, rear drums

Electrics
12V with 33Ah battery capacity

Dimensions

Wheelbase	2,120mm (83in)
Track	1,300mm (51in)
Height	1,119mm (44in)
Top speed	166km/h (103mph)

added a shapely curved line to the rear side windows and panels to create a design that was clearly Saab-based, yet a touch exotic. There was an increase in cabin length to create a 2+2 that had a hint of the Lamborghini Espada. The original 1968 design drawing is shown herein, and the reader can reach his or her own view as to whether Sonett would have been better served by Andreasson's neat and trans-European styling with its shades of Italian coupé style. Looking at the Cogglia-designed Sonett, with Saab's input via Gunnar Sjorgen that became Sonett II, it is, however, possible to observe some of Andreasson's themes, notably the rear panel treatment. Andreasson's pitch for the Sonett III's design has received little coverage, but it represented an example of the enthusiasm within Saab for the Sonett concept, and his design drawing makes its own statement.

The year 1969 was also notable for Saab's amalgamation with the ancient firm of Scania (Scania–Vabis AB), to form Saab–Scania in an 800-million Swedish krona deal, at the time Sweden's biggest-ever corporate merger. Saab–Scania decided to fund the continuance and updating of the Sonett. Given that Scania–Vabis were both long established, heavy engineering companies, their commitment to the plastic Saab for 1970 was noteworthy.

Looking somewhat shrew-like, the new Saab–Scania company's Sonett III had a long, elegant bonnet/trunk leading back into a carefully detailed cabin that featured a modern Kamm tail and clean detailing. The drag figure was tuned to Cd 0.31, which was what you would expect from a low-fronted, Kamm-tailed, smoothly finished coupé. However, this applied to the early cars with their simple yet stylish front and rear designs that had no bumpers, but instead rigid rubber trim edging the panels. The addition in 1973 of the 8km/h (5mph) impact-absorbing cellular bumpers to the Sonett would have an adverse effect on its Cd. The car boasted three transversely placed, aerodynamic blades

RIGHT: **Early Sonett III on the rare original alloy wheels and without the later bumpers – so with less aerodynamic drag.**

BELOW: **American Saab legend Tom Donney took his Sonett II to Bonneville in 2012 and broke records with 115.619mph from a 2-stroke engine. Also seen, a 93 that ran on the salt as well.**

recessed into the nose cone, behind which were hidden large auxiliary driving lamps (in case the main lamps failed). The grille blades kept snow and ice off the lamps, and funnelled air into the engine bay. Underneath the glassfibre body could be found numerous Saab 96 and 95 floorpan and structural pressings.

THE YEARS 1970 TO 1974

Sonett III was launched in early 1970 at the New York Motor Show. The early 1970 cars had a rare alloy wheel design from a Swedish company named Tunaverken of Eskiltuna; these wheels were changed to the 'football'-type design that became so familiar on other Saabs. From 1971 to 1973 they were silver grey – alloy coloured – but for 1974 they assumed the part-painted design with black-painted segments, as seen on the 99 EMS.

America was the Sonett's main market, and certain parts of Europe were also targeted; strangely, the Sonett III remained unlisted as a British market model, though probably the costs of re-engineering to right-hand drive were deemed too expensive. The Sonett sold well in France, the Netherlands, Denmark and Germany, and even a few Italians ordered them in bright red.

Some loved the styling of the car, others hated it: America's *Car and Driver* suggested to Sonett buyers that they could remove the Saab badges and tell people that they had built it themselves! So Sonett III created divided opinions, although seen from today, it has aged well. Cogglia's ideas had to be 'Saabized' and turned into production reality. Saab's requirement for keeping the Sonett II's central tub and windscreen had not helped, but inside Saab there was Gunnar A. 'GAS' Sjögren, artist, designer, illustrator and a Saab man since 1959. It was he who guided Sonett III's difficult birth from plastic to something less than fantastic. Many feel that the passage of time has shone a better light on Cogglia's and Sjögren's combined efforts, and Sonett III is now regarded as a clever and unusual moment in Saab's story.

The Sonett III spec included moulded seat pans, and trim items from the Saab 96 and 99 ranges – including those 'football' or 'soccer'-style alloy wheels from the 99 EMS. The Triumph-style flip-top bonnet of the Sonett II had gone, and there was now a bonnet/hood that was more of an inspection hatch. A better trimmed 1971 'luxury' model with leather trim, 'Coolair' air conditioning and extra brightwork was made available in America.

All Sonett IIIs had racing car-style wishbone suspension at the front and a well tied down tube axle and coil spring/sports damper combination for the rear. The vital 0–60mph time was 11sec, but once stoked up, the car could be made to feel a lot faster through the gears. Sonetts stopped well, too, as the brakes were taken directly from the larger, heavier Saab 96.

For 1971, the capacity of the Saab V4 was enhanced to 1.7 litres at 1698cc with 65bhp at a rather noisy 4,700rpm, though the new engine managed to meet new emissions standards. With 85lb of torque from a 65+ bhp engine, Sonett III proves the old engineering adage that when torque exceeds bhp by a significant margin, rapid progress can be drawn from the drivetrain. Lifting the engine hatch revealed two air cleaners mounted on long arms, angled downwards either side of the low bonnet line in a curious cow horn-type design.

In 1972 a new grille design was added to the Sonett's front end, while at the rear, the back panel was painted matt black. Tyre size was increased from 155 to 165 aspect ratio on the same 15in wheels. The new Saab corporate grille was first used on the 1973 models.

Despite the addition of this grille for 1973 models, and also US-style 5mph impact bumpers taken from the 99, the Sonett still had an elegant style and sold well, most notably in the eastern seaboard states of the USA. The cellular, self-repairing bumpers were taken from the Saab 99 parts bin, cut in half to shorten them and then re-joined back together with the moulding join covered up by a finishing plate. This was money-saving engineering, but very few people noticed. However, with these new bumpers weighing 25kg (55lb) each, hanging them off each end of the car did affect its balance. But whatever Saab's penny-pinching, at least the Sonett now had a proper floor-mounted gearshift!

The 1973 cars also sported side stripes along their lower flanks, with the Saab name designed into their motif: light-coloured cars were given black stripes and darker-coloured cars white stripes. The Sonett III was briefly available in a rare purple/mauve colour for the European market. The glass rear hatch was given spring risers in place of the previous struts.

For 1974, the Sonett's paint range was Baja Red, Burnt Orange, Mellow Yellow and Emerald Green. Whatever colour you ordered your Sonett III in, it came with a quintessential 1970s brown and orange-hued interior trimmed in vinyl and corduroy, complete with a matt black crinkle-finished instrument cluster and 'pop-up' headlamps. Somehow Saab fitted headlamp wipers to the retractable main lamps, which also had a very practical hand-cranked deploy and retract mechanism for their 'pop-up' function.

Sonett III survived, latterly in 1.7-litre guise, until 1974, with the final cars mostly being sold in racing-style colours of blue, orange and green. For its last year, the Sonett's weight had gone up, especially with larger tyres and air conditioning added to the spec (maximum weight 766kg (1,945lb)). For 1974, Sonett's price in America was just under a heady $5,000, at $4,898. Sonetts scooped up many sports car racing wins in the 1980s, with Jack Lawrence and his tuned V4-injection Sonett proving that although it might not have rallied, it could race. Sonetts

RIGHT: **Saab often used gliders in their publicity shots. This is classic 1970s marketing imagery.**

BELOW: **A forgotten face of Saab: the Sonett III in typical 1970s orange hue, and looking great.**

were also seen on the Swedish rally scene, but not to the degree of the 96. A one-off soft-top was also created by a private owner in the USA.

In their production life, the Sonetts II and III had few problems with their glassfibre, which was thickly moulded and of high quality, but today's Sonetts sometimes need deep repairs to the

LEFT: **Sonett lineage – the II and III. The forgotten side of Saab, both looking great over forty years from their inception.**

BELOW: **Sonett III – Saab's great wasted opportunity.**

fibre construction. The Saab steel in the floorpan resisted rot, but by its nature was not immune to corrosion – especially as in Sonett III, Saab used a panel-joining sealant that over time allowed moisture ingress. With the ubiquitous Ford 91H V4 engine, spares are still available, but as with the Saab 96 application, replacement of the fibre timing gear wheel was a known issue in the Sonett's production life, and subsequently. In hot climates with hot-running drivetrain components, the Sonett's Achilles heel proved to be its gearbox, and without regular oil inspections, the noisy-by-nature transaxle unit could overheat and break. Cars in a cold climate suffered to a lesser degree, but as with other Saab models, the gearbox could become an issue.

AMERICA AND JACK LAWRENCE'S SONETTS

It was in America that the Sonett became more widely known. There, private individuals fettled and modified their Sonetts and some, like Jack Lawrence, even went racing. Two Sonnet soft-top or convertible conversions were also undertaken, one based on a Sonett II and the other on a Sonett III.

One Sonett III 'tweak' emerged from America's band of Sonnet enthusiasts, notably Sonett guru Bruce Turk, who worked out that increasing the car's track by using wider wheel rims and increasing the front tyre pressures by 5lb more than the

SONETT SAFETY

As a glassfibre or 'plastic' car Sonett could have fallen into the trap of having a weak, thin-skinned, one-piece synthetic shell draped over a central chassis tube or rail – this would leave the occupants very vulnerable to crash impact intrusion and energies, particularly in side, roll-over and offset impacts, as is the case in so many glassfibre cars. However, Saab did all it could to make its plastic car safer.

The Sonett was not a glassfibre one-piece shell in the manner of Lotus, Reliant or TVR: instead the Sonett's synthetic body was bonded and joined to a solid steel underframe and floorpan taken from the steel production Saab pressings. So the Sonett II and III was a truly composite car – a blend of steel and glassfibre monocoque that was torsionally rigid and very strong. It had a thick metal floorpan tub, steel front inner wings and strong floor longerons and rear end, taken from the Saab 95 and 96. These gave the Sonett a very stiff basis across the car – not just down the middle where a normal backbone chassis provides strength to glassfibre-based car bodies, leaving the cabin and its occupants highly vulnerable. Saab added a roll-over bar, and actually created glassfibre panels that were zoned for progressive deformation; it did not rely solely on a whole-body one-piece moulding normally so typical of glass-reinforced plastic car, yacht and glider design.

Impact Forces

This design technique meant that the deformation caused by impact forces at one point in the plastic shell could be better controlled, and did not lead to the glassfibre shattering at random and at crucial locations elsewhere in the body in a way so often associated with plastic construction. Saab also added side door beams to the Sonett, and made sure that the car was not a fire risk. Sonett might not have had the 'hewn from rock' feel of Saab saloons, but it was far from being a 'kit car' structural nightmare.

Saab sold 10,219 Sonett II, V4 and III: for a niche model it was probably an expensive experiment. Yet hidden in the Sonett there lies the spirit of Saab, and those who have driven or owned a Sonett know that it is a car of immense character and joy. The handling, the driving and the essence of the thing, speaks of a world of cars long gone. Was it a Swedish Lotus or TVR? A baby Corvette? Perhaps not, but like those cars, and the early Porsches, Sonett encapsulated not just a Saab ethos, but an era of driving now dismissed as too simple for today's tastes.

---

rear tyres transformed the Sonett III's handling and added balance to the car's dynamics. Understeer was reduced, steering sharpened, and the rear end remained planted on the road with more grip from a flatter tyre footprint.

The VSRG and Sonett's American Friends

From the 1980s right up to the present decades a 'Vintage Saab Racing Group' (VSRG) campaigned highly modified Saab Sonetts (and other Saabs) across North America. A long list of engineering modifications was carried out, and the lead names in the US Sonett privateer racing teams included Randy Crook, Charles Christ, Steve Church, Ed Diehl, Mary Anne Fieux, William Hardy, Chris Moberg, George Vapaa and his son Stefan, and Bruce Turk. Dr Richard Thomson also raced Saabs, and went on to drive Corvettes in competition. Father and son George and Stefan Vapaa became well known Sonett racers and restorers.

In California, in 1959, a young car enthusiast named Bud Clark was taken for a ride in the screaming two-stroke Saab 93, and a lifetime's passion for Saab was born. Today, as the man behind J & B imports of Orange, California, Bud Clark is a high priest of all things Saab and most things Sonett. He also owns a Saab 9000 with 750,000 miles on the clock. Across America, Saabism still rules: Tom Donney from Iowa set a new speed record for a 3-cylinder engine at the Bonneville Salt Flats in 2011 when his 748cc 1967 Sonett II reached 159.234km/h (98.968mph).

George Vapaa was also part of John 'Jake' Jacobson's Saab racing crew in the 1960s; he also built and modified his own personal Saabs for autocross. But it was under the aegis of the Sports Car Club of America (SCCA) that the Sonett II, V4 and III went racing.

The American Saab enthusiasts made major changes to the design and specification of the Sonett's V4; principal amongst these were the changes created by the well known Saab dealer and Sonett aficionado, Jack Lawrence. The idea of improving the power output of the V4 started not with Lawrence but in 1969 when the Saab competition department under Bo Hellborg had increased the V4's potential to 125bhp via various changes to internal engine specifications – effectively 'blueprinting' the engine. But could the V4 be force-fed? One of Saab's members of the 'Aeroplan' family was Sigge Johansson, who was working in the department and spent most of 1970 trying to perfect a fuel injection system for the V4. He used a Lucas mechanical injection unit, which with the engine in race-tuned trim created 185bhp! Johansson also turbocharged a V4 and went on to 4WD design fame.

Two years after his fuel injection experiment, the V4 achieved 165bhp with a Weber 45DCOE dual port cross flow specification. The Weber specification was made available to Saab enthusiasts through Saab's 'Sport and Competition' catalogue.[11]

The problem for the fuel injection experiment was that it could not react to the varying air densities and extreme airflow temperatures encountered during rallying, particularly at high altitudes. Saab was to learn a lot about this subject from these experiments – knowledge that would later manifest in the engines fitted to the later 900 and 9000 cars.

Ultimately the V4 fuel injection experiment was abandoned, but not before one unit found its way to a well respected Saab race and rally privateer in the USA. There, Glen Bunch campaigned a standard V4-powered 96, but there is no record of the fuel-injected version of the V4 making it on to race track or rally stage. The V4 fuel-injection device finally made it into the hands of Jack Lawrence, who over the course of a decade between the mid-1970s and mid-1980s developed a series of improvements to the V4 and to its fitment in the Sonett II and III, resulting in a strong series of successful competition results for the Sonett – far beyond Saab's own dreams.

Lawrence poured time and money into developing the V4 for his racing Sonetts. The key areas of design and engineering works included a machined head, hardened valves, re-flowed and re-radiused internal components with all edges smoothed, clamped gasket, bronzed valve guides, two-port exhaust manifold, Solex 40 PII-4 with revised internal airflow vanes, two electric fuel pumps, lighter camshafts and pushrods, increased oil flow to crankshaft with elliptical internal flow outlets, and the flywheel lightened to 5.33kg (11.75lb).

The pistons were replaced with forged, aluminium hand-built devices using a specially quantified alloy with a lower coefficient of expansion. Dome heads and special shaping to the pistons improved swirl and combustion. Three balanced piston rings were fitted, each calibrated to a fine degree. Jack Lawrence designed his own oil sump and oil pump to ensure better flow and performance within the engine's lubrication; oil temperature was regularly monitored via sensors placed in the system, and oil intercoolers and an extra header tank to the main cooling system increased the life expectancy of major components.

Lawrence also recalibrated the gearbox/transaxle drive ratios with an ultimate possibility of achieving 228km/h (142mph) – and he managed 220km/h (137mph) on a racing circuit. By adding sealed bearings and carefully machining all components, the gearbox was made to last longer and perform with a quicker action than Saab's more usual, slightly ponderous gearbox characteristics.

All these changes were accompanied by a host of further Lawrence-designed modifications to gauges, settings, radii, component weights, and gas and fluid flows, all of which represented a significant investment of private time and money in the V4 and the racing Sonetts.

Lawrence's hard-charging, tweaked Sonett V4s campaigned in the SCCA production and GT-4 classes. Lawrence was production car class national champion in 1982, and the national sport Light GT-4 champion every year from 1990 to 1995. He was a regional race champion who also took national honours in a Sonett. As recently as 2010 at a meeting of the New York Saab Owners Club at an upstate gathering, Sonetts appeared en masse – including two Jack Lawrence spec, bright yellow Sonett IIIs.

SONETT: SUCCESS, OR TOO SHORT A POEM?

Can the Sonett story really be called a success? If Saab had been making half a million cars a year, such a limited production run involving several bouts of re-engineering would have constituted a failure. But for Saab, producing a smaller number of cars overall, the Sonett and its 10,000 sales created valuable profile and expanded the company's design knowledge. Saab's Sonett survived the critics and earned export currency for Saab. It was fun to drive, rewarding to own, and although not without its faults, proved that Saab could carve its own path. In its own Saab way, Sonett contributed to the Saab story.

Saabists will call Sonett a success, but more dispassionate observers might well opine that the Sonett story was also typical of Saab in its myopia and development struggles. But Sonett, especially in its early forms, was great to drive and fun to own, and it represented a truly deep form of alternative thinking – a car of de Bono philosophy in its lateral design psychology, perhaps?

In the late 1980s, a car resembling a cross between a Fiat 130 coupé, a Renault Alpine A610 and a Saab Sonett III emerged as a Skoda-based prototype from a Czech design group. Some Saabists saw more of the Sonett in the design proposal than may have really been present, but it did have the ideal long-nose, Kamm tail, high rear-decked styling so appropriate to coupé design.

As late as 1984, privateers were still wanting to build a sportier soft-top Saab. In that year, the Swedish magazine *Tecknikens Varld* used a Saab 900 as the underpinning for a sporty soft-top Saab. This was designed and built by Leif Mellberg (who had also built Bjorn Envall's sensational Saab EV1 concept car). In America, Brent Ellasson built a turbocharged Sonett II, and people still believed in the Sonett concept having a Saab future.

Now, the Sonett is becoming a much sought-after classic car, values are rising dramatically for early Sonett II two-stroke cars, and the Sonett II and III is appealing to a wider audience. That audience includes those people who have driven a Sonett, for once you get to drive a Sonett, especially a Sonett II, you emerge with a smile on your face and reborn enthusiasm for small,

TOP: **How to shoe-horn a V4 under a Sonett bonnet! These were the 'cow-horn' air filters.**

ABOVE: **Shades of Porsche, perhaps: the Sonett III command post.**

LEFT: **Stylish Sonett rear with Kamm back aerodynamics off the inclined canopy.**

lightweight, sharp-handling cars that react to the merest touch. If only GM could have created for Saab a 'new' Sonett in the 2005 era from the skeleton of its Lotus-inspired, composite-built, VX220 mid-engined open-top roadster.

As the record stands, the last Sonett was a bright yellow car that was consigned to the Saab Museum, so ending an expensive yet rewarding experiment, which, sadly, saw the public being allowed to forget that Saab had once made a true two-seater sports coupé. It was a style of Saab that has only been subsequently hinted at in the company's design concept cars.

The family of fronts.

THE 99

A 99 EMS with all its compound curves and parabolic style.

FROM X7
TO TURBO

THE 99 | *FROM X7 TO TURBO*

WHAT FUTURE FOR SAAB? This was the question in the minds of the men of Saab as early as 1962. They knew that they had the 96 to be going on with, and some of them knew that Saab would have to re-engine that car with a four-stroke, 4-cylinder engine very quickly. If they did not, Saab would lose market share and fade away, as buyers, even loyal Swedish buyers, took to the efficiencies and low maintenance of the new lightweight, 4-cylinder cars that Europe was honing.

But even with a re-engined, 4-cylinder power plant under its bonnet, the 96 would still be old. Its renaissance would be short-lived from 1967. By 1964 Saab was selling 30,000 cars a year, yet that would begin to decline. Something utterly new and different was needed for Saab. Ljungström, Sason and Mellde all knew this. Sason, forever heading south to Germany and Italy to visit motor shows and his friends at the design houses, knew that other rival car makers were planning an onslaught, and that wave after wave of new cars were due to come out. Fashions were changing, and design as a marketing tool and not just an entity was becoming more and more important. Ford was refining the Cortina for Britain and the related Taunus for German tastes, Peugeot were turning to Pininfarina, and Triumph and many others were using Giovanni Michelotti to update and fashion their cars.

Michelotti was even assisting the growing Japanese car industry, although unlike other designers' works, his name did not appear in 'Designo di Michelotti' badges on the sides of the cars he styled. Bertone were busy as well, as were independent designers. Even staid old Austin of England were to follow the Italian styling trend. It would not be long before cars such as the accomplished Citroën GS, Peugeot 504 and Fiat 132 made their mark. Surely we can speculate that if the incredible design of the NSU Ro 80 (under the pen of Claus Luthe) had not been tainted by its Wankel engine's problems, would it, with its advanced aerodynamic styling, safety body and sheer futurism, have swept aside Saab's own attempts at a similar interpretation of design ideals?

The fact remained that if Saab failed to do something, it would contract, maybe even falter. Just over the horizon lay the likes of the Renault 12 and 16, the new Volkswagens and the threat of Datsun. Meanwhile in Germany, BMW was planning a range of small cars, and had bought the small German car maker Glas to attend to the family sector.

And the British? They were persevering with the conceits of a dated, inward-looking school of design thought. For all their clever packaging, the Issigonis-influenced cars were hardly stylistically attractive. But over the British horizon lay such delights and disasters as the Rover 2200/3500, Triumph Dolomite, Jaguar XJ6, and then the dubious Morris Marina and Austin Allegro. And what of Americana? How would Saab fare against the shiny steel and vinyl of the American-inspired works of Ford, Chrysler and GM? Cortina, Capri, Escort? Avenger? Viva Victor?

IGNORING FASHION

Saab knew that it did not need to pander to short-term fashion, and within Saab, unlike many car makers, the engineers were not told what to do by marketing men and focus group survey results. At Saab, the engineering and design teams discussed their ideas, put them forwards to a small, select group of highly informed directors, and proceeded to create a car.

Sixten Sason's original sketch for the genesis of the Saab 99, drawn on Hotel Bele notepaper! Aribert Vahlenbreder, Ralph Jonsson and Bjorn Envall were Sason's design team.

Sason had begun sketching an idea for a totally new Saab saloon – a mid-sized car that was a class above the 96 – as early as the winter of 1961–62, and by 1964 he had developed an idea for a pretty two-door car with definite Italian overtones. For example, it had faired-in headlamps, an Alfa Romeo or Lancia effect that may have grown from his ideas for the 1993 'Italian' front. There was a touch of Citroën in the mix, too, a definite French feel that was reflected in his styling drawings. At the rear of his proposals a stylish glasshouse with a fastback hinted at a truly European style. Yet the shape was a copy of nothing, more an amalgamation of themes with the designer's own hallmark added in. Some of the themes evident in Sason's concurrent 'Katherina' two-seat prototype were evident. Even in the early sketch shown here, the concave boot line, dart-shaped front and cabin 'turret', which marked the production Saab 99, were evident.

Thus the shape that would become the 99 was a mature and expertly tailored piece of product design, yet not one that followed fashion. Sason also sketched a smaller, downsized idea for a new small Saab, one that also used a concave rear end and small rear side windows in the style of a modern three-door hatchback.

For the definitive, larger Saab shape, the real moment of definitive design inspiration seems to have come in Trollhättan. There, in a quick pencil sketch on a piece of the Hotel Bele's notepaper, we can see the strong C pillar, swept rear and dart-shaped front of the 99, being born from Sason's hand.

By this time Sason was not alone as the design figure. A young man named Björn Envall, who would go on to become a highly respected industrial designer on the global scene, joined Sason in 1960 as a Saab design junior. Envall had sent Sason some of his sketches, and received an invitation to visit the studio. He was taken on – but by 1966, Sason's health was failing. Despite losing a lung early in life after a flying accident, he had remained a smoker. He also enjoyed the finer things in life and lived it to the full. His young protégé would soon find himself steering design themes, and not just for the details of the new car. Ljungström, Sason and Mellde were putting together their thoughts for a new car, and the idea was informally known within the company as 'Project F'.

Through this early work and the efforts of Mellde and his men to come up with their own new Saab-designed, 1.2-litre, 4-cylinder engine, the beginnings of a bigger, more luxurious, more contemporary new car for Saab were started. It wasn't a 'Eureka' moment of marketing department-led desire, but a solid, safe evolution of themes that would come together to form a new project for Saab.

GUDMUND'S DAY

By 1964 Saab management had given the go-ahead for the new car. The auspicious day was 2 April 1964 – 'Gudmund's Day' in the calendar, and so the new car became 'Project Gudmund'. It came nearly thirty years after Saab itself had been born, on 2 April 1937 – another auspicious Gudmund's Day.

For the 99, 150 and then a total of 300 men were to spend 400,000 man hours and four years developing the new car project. The design of the body was well within the company's talents, but having stayed loyal to the two-stroke for so long, and having had to buy in the Ford V4, Saab was short of research

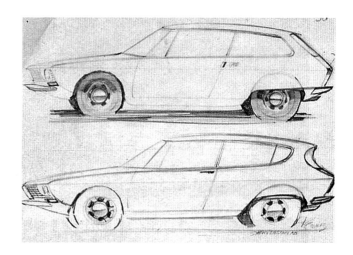

ABOVE: **Saab 99 early sketches, with shades of 1960s styling themes. The strong C pillar is emerging.**

LEFT: **As early as 1964, this 99 three-door estate was drawn up.**

into engines. Luckily, alongside Mellde as the 99 project manager there were others with engine obsessions, namely Per Gillbrand, Josef Eklund, Lennart Rosen and Karl Rosenqvist; Bengt Gadefelt came later, from Scania. The engine was to be a crucial theme and one that would require money. Could Saab collaborate with others and save money?

Whilst the engine boffins got on with designing their powerplant, the body design team started to create the new car, which was to be wider, longer, even stronger, and completely new in all respects. Carrying over items from the 96 was avoided, except for a few minor trim items such as the clock.

In planning the 99, Saab had to assess its future needs from a future perspective: the new car needed to be new for the 1970s, not contemporary with 1965. The home, core Swedish market had to be satisfied, and a wider, global market secured by the car.

Whatever the needs of a wider market, the Saab would still be a Saab, with front-wheel drive, a reinforced cabin made from extra thick steel, attention to aerodynamics and detailed design, and sporty-feeling steering, brakes and suspension: these were the Saab ethos essentials, and no international corporate-speak focus group 'spin' was going to change these core values in a Saab car. The Saab management and the Saab engineers were of one mind: they were all Saab men. So the 99's designers worked with a degree of freedom rare in the motor industry, and the correctness of their decisions about the 99 was proven by its longevity.

At its launch in 1967 it was competing against some 1950s and 1960s-era cars such as the Triumph saloons, Mark I Cortina, Fiats, the Austin-Morris ranges and rear-engined VWs such as the 411. But soon it was the cars of the 1970s – the Renault 12, Austin Maxi, Ford Escort, and the likes of the Citroën GS and Peugeot 504 – that were the mirrors against which the Saab 99 was set. Beyond these, the cars of the early 1980s, and the arrival of Datsun and Toyota, would change the landscape of competition once again. And what of the VW Golf, Alfasud, Volvo 240 series, Fiat 131/132, Lancia Beta, and the host of others below and above the 99's niche? Over them all, with its unique design, the 99 rode out the swamping of the world car markets and endured well beyond its sell-by date: only good design could have ensured this, and as proof of concept, it did.

The original development team included the Saab stalwarts – Ljungström, Mellde, Sason, and also in the blend were Olle Lindqkvist, Lars Nillson, Olle Granlund, Sperr Gustav and the young Bjorn Envall. Erik Carlsson was not forgotten, either, as he could contribute much to the 'feel' of the car. Saab aircraft designer Ragnar Hardmark was also transferred to the car division to assist with the 99's development. A test 'mule' was constructed from a 96, specially welded up: this car was 20cm wider

ABOVE: **The first 99 prototype featured quarterlights and a Daihatsu badge as a disguise.**

LEFT: **A rare view of an early Sason frontal proposal for the 99, circa 1964. The separate front wings and round headlamps date the car. Thankfully a more modern approach prevailed.**

and longer than the 96, yet was a perfect disguise for testing out the 99's components without letting the competition know what Saab was up to. Named 'Toad' ('Paddan' in Swedish) as a result of its green paint and exaggerated stance, it was finally spotted by a local news photographer.

ENVALL AND A EUROPEAN SHAPE

For the 99's shape, Sason's sketches of 1961–63 proved the basis, and somewhat Italian and French early themes were merged into a distinct Saab style. The front grille and headlamp shapes took their cue from a blend of Saab 96 themes and external influences. Björn Envall remembers sitting up late into the night with Sason, refining the details and working on the cabin glasshouse and the concave rear. Envall says Sason was a man of humour and great company. Fine wines and fine dining also seem to have been a trait – something Sason must have picked up during his times in Paris and Turin. Envall told the the author about the 99's genesis:

> We had real trouble with that one. Sixten was up all night trying to get the back end right. I was just the new boy, the assistant. What he really wanted was an Alfa-style glassed-in rear boot – a sort of hatchback coupé. It's funny how years later we got closer to his original idea with the three-door 99 bodyshell. He was never really happy with the original idea for the rear end of the 99, and it gave us lots of aerodynamic problems, but we solved them in the end, and the rear grew on you.[12]

The 99 soon gained a 'cab-forward' stance with a wedge- or arrow-shaped bodyline. The concave rear needed an airflow separation line at its roof lip, to tie down the critical airflow separation trigger point and avoid a flexible, drag-inducing vortex pattern off the 99's rear. Unlike the 92–96, the rear deck angle was too steep to keep the airflow attached to the base of the boot – there was no sense of 'fastback' to the design. So managing the airflow off the top of the roof became vital, just as it did in the contemporary Giovanni Michelotti designs. Once separated, the broken airflow had to be managed down the rear of the car to achieve good side-wind stability, low wake drag, and to keep the rear windscreen from becoming dirtied by the threat of turbulent air enveloping the back of the car.

Using the Saab wind tunnel, the airflow pattern was teased to roll and swirl inwards and downwards over the 99's tail, reducing wake vortex and 'base' drag levels as well as negating unwanted lift. All these factors had to be tuned in, or tuned out, of the tricky rear-end design. The later, Envall-designed three-door

Combi Coupé 99 with its longer tail – which was still too short and steep to persuade the airflow to remain fully attached down to the boot lip – did assist that need, and allowed more aerodynamic tuning to take place, and gave better side-blade angles to slice the airflow Kamm-style, improve side-wind resistance and reduce lift and wake drag. As can be seen in the accompanying photos, Saab even dreamed up an unusual rear-deck spoiler for the 99 two-door, unusually mounted under the rear windscreen as opposed to the boot/trunk trailing edge.

Other cars also featured the concave, 'swept' rear design treatment, the later Ford Zephyr and Renault 12 included.

In the Saab 'barn' design studio there was an overhead gallery, which allowed Sason and Envall to see how the car looked from all angles – and not least from above. With clean and smooth panelling, one-piece rear wings, and with its taut lines and highly curved windscreen design, all the elements of the 99 were drawn together to form the cohesive, organic whole that the design became. The stance, the down-the-road graphic (DRG) of the car and the way in which the panels caught the light, were all worked on. Of note, the door frames overlapped the windscreen pillars and sills, a most unusual technique for the time. The extra strong, 2.5mm steel sandwiched windscreen posts or A pillars had their narrowest section towards the interior, allowing the widest possible view out with minimal sight-line obstructions. Hinged front window quarter lights were dispensed with, and a smooth side panel to the cabin created. The domed roof of the 92–96 was also hinted at, adding headroom and aerodynamic benefits.

The narrowed and faired-in frontal aspect also went towards creating the new 'face' of Saab. Significantly, the 99 introduced the idea of a bonnet or hood line overlapping the crowns of each front wing and rolling the bonnet edges down on to the side panels, giving a very smooth look and a smooth skin for reducing drag. This was the birth of the Saab 'clamshell' bonnet, which so many now see as a defining Saab design motif, and yet it is one that only came to Saab in the 99, twenty years after the first Saab car was born.

The other key design motif was the shallow and deeply curved windscreen, cited by many as a defining 'beetle-browed' Saab design marker. This windscreen shape made the most of previous research into reducing the pressure bubble and airflow separation that normally occurs in front of most flat, sharp-cornered front windscreens. Using aerodynamic techniques found on aircraft, with their curved cockpit windscreens and canopy bubbles, turbulence, noise and drag were greatly reduced over the 99's bonnet/hood area and down its side panels. The super-curved windscreen of the 99 – only exceeded in its radius of curvature by that of the limited production Lancia Stratos – allowed the air to split cleanly and sweep round the front of the car in a manner not seen on the

Sixten Sason drew up this proposal in the 1960s. Some say it is the 99, but it looks more like a design proposal for a smaller 99 theme – a new small Saab – the one that should have replaced the 96?

flat or mildly bowed windscreens of all other cars. With its dart-like, cab-forwards frontal design, domed roof and bladed rear pillars, the 99 had airflow control in a 'three box', non-fastback design, detailed down to a forensic degree.

The first 99 had conventional steel bumpers with a shiny 'chrome' brightwork effect, where stainless steel was sheathed in clear plastic – this eventually became opaqued by time – a technique also used on the steel brightwork seen round the window frames.

After less than three years in the market place, the 99 was revised for the dawn of a new decade. It was a minor facelift involving no metal changes, and yet the 99's whole image and graphic changed after Envall restyled the front grille and head-lamps, added smart self-repairing bumpers, deleted some shiny trim, and brought a new dashboard into the interior. It was as if the car had been meant to look like this from the beginning. Envall also created a crescent-shaped, side indicator light cluster design, which became a Saab hallmark. Thus Sason's 1960s front with its Franco-Italian feel was gone, replaced by a fresh new style of lamps and grille, which became a bolder international image for Saab.

Originally launched with two doors, the 99 was planned for four doors, and as a three- and five-door estate early on. Two extra side doors were introduced on the four-door 99 saloon for the 1970 model year. If anything, the strength of the shape of the C pillar became even more pronounced as a design theme – one later echoed by the Saab 9-5 of 1998.

Construction Issues

Before that 1970s makeover, the 99 Mark 1's first completed production-test bodies were ready on 5 June 1967. Although the car was to be publicly launched in November 1967, Saab would have another year in hand before any final, customer-ready production cars were on sale. In that time, vital testing of development cars and cars placed with specially chosen members of the public would create helpful feedback.

One issue that came up when testing the new 99's body for strength was that some fatigue-induced cracks appeared in the area of the one-piece, rear three-quarter side panels, notably in the rear wheel arches. The metal in the panel was 0.94mm thick, so Saab increased the thickness to 1.06mm – but fatigue-induced problems still occurred, and Saab had to increase the metal thickness to 1.21mm, which cured the problem. The engineers also devised some additional strut braces and flanges for inside the rear wheel-arch area, though not all of these were required. The rear wheel-arch metal gauge was, however, increased.

In the autumn of 1967, the final production gauges of metal in the front bulkhead and floor were set; these were later increased on production cars in late 1968. Further changes were made for the 1970 models. When the four-door 99 was announced in April 1970, further refinements to the thickness of metal used in parts of the car were made. The shorter front doors were stiffer, but the apertures in the hull for the new rear side doors reduced torsional rigidity, so extra sill fillets were added and the C-pillar strength increased. The new B pillar was also given a special flange at its mid-height point in order to reduce twist and intrusion.

Intriguingly, the tooling and jigs for the four-door 99 came from Turin via a Fiat subsidiary, and the components were trucked back to Sweden via a route that avoided German regulations and tariffs.

When the 99 was revised with its Envall-designed new front and bumpers, Saab handled the minor tooling changes, but for the three-door 99 Combi-Coupé, launched in August 1973 and on sale in January 1974, Saab contracted out the building of the new rear side panels and tailgate to a company named Lapple in Heilbrunn. Whereas the 99 saloons had been constructed on a moving production line in traditional manner, Saab introduced the group construction method for the three-door car, where teams of multi-skilled workers built the car on a static jig.

A series of early test cars was produced, one of them with a script describing it as a Daihatsu, stuck on as part of a disguise; however, way back in 1966 it was unlikely that anyone knew what a Daihatsu was.

SAFETY, HALLMARK OF THE 99

Today, safety is taken for granted, and no car manufacturer would risk the commercial, PR and legal consequences of producing a car that was wilfully less safe than knowledge would allow. But before safety became both a marketing-led tick-list item and an expectation, there was an era when many cars had many different, varying rates of safety in terms of occupant protection or 'crash-worthiness'.

The power of consumerism and the media has forced all car makers to provide better structural or passive safety standards, and the recent work of the FIA and its EURONCAP initiative has saved many lives. But even before these things happened, Saab was one of the very few car makers to study safety in a laboratory, and to study real-life car accidents and spend money on making stronger, safer cars. Such safety standards have saved many lives and are a core foundation of the Saab ethos. In the 1960s, the Saab 96 was the strongest car of its class by a wide margin, and in the 1970s the Saab 99 was far ahead of its competitors in terms of its crash safety. Only the likes of the Volvo and Mercedes could match the 99's standards, and the 99 was smaller than such cars. The contribution to car safety and occupant protection made by Saab in the 99 cannot be underestimated.

The MkI car shows off the early rear panel and Sason's curved rear windscreen motif.

Roof and Sill Strength

All the 99s shared the highly unusual A pillar and front bulkhead design. The fact that the windscreen was highly curved had little influence upon the choice of structure beneath it, and Saab could have used conventional construction techniques and created a series of pillars and pressings made from thin gauge, hollow, light steel spot-welded into a normal monocoque. Instead it turned again to aviation practice, and where there was an aperture in the hull, the edges or panels around that opening were strategically reinforced with very thick metal and load-bearing reinforcing posts. In this way the 99 copied the construction technique of the 92–96, and it also saw the use of the 2.5mm high-tensile strength, triangular steel sandwich design for the A pillars at the sides of the windscreen. These were the strongest, thickest metal-gauge windscreen pillars ever seen on a car at that time and for years afterwards, and their resistance to twist and roll-over crushing became legendary. So strong was the 99's windscreen frame that, unlike most other cars, its windscreen glass did not need to be glued or bonded into place, but was retained by its sealing strips.

In 1967, the 99 was drop-tested on to its roof from a height of 8ft (2.4m). The roof stayed upright and intact, and did not impinge upon the occupants. Notably, those 2.5mm rolled steel, triangular-section windscreen posts stayed taught and straight. It is doubtful if any other car of 1968 possessed such inherent roof and roll-over strength. The reader can only begin to imagine what would have happened to a Triumph Herald, Ford Cortina, Renault 16 or Fiat 128 if these were subjected to similar roof impact loads.

The 99 had thick strong doors, and steel box-section sill beams that allowed the cut-way floor and turned-under door design so that occupants could get in and out of the car without having to step over a conventional, thin, spot-welded sill panel. Under the bonnet there were huge steel wheel-arch housings and double-skinned front wing panels. A series of beams and supports, allied to a steel-chambered engine bay design, meant that there was a large amount of steel square footage under the bonnet to absorb crash impact forces. The deep and double-skinned front wing and wheel-arch designs offered widely spaced impact crush zones leading into those massive wheel arches to create effective 'offset' crash-impact protection years before other car makers created stronger corners and outer wing sections for their cars.

Saab therefore avoided the 'battering ram' design technique that so often produced two steel supports close to the centre line of the car, which, although they performed well in a full 100 per cent overlap crash, left the outer corners of a car vulnerable to the very common lozenging or peeling effect of an 'offset' or driver's side-only crash impact, a crash that was harder to engineer for.

Torsional Rigidity

At the rear, the fuel tank was well protected up by the rear axle, and three impact beams reinforced the rear floor. The rear roof C pillar was also made of thick steel and had internal support struts. The rear side panels were one piece pressings, as was the roof – this avoided a loss of rigidity, as was so often found in the roofs and panels of cars of the 1960s and 1970s, where thin steel sheets were joined by welds and then smoothed over with lead filling. Much of the 99 was constructed from steel thicker than on most other cars. The torsional rigidity rating was in excess of 5,000lb ft/sq in at a time when 3,000lb ft/sq in was deemed a good result. The Saab resisted twist by up to 30 per cent more than its closest rival. Saab called the 99's in-built design 'steel basket construction'.

While any car maker can create a so-called 'safety cage' of thin, welded steel panelwork around the cabin area, in reality few car makers of the 1960s actually used stronger, thicker steel to reinforce the key elements of a car's cabin design in the manner that Saab did in 1967. The 99 also pioneered a design of side sill to footwell/front wheel-arch design that reduced intrusion and created lesser rates of leg injury. Both of the above-described techniques are now widely copied across the car industry.

By 1972, the 99 had been equipped with properly integrated side-impact door beams that transferred impact energy through lateral compression. Unlike some other car makers' claims of side-impact protection, which consisted of a thin strip of corrugated mild steel tack-welded on to the inside of the door skin, the Saab side-impact beams were box-section steel structures mounted into the door frame and therefore linked into the car's A and B pillars. At this time, only Volvo were thinking the same thoughts, but the Saab 99 innovated such side-impact protection. Interestingly, British Leyland was to use similar techniques on its ill-fated, late 1970s large car design for the Australian market, yet not in its domestic British products.

From 1972, the Saab 99 was equipped with a thickly padded, glassfibre layered, impact-absorbing roof lining designed to reduce head injuries. The three-door 99s with longer side doors were equipped with a thick, padded, collapsible, impact-reducing interior door panel, which had a moulded armrest designed to avoid the ribcage and spleen injuries found to occur with the industry standard, sharp-edged armrest designs of the era.

The 99 also had a collapsible steering column, and padded facia and pillars, as well as very strong seats with integral headrest, which offered a far higher degree of neck protection than the industry's standard 1970s designs. Saab's heavily padded and cleverly designed steering wheel was also shown to be the safest design for reducing head injuries in the days before a steering wheel-mounted airbag became an expected normal fitment. Saab invested much time and money in creating a cellular deformable pad for its steering wheels, which drastically reduced the likelihood of facial injuries.

Awards

On a visit to Saab's safety centre to see its work, *CAR* magazine's then editor, Mel Nichols, stated that the 99's strength and safety was incredible.[13] To underline the point, the Saab 99 had won the British Don Safety Trophy in 1972, for delivering what the award committee called the 'most remarkable safety package'. The safety-conscious Germans also awarded the 99 an 'Auto Oscar' for its safety features and crash strength. In the USA, the magazine *Motor Trend* told its readers that the car of the future had arrived in the form of the Saab 99. Given that the 99 was designed before the crash test or safety revolution, and before the safety advances that car manufacturers embraced in the late 1970s, the 99's total commitment to advanced safety design cannot be ignored.

Key names in the Saab 99's safety features and development were those of Olle Lindqvist as chief body engineer, and senior safety engineer Lars Nilsson. Saab's Christer Nilsson also made

A 99 soaking up the impact. This 1970 crash test shows how Saab kept the cabin intact with minimal intrusion and deformation. Few other cars of the era could manage this level of protection.

SAAB 99 KEY PASSIVE SAFETY ATTRIBUTES

- Steel in key body panels thicker than was motor industry practice at the time
- Unique 2.5mm steel sandwich windscreen pillars give in-built roll-over bar design
- Single-piece roof and panel design increases torsional rigidity to over 5,000lb ft/sq in
- Double-skinned front wing structure
- Wide-section 'offset' crash zone with very large steel wheel arches to absorb impact
- Reinforced bulkhead to resist intrusion
- Windscreen pillars extend down into the sill area, welded to the rear of the front wheel arch to resist intrusion
- Advanced roll-over roof deformation resistance and anti-crush roof supports
- Unique box-section steel sills

- Reinforced floor cross-members
- Innovated high strength box-section side-impact struts in doors
- Anti cabin-intrusion design to wheel arches
- Protected fuel tank
- Very strong steel tube seat design with strong, high-backed, static head protector
- Unique safety design of roof lining and interior door panels to reduce specific crash injuries
- Collapsible steering column with head injury-reducing padded cellular design
- Padded dashboard
- Headlamp wipers
- Dual split braking system
- Heated seats

This Mk1 four-door has the extra 'nostril' air vents let into the front panel to better cool the gearbox and engine bay. It retains the steel 'chrome' bumper design.

a mark on the 99's safety development. Thanks to their work, and that of their Saab safety centre colleagues, the 99 exceeded all known and much subsequent safety legislation at a time when building in safety was not the fashionable marketing tool it has now become. Perhaps no other car of the late 1960s and through to the 1980s had this much safety and occupant protection engineered into it. And it was not just such passive safety that was part of the 99: the car had excellent handling and accident-avoiding, active safety characteristics as well.

However, there was a small problem for the development of the 99, and that was the matter of a powerplant.

AN ENGINE WAS EXPECTED

Under Rolf Mellde's lead, Saab had finally made the move to the four-stroke cycle via the Ford V4 engine agreement. In 1964–66 that agreement would create the 96 V4, but for its new model Saab needed a new engine for a new car: the V4 could hardly be used in the new mid-range Saab, and Ford would not countenance its use in a direct competitor in its most vital European market sector.

Not for the first time, money was an issue. Saab would be hard pressed to fund the design and development of its own completely new engine, although it surely had the skills in its toolbox to do so. Indeed, from the early 1960s, Mellde's department had been working on a 1.2-litre engine of in-house design, with a gearbox to go with it. This was the engine that might have gone into the 96 if the move to four-stroke cycle had been made early enough. During this process, the Saab team, including Gunnar Ljungström and Karl Rosenqvist, had consulted with a British engineering firm named Ricardo. This long established

(1919) and well-respected British engineering concern was also contracted to the Standard-Triumph car company to help them create a new series of mid-range engines. Saab's director, Tryggve Holm, spoke with Triumph's new British Leyland boss, Lord Stokes, and Triumph's legendary engineer, Harry Webster, talked to the Saab men. Both companies were aiming for the same thing, and Saab was a big customer for British-supplied steel and trim items. The outcome was obvious: could Ricardo put Saab and Triumph together? Could a collaboration be considered?

Ricardo and Standard-Triumph

Saab, like Ricardo, had years of study of combustion cycles and efficiencies behind it; it had also decided that 1.2 litres was a good capacity for a small car, and that such an engine could be safely enlarged to 1.5 litres. Yet given the weight of the new Saab 99, 1.2 or even 1.5 litres was not going to be enough – the game had moved on since Mellde had started to draw up the 1.2-litre idea. Triumph wanted an engine in the 1.5-litre range that could ultimately share its component costs with a larger version. After early discussions, the new jointly developed engine became a unit of just over 1.7-litre capacity. The lead name in the new engine's life was to become that of Per Gillbrand, and his influence was to go far beyond the new 4-cylinder engine: under Gillbrand's expertise, the engine would become something much greater.

Saab signed a deal for 50,000 of these engines to be built in, and supplied from, Great Britain. The resulting engine proved to have strong, smooth torque and economy traits that reflected the driver's style, but in its Triumph guise it suffered from pressure concentrations in the cylinder head to engine block joining, and it also required very efficient cooling. Triumph took their version of the engine, mated it to an identical block and created a V8 unit for the Triumph Stag, an engine idea that was beset with problems.

Iron-blocked, alloy-headed and large in its dimensions, the engine was rated at 1709cc and had 87bhp. But it was a slant-block or canted over design with internal thermodynamic problems that led to isolated hot spots in the piston chambers and head structure. Getting the tensions of the cylinder head-to-block loads also proved difficult. But the engine did have a chain-driven cam, so there were no concerns over cambelt failures for owners.

Saab fitted the engine at an inclined 45-degree angle under the bonnet of its new 99 and, most unusually, bolted the gearbox on to the front of the engine; it then made some head gasket alterations, and generally applied its knowledge where it could. It also put the clutch and gearbox up front, creating a 'wrong way around' configuration for an in-line but front-wheel-drive engine – but that certainly improved the cooling situation.

After early production issues and Triumph's own problems with the engine, Saab decided to modify the unit and recreate it as a larger capacity, Saab-branded engine – yet in its first reincarnation it retained its Triumph origins. First Saab tweaked the engine to produce 1854cc: the '1.85'. Fuel injection was soon added, raising the output to 95bhp, or over 100bhp by the SAE measure. The original engine remained carburettor-fed, but the fuel-injection unit soon found its way into the 99 automatic.

The Saab 99 US specification included the round headlamps that changed the 'face' of the car, and the safety hoop headrest design.

FROM 1.85 TO 2.0 LITRES

Within three years of launch, the engine would be greatly recast as a revised Saab design and reach 1985cc and 110bhp. Also production would be transferred out of Triumph and into a new Saab-built engine factory in Sweden. With Saab giving redesign attention to valves, cooling and combustion characteristics, and numerous block changes, including cylinder dimensions, crankshaft and clamp loads in the new Saab-engineered alloy head, there was very little left unchanged and a 'new' Saab engine finally emerged from the origins of the Triumph block. Saab had also added a new valve mechanism and redesigned, reflowed combustion chamber: this stemmed from its years of accumulated research into engine design. This special combustion chamber design reduced emissions, notably for the American market, and was an example of the engine design genius hidden within Saab for so long.

The Saab 99 therefore started life with what was undoubtedly a British engine, but one that was developed and enlarged to a greater potential by Saab, not as originally intended by Triumph under Harry Webster and as planned by his predecessor Lewis Dawtrey. By 1970, with the merger of Saab and Scania leading to a big increase in available engine development resources, Saab had bored out the original engine to give 1854cc to create the 1.85-badged cars, known as the 'EA' model. For 1972, Saab created from the Triumph base unit its new, heavily modified, larger bored, lower compression, bhp, 1985cc engine. This was first fitted to the new four-door variant technically defined as the 'CM4' model, and then 'CM2' for the two-door. The 1973 model year cars, which began production in late 1972, had a number of revisions and were reclassified with the 'LCM' prefix in front of their model variant.

In 1972, the thought of this engine becoming the base of a turbocharged unit was an unlikely dream. Meanwhile Triumph, with its Dolomite and Stag, struggled to solve the problems they had encountered with their versions of the original jointly developed engine, notably in terms of head, valve and V8 design.

HANDLING

With the legacy of Mellde's focus on handling that built the Saab rallying reputation and which was delivered by the hands (and feet) of Erik Carlsson, the 99 had no excuse for not continuing the tradition. The 99 had wonderfully communicative steering and levels of feel and feedback to the driver, which really were above the norm: here was a rally-tuned car that told you what was happening. Steering, brakes, damping, stability, all were driving characteristics honed to a degree that lifted the 99 above the average standards of the era. A Porsche driver would immediately have felt at home with the feel of the 99, despite the difference in styling and layout. It was that old Ljungström, Mellde and Carlsson magic at work again.

Through thousands of hours of test driving, the feel of the car was honed. The steering was weighted to both communicate to the driver and provide feedback, the brakes and their pedal action was tuned to provide good response, and the car's ride and handling compromise was excellent. Saab equipped the 99 with the rare, expensive and time-consuming fitment of double wishbone suspension at the front, giving the kind of wheel location and suspension control normally reserved for racing cars and a few very fast coupés. Double wishbone, multi-linked suspension was very unusual in a saloon car of the 99's segment – it was a race-car element in a saloon.

Add in coil springs with top quality telescopic shock absorbers at the front, and a dead axle located by longitudinal

ABOVE: **The revised 99 dashboard circa 1970, with period cowled instruments and 'fake' wood.**

LEFT: **This is the Saab 1.85-litre modified engine from the original Saab–Triumph origins.**

arms, a Panhard rod and coil springs at the rear, with a small degree of self-steer in the geometry, and the 99 offered well-controlled suspension behaviour. With its direct rack-and-pinion steering as opposed to the more conventional but vaguer worm-and-roller mechanism, as well as large 15in wheels and a very stiff structure that did not flex under chassis loads, the 99 met the Saab-inspired handling traits that were an essential part of the ethos. Only the heavy low-speed steering represented a degree of compromise. The car would understeer, of course – as a front-wheel-drive car it would – but there were no nasty 'lift off' effects if the driver reduced power in mid-bend, and the rear of the car stayed firmly planted down and did not react adversely to such dynamic changes. Bounce, rebound and damping were all well controlled and absorbed, with no 'patter' coming up through the structure as can be found on some cars of thinner-gauge build quality.

On ice and snow the front-driven, expertly tuned 99 romped away, leaving rear-drive rivals (and Volvos) slithering in its wake. In the dry, wet or on ice, the 99's limits of adhesion were high, and it also had the press-on feel of the old 96 cars. Like its forefathers, the 99 was communicative and responsive, traits tuned during thousands of miles of testing that took place with a group of early production cars for a year of trials after the car's announcement. Only then, after proper fettling of its settings, did Saab settle on the final production parameters. Of note, despite its weight and front-driven configuration, the 99 was not to suffer from the usual affliction of front-driven power, in that it did not consume drive shafts at regular and expensive intervals. Saab saved the customer money by fitting heavy duty, long-life drive shafts that could take a pounding – unlike so many of the 99's front-driven 1970s competitors. It was during CV joint and drive-shaft durability testing that a prototype 99 crashed and became the first 99 to be involved in an accident. Happily, no one was injured.

DETAILS OF THE 99

The 99 continued the Saab theme of intelligent design. It was a saloon car, and yet the wide rear seat back could be folded down to provide 6.5cu m (23cu ft) of cargo space and a 1.75m (5ft 9in) cargo bay. There was also room for three adults in the back. Proper safety-tested headrests could be ordered, and the front seat occupants sat a long way back from the curved windscreen – far back from the glass and the impact zone of the bonnet. In comparison, many of the 99's competitors placed the front seat occupants close up to a very thin, short-depth dashboard and close to the windscreen and bonnet, nearer to the front crush zone of the car. The front seats also came with a degree of height variation via a small wind-up (or down)

catch, which tended to make up for the lack of steering-wheel adjustment.

The early dashboard was well padded and had a 'coaming' effect to its wrap-around design, which led back into the doors. This would soon be replaced by Bjorn Envall's revised 99 design for the 1970s, which featured a new interior.

Other details included the effective heating system. The ignition barrel and key were placed low down between the seats to avoid slicing open the knees of the driver, which had been a common factor with dashboard-mounted keys. The car also had to be placed into reverse and its transmission selector unlocked before it could be started – a crude but effective anti-theft device.

The aerodynamics kept the rear windscreen clean, and a drag coefficient of Cd0.37 was better than any other saloon car of the era, apart from the larger Citroën DS, NSU Ro 80, and the fastbacked Saab 96. It took a long, low-bodied coupé to rival the 99's air-cleaving abilities: most saloon cars had a Cd range of 0.40–0.50, and it would be the 1980s before a Cd of around 0.35 would become the standard. The 99 was also tuned to avoid aerodynamic lift, and had a very smooth undertray and strategically placed vortex generators to reduce turbulence and lift under and behind the car.

The 99's chromework was in fact clear pvc-coated stainless steel, while the thick-layered rust proofing under the car was far more comprehensive than anything the likes of Ford, Fiat or Renault might offer at the time. Rear windscreen demisting was by hot air venting; this was less of a drain on the car's electrics than a heated element, but slower to work. Eventually, an electric glass heater element was specified.

Overall, the 99 had a quality feel and an interior of rare thought and concern for the driver and passengers. As was usual with Saab, this was a car designed by people who cared, a thoroughly modern car that was ahead of its time in terms of safety, aerodynamics and cabin features.

From 1968 to 1984 the 99 was modified, improved, detailed and worked on by Saab to create a range of two-, three- and five-door cars that managed to project a 1960s design into a 1970s and even a 1980s car that remained competitive in terms of safety, style and capacity. There were two key elements to the 99 being able to do this: the first was Saab's technique of building a car that did not reflect the fashions of its time, but which set a new futuristic set of consumer and safety standards that would come into their own; and secondly, Saab spent time and money concentrating on the details of design and in developing them. These two characteristics explain how a model as old as the 99 managed to survive for so long as a competitive, safe and rewarding car. If any Saab encapsulates the ethos of Saab's obsession with the details of design, the 99 must be the prime example.

LAUNCH

Saab's new mid-size, two-door saloon was very different from the vast acreage of Volvo's 144 and 142. The pert little Saab had a unique identity that was backed up by its list of carefully designed features. It was officially launched on 22 November 1967, but it was 1968 before things really got going in terms of production and sales, and early 1970 before British buyers really got to grips with the car. In that intervening year, Saab and selected customers honed the car to new standards. After these early customer trials, Saab finalized production details in the autumn of 1968. By late 1969, Saab had sold 19,411 examples of the two-door 99, and by 1971 its new Finnish Valmet OY factory at Uusikaupunki on the Baltic coast had produced 7,781 cars.

The Swedes loved the new, characterful Saab, but there were a few teething problems with clutches and brakes, and the European motoring press seemed interested but not bowled over. The problem lay in the fact that Saab's first car, the 92, had been a significant advance, a major step in car design and utterly unique. That original Saab 92 was a car that 'wowed' the media and public alike – just like the later Citroën DS – with its spaceship looks and handling qualities. The 99, honed, tuned and deeply designed as it was, did not look so radical, and its qualities were not so immediately obvious through its shape. But it was a timeless design statement, and not a fast-dating flash-in-the-chromed-pan of 1960s design.

But there was another issue: the Triumph-derived engine was quiet, sound and strong, but it struggled to haul the heavy bodyshell around. The 99 was no slowcoach, but it lacked verve. Acceleration through the gears was thoroughly normal, and the

fuel consumption, especially in the winter, hovered just under the 9.4ltr/100km (30mpg) mark. The gearbox, actuated at length from the cabin to the very front of the car, had a gear-change mechanism that required care, and the steering at parking speeds was very heavy indeed, especially if the tyres were not pumped up sufficiently. So, good as it was, for the 99 there was room for improvement. The aerodynamic quietness of the car and the low wind noise from the curved windscreen also seemed to focus attention upon the gearbox and front-wheel-drive noise problem that every such car contained.

For the press, especially the British magazines, Saab's sound and secure design for its new car was to be admired, but it needed more power. There was much to be admired about the 99's design, commented the British motoring pundits, but fast the 99 was not.

EARLY CARS 1967–69

For its press cars and brochure photographs, Saab focused on displaying cars in a very strong red colour known as Toreador Red. Other early colours were green, white, blue and an unflattering creamy beige. In the main, the interiors were cloth trimmed in a black colour with a synthetic cloth seat-covering called 'nylon tricot'. A grey interior trim colour complemented black-painted cars, and a pale blue colour for the doors and side panels was also seen on blue cars. The launch brochure showed a car with a bright red interior trim colour for the seats and carpets, although few were seen in early production. There were also some black cars produced with a more luxurious, woollen-type seat cloth; a red interior trim and red seat trim

The revised 99 with its styling update and 'rubber' bumpers. Henrik Gustavsson was 99 technical director. The 99 with four doors signalled 99 development.

Saab seemed to like brown, and
this 1970s shot of the four-door
99 sums up the styling of the car
before it became the GLE and
had nicer colours. Anders
Hansson was 99 production
director.

was also shown in the early brochures, but it was some time
before this was widely available for the 1971 model year. Certain trim items from the Saab 96 were also used, including the
clock and cigarette lighter.

Despite the year-long pre-sales trial period, early 99s did have
some issues: brakes and clutches were of inconsistent quality,
and engine cooling issues were not unknown – indeed many
99 owners of later decades fitted large radiators to reduce the
operating temperature.

'JENKS' AND A 99 ACROSS EUROPE

Saab gave the leading British motoring writer Denis Jenkinson
of *Motor Sport* fame a new 99 to drive through Europe. 'Jenks'
is likely to have driven the Saab hard all the way down to the
Turin Motor Show and back, but his particular 99 never faltered
– which, in retrospect, must have been a relief for Saab. 'Jenks'
loved the 99 and its handling responses, but he noted that the
steering was hard work.

All the early cars had the 'klippan' buckle-less seat-belt design
that featured an easy-to-use clamp retainer between the
front seats. Headrests of the Saab-named 'art deco' design were
offered as optional extras and as standard fit on the first American market cars for 1970. Saab also made specification changes
to various items, and trim choices ranging from the shape of
the door mirrors to the choice of tyres and carburettors.

As early as the 1970 model-year cars, built from late September 1969, running changes were made to the 99: a third
engine mount was added to reduce vibration and drivetrain
'shunt', rear seatbelts were offered, and new colours added
to the paint palette. An injected, Borg-Warner three-speed
automatic gearbox was also announced, making this the first
automatic Saab. The side indicators were increased in size but

still low-mounted on the front wings. New wheel trims were
created, and stylish new 'SAAB 99' badges in brushed aluminium appeared at the rear edge of the clamshell bonnet. Thus,
slowly, the 99 was getting a make-over.

The first cars were two-door only, but in April 1970 for that
model year Saab sprung a surprise by announcing a four-door
version. This added a new dimension to the 99. With a strong
styling motif to the rear C pillar and stronger lines framing the
new rear side doors, the 99 looked tougher and larger, and it
had a new stance and a new look to it – yet the first four-door
cars retained all the original styling cues of the original 99; however, this was not for long.

Behind the scenes, Envall, now back from working for Opel,
created a new 1970s facelift for the 99. For the 1971 model year,
the car's look and image was transformed. First, Envall created
a new interior with a very smart dashboard moulded in a high
quality synthetic material. Ergonomic, aircraft-inspired, zoned
design went into the layout, and the car had the 'cockpit' look
that became a Saab motif. The late 1970-build, 1971 four-door
cars were first to feature the new dashboard, but within months,
the new interior was fitted across the 99 range – which at the
same time was also fitted with Envall's new frontal design
treatment of a revised grille and much bolder side indicator
lamps. Extra air grilles were added below the main grille to
increase cooling flow, especially for the hard-worked three-
speed automatic gearbox. The famous, cellular, self-repairing
black '5mph' bumper also appeared. Another innovation at this
time was the Saab-designed headlamp wash-wiper system for
the 99, another 'first' for any car.

Such was the success of the 99 and its development needs,
Saab set up a separate development bureau and factory at
Halvorstorp. There, 115 staff, including engineer John Ahs and
foremen Bo Lundh, were involved in product development and
testing under their manager Gosta Svensson and director Rolf
Sandberg.

Saab 99 branding seen on the lower facia panel.

SPECIFICATIONS SAAB 99 (1968)

Body

Aerodynamic, reinforced bodyshell with 2.5mm rolled steel strengthening beams and box sills. Crumble zones, protected fuel tank. Anti-crush roof

Engine

Type	Front-wheel drive to Standard Triumph–Saab Ricardo design; 2 valves per cylinder, overhead cam; chain-driven camshaft
Cylinders	4-cylinder longitudinally mounted
Cooling	Water-cooled
Bore & stroke	83.5mm×78mm
Capacity	1709cc
Compression ratio	9:1
Carburettor	Stromberg
Max. power	80bhp (59.5kW) @ 5,200rpm
Max. torque	98lb/ft (131Nm)

Transmission

Type	Front-wheel drive with four-speed full synchromesh gearbox with column shift. Freewheel device
Clutch	Single dry plate

Suspension and steering

Suspension	Independent front suspension with double wishbones, coil springs and absorbers. Rear tubular axle with twin link location and Panhard rod
Steering	Rack and pinion

Wheels and tyres

4.5J × 15; tyres 155 × SR15

Brakes

Hydraulic brake discs all round with split diagonal system

Dimensions

Wheelbase	2,473mm (97in)
Length	4,354mm (171in)
Width	1,676mm (66in)
Height	1,450mm (57in)
Weight (net)	1,030kg (2,271lb)

Top speed

145km/h (90mph)

POWER ISSUES

In 1970, *Motor* magazine described the Saab 99 as 'an extremely well designed 4/5 seater that doesn't go fast enough'.[14] Saab reacted to media and buyer complaints about a lack of power by quickly developing its 1.85 and then the 1985cc, or '2.0-litre' tagged engines. Adding fuel injection and luxury trim for the American market cars soon created a new theme for the 99, as a faster, better trimmed, more upmarket car. By late 1971, the 99 had heated seats, headlamp wipers, more sound-proofing, chrome wheel trims and new badging.

The original 1.7-litre engine was phased out, as was that old Saab favourite and a carryover from the 96, the freewheel gear disengagement device – though before it went, Saab GB offered an SAH company tuning kit (now long forgotten) for the 1.7-litre engine. This added two Weber DCO40E carburettors, a new inlet and exhaust manifold of less tortuous flow design, a 'stage one' revised profile camshaft, a free flow main exhaust and a Koni sports damper set off by new wider wheels. A podded facia-mounted rev counter was fitted. Surprisingly, the air filter remained standard specification, an unusual tuning omission. With the tuning kit fitted, the 99's 0–60mph time went down from 15.2sec to 10.2sec, but sadly fuel economy plummeted as consumption dipped to 14ltr/100km (20mpg). The cost of the tuning kit was £200 in 1970.

Such changes and customer demand set the men of Saab thinking: could they create a sportier Saab?

EMS – STEPPING STONE

By using the two-door body shell, adding the new Saabized fuel-injected 2-litre engine – built at Saab's new engine plant at Sodertalje, and mated to a manual gearbox – and creating unique trim and specification items, the Saab team created a 99 with electronic injection (E), manual gearbox (M) and sports trim (S) – an EMS.

Announced in January 1972, the 99 EMS had a smart, black-painted grille, an unusual new type of alloy wheel design (the 'football' design), and it came in only one colour – a warm, reflective hued silver with a hint of warm orange known as Copper Coral Metallic. The next EMS-launched colour was 'Silver Mink'. The EMS had a tachometer, radial and sports-grade Pirelli tyres on wider wheels, halogen headlamps and a leather-rimmed steering wheel. With more power, Bosch Jetronic (pulsed) fuel injection (later modified), the 99 had met the critics' demand for something faster, and the new engine would improve things lower down the range, too.

For the British, 0–60mph came up in around 11sec (later improved down to 10sec), so the important European 0–100km/h took 11.3sec. The top speed of 177km/h (110mph) was very respectable. Saab's new 1985cc engine was smooth running and quite happy to be revved in normal, sports driving use to 6,200rpm.

By 1974, the EMS had been further improved with the addition of Saab's new high-backed safety seat design, a centre console, pivot-mounted front coil springs, a vinyl roof, optional sports side stripes, and a new colour for the EMS only – Silver Crystal. For 1975, the EMS changed from electronic pulsed injection to a continuous fuel injection system. Power went up from 110bhp to just nudging 120bhp, at 118bhp.

At its launch, the EMS was deliberately pitched by Saab as a competitor to the venerable BMW 2002 range of two-door sports saloons. Saab decided that the BMW 2002 was 'the

Saab 99 EMS – or electronic-manual-sport specification.

toughest competition around', to quote a Saab advertisement for the important American market. The 99 EMS, much heavier in the body than the thin-pillared, lightweight-panelled BMW, managed to compete in performance terms, let alone out-handle the BMW's somewhat twitchy, rear-driven design characteristics. In independent tests carried out in March 1976 by the American Testing Institute, the public perception of the more 'sporting' BMW was challenged.

EMS VERSUS BMW

Below are the performance figures for the 1976 US spec model Saab 99 EMS versus US spec BMW 2002.

	Saab 99 EMS	BMW 2002
0–60mph:	11.8sec	12.00sec
0–30mph:	3.8sec	3.5sec
¼ mile:	18.27sec	18.33sec
¼ mile km/h (mph):	119.4 (74.2)	117.5 (73)
Slalom km/h (mph):	74.9 (46.55)	72.9 (43.13)
Skid pan km/h (mph):	52.5 (32.63)	52.7 (32.77)
Skid pan G-force:	0.711	0.717
Braking		
30mph–0mph:	40.4ft	40.3ft
60mph–0mph:	154.7ft	153.2ft

Per Gillbrand – the Saab turbo man.

So the Saab, front-wheel drive and heavily constructed, could take on the best. And by 1977, a three-door version of the EMS using the new Combi-Coupé body was announced – but it was not widely available in all markets, and there was a reason for that: Saab was going to go 'Turbo'.

In Britain, by 1977 the EMS was priced to match the very latest new models from BMW, Audi and others such as Renault. Pitched at a British sales price of £4,900 in 1976, and increased to £5,540 in late 1977, the EMS was, alongside the Triumph Dolomite, an expensive old car facing new competitors – yet unlike the ancient, upright Dolomite (with its original Ricardo/Saab/Triumph-derived engine), the 99 still looked fresh and modern. Saab's technique of avoiding fashion and designing for the future was proven. But set in 1977 alongside BMW's latest Three Series that was sold for the same price, in the form of the 320i and its superb style and class-leading interior, the EMS relied on its depth of engineering rather than its 'of the moment' style.

EMS opened up a whole new customer base for Saab, especially in Great Britain and the USA. EMS was less wooden than the feel of a normal Saab, it had an air of excitement. It was no Ford Capri, of course, but you would not expect that from Saab.

Now thanks to EMS, for the first time a younger or more sports-oriented car driver was both targeted and captured. The 99 EMS brought Saab closer to the market place and extended the Saab brand's recognition to new fields. In the 99 EMS, Saab had a fast, classy, decidedly niched product that could tackle the rise of competing sports saloons and even begin to play BMW at its own very successful marketing game, which had seen the two-door BMW saloons secure a wide following. EMS also had royal approval when HRH Prince Bertil of Sweden took delivery of his own 99 EMS on 30 October 1974. The car was delivered by Saab President Curt Mileikowsky and who else but Erik Carlsson – 'Mr Saab' – and the brand's roving ambassador.

WIDENING THE RANGE

Further down the model scale, with the ageing 96 beginning to look dated by 1973, Saab created a new economy-class special from the 99 two-door bodyshell using the 1.85-litre engine. This was the curiously tagged 99 'X7'. Stripped out and down to a basic specification, the X7 strangely reverted to using steel, chrome-effect bumpers – which saved Saab money and reduced the car's weight (the bumpers weighed 25kg (55lb) each). X7 retained the brightwork trim of the 99 around its front door windows, but used black rubber trim without shiny chrome effect for the windscreen and rear side windows: this strange mismatch looked very odd indeed, as if someone had fitted the wrong doors to the car!

X7 featured an even stranger economy measure – it had the old seats from the Saab 96, and no carpets. The 99 X7 was a Scandinavian market special model and not seen in Great Britain or other markets, although some Dutch sales were rumoured via Denmark. But X7 was short-lived, and by late 1974 it was gone. Given that the true base model 99 variant the 99L had been so good, the point of X7 was soon lost. A Nordic market 99 base model with the rubber bumpers and fitted carpet soon banished the memories of the X7. In Britain a basic spec L version was as close to an economy model as the 99 would get. It is rumoured that due to shortages at the factory, a small number of British market 99 L cars were fitted with the seats from the 96, as the X7 had been.

Across the 99 range, complaints about the heavy low-speed steering had become a consistent theme in media road tests and customer feedback. For the 1975 model year, Saab quickened the steering rack ratio, and shortened the steering arms for all 99s except the EMS. The EMS had originally been given a steering rack with 3.4 turns of the wheel from lock to lock, as compared to an original 4.1 turns for the standard 99s. With 165 x 15 wheels and Pirelli CN 36 tyres, the EMS retained that old issue of heavy steering: it was hard work to park, or steer at low speeds. But the feedback from the front wheels was the stuff of race and rally-tuned excellence.

For the American market, the 99 came with four round headlamps due to legislative requirements. Early cars had the 'art deco' headrests fitted, and by the mid-1970s, with high-backed 'tombstone' seats, special wheel trims and an 'LE' brand designation for 1974, the 99 sold well to a certain type of American buyer who, like their European counterparts, wanted a long-term relationship with their car.

THE GLE GENERATION

Beyond the decidedly penny-pinching economy of the X7, the EMS had engendered demand for a sportier *and* more luxurious Saab. Could the EMS formula be adapted to the four-door version of the 99, to focus on luxury with power? So was born the ultimate, most expensive pre-Turbo era Saab 99: the 99 GLE. Based on the 2.0-litre, four-door GL bodyshell, the GLE was a luxury-trimmed, fuel-injected, alloy-wheeled Saab of a character never before seen. Here was the first step towards a more upmarket Saab, even if it did utilize an existing Saab body.

Launched at the Brussels Motor Show in early 1976, the Saab 99 GLE was lavishly trimmed with a specification that included pleated velour seat coverings, rear headrests, heated front seats, centre console with stereo, tinted electric windows, alloy wheels (from the EMS, but gold painted), an automatic gearbox (manual was later offered) and lighter steering. Electric mirrors

and a new, even larger front-indicator light-cluster design made its debut on the GLE. A range of new, upmarket colours such as Cardinal Red, Anthracite Grey, Dorado Brown and Astral Blue were soon available. By 1976 the GLE would feature new, larger rear lamp designs, pinstripe chrome-effect steel bumper trim lines, a steel sliding sunroof and a new steering wheel, which by 1977 would feature across all Saab cars.

The 99 GLE four-door sold well, particularly in Great Britain, Germany, Scandinavia and the USA. It might have been smaller than the likes of the Volvo 144/244, the BMW 5 series or other competitors, but the GLE was like most Saabs: well conceived, well thought out and properly presented. Certainly, if the streets of London's Mayfair or Frankfurt's financial quarter circa 1977 were evidence, the sight of alloy-wheeled, brightly trimmed, dark blue, dark crimson and dark brown-hued 99 GLEs swishing along amid the acres of Rover, Volvo, BMW and Mercedes steel was very pleasing for Saab's sales managers. GLE was a new theme for Saab and, like the EMS, laid the foundations for a wider brand awareness and sales success around the world. The GLE was a class act and defined a new era for Saab. By the time the GLE became available in three- and five-door bodyshells, two things had happened at Saab: first, the hatchback derivative of the 99 bodyshell had been born; and second, the Turbo era was about to begin.

For the 99 hatchback, orange was a big theme for Saab in the mid-1970s. It has made a comeback more recently across the motor industry. Here the 'Combi' looks the part.

BACKING THE HATCH

As the two-door and four-door 99 ranges matured, Saab did what it had always done: it tweaked and improved the car's engineering and trim specifications as each subsequent model year was announced. Wider wheels, better steering, new seats, improved gearboxes – including the cold chill-cast gearbox housing that was designed to improve the strength of the 99's gearbox and its reputation for trouble if abused – all these measures created a car that matured over time. But around it, other manufacturers churned out a relentless diet of easy-to-make, disposable cars, which were snapped up by buyers interested less in a depth of engineering and more in the latest fads in plastics, chrome and gadgets.

Without joining this club of mainstream manufacturers, Saab could see that it had to do something, and so was born the idea of a three-door hatchback version of the 99. For the 1970s, the hatchback became the car-sales tool of the moment – even the American market embraced the practicalities of a combined saloon/estate. Renault's stylish 16 hatchback had set European hatchback buyers' hearts a-flutter, and in Britain, the incredibly dull but very practical Austin Maxi hatchback was selling well, despite being based on an ancient set of doors, body panels and even older engines all inherited from its predecessors.

Saab sat down, studied the themes, and then came up with an unusual take on the idea: how about a modern, contemporary hatchback with the space of an estate and the looks of a fast-backed coupé? Would such a car not be uniquely Saab?

It was Bjorn Envall who dreamed up the shape of the 99 three-door and then the 99 five-door, with its 'love them or hate them' 'opera' windows in the C pillars. Achieving a proper rear hatchback that opened, estate car-style, down to the bumper was not easy in a bodyshell, the big hatchback aperture and lack of a high cross-brace at the boot/trunk height left the rear of the car vulnerable to twist and flex, not to mention the dangers of it literally peeling open in a rear-end crash. Hatchbacks had fewer crush zones, too, as the traditional boot/trunk was sliced off.

Over hours of styling, computerized aerodynamics tuning and wind tunnel-tested modifications, and structural engineering work, Envall and the Saab body design team came up with a way of bracing the rear C pillars and having a proper estate car-style rear hatch aperture. By inserting a web of steel and a strong frame, the new rear end was made to meet Saab's stringent safety requirements. Saab also fitted a box-section steel beam across the top of the folding rear seat, which added passenger protection when the seat was upright and in use by bracing the two C pillars across the hatchback's void. The fuel tank was well protected up by the rear axle, and a thick steel floor isolated the cabin from its danger.

With a swept rear end and large, lift-up tailgate, the 99 had gained modern good looks and a massive rear cargo bay, even with the rear seats in place. Folding the seats down created an even bigger load bay. The carrying capacity of the car, christened 'Combi-Coupé' by Saab in Europe and 'Wagon-Back' in the USA market, at nearly 2m (1.85m) long and 90cm high, was enormous and resulted in a massive sales 'bounce' for the 99. You could even sleep two people comfortably in the back of the new car – although the owner would need to supply the mattress.

1970s Fashion Item

Unveiled in 1973, the 99 hatchback did not go on sale until well into 1974. Although very popular as a workhorse family car (some 99s were even made to van configuration for the tax advantages of the Danish market), the three-door, or Combi, soon found itself trimmed for upmarket placement in various GL, GLE and EMS guises. In its early life the car was available in a 1970s hue of bright orange, which did it few favours, but by 1976 the fitment of alloy wheels, stainless steel trims, spoiler kits front and rear and a range of metallic colours took the new car into more expensive territory.

In 1974, Saab sold over 62,000 examples of the 99, many of them hatchbacks. In 1976, the effect of the EMS, GLE and Combi had created 72,819 sales worldwide of the Saab 99; compare that with the 35,136 basic 99s sold in 1971, and the effect is obvious.

For the Geneva Motor Show in March 1976, Saab unveiled a new five-door version of its hatchback concept, which kept the long tail but initiated one of the earliest elements of a new market sector: the executive or luxury trimmed, large five-door hatchback. Ford, Opel, Volvo, Mercedes, BMW and others had no answer, stuck as they were in a world of 'three-box' design, booted saloon thinking. But Rover, Audi and others were soon to produce their own large five-door hatchbacks.

For the late 1970s, Saab updated the 99 again, with larger rear lamp clusters, new colours, new seat designs with less intrusive headrests, and an array of wheels and body trims. New grilles, new materials, and such oddities as large but aerodynamic 'elephant's ear' door-mounted rear-view mirrors, all came and went. By 1980, after the debut of the new, larger Saab 900, the 99 inherited some of its improvements, principally the seats, wheels and revised gearbox. For 1980, the 110bhp-injected Saab 99 GLi in manual or auto form was supplied to North America. By 1982, the 900's 'H'-version engine was fitted to the 99, the engine being 12kg lighter and with higher compression. In five-door guise, notably painted in the dark hue of crimson known as Cardinal Red metallic, or perhaps finished in dark grey or dark blue, the five-door 99 took on a new life.

The rarest 99 of them all, the pearlescent white 99 Turbo three-door
on Inca wheels, as also seen at the Frankfurt show launch.

TURBO: THE MOMENT ARRIVES

The men of Saab it seemed never rested. If the growth of the
99 into a new version of an old car was both clever and well
executed, the next thoughts for what to do for the 99 and for
Saab were both risky and a spectacular success. Saab was about
to crack a code that had defeated even major players in car
design, and the inspiration came from aircraft and from heavy
trucks. Here began the Turbo years, arguably Saab's greatest
chapter.

Although often cited as the world's first turbocharged mass-
production family car, in the 99, Saab was not the first car maker
to pursue turbocharging. BMW spent millions of Deutschmarks
creating its own series of race and production turbo two-door
cars, and way back in 1963 the Oldsmobile Turbo Jetfire had
beefed up its name with a bolt-on turbo. Chevrolet also produced a limited number of turbocharged cars, but neither
these nor any of the other applications were designed for
mass market, mid-range power enhancement. The thought of
having a high-powered turbo boost bolted to a standard 1970s
American chassis can only be guessed at.

Other car makers had tinkered with turbos, but the concept remained a bolt-on item that remained at the periphery
of the car market. But the science of turbocharging was not
new, and trucks, tanks, racing cars and wartime military and
civil aircraft had all used force-induction turbocharging or

supercharging to force greater pressure into the combustion
process. Thus turbocharging was not new – but what Saab did
to it, and with it, was.

Turbochargers, or turbos, had 'blown' extra air pressure
into aircraft combustion chambers throughout World War II,
the turbo being a 'free' gain in that it used exhaust waste gas
to pressurize the combustion charge into the cylinder head.

AN OLD IDEA

In the early 1930s, superchargers had worked for Bentley, and
in the 1920s French and German engineers had added extra
induced 'breathing' to the inlet mixture flow via a forced car-
buration device. In fact it had been the Edwardian engineers
of England and early American engineers who dreamed up
impeller-type wheels driven off the engine to provide extra
power. These early devices were a sort of combined supercharger and turbocharger compressor, belt driven and then
impeller driven. By 1940, reliable super- and turbocharging that
did not explode the engine was achieved, and aviation only
hastened the development of such technologies.

Big turbos could be engaged via a *de facto* clutch-effect
mechanism, just as an engine crank-driven supercharger could
be, or they could be constantly plumbed into the power system.
The issues were weight, temperature, combustion chamber
pressure, reliability and the 'lag' – the time it took the turbo

wheel to speed or spool up to a point where its inlet efforts could be translated into outlet performance. At high altitudes and in low-revving diesel truck engines such lag effects did not matter, but in a mass-production car they could be annoying, if not dangerous.

But the Swedish engineers of Saab, Scania, Volvo and other companies all had experience of forced induction through their aircraft, truck, marine and hydrodynamic experience. Even Trollhättan itself had mastered the art of impeller blades, rotating wheels and turbos in its hydroelectric engineering output. It seemed obvious that Saab should try and tame the technicalities of the turbocharger.

The Saab ethos would avoid building a large cubic capacity 6- or 8-cylinder engine – such things were too 'lazy' for the Aeroplan men and their ethos. And simply bolting on a turbo to create top-end speed for racing or rallying, in the fashion of BMW or Porsche, was not what Saab was looking for. Saab's engineers reckoned that mid-range overtaking performance was where the safety advantages of turbo power lay. By spending less time on the wrong side of the road, a Saab car and its driver would be less exposed to danger. The vital 48–80km/h (30–50mph) and 80–113km/h (50–70mph) speed bands were where the fusion of a flatter, less peaky torque curve and a tuned turbocharger that kicked in below 2,500 revs would be played to best advantage.

Inside Rolf Mellde's engine division there was Per Gillbrand, and soon the top ex-Scania diesel engineer Bengt Gadefelt. Saab's Josef Eklund was also in house, as was Karl-Erik Petterson, and before long an English expert from Turbo-Technics Ltd joined the development team, Geoffrey Kershaw who was

Rolls-Royce trained. Kershaw and Scania had worked with Garret AiResearch on turbocharger development for trucks, and Saab had itself turbocharged a 96 V4 rallycross in 1974. Saab executive vice president and general manager Sten Wenlo was the management name who backed the turbo idea, but it was an idea and a project that existed long before he was promoted within Saab to manage and frame the turbo era.

Reinventing the Application

Saab soon defined its cause: to create a new type of effectively 'geared' turbo – not some large dustbin-sized box in the engine bay designed to create a high-revving burst of top-speed power enhancement, but a more subtle, cleverer device. So began the quest to develop a lightweight, smaller-sized turbine impeller wheel inside an exhaust gas-driven turbocharger unit that would contain the massive forces created, and not overstress the engine block. These were the key issues: BMW and Porsche had seen poor reliability on their early road-going turbo cars, and warranty claims to match. The old, full bore, on-off power switch-type turbo performance was also dramatically devastating in its effects on a car's dynamics and the driver's reactions, and Saab needed to avoid any potential huge PR, marketing and financial disaster as a result of getting its turbo application wrong.

Thus began another search within Saab, one that led to the adoption and 'Saabification' of an idea of a smaller turbo unit with a lightweight turbine, which would then protect its innards and its reliability by bleeding off or dumping its excess energy

Turbo in black: the essential Saab. Curiously for a Saab shot, the wheel caps are missing!

or pressure at very high revs. GarretAiResearch had already been studying this technique and Porsche was aware of it, but nobody had applied it to a mid-range production car. This was what Saab decided to do, and was the 'waste-gate' idea in its genesis. This was a step head of the production turbo fitted by BMW to their 2002 Turbo models of the 1972 model year; only 1,673 such BMWs were sold until the model was withdrawn. Going turbo had not worked even for the likes of BMW who had been building car, motorcycle and aircraft engines for decades, so clearly the turbo was a tough nut to crack in car engineering.

Another way of protecting the turbo unit against its self-created boost pressure was to have a valve in the internal flow stream, which could be weighted to activate at a certain pressure when it would dump or waste the boost charge. This was the blow-off valve equivalent of the waste-gate idea, and had been investigated by engineers for some years. By spilling off air upstream of the turbine, excess revolutions and created boost pressure were reduced, but the trick was to keep the turbine spinning at low speed so that it could respond quickly upon demand but not create overboost downstream of the unit. Herein lay the paradox and the problem, and Saab set to work to focus on this key characteristic.

Because Saab had modified the old Triumph/ Ricardo engine as early as 1972, it had considered adding power to the engine for future applications. This was why Saab had specified an extra strong forged crankshaft and very high quality alloys for the internal components. Over at Saab's Sodertajlie engine plant, Saab's old engine group and their new Scania-Vabis colleagues put their heads together.

Vital Testing

Over many months of testing, the team selected the ingredients for what it needed and then set about gauging the strengths, tolerances, pressures and behaviours of each component. Cylinder heat pressures, gaskets, cooling and valve stems and seats were all critical factors that needed defining for long-term reliability. Heat-shielding would also be required for a turbo turbine that would spin at 50,000 to 80,000rpm. Saab tested its little turbine up to 20,000rpm. Fuel injection would also be a vital key ingredient to the measuring of tuned, impelled combustion.

The costs were huge, and the engine team had a fight on their hands as development time and development costs rose. Six rather grubby 99 EMS cars were used as development mules – the brains went on under the bonnet. Saab made the exhaust's 'back' pressure the activating parameter.

Other changes would include a stronger camshaft, the sodium-treated valves with altered cam timing, strengthened

gears and a different final drive ratio, and forged pistons with better thermodynamics for improved heat dissipation. The experimental, US specification, oxygen-sensing Lambda probe or sensor in the exhaust gas also allowed the first steps at engine combustion monitoring and self diagnosis – altering the fuel/air mixture. From these early tests would come Saab's highly advanced APC – automatic performance control – system.

By 1975–76 Saab had perfected a turbo application that delivered mid-range power in a torque curve that although achieving a peak, had a broader gradient and descent than a normal top speed-biased turbo. A special gate or valve ahead of the turbine remained open, leaving the system unpressurized or unturbocharged by allowing the exhaust gas to bypass the turbine. On demand from the accelerator pedal, the gate or valve would close, forcing the exhaust gas to divert on to the turbine wheel and spinning up the turbo, thus pressurizing or charging the system into action. Then after the required 'charge' the turbo effect wasted or dumped the charge to avoid over-stressing the application and its components. Above all, Saab wanted to achieve actuation of the turbocharger via the exhaust back-pressure, rather than the previously accepted inlet manifold pressure.

By late 1976 the Saab team had defined their new take on the science of the turbocharger as a concept, and the first engine was presented in 1977.

The mid-range pressurization also smoothed out the exhaust vibrations and dynamic harmonics, which created the Saab turbo's unique sound, accompanied by a turbo 'whistle'. Spilling air away from the turbocharger preserved reliability – and the whole thing was bolted to a Saab-modified engine that had started life in the 1960s in Britain, an engine that had been effectively reinvented.

The results were astonishing. Torque was up by 45 per cent, power up by 23 per cent – in fact the torque at 175lb ft, or 245Nm/kg, was way in excess of the 145bhp horsepower rating. Furthermore Saab's tuned turbo only cut in for approximately 20 per cent of the time in normal driving, so fuel economy was not devastated. So tractable was the 99 Turbo that there was rarely need to drop down a gear in order to gain power, and this aided fuel economy; however, maximum performance did come from making use of the gearbox and keeping the turbo spinning.

The driving characteristics were simply astounding. Once the issue of the low revs 1,500–1,850rpm 'lag' had been driven around, the afterburner effect of the development cars was incredible. Acceleration, and particularly overtaking performance, was on a par with supercar performance; thus by 2,500rpm in the engine, the turbo would be spooling up beyond 55,000rpm and getting ready to deliver the 'shove' or rocket ship surge for which the 99 Turbo became known. Thus the 99

Turbo could see off minor Porsches, old Ferraris and a host of 1980s 'hot hatches'. A new driving technique had to be learned in order to make the most of the 99 Turbo, anticipating a need for power and giving the turbine time to spool up or charge prior to the manoeuvre – or keeping the car 'on the cam' in the old-fashioned sense.

The motoring press would make something of the early engines' turbo lag, but as it was less than in any other

---

SPECIFICATIONS   SAAB 99 TURBO 1978

Body

Three-door bodyshell 'Combi' with special aerodynamic aids: front valance spoiler and rear tray spoiler for wake vortex tuning

Engine

Type	Longitudinally mounted iron block/alloy head chain-driven ohc 8-valve engine
Cylinders	4 cylinders
Cooling	Water
Bore & stroke	90mm×78mm
Capacity	1985cc
Turbo	Bosch Jetronic fuel injection, Garrett AiResearch turbocharger with 0.09 bar (1.2 bar max. rated)

Max. power	145bhp (DIN) (108kW) at 5,000rpm
Max. torque	174lb ft (233Nm) @ 3,000rpm

Transmission

Four-speed gearbox mounted at the front of the engine

Suspension

Double wishbones and coil springs/dampers to front, Panhard rod and tube arm links to rear with dampers

Tyres

Pirelli CN 36

Black paint, Inca wheels: this is a Turbo two-door moment.

LEFT: **The classic 99 Turbo interior of pleated velour and a uniquely Saab steering wheel. This is the later, revised seat design with the 'collar' headrest.**

BELOW: **The engine bay from the 99 Turbo: pure Saabism.**

application they had encountered in a road-going saloon car, it sounded like nitpicking. It would not be long before Saab lightened the turbine blades, altered the airflow, and then went on to create the 'LPT' light pressure turbo itself – another new era in turbocharging that was a Saab development.

EMS-TURBO BRANDING

Prior to the launch of the definitive 'Turbo' brand, the early 99 turbos had all been based on EMS-trimmed cars, and indeed for some time the project was tagged 'EMS-Turbo'. Saab let it be known that the EMS-Turbo was an American specification designed to meet new emissions legislation, though clearly this tactic was that of a ruse in marketing terms. The additions of a three-way catalyst and Lambda sensor were to be expensive engineering solutions for California specification cars, which at 132bhp had 12bhp less than European specification cars.

In early 1977, Saab produced a batch of 100 EMS-specified Turbo development cars using the three-door Combi-Coupé bodyshell, which was to be the base of the first Turbo models. But wise heads soon saw the advertising and marketing benefits of complete reinvention, and EMS-Turbo soon became Turbo. The early development batch of 99 EMS-Turbos allowed Saab to iron out any problems and sort out the US specification cars in terms of injection, turbo settings, compression and emissions.

The full production specification 99 Turbos were all finished in jet black with crimson pleated velour seats. The new 'Inca' wheels – reflecting either ancient South American architectural motifs or turbine blades, according to two differing legends – marked the car's unique style, as did a new rear-window lip spoiler – this was a Saab take on the Porsche-style tray or ledge spoiler design.

Upgrades to the full Turbo specification at launch 1978–81 included the addition of superb Bilstein shock absorbers and Pirelli P6 tyres, which gripped well but soon wore out their shoulders under turbo-powered loadings. These were the original, three-door bodyshells of the first 99 Turbo incarnation, but the need to homologate the 99 Turbo for rallying using the stiffer, two-door booted bodyshell meant that Saab latterly manufactured 1,000 of the two-door 99 Turbos. Of these, 600 were imported into Great Britain, with 200 being painted red, followed by a mix and match of black- and red-painted cars. A later batch of these cars received suspension upgrades from the 99-derived Saab 900. Because these two-door cars were lighter, shorter and stiffer, they were also faster with a 0–60mph time of 8sec (over a second quicker than a three-door with 9.2sec) and a top speed of an actual 193km/h (120mph) rather than the 188km/h (117mph) of the three-door car. The vital 100–130km/h (60–80mph) overtaking time was down to 6sec – real performance.

In the early days of the Turbo, a handful of Cardinal Red metallic 99 Turbos were brought in by Saab GB to their new Marlow head office. This included twenty-five five-door 99 EMS

Not all Turbos were black or Cardinal red, and two-door cars were often red or Acacia Green, as here.

cars branded as Turbos, which were essentially late model EMS variants fitted with the turbo engine and trimmings. Legend has it that three black five-door Turbos were imported into Great Britain. Other rarities were pearlescent white-painted three-door 99 Turbos that mirrored the original launch car from the Frankfurt Motor Show.

Launch price of the 99 Turbo three-door in Great Britain was £7,850, which was £250 more than BMWs brand new 3 series, 2-litre 320i model. Given the Saab's age and the BMW's modernity and stunning cabin, the Saab had a fight on its hands. But the Saab had four proper seats with ample room, faster performance and front-drive handling to shame the BMW's rear semi-trailing arm limitations. BMW's other tail-happy super saloon, the quick 528i, only cost £8,128 for British buyers, so potential Saab Turbo buyers had a real performance versus brand perception choice to make.

The eager Saab buyers of Finland were treated to their own special Saab-Valmet specification version of the 99 Turbo as early as spring 1980. This was a base-model variant of the two-door shell, fitted with the standard 145bhp turbo engine, Inca wheels and dechromed trim. Cars were sold in white and pale green as well as black. Some 300 of these cars were exported by Saab-Valmet to the Swedish domestic market.

The sheer power going through the front wheels and unequal length driveshafts led to torque steer, yet rally specification 99s had differing diameters for their driveshafts to avoid such steer effects – so why not the road-going models, asked the critics? Early cars had a few problems, and Saab had not quite cracked the nut, but within months, tolerances and specifications were improved. Owners had to let their turbo cars run for a couple of minutes at idle after a high speed run in order to lubricate the oil flow in the turbo unit: if you simply turned off a hot turbo, the oil would boil, carbonize, and cause wear. Saab came up with a water-cooled jacket for the turbine; it also reduced the weight of the turbine blades, and made some

changes to their aerodynamics in the exhaust gas stream. Apart from the occasional stuck waste-gate valve mechanism, the turbochargers began to be seen as reliable.

Failures to hard-driven or poorly maintained cars did occur, but in the majority of cases the turbo unit was good for 112,600km (70,000 miles) without problem – many reached 194,000km (120,000 miles) before needing repair. Like all Saabs the key to turbo reliability was regular servicing, clean oil and tuned fuel injection. A regular 9,650km (6,000 mile) service was the key to early turbo security. These were vital factors in prolonging the turbo engine's life – keeping it cool was another aspect that would soon lead to the addition of the intercooler to the 900 Turbo by Saab.

Before that happened, failed water pumps in the 99 were a sign that the turbo's latent heat was an issue. A Saab water injection kit reduced the turbo's operating temperature and increased the volume of the turbocharge. A large plastic fluid reservoir was plumbed in with a small motor to inject water upstream of the turbo; the boost could then be turned up and up to 45bhp extra secured. However, failure to monitor the supply of water meant that if it ran out, serious damage could be done to the unit. Saab fitted a cut-off device that activated when the water level dropped.

The British firm of Viking Motors designed a Ford Cosworth-based turbo intercooler for shoe-horning in under the 99's bonnet, and they and others fitted faster camshafts to boost top-end performance at the expense of low speed lag. Many private owners and race and rally drivers altered the boost pressure of their 99 Turbos. In the main the Saab engine handled the increase, but spectacular over-boosted failures were hardly the fault of the factory.

The usual Saab engine bugbear of a small oil leak did not disappear with the turbo unit either, but the engine had been around long enough for Saab and owners to know that it was not a terminal fault.

Inca wheel, iconic Saab design, and one of many great Saab alloy wheels.

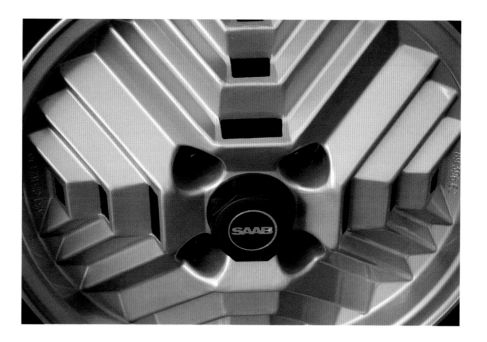

AN OWNER SPEAKS

Gary Stottler, owner of a Saab 99 EMS and a 99 Turbo, spoke to Mark McCourt, editor at *Hemmings Classic and Sports Car*, as follows:[15]

> To me, the Saab 99 is really all about the feel for the road. Saab did a really superb job of designing and building a car for people who are interested in driving – it's a car that communicates every nuance of the road to the driver. I think this is one reason that Saabs are so good in poor weather conditions. The 99 EMS is smooth, but it does not isolate the driver. You can hear noise, certainly louder than in a modern car, but it's 'good' noise that lets you know the details of what is going on with the machine and the road. In the EMS, you are very aware that the engine is spinning 4,000rpm at 70mph, but it's not bad or intrusive unless something changes that you need to know about. You hear wind rush, not in the sense of 'wind noise' that would imply a leak, but the air flowing over the car, alerting you to your speed and any crosswinds you might need to know about.

> The Turbo is also a very 'tactile' car in terms of its feel for the road, and the turbocharged torque is fantastic. The driving dynamics are truly superb. It is firm but not harsh, and the combination of the quick ratio manual steering and the crisp, direct four-speed gearbox makes it an extreme pleasure to drive. Those features did not translate entirely into the 900 Turbo, and I've never liked that as well as this. I remember driving a friend's 1976 BMW 2002 in the early 1980s, and thinking how twitchy it was compared to the Saab 99.

These words sum up what the feel of a Saab means. The essence of Saab, captured by the 99 EMS and 99 Turbo, really do come through, as does this owner's love of the marque and its cars.

Gearbox Troubles

The original four-speed gearbox and standard 99 clutch were tested by the torque of the 99 Turbo, and this was an area where the car developed issues in the long term. Stronger clutches and stronger gearbox components were the only answer.

As early as 1971, Saab was experimenting with a special casting technique for alloy gearboxes. By reducing and controlling

The 99 spirit captured by a Turbo rally car in Clarion colours.

temperature during casting, a more even, less porous casting could be made. This technique was known as 'chill cast', and created a stronger gearbox and pinion housing, but it made for a heavier gearbox. However, later changes to the blend of the alloy used in the gearboxes for the 99 and later 900, designed to be lighter by using a higher magnesium content, created some brittle casings that shattered spectacularly. If a Saab owner saw their gearbox strewn in pieces across the tarmac, they knew it had 'let go' in some style.

For the 900 Turbo from 1988, Saab fitted its gearboxes with a larger input shaft and more bearings in the primary gear, but from 1977 to 1980 it made very strong, non-brittle, chill-cast gearboxes, which served the EMS and the harder and hotter running Turbo very well indeed. Adding a fifth gear failed to upset the balance.

TURBO – THE 'HALO' EFFECT

Through the 99 Turbo, and through intelligent marketing, Saab managed to achieve a deep-seated change in the motoring public's perception of the Saab brand. The Turbo for the mass market had delivered a new, de-chromed, all-black, alloy-wheeled performance car aura to the previously solid but staid Saab brand image – even if decades of rallying had already changed the perceptions of the Saab cognoscenti.

In the 99 Turbo, Saab's image was comprehensively changed in one go by a single act. Few brand and marketing men could ever dream of transforming a product in such a manner. Through the increased sales (up by over 10,000 cars) the aged Saab 99 in Turbo guise not only earned money for Saab, it gave it international profile and credibility within the motor industry

LEFT: **The 99 Turbo rally spec. Beware: hot!**

BELOW: **The 99 Turbo. Red, not black, and a two-door. Seen blasting along, as intended.**

as well as in the minds of the media and public. By the time Saab had applied its turbo concept to the 900, and added a range of refinements from APC to a 16-valve head and up to 185bhp, the 900 Turbo would sell over 200,000 examples and become a definitive item, worldwide. Other car makers could now see that the Aeroplan men were serious scientists, engineers and designers across a broad spectrum of technology. If the Turbo concept did one thing for the Swedish marque, it made people take Saab seriously.

99 SPECIALS

In its eighteen years of life, the 99 was tweaked and modified by Saab to create a range of unusual models, limited editions, specialist cars and VIP transport. From a long-wheelbase 99 royal limousine GLE of 1976, to a panelled, van version of the three-door, 99s performed many roles. Tuned examples were great favourites of the Swedish and Finnish police forces. Saab's 99 build partner, Valmet of Finland, built stretched-wheelbase 99 five-door Combis with a curious double-B pillar enclosing a small extra window panel. This was the original 'Finlandia', and it was also fitted with two front seats in the rear, both divided by a centre console. With 20cm (8in) more legroom, in 1977 these cars were a precursor to a longer-bodied 99 four-door, and then the 900 with 20cm (8cm) extra in the wheelbase, which was added by making each specially built side door 10cm (4in) longer.

Saab built airport runway friction testers based on the 99 three-door, which sold well. These cars had a modified floorpan to accommodate the sensing probes and equipment, and were not cheap to manufacture.

Saab got as far as building full-size prototypes of a long-bodied 99 estate in both three-door and five-door variants. As late as 1974, speculation about the launch of a 99 estate continued, and Saab teased its enthusiasts with leaked images; the British Saab owners club even ran a drawing of the car, labelled 'X14', on the front cover of its magazine. Of note, there were two distinct Saab 99 estate cars built as prototypes: the first was from 1974 – a green 99 with chassis number 99022950 – and had a long rear estate section with large rear side windows rather in the manner of the Volvo 245 estate.

Then in 1977, Saab also built an unusually styled fastbacked or sports-tourer estate based on the 99. This brown, one-off car was known as the 'Multikaross' and hinted at a flexible sports tourer for suburban and outdoor or sports users, years before such a concept became popular. Of note, the 'Mulitkaross' or multibody style kept the 99's concave C pillar, and featured swept and angled rear side-window styling that aped the concave line of the existing panel. As such it looked remarkably similar to the later 9-5 estate's elegant rear side-window treatment. This shorter, sleeker, sports tourer-type estate car remained for many years in the Saab Museum store, undisplayed and forgotten. But Saab never did make the 99 estate, and missed out on the estate car boom of the 1980s. It was a lost opportunity to make more much needed money.

RIGHT: **An earlier incarnation of the 99 Turbo with the Saab bodykit.**

LEFT: **Fully blown! The 99 Turbo rally spec underbonnet delights.**

BELOW: **Sten Wenlo, who took Saab from Turbo to 9000.**

A strange V8-powered 99 was also built by Saab in the early 1970s. Chassis number 99102791 was a red 1972 car with an oddly extended long nose to house a single V8 engine development. Thankfully it did not get past the rough prototype stage.

Some 99s were fitted with faster steering racks, others in later production days received changes to the settings and weights in swivel arm bearings. A few 99s were fitted with power steering, shoehorned under the bonnet. Tropical market cars often saw the battery removed to the boot to reduce battery temperatures, and air conditioning could also be plumbed in. Many of these changes were not official factory specifications, but dealer and owner options. Many Turbo cars received water-injection kits to aid running and add to the boost, and numerous after-market performance kits were offered by a range of specialist suppliers such as Trent, Viking, Abbott, DCA, ANG in the UK and others in Europe and the USA.

Saab also launched a 99 special accessories catalogue that included a lower and wider front apron/spoiler, a mid-point rear wing for the two-door, and a three-piece rear lip-spoiler for the three-door. Special low-drag, stalk-mounted, rear-view

Peaceful Turbo seen at Swedish Day UK, in the elusive Acacia Green metallic.

LEFT: **Saab 99 Turbo with the Airflow bodykit and US spec lights.**

BELOW: **The 1980s face of the Saab 99 Turbo in black, green and red.**

TOP: **Two-tone Turbo. A French setting for a Swedish icon.**

LEFT: **The full Saab bodykit as seen on a rare sunroof-equipped 99T.**

BELOW: **The rarely seen 99 saloon rear deck spoiler made by Saab.**

99 SPECIALS AND MARKET VARIATIONS

Swedish market

- 99 four-door automatic, taxi specification 1972 onwards
- Police specification 99, two-door and four-door 1971 onwards
- 99 X7 base model, 1973
- 99 stretched royal limousine for King Carl Gustav XVI tour of America 1976
- 99 'Ronnie Peterson' F1 driver special build cars with autobox, air con, special handling kit, side stripes, also sold by Saab UK in RHD
- 99 EMS-Turbo, 100 pre-production cars special chassis nos 900–999
- 99 Rally and 1978 Turbo Rally 246bhp, prepared cars delivered to Saab Competition Department
- 99 five-door long-wheelbase Combi 1977: Valmet built 'Finlandia' for Swedish/Finnish market. 20cm (8in) extension at B post with two B pillars and extra side window slot. Two front seats in rear with centre console. This car led to a 99 stretched saloon with 10cm (4in) added to each door giving a 20cm (8in) stretch, followed by a stretched 900 CD branded, long body derivative
- Finlandia Turbo specification. Saab built three 99 Finlandia Turbos to full 99T spec

Denmark and Belgium

- 99 three-door Combi panel van 1975

USA market

- 99 E model 1971 injection engine on US cars
- 99 LE model with fuel injection, special trims 1973.
- 99 engine California spec for 1974 emmissions laws: catalyst and lambda offered, 1978
- 99 EMS in two-door style. Special accessories version for US market includes side stripes, and rare low-drag door mirror options. Under-bumper front spoiler and rear lip spoiler
- 99 EMS three-door styles. Three-door shell branded 'WagonBack' 1974
- 99 GLi auto and GLi two-door USA and Canada 1980
- 99 GLi to Aspen and Vail Police Department Spec 1980s

UK market

- 99 Turbo five-door EMS-based model, twenty-five cars imported 1980, three cars in black, others Cardinal Red metallic
- 99 Turbo 400 extra cars with two-door shells sold after original three-door Turbo brand
- 99 SAH power and handling kit 1.7-litre model 1970
- 99 Saab GB 'special' with Saab bodykit and A-pillar trims 1984

- 99 various dealer 'specials' in various body shapes and equipment specifications

Finland market

- 99 Kerosene-powered base model 'Petro' 1981
- 99 Finlandia, long-wheelbase 99 limousine details as above in two versions
- 99 Turbo base spec special two-door 1980
- 99 Turbo two-door base car. 300 exported. 1980

Norway market

- 99 four-door special base model 1978
- 99 Gli direct injection 118 bhp, with extra brightwork, special interior colours, 1981

Scandinavian/ Nordic market special

- 99 Economy model two- and four-door, five-speed, with low rolling resistance compound tyres 1982
- 99 GLi with injection in two- and four-door; 1,600 made, 1981

Australia market

- 99 EMS three-door with air con aftermarket option 1976
- 99 Turbo range includes Cardinal Red and air con cars

Africa market

- 99 base spec four-speed imported cars in East Africa. Some private imports to South Africa

Uruguayan market

- 99 produced from 100 kits delivered 1970, and *ad hoc* from kits thereafter. 100 Uruguayan 99s built. Sales in Uruguay, Argentina. Some cars finshed in BMW or Alfa Romeo paint shades. Locally sourced trim and fittings

Worldwide market

- 99 Saab Sport kit for 99 and 900 Turbo adds 30bhp 1982
- 99 'Airflow' after-market body kit from the Scandium company 1977
- 99 striping decal kits from Saab, popular in the USA and UK 1975
- 99 LEA4 fuel-injection automatic stops December 1974
- 99 LCA4 carburettor automatic starts January 1975

Note: Various Saab dealer trimmed and equipped specials and tuning specialist 99s were also created across Saab's global market place, notably in the USA, UK and the Netherlands. Production figures for the Saab 99 were 588,643.

THIS PAGE:

TOP: **The 99 in later form with 900-style bumpers and trims, and fitted with Inca wheels from the Turbo. A modern looking car yet one actually styled in 1965.**

ABOVE: **Reflecting light from a popular Saab colour, the pert rear styling of Sason's 99 captures the feel of the car.**

OPPOSITE PAGE:

TOP: **A 1970s interior fit for the 1980s. This one has a Turbo wheel fitted and has also been converted to automatic transmission using the correct gearbox and fuel-injection specification by Alan Sutcliffe.**

BOTTOM: **From the passenger seat, the 99's late model interior still looked great.**

door mirrors were also available in body paint colour. An EMS, twin side-stripe decal kit was also offered and was popular in the US market. Later in the 99's lifespan an Airflow body kit and Saab-manufactured A-pillar air slicers were marketed.

Saab built over half a million of its 99, and did so in Sweden, Finland, Denmark, Belgium, the Netherlands and Uruguay. Saab's one millionth car ever made rolled off the production line in the winter snow of 1976; fittingly, it was a 99 three-door Combi, finished in alabaster white. The first 99s were twenty-five development test cars hand welded up in 1967, the last 99s were the 7,145 cars sold in the 1984 model year, but in a strange tale of a seemingly alternative dimension, the 99 refused to die; it was about to morph into its own ghost.

Saab 99 detail: the revised rear lamps and 'five-speed' badging.

SAAB 90 – ABSTRACT ART

In 1984, Saab did what no other car maker has ever done in order to create a new model. Saab took two cars from its range, sawed them in half and built a 'cut and shut' special that was a weird and only slightly wonderful attempt at a stop-gap car in its model range.

The claims bears repetition: a major car manufacturer took the front and back of two different cars and welded them up to create a new model. Saab, in a play on words, called the 90 a 'prolongation of a classic', but it was a game of smoke and mirrors, the 'new' small Saab pitch for the 90 that Saab tried was a marketing hoax and everyone knew it. Yet Saab sold over 25,000 of the 90 in its short life (mostly to pensioners it seems), but the motoring press and the new, upmarket Saab client base, were not impressed. Saab forgot a vital question, if you had just bought a new 'prestige' branded big Saab, how would you feel to see the company trying to market an old 99 as a 'new' 90 alongside the upmarket branding? Saab 90 may have been a decent enough car, but it was a sign of desperation and a lack of planning.

Thus was the Saab 90, a car that was almost twenty years old when it was born. Somehow, it worked – but it was no real answer and it reflected a cash-strapped myopia that was and remains typical of a certain period at Saab. The Saab 90 was the front of the old Saab 99 two-door, conjoined with the back of the longer, newer, Saab 900, which although originally derived from the 99, did in two-door and four-door form feature an entirely new rear end design and tooling. The result was a long tailed thing that had the Sason and Envall short-nosed 99 front and curved windscreen slot, with a long Envall designed 900 tail stuck on the back. The rear side windows

Here is the 90 from the front – when it thought it was a 99.

The Saab 90 – when the front of the 99 was welded to the back of the new 900 two-door to create a new economy special for Saab. It was the world's weirdest 'cut and shut' car ever, but 25,000 were sold.

came from the old three-door 99/900 bodyshell and the rear windscreen from the newly tooled 900 four-door, as did the rear lamps.

Saab gave the 90 twin-tube sports dampers, shorter gear ratios, a re-angled steering rake that was 4 degrees steeper, automatic fuel cut-off and 900 style badging – minus the last zero – so they did not even have to tool up for new badges!

Inside it was pure 1970s Saab 99 right down to the fake wooden strip of exotic veneer that ran along the base of the dashboard, and the 90 still lacked power steering. There was a bigger 13.9 gallon fuel tank (with 400 miles range) – a good thing as this old, heavy gauge car only just scraped home to 30mpg; 0–60mph took a lethargic 12 seconds plus and the mid-range overtaking performance was near the bottom of the class. This was the Saab 1985cc engine without the turbo and tuned for economy.

Saab did nothing with the 99 and the 900s' old bug bear, the gearbox, and the handling remained slow-geared in steering terms, but it was not bad for a chassis that was two decades old, a fine testament to Saab's original work and the simple rightness of a rigid body and double wishbone suspension (long before Honda spend millions advertising their use of such suspension).

The headlining still dropped – even though Saab had twenty years' knowledge across two car ranges about that problem before they stuck it into the 90. The windscreen was not

deepened as it had been for the 900 – so the driver's view out was still like sitting in a deep Victorian bath tub looking out through a visor. As they had for the 99, Saab specified the kit from the 900 for the 90; the door mirrors, seats, rubbing strips, and so on. One non-900 delight was a choke lever – a manual choke, big enough to be pulled by a gloved Swedish hand. There was a five-speed manual gearbox and a top speed of about 100mph.

The car was overly rigid, crash safe, reliable and character-ful. But that was not enough and was never going to be. Many customers, press men and industry observers, wondered how on earth could a car maker survive by creating a new small 'bread and butter' model by welding two other models togeth-er? The 90 was old, heavy, slightly clunky, and unlikely to win 'convert' customers over from other brands. Yet it steered, rode and drove with aplomb, like a true Saab should, but it was also a curiously long-tailed, short-nosed beast.

Saab did what it always had done in development terms, and from 1985 to late 1987 tweaked the specification, throwing ever more luxurious fittings onto and into the 90. Saab even went to the expense of a new interior colour for the 90 – Bokhara – but the dashboard remained black, as it had for the eighteen previous years of the 99's life; even the 'fake' wood strip across the dashboard remained from its 1972 launch on the 99: this was a reincarnated car.

Snow Weasel

To prove the point, after three years on the market, the 90 died. Just before it died, though, the Finns had something special in mind, the Lumikko or "Snow Weasel" special edition Saab 90. Saab 90 enthusiasts now had their very own limited edition, with only ten examples made and finished in an all-white, body-kitted treatment that smacked of something very tacky indeed.

In total, 25,378 Saab 90s were made. It was sold in selected European countries only from 1985 to 1987 but actually began life in late 1984 as a 1985 model year offering, and the Swedes and the Dutch loved them. In Britain in 2012, just a handful remained registered. Many are still in use in rural Holland. In America, the 90 is almost unheard of amongst the Saab cognoscenti. The Saab 90, solid and dependable was the automotive equivalent of a reproduction antique. It was a brand-new car based on a car first engineered in 1967. Saab purists will argue that its reality and success in 1985–87 speaks volumes for the integrity of Saab engineering, but those with less rose-tinted glasses will remember the 90 as marking a decline; it was not Saab's finest hour, however good the lineage. Ultimately, the 90 was neither fish nor fowl and in marketing terms was an oddity.

99 NOT OUT

It is with the 90's lineage of the Saab 99 that the 99 story should end. Surely the Saab 90 was a strange moment, if not an aberration, amid Saab's glittering history of innovation. It was the 99 that really took Saab onto the international stage and, in Turbo guise, created a new era and a new story for Saab. Without the 99 and the 99 Turbo, Saab would never have survived. Few other cars gave the motoring public what the 99 delivered. For its style, safety, speed and sheer character, the 99 was a car that sold across the world and became a long term member of many families. Many children grew up with their parents' 99s and then took their first driving lesson in the same family car. The Saab 99 was one of Saab's finest achievements, and then incredibly, its origins lived on as the Saab 900. No other car can claim such a record , not even the icons of motoring longevity. For Saab and Saab fans, 99 was and remains, a special number.

And the 99 begat the 900… These two members of the international Saab family are seen in an English country pub setting in Somerset.

THE 900

Silver blue paint, flat front, 'Bugatti'-type
brushed aluminium wheel trims – a stunning
early 900, and one of Bob Sinclair's favourites.

EIGHTIES ICON OF STYLE AND SAFETY

THE 900 | *EIGHTIES ICON OF STYLE AND SAFETY*

BY 1979 THE SAAB 99 Turbo – over ten years old as a production car at its launch – found itself pitched in a price comparison with the likes of the Ford Capri, newly launched BMW 3 series, and Volkswagen Scirocco, followed up by truly new generation cars such as the Audi Coupé. Saab's top-of-the-range luxury 99 'GLE' and 'Turbo' 99s also had to fight off the likes of the superb revised Audi 100, Volvo's old war horse the 244, the newer Renault 30 and the Peugeot 604, both with the Volvo co-op Franco-Swedish V6 engine. The Peugeot 604's elegant Paul Bracq styling and interior tempted many buyers (Bracq being the man who designed the timeless perfection of the nose and cockpit shaping of France's TGV train). And what of the Robert Opron-styled Citroën CX Gti, or the BMW 5 Series, or the ancient Jaguar XJ6, all priced within a few pounds of a top-of-the-range Saab? Even the Ford Granada of the 1980s looked sharp and modern, although it was, in fact, via Uwe Bahnsen's lightly re-skinned version of the original late 1960s Granada Mk1, identical in its underpinnings hidden behind its flash new plastic dashboard and 'Ghia' trim badges.

Into this changing world, against shiny, sharp-edged, brand new cars, Saab and its old but excellent stagers, honed and refined as they were, not least as the stunning 'Turbo' range, carried on towards a crisis as then unsighted upon the horizon.

With its focus on more sales, building more cars and driving costs down, the 'prestige Saab' took over as the mindset. In the expanding American market, under Bob Sinclair's guidance, a more upmarket Saab was a tempting prize, not least as the car would, perhaps like BMWs, have a defined niche of its own. If ever there was a moment when, after the Saab 92 of 1949, a Saab car would encapsulate the ethos of Saab, and that spirit of Saab, the 900 was that car.

Before it was designed, the genesis of the Saab 900 began with a rare process. Saab's design engineers did not sit down with a budget to create an entirely new model, they sat down to create a new version of a basic design that was already old. How on earth were they going to pull off this trick? Could a new car be created? The answer was that it could, and it would be more 'new', more re-engineered, than the so-called 'new' Ford

The 1980 900 Turbo in black on Inca wheels. Launched in Monte Carlo.

Granada Mk2, a car that was nothing more than a re-skin of a decade-old design, with only the outer skin – the icing sugar – re-coated. Saab were going to do more than Ford had so cleverly got away with: Saab were, to use an architectural or builder's analogy, going to do more than repaint the walls, they were going to rebuild the structure but leave the roof alone. Factors to be considered included new US safety legislation – an irony not lost on the men of Saab who had been building in safety long before it became fashionable to do so.

Saab's existing top-of-the-range non-Turbo model in 1977–78 was the 99 GLE, a luxury-trimmed four-door 99 that came with all the bells and whistles, yet in effect was still a medium-sized car – and a smaller one, at that, in comparison to the acres of steel framed by the likes of the Ford Granada or Volvo 164.

And how long would any heavily revised, new Saab, have to survive in the market place before a totally new Saab saloon for the late 1980s would emerge? Was the new car – to be called the 900, in a prolongation of the '9' series theme – a stop-gap or a long-term product plan?

One thing was for sure, Saab could not use the old 99 saloon shape with its 1960s concave rear end as a basis for a modern car. So back in 1977, Saab decided to take Bjorn Envall's 99 five-door 'Combi' bodyshell and create a classy hatchback for the 1980s. Other car makers were also taking the fastback route: the Lancia Gamma, Rover SD1, Audi 100 Avant, Renault 30 and others were all waiting in the wings. Executive fastbacks were the theme of the era, even if Ford, BMW, Mercedes, Peugeot and Volvo all eschewed such temptations for many years to come.

THE 900 MEN

The team that created the first Saab 900 – correctly conceived and thoroughly engineered – were as follows:

Stig Norlin: head of 900 development
Björn Envall: design and styling
Harry Eriksson: interior and climate
Bernt-Ake Karlsson: modelmaker (clay)
Lars Nilsson: safety features and engineering
Magnus Roland: test and development
Per-Borje Elg: marketing/brochures
Dick Olsson: bodywork design/engineering
Hakan Danielsson: aerodynamics
Olle Granlund: motor and turbo installation

THOROUGHLY RE-ENGINEERED

Saab undertook a fundamental reassessment of the 99. From seats to safety, from cabin to wheels, everything would be improved upon. The first major decision was to add 50mm (2in) to the wheelbase and just under 10mm ($\frac{1}{2}$in) to the track. This delivered two major benefits: more cabin legroom and a longer body, and with better handling from the wider axle. But where to add that length? Using the 99's door pressings and rear panels meant that the cabin itself could not be stretched, but cleverly, Saab added the extra space within the cabin at the junction of the front bulkhead and front wheel arches, thereby creating more room in the front of the cabin.

A Rony Lutz classic drawing – a 900 Turbo in Acacia Green.

Adding Length and Solving Problems

The immediate effect of this was to create a problem with the windscreen pillars or A posts. Previously on the 99 these pillars had been an unbroken, 2.5mm rolled steel, triangulated beam running from the top of the roof down to the back of the front wheel arches. This beam, far stronger than any other car windscreen frame, gave a solid, steel cage effect to the front of the cabin. But moving the wheel arches forwards by 50mm left nowhere for the beam to be tied down to at its bottom end, as the old mounting point was gone.

The answer was to cut off this beam at the scuttle/firewall and securely weld it to the bulkhead and inner wing rail where these major panels met at the corners of the windscreen. Saab then beefed up the area by inserting a tubular steel cross-member transversely across the car behind the dashboard. The 99's old narrow slit of a windscreen was deepened by 37mm (1.5in) across its curved lower edge, adding better visibility and style. Behind it, the 99's curved steel dashboard panel was removed. The 900 was also given a new toe-board floor panel and inner front wing panels.

Under the bonnet, Saab removed steel to soften up the new longer front end to add better impact-absorbing capacity. The 99 had had a sealed steel vault of an engine bay, and by reducing its rigidity in key areas it could be made to deform more progressively. However, the massive wheel arches, hewn from solid steel, remained – they offered great strength and lots of impact-absorbing metal. Down in the lower engine bay, up near the new, longer nose, Saab added special Z-shaped beams to transfer crash energy down into the core of the car.

One problem with front-hinged bonnets was their tendency to lift their rear trailing edges in a crash and push the sharp, rear edge of the bonnet into the windscreen. Saab had developed a way of stopping this happening with the 99, and further refined it for the 900 – each rear corner of the bonnet was mounted with wheels that ran on a miniature, tracked locking device.

For the cabin, thicker under-floor cross-members were added – but the unusual boxed steel, side sill beams and cut-under door apertures remained. Like the 99, the 900 avoided spot-welded, thin steel sills of normal monocoque car design. The gauge of the roof steel was increased – you could hit the roof of the 900, hard, with a clenched fist directly over the front and rear doors, and the roof panel would not flex at all. Saabs already had proper steel beams inside the doors to offer lateral compression, increasing impact intrusion resistance and channelling crash forces away into the door frames, but for the 900, Saab made another industry first: it added large foam pads into the doors to further absorb side-impact energy in the vital chest and hip region of the occupants.

Alpine setting for a 1981 900 Turbo, really looking the part.

The rear of the car – designed later in the 1970s as the 99 three- and five-door – featured a predetermined collapsible rear impact zone and very strong steel liners to the rear or C pillars. The fuel tank was, as ever, protected between the rear wheels, an obvious move perhaps, but not all 1970s and 1980s cars had learned that lesson, and there was one, newly designed, iconic car of the 1980s that still had the fuel tank mounted at its rear corner directly behind the bumper, despite its manufacturer's previous and much publicized experience of the issues involved.

Along with an under-dashboard 'knee roll' to protect the legs of unbelted (American) occupants, there were padded B pillars and a thick, head impact-reducing glassfibre roof lining that extended down over the roof pillars and roof side rail reinforcements in a manner not practised in other cars. The steering wheel was not only collapsible as per the norm, but had a three-section impact-absorbing chest pad to reduce injuries to the driver. The steering wheel was also graded to offer differing rates of compression to reduce chest and head injuries; this was achieved through using a 'bellows'-type steel mesh in the column, and cellular plastic and rubber chambers in the hub. Saab's 900 steering wheel design was the safest in the world.

The lower dashboard 'knee roll' was designed to spread impact loads along the leg bones of impacting occupants and to avoid localized concentrations of energy, which would normally snap leg bones. By preventing serious injury being transmitted in 'hot spots' to lower leg, thigh and hip bones, occupant protection and survivability was greatly enhanced as compared

ABOVE: **Elegance and aerodynamics exemplified. The Saab 900 MkI 'flat-front' three-door coupé.**

LEFT: **The 1981 900 T interior.**

BELOW: **Saab style by night. 900 T circa 1981.**

to normal cars. So effective was this Saab measure that at 50km/h (30mph), an unbelted front seat occupant impacting the dashboard with their legs would not suffer a thigh bone fracture. In 1979 this placed the Saab 900 well ahead of leg/thigh bone injury criteria measurement levels proposed in US crash safety legislation for 1984 and beyond. This singular example of Saab's research work provides the reader with tangible evidence of how Saab's superior safety ethos was real, and not a piece of marketing spin.

Clearly the Saab 900s interior was a very safe place to be. This was enhanced by the very strong, tubular steel-framed seats and high-backed integral headrests. Unlike most car makers, Saab (and Volvo) had discovered that soft, round-shaped headrest 'pillows' that jutted out of the seat backs on thin, flimsy metal supports, were not just useless in a crash, they could, by encouraging the neck to pivot around their pillow-type design, increase neck injuries and in some cases cause them. Strangely, even the safety-conscious German car makers were still persisting with round pillow-type headrests at this time, despite their dangers. Saab's own real-life crash investigation unit (along with Volvo's) had made this discovery early on, and the 99 had been given the much safer 'tombstone'-type solid high-backed seats with integral, solid head supports. Soon the 900 would get a revised and even safer version that would be a hallmark of Saab seat design for the next thirty years.

The 900, based on the foundations of the 99, yet improved upon, was crash tested at full frontal and 30 per cent offset or overlap barrier crash testing at over 50km/h (30mph) as early as 1977. In all cases the key advanced Saab criteria were met, namely:

- The passenger cabin remained intact
- The doors retained their shape, remained in the closed position and could be opened by hand using the handles
- All window glass remained in place
- The floorpan did not buckle or split
- Wheel-arch intrusion was minimal
- The bonnet (hood) must deform as planned yet retain its position
- The occupants must remain within the passenger cabin and not be exposed to lethal impact forces

These were the vital safety parameters that a Saab had to meet, and were set long before any subsequent legislation to make such requirements law. Such attention to passive occupant safety was still rare in 1979; Volvo and a few other car makers were there, but Saab's 900 offered state-of-the-art protective crash safety that was so advanced it kept the car safe and safety legal for years to come in the face of ever-increasing legislation.

With its uniquely constructed and very strong windscreen pillars and padded, safe fittings, the Saab 900 offered excellent frontal, roll-over and side-impact protection at a time when many car makers were building thin-skinned, low-fronted, soft metal, lightweight cars that simply folded up if you crashed them. Like any car, the 900 was no guarantee of survival, but its injury and fatality rates were very low in comparison to some of its more fashionable competitors. Your chances of surviving a heavy crash in a 900 were several times better than in certain similar-sized cars of its era, and the official safety survey figures confirmed it, as did the experience of many owners who upon surviving a major crash in a 900 were often told by the rescue services of their having been fortunate to have been in a Saab. It was not marketing hype, it was simply true, and stemmed from sound Saab engineering.

PROPERLY BUILT

Having been subjected to extensive under-sealing and the application of chemical paint application, and with all brightwork sealed under a pvc skin or dechromed in black, 900s resisted rust and remained sealed throughout even the harshest of Scandinavian weather conditions. When rust did occur, it was in door bottoms and front wing crowns and along the edges of the bonnet.

Other high quality touches to the 900 included the world's first cabin air filter, which would remove pollution and pollen provided the filter was kept clean. The cabin air and heating

---

SAAB 900 LAUNCH MODEL LINE-UP

This is the range unveiled in May 1978 for the 1979 model year, with sales commencing in late 1979:

900 GL three-door 100bhp (73kW)
900 GLS three-door 108bhp (79kW)
900 GLS five-door
900 GLS five-door with three-speed auto
900 EMS three-door 118bhp (87kW)
900 GLE five-door 118bhp (87kW)
900 Turbo 8-valve three-door
900 Turbo 8-valve five-door 145bhp (107kW)

British price range in £ sterling at launch:
900 GL base model: £5,525. Top Turbo model: £8,995.

system was the most efficient in the world, with a maximum cabin airflow rate of 6m/3min via a vacuum-controlled system operated from an ergonomically designed control centre on the facia.

Saab's claim was that the 900 was the most thoroughly engineered quality car on the market. Every aspect of the car – safety, handling, engine, noise, harshness, vibration (NVH) and all the key areas of dynamics – even the interaction between the suspension and the seat cushioning – was tuned as never before in a Saab or any car. The 900 boasted over 800 detail improvements over its 99 model ancestor. Saab proudly said of the 900:

> Each of the 900 models satisfies strict demands on safety and road behaviour. They are created and designed on the basis of expected regulations on various markets up to the mid-1980s. And they satisfy with a wide margin the stricter collision safety regulations coming into force in the USA in the autumn of 1978. But merely keeping pace with the legislators has not been the aim in the development of the Saab 900 series. Closer study will reveal that the cars are the result of innovative work aimed at keeping them ahead of legislative demands and of the competitors.

These were not hollow, marketing hype words: they were facts. The Saab 900 exceeded all known and impending safety requirements not just by a few per cent, but by a large margin. Very few other car manufacturers could make such a bold claim of fact. Björn Envall was the 'father' or 'godfather' of the 900, and he and his team of about ten people created the best car they could. It was a car built up to an engineering target, not

down to a cost, as Envall always proudly said. And even though Saab spent money on the 900's exquisite detailing, it still made massive profits from the car.

AERODYNAMIC EXCELLENCE

In 1978 most executive or prestige class cars were three-box design shapes, with bonnet (hood), cabin turret and then boot (trunk). The average aerodynamic drag coefficient of such cars, whether they were Volvo, BMW, Mercedes Benz, Rover, Fiat or Ford, was about Cd 0.44 to Cd 0.50, and these figures had not really changed in decades. Volvo's Saab 900 rival, the 240 series, wafted along with an aerodynamic 'barn door' of Cd 0.44. Only Citroën, in 1978, was producing truly low drag cars with a Cd range of less than Cd 0.39. The NSU Ro 80 had been another glorious, low Cd exception at Cd 0.37, and Rover's new SD1 shape, and certain Audi fastbacks, and super-smooth high-tailed saloons, including some Mercedes cars that were soon to be announced, were achieving the lower Cd 0.36 to 0.39 figures. But in the main, cars remained unaerodynamic lumps trailing vast wakes and vortices of lift and base wake drag and dirtying eddies.

Not so Saab, however. The 99 three- and five-door shell had a low Cd of 0.35, though the 99 saloon with larger bumpers worsened to Cd 0.37. But the new 900 had a low Cd range of just below Cd 0.36 for the hatchbacks to Cd 0.37 for the later saloons. The 'slant front' styling revision of 1987, with a 28-degree sweep back and smooth, curved, integrated bumper mouldings, brought the drag coefficient down to Cd 0.35. Just as importantly, the 900 had excellent side-wind stability, clean separation points for the airflow, and pressure-control vanes

Bluebird, Saab style.

under the car to reduce lift and yaw. What other car could boast such technology? And just like the Citroën CX and later C6, the 900 offered self-cleaning windows and 'clean' side airflow and tail separation. The rear 'lip' spoiler at the base of the 900's rear hatchback windscreen was the result of many hours' work. By tuning its shape, Saab reaped a massive 25 per cent drag reduction from its effect; this was approximately four times better than the usual effect of a rear spoiler.

SPECIFICATIONS SAAB 900 TURBO 1979

The new 900, presented in May 1978 for the 1979 model year launch in late 1978.

Body

Base 99 unit re-engineered and lengthened. Increased reinforcements and improved crush zones. Side-impact bars in all doors with transverse steel beam cross-brace under facia and in rear seats of Combi-bodied cars

Engine:

Type	4-cylinder longitudinal turbocharged engine. 8-valve ohc and chain-driven cam
Cylinders	4
Bore & stroke	90mm×78mm
Capacity	1985cc
Compression ratio	7.2:1
Carburettor	Mechanical fuel injection: Garret turbocharger with waster gate and charge regulation with 0.70 to +/- 0.05 bars
Max. power	145bhp (107kW)
Max. torque	175lb ft (235Nm) @ 3,250rpm

Transmission

Front-wheel drive via four-speed manual gearbox or three-speed automatic

Suspension and steering

Suspension	Front double wishbones with coil springs and damper. Rear beam axle with tube link locating arms and Panhard rod. Bilstein gas shock absorbers/dampers all round

Wheels and tyres

Light alloy vented rims on 195/60 HR Pirelli tyres; five-door uses Michelin TRX 180/65 HR tyres

Brakes

All disc, diagonally split system

Dimensions

Wheelbase	2,525mm (99in)
Length	4,739mm (187in)
Width	1,690mm (67in)
Height	1,430mm (56in)

Top speed

195km/h (120mph)

The later model, flat-front 900 Turbo with the body cladding kit. In the USA this was the 'SPG' model.

Saab's own unique GLE variant style is well captured in the 'blinged-up' 900 saloon. Lots of stainless steel addenda and brushed wheel trims.

Wheels, Seats and an Array of Trims

A vast range of alloy wheel designs was created during the 900's long life, but perhaps the 'Turbine', 'Super Inca' and 'Three Hole Teardrop' wheels were the most famous. A range of alloy wheels from the 9000 also looked good on 900s, and early 900 GLE models could be had with smart, brushed alloy wheel trims that were likened to a Bugatti design motif. Latterly, cross-spoke alloys were a common choice, notably on US cars. The three-door Turbo version was launched with the 'Inca' wheels from the 99 Turbo, whereas the five-door 900 Turbo was equipped with the elegant new 'Turbine' multi-spoke, aviation-inspired wheel design.

The 900 had room under its better visually balanced, longer nose for a range of improvements, not least power steering. In the cabin there was a high quality moulding for the one-piece dashboard unit, which followed aviation design principles in its ergonomics. The entire dashboard was hoisted into the car in one go during build, using a special tool. All fittings and connections were installed beforehand and just had to be plugged in when lowered into the car.

Saab tuned the wishbone front suspension and the steering geometry to provide the best possible recovery characteristics in the event of tyre blow-out. The front coil springs, were, importantly, pivot mounted, which allowed them to work without deflection.

The new car was built and trimmed to high standards. Restful interior colours were used, such as pale blue, mid-tan and emerald green, and in Turbo guise, the bright crimson previously seen on the 99 Turbo. A chunky three-spoke steering wheel of high quality moulding was used on the Turbo, whereas lesser models received a simpler steering wheel. Later models benefited from the four- and three-spoke wheels fitted to the new Saab 9000.

US specification cars were the first 900s to receive an airbag-equipped wheel. This came from an external supplier, and was similar to the ungainly steering wheel seen on several American cars of the 1980s. Many 900 owners fitted the three-spoke wooden Nardi or Mota-Lita type wood-rimmed, alloy-spoked steering wheel first seen on certain factory-spec 900 Turbo models. This often matched the grain and colour of the darker wood used on 900 facia and centre console inserts.

Early 900s were fitted with 99-style high-backed 'Tombstone' front seats, fitted with plug-in headrest cushions. By 1981, however, a newer headrest design was introduced, allowing better visibility. This featured a rolled or horizontal 'collar'-type head protector to the top of the seat. In the early 1980s the 900 retained Saab 99-inspired seat coverings and patterns, but by the mid-1980s new leather coverings, and revised seat-cover patterns for both cloth and leather, were introduced. Dove Grey became a very popular trim choice, being more subtle than some of Saab's brightly hued, strong browns, greens, reds and blues used in the 99s and earlier 900s.

Though launched with an 8-valve engine, the work of the Saab engine designers under Per Gillbrand at Sodertalje on the Saab engines and the new 9000's power plant soon resulted in a superb, 16-valve head design that beat Mercedes-Benz to the finish line – Saab's 16-valve unit was launched first, and the Germans came in second. Gillbrand had predicted the multi-valve technology.

LEFT: **900s of all types descended on Paris in 2010 for a rally that ended at Le Bourget airport. Here we see flat-front, convertible and slant-nose 900s.**

BELOW: **The 28-degree slant-nose styling changes to the classic 900 shape brought a fresh look for the late 1980s.**

16-valve slant four – all of Saab's expertise framed.

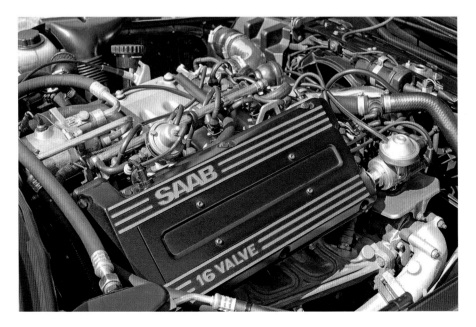

The Saab 900 was a forensically designed car with a range of characteristics topped off by the sensational, almost supercar performance of the Turbo models. As Saab said on the front of its highly detailed and intellectually appealing car brochure, the Saab 900 was 'correctly conceived and properly built'; or as it also put it: 'The most intelligent car ever built.' Saab also produced the most intelligent sales information and brochures for the 900: it issued a beautiful range of brochures for the 900's launch, and with each new model or revision, further publications, packed with details and fine photography and drawings, were issued.

The key figure in Saab's artwork department and graphics portfolio was an artist with the skills of an engineer, and his name was not Sason, but Rony Lutz.

900 special edition – named after the Saab Scarab green paint and wearing special 'Scarabee' badges.

RONY LUTZ – THE X-RAY ARTIST

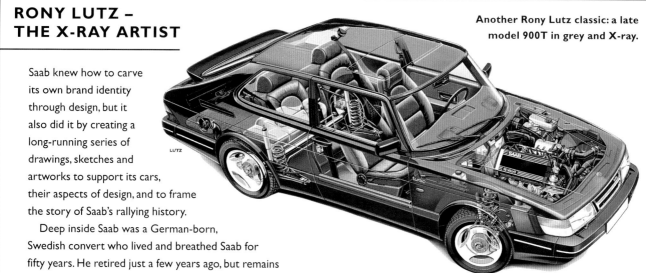

Another Rony Lutz classic: a late model 900T in grey and X-ray.

Saab knew how to carve its own brand identity through design, but it also did it by creating a long-running series of drawings, sketches and artworks to support its cars, their aspects of design, and to frame the story of Saab's rallying history.

Deep inside Saab was a German-born, Swedish convert who lived and breathed Saab for fifty years. He retired just a few years ago, but remains a hero of Saab, albeit in a way that is less well known beyond the Saab *cognoscenti*. The man was Rony Lutz. His work carried on the graphical representations of Gunnar Sjögren – otherwise known as 'GAS' – but in a new style and to a wider global audience. From the 99 in its pre-Turbo days, through to the 9-3, Lutz gladly drew Saabs – and Saab under GM also benefited from the profile created by Lutz's artworks.

It was Lutz who produced the exquisite x-ray drawings of styling, engineering sub-structure and engines that Saab produced with every new model launch. But although Lutz became famous for the X-ray views, his artworks ranged far wider than just those drawings, and he produced paintings, posters, graphic design images and a whole wonderful collection of what might be called 'Saabology'.

Lutz used to take car components back to his studio, including doors and aerodynamics addenda, and would then sketch in the foundations of the drawing with a pencil. His next step was to build up the colours and depth of field with pencils, inks and water-based paints applied with a brush. Then he gave his works that feel of slick industrial design graphics with an airbrush. Sixten Sason drew an X-ray image of the 92, Gunnar Sjögren made coloured paintings of the 93 to 96 ranges, but Rony Lutz produced what must rank as one of the motor industry's greatest portfolios of automotive art. Only a company such as Saab would have supported such a man and his talent, and his drawings featured in all Saab's brochures and PR material.

Rony Lutz might therefore be called the art of Saab.

A WORLD CLASS CAR

The 900 received great reviews all over the world. Here was a genuinely safe, yet sporting car, with panache and style and a class that took it beyond the clichés of BMW or Cadillac. In Britain, *Autosport* stated in its review that the 900 owner would be correct in thinking that it was 'Just about the best motor car which is at present being made, anywhere.'

By 1982, after its full US launch, Saab had sold 63,400 of the 900 range worldwide; this included the new four-door or 'booted' saloon that was launched across the range in 1981. In the USA, the 900 sold 18,003 in 1982, and that figure rose every month for over five years. In 1982 the British bought over 7,000 of the new car, and an LPG-powered version was also announced for the Swedish market. The new Automatic

Performance Control (APC) system, unveiled by Saab in 1980, found its way on to the Scandinavian market 900 Turbo by mid-1982, and worldwide within eighteen months. This system automatically sensed states of tune and combustion within the cylinder head created by variations in grades of fuel, and adjusted turbo and fuel settings in response.

Throughout the 1980s, Saab did what it had always done: it refined its car. The B-series engines gave way to the H-series, with improvements to major components and changes in compression and weights. The H-series engine weighed 12kg (26.5lb) less than the early engine. Changes were made to the turbo unit's size and actuation method. Water pumps were improved, and a series of bumper moulding and side trim changes were made, leading to smoother styling and panel surfacing with a reduction in local boundary layer disturbances.

The 900 T trio. Note the larger rear deck spoiler and side vent styling.

The ultimate 'real' Saab perhaps: the 900T 16S with everything on it, also seen in the similar 'Carlsson' spec.

RIGHT: **The real deal. Classic 900 Turbo S with larger rear spoiler and bodykit.**

ABOVE: **The stunning paint finish of this 900 T16S is matched by what is under the bonnet.**

The biggest news was in 1984, when the 8-valve head became a 16-valve unit – and so was born the 900 Turbo 16 with 175bhp (129kW), assisted by an intercooler and the domed cylinder heads of the revised engine. Double overhead camshafts and hydraulic valve lifters all helped the 900 breathe with cleaner, smoother, more efficient combustion. By 1986 Saab had fitted the intercooler to the 8-valve base engines too, and from 1987onwards the US specification catalysts were fitted to European cars. In 1988 a significant change to water cooling of the turbo housings was added to prolong turbocharger life. In 1989, 8-valve Turbo engines were faded out. Anti-lock brakes became a standard fitting from 1992.

SAAB 900 TURBO 16 (1984)

Engine	
Type	16-valve Automatic Performance Control (APC) system. Garrett Air Research T3 model turbocharger with intercooler. Waste gate control
Cylinders	4
Max. power	175bhp (130kW) @ 5,000rpm
Max. torque	202lb/ft (274Nm) @ 3,200rpm

THIS PAGE:

ABOVE LEFT: **A rare 900T16S two-door undergoing repair; note the massive inner front wing housings and double-skinned wing panels. The cross-member also ensured efficient energy absorption.**

ABOVE RIGHT: **The 900 engine bay, with impact beams and front wing crown structure clearly visible. Few other cars had this amount of steel under the bonnet. The complete car is seen in the following photographs.**

BELOW: **Back to black, or not. The 900 T16S with bodykit two-door shell in Odorado grey. Only 263 of these exact spec cars were made by Saab, solely for the British market.**

OPPOSITE PAGE:

TOP: **The stylish rear design of the saloon was another piece of Bjorn Envall excellence, also seen on the four-door shell.**

BOTTOM: **Leather-lined cocoon. The later model 900 interior, this time from the 900 T16S featured.**

RIGHT: **The British market 'Jubilee' edition 900 three-door with special stripes, sunroof, larger spoiler and 'Super Inca' wheel upgrades.**

BELOW: **Turbo blues are not likely under this bonnet.**

AMERICA AND A SOFT-TOP

The idea of creating a sportier Saab, or something special, had been bouncing around amongst the petrol-heads at Trollhättan for some time. But any variation on the 900 theme would be based on a car already into its prime, so what expense on body style or structural changes could be justified?

Inside Saab, the idea for a soft-top – a full convertible, or cabriolet – was already known; indeed, Sixten Sason had dreamed up a 92 convertible soft-top in 1951, and a Saab

employee had built a soft-top 96 in the 1970s as a private venture. But Saab had ignored the convertible or cabriolet, just as it had ignored the estate car market.

In truth a cabriolet was a description that originally applied to open-top cars that retained a portion of their roof, in the manner of the style that became known in the 1970s as the 'Targa'. A full convertible or a partial convertible retained a roll-over hoop at the B pillars or a Triumph Stag-style 'T'-bar bracing structure. A British firm, Lynx Engineering, had also experimented with a soft-top 900 idea, and created two such targa-topped cars that kept their B pillars with a cross-brace roof bar, and had a specially made soft-top. At a fee of £4,000 per conversion, the buyer base was all but invisible.

In America, Bob Sinclair – ever wanting to push the 900 upmarket – had conceived and rejected the idea of a fully convertible 900, albeit lavishly trimmed and able to earn strong profit margins. The trouble lay in the three-door 900's rising waist line, since any 'chopped' version would look ungainly. But Saab solved Sinclair's problem for him, by coming up with the new rear styling of the 900 two-door saloon, which made a soft-top restyle much easier.

In 1979 Saab in the USA had rarely made a profit, but in the 1980s that was all changed, as a near-1,000 per cent increase in turnover was created. For 1982 Saab had wanted Sinclair to accept a batch of basic two-door 900-series cars for the American market place. Sinclair, summoned with Sten Helling to a sales conference in Sweden, saw no such market for an 'economy special' – the 900 was too big to be an economy car, and any such branding would damage all the work Saab America had done to reposition Saab in the market place. Saab wanted Sinclair to take 1,000 or maybe even 2,000 extra Saabs a year, and told Sinclair that they could be kitted out with whatever he wanted. This led Bob Sinclair to conceive of a luxury,

The prototype that won the day and added allure to Saab on a world stage.

leather-lined, alloy-wheeled, turbocharged limited edition two-door Saab for his American customers – and the key attraction was that it had to be a soft-top. Saab's Sten Lundin was shocked, but soon came back with Sten Wenlo to assess the idea.

So was born the 900 convertible. With the go-ahead from Wenlo, and up to $20,000 dollars as start-up fund, in 1983 Sinclair commissioned the highly experienced American Sunroof Company (ASC) to build a prototype. Meanwhile Saab held an internal competition, and the Swedes created a targa-topped 900 convertible that retained the existing windscreen pillars and B pillar to provide a roll-over hoop. However, it lacked the style that Saab knew such an expensive re-working of the 900 needed.

The Americans, meanwhile, despite the poor offer of a few thousand US dollars, went on with creating a true California-style soft-top. The ASC knew a good opportunity when it saw

it, and Sinclair was a consummate persuader. The car was built under the leadership of Steven Rossi, though the men in Troll-hättan wanted to build the new car themselves. But Sinclair and the ASC came up trumps, producing a well engineered, triple-layered, winter-proof soft-top, which also had major structural reinforcements.

Uniquely, the car also had its A pillars, the entire windscreen surround being re-angled to a faster rake than the donor 900 design. Few people spot this major design and styling difference in the classic 900 convertible – significantly more steeply angled A pillars. This was not an easy task, as the 900 had aviation standard, 2.5mm rolled steel sandwich A posts that no other car maker had ever used. ASC had a tough time resetting them and adapting the curved windscreen to fit, but the change was made nonetheless. The windscreen shape also had to be changed to fit the new rake angle, an expensive alteration.

The alternative cabrio-type Saab proposal.

A Saab 900 T, the roof down and with unique Saab parts styling modifications, including headlamp shrouds.

The interior of the car, with the thick-rimmed wooden steering wheel.

Although lacking a targa or T-bar roof brace, and also lacking a 'pop-up' roll hoop, the soft-top 900 did offer its occupants the incredible strength of the 900's steel sandwich-type, reinforced windscreen pillars. ASC had also further strengthened them, and the scuttle and sills, and had also increased the steel gauge used. For safety-obsessed Saab, the 900's windscreen frame provided acceptable roll-over and frontal crash protection. Scuttle shake – that old bug-bear of soft-tops – was, however, unlikely to be eliminated, and some did indeed remain. The car was finished in a stunning pearlescent white, with a white hood and burgundy leather interior.

The new soft-top was displayed at the 1983 Frankfurt Motor Show, to great acclaim, and the go-ahead was then given for a limited series production of 2,000 cars to start in 1984. First US deliveries of the Finnish, Valmet-built 900 convertible began for the 1986 model year – appropriately enough, in the American market. The reaction was massive, and Saab sold 10,000 of the convertible 900s in 1991. A special 10,000 edition, one-off car was created with a unique Pierre Olofsson-designed interior and exterior colour scheme. For 1992, a 900 Turbo 19S Aero convertible was Saab's highlight on the world market.

Altogether Saab sold 48,888 convertibles, and it was the last 900 left on sale after the Ruby models signalled the end of production. Demand was so strong that the new GM-based 900 was soon subjected to the convertible treatment, and went on to be a bestseller for Saab in all its subsequent incarnations.

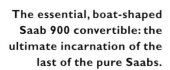

The essential, boat-shaped Saab 900 convertible: the ultimate incarnation of the last of the pure Saabs.

The increased A-pillar rake of the convertible is shown here as a 900 T poses in La Roche Bernard, France.

SAAB 900 SPECIAL/LIMITED EDITIONS FROM MANUFACTURER OR DEALER/CONCESSIONAIRE

The 900 was available in an amazing number of factory and dealer special trims and editions. This listing also includes factory prototype and one-off car build information:

- **Sweden and Britain 'EMS' 1979–80:** Very rare, limited production EMS continuation from 99 into 900. Cardinal Red, Acacia Green or Grey
- **Europe market: 900 'Pansar':** a one-off bullet-proof and reinforced 900T executive car proposed at the height of European terrorism and kidnap fashion. One factory spec car built by Sandvik and finished in blue, registration number GGY 471. Last seen in Saab Museum private store
- **Sweden/ Finland 1979 'Finlandia':** Developed from the 99 'Finlandia' extended wheelbase Combi GLE; 20cm (8in) longer in the body, giving extra leg-room to both the front and rear seats through lengthened front and rear doors
- **Europe markets 1979 'Super Turbo':** SAAB's latest concept car, launched at the Geneva International Motor Show in 1979. 175bhp high-pressure turbocharging and water injection
- **Australia 1980: Saab 900 'Enduro':** eleven or twelve cars with flared arches to accommodate wider wheels. Extra instruments pack in centre of dashboard with oil pressure, ammeter, voltmeter. Stiffer shock absorbers. The wheels to fill the extended arches were 15in in the Saab tradition but had 7.5in rims with 225/50 VR-rated

tyres. The car was 9in (230mm) wider at the rear. Changes to suspension settings and the turbo was blown to 1.7psi. The cars were painted in red, green, blue and white, and a black car was rumoured. Special decals were applied. The 8-valve engine was given a water-injection system for the turbocharger
- **Sweden 1981: 900 low price edition for domestic market.** Used steel wheels with Bugatti-type GLE model alloy clip-on trims, B-spec rather than revised H-spec engine. Deleted rear spoiler. Solid paint
- **British market 1981: 900 'Gold' edition.** Vinyl and graphics pack with gold stripes and gold-painted Minilite design wheels. Pine Green metallic paintwork. Available as three- and five-door
- **Sweden 1981: Turbo 'S' model.** Water injection with 1 bar turbo pressure setting
- **USA 1982: American 'Anniversary Edition'.** 400 specially equipped 900 Turbo cars with Slate Blue paintwork and four-door bodywork, with a black bolt on the spoilers and light-coloured floor mats. Special badging
- **USA 1984, SPG – Aero-based prototype:** three-door 900 in pearlescent white paint with body kit and 175bhp B-series engine. Twenty-two were built. Full production 'SPG' was a USA-only badge tag, the meaning of which has long been argued over; most have settled on 'Special Performance Group'. Effectively, SPG was 'Aero' by another name. 7,625 examples of the 900 Aero-SPGs

Classic silhouette of the C900 with its roof up.

were imported into the USA 1985–91. Interior trims of Buffalo Tan and Dove Grey replaced the crimson swathes of the twenty-two prototypes

- **Britain 1984, 900i 'Lynx' convertible:** 900 three-door-based cabriolet with fixed B pillar and lift-out roof panel. Two examples were constructed
- **Canada 1984, 900 'Sport':** Based on the 8-valve GLi model with 'Ronal'-type wheels; special low-mounted rear lip spoiler. Special badging
- **Britain 1984: Two Saab Wimbledon dealer special models 'Sprint' and 'Sport'** based on the 900 using GLi or Turbo base cars. Cars were supplied to Profile Styling Company for the creation of the first Saab 900 bodykit
- **Britain 1985, 'Tjugofem':** 25th anniversary of Saab GB, 300 special edition models. Metallic silver with side vinyl stripe labelled 'Tjugofem', or 'twenty-five'. Electrics pack and rear décor panel. GLi engine, and a plaque on the gear knob
- **Belgium 1986, 'Beverley' edition:** four-door saloon shell with sunroof, alloys, silver-grey paint and dark grey leather interior. US Turbo-style alloys. Sunroof with plastic wind deflector. Based on the GLi
- **Switzerland 1986, 'Commander' edition:** two-door 900 in Malachite Green only. 8-valve Turbo model with red side stripes. Wood interior panels fitted. Super Inca wheels
- **'Executive' edition, USA 1986:** Turbo body with burgundy leather-trimmed interior, electric pack, air conditioning, no bodykit. B-series engine
- **The Netherlands 'Silver Arrow' 1986:** Special stripes on 900 injection model. Trim upgrades
- **Britain 1986, James Bond 'Silver Beast' edition:** commemorative model to mark the use of silver 900T 'flat-front' in John Gardiner-authored Bond novels. Trim upgrades and unique decals
- **Canada 1986, 'White Knight' edition:** Cirrus White with Airflow bodykit. Plastic sunroof deflector. Body-coloured mirrors and grille. 'Super Inca' wheels
- **Belgium 1987, 'Jubilee' 40th anniversary 1987:** 900 8-valve Turbo with Rodonite paint. Tan leather or velour. Chrome pack. 'Super Inca' or cross-spoked wheels. Decals, numbered plaque
- **Sweden 1987, 'Jubilee' (50th anniversary) 1987:** special edition model to celebrate fifty years of Saab in 1987. 'Super Inca' wheels, Gli. Side stripes and decals on front wings and rear panel. 'Jubilee' label also applied

A Nardi 'Turbo' steering wheel looks just right on this 900 T convertible with its grey leather trim and wood facia kit.

to forty years of car production (as opposed to overall Saab production)

- **Britain 1987, 'Jubilee' 50th 1987 version of above car:** in Odorado Grey with red and silver striping. Trim upgrades. Wreath motif in vinyl
- **USA 'European edition' 1987:** US market car with European spec trim kit upgrades from Airflow bodykit to leather interior, electric pack, larger spoiler at rear, rear vent shields. Various wheel options, from 'Super Incas' to teardrop three-holers. Wood dash kit and centre console
- **Belgium 'Racer' 1987:** bodykit, special badges, larger rear spoiler
- **Netherlands 'Red Arrow' 1987:** special 60th anniversary car with range of upgrades. Some with larger or standard rear spoilers. Special logos
- **Sweden 'Springtime in Sweden' 1988:** special edition of the SAAB 900 Turbo convertible finished in black with SPG trim and three-spoke Aero wheels
- **Britain 'Sport' 1988:** Odorado Grey-painted GLi-type spec. Sunroof, electric pack. Larger whale-tail spoiler. Rear décor panel. Side stripes
- **Sweden 'Vinga' 1988:** Gothenburg-produced Vinga special with logo of a lighthouse on rear panel. Airflow bodykit
- **Sweden 'Ving' (or Wing) edition 1988:** not to be confused with Swedish 'Vinga' edition of 1989. 'Ving' built in thirty-car run. Wing-type logos and side decals: Cirrus White with red stripes

Continued overleaf

SAAB 900 SPECIAL/LIMITED EDITIONS FROM MANUFACTURER OR DEALER/CONCESSIONAIRE

The essential innards of the Saab turbo installation.

- **France 1989, EIA Motors '158 BHP' edition:** French concessionaire with blueprinted uprated engine 16v fuel injection. Uprated camshafts, shorter gearbox ratios made by EIA Motors France
- **Britain 1988–90, T16s two-door:** 900 T16S two-door, of which 263 of this limited run were produced and sold in the UK. Series of 300 cited by factory sources: produced in black and Odorado Grey, this T16S model has Super Aero wheels. 150 were fitted with the factory-option sports pack, and fifty with the Airflow bodykit. Full grey leather interiors. Rear bootlid wing fitted
- **Netherlands 'Forty' edition 1989–90:** Netherlands dealer model based on 16v. Three-door cars with Le Mans blue paint and special graphics and decals. Turbo spoilers, electric pack
- **Britain 1989, 'T8' Special 1989:** to mark ten years of Turbo. B-series 8-valve turbo engine with black paint, silver stripes, larger rear spoiler and décor panel
- **France 1989, 'Yacht Club' edition:** 16-valve, three-door cars with Embassy Blue or Ultramarine Blue on 'Minilite'-type alloys. White vinyl graphics pack with sail motifs on C pillar. Special radio pack fitted. Estimated seventy cars ordered
- **Britain 1989, 'SE' Model 1990–91:** five door-based 900i with Dove Grey leather trim with exterior green or blue metallic only. Wood-kit interior upgrade including door caps. Gold coachlines and cross-spoke alloys
- **Britain and selected European markets only, 'Scarabee' 1989–90:** special Scarab Green edition 900 three-door and convertible Turbos with side stripes, special 'Scarabee' badges, and interior upgrades with tan leather trim
- **Europe/ USA 'Monte Carlo' edition 1990:** 300 cars with numbered plaques. Platan Grey or Monte Carlo yellow with bodykit
- **Britain 1990–91, 'Carlsson' edition:** this UK market special was named after rally legend Eric Carlsson. Based on the three-door shell and launched in 1990, it had an uprated 1985cc turbocharged engine with APC, and 185bhp pumping out through twin chrome exhausts. A special bodykit consisting of front and rear under-bumper aprons, and side skirts based on the Airflow bodykit, distinguished it from the T16 or 'Aero' bodykit. Available in black, white or red, the first batch had enlarged rear spoilers, rear infill lamp panels, 'Carlsson' stickers and red side stripes. The car also had lowered suspension. In 1991 for the 1992 model year the 'Carlsson' edition had part suede/leather seats, and in 1992 a changed wheel specification. Many came with a three-spoke, wood-rimmed, Nardi-style steering wheel
- **Britain 1992, 900i 'Aero':** an Aero kit-styled 900 I 16v. Also available in Australia with a 2.1-litre special engine, as also used in California
- **Britain 1992, 'XS' edition 1992:** five-door, 900 injection with special stripes, rear décor panel, interior trim upgrades and electric pack. Some with alloys, some with wheel trims
- **Norway 1992, 'Griffin':** four-door 900 bodyshell with the 2.1 litre 16v export market engine. Special stripes and 'Griffin' logos. Chromed grille
- **Britain 1993, 'Ruby':** the 900 'Ruby' was the ultimate Classic 900. Offered in metallic Ruby Red, it used the 185bhp turbo engine, but kept the basic shape of the unadorned earlier 900 shell with no bodykit. Features included air conditioning, Zegna wool seat-trim inserts,

lowered suspension, and three-hole alloys with unique two-tone graphite finish, and the car was packed with electrically powered options. The UK price of £19,995 made it the most expensive 900 ever. However, it suffered from poor paint adhesion and unexpected rust, and seat trim wear

- **Sweden and Germany, 'S' 1993:** 900 T16S-based car with Ruby paint and interior. Known as 'Last Edition' in Germany
- **France 1993, 'GT TSR' 1993:** a French market Ruby yet with black paint, but similar interior and trims. Extremely rare run of up to seventy cars
- **USA 'Commemorative Edition Turbo' 1993:** three-door Turbo. Black paint. 185bhp. 325 cars imported. Numbered plaques on wooden dash kit. Rumoured to have become a 1994 edition during the wait for the new GM 900. Rare USA manual gearbox five-speed. Available as a convertible. 500 said to have been created in late 1993 to early 1994, US market only. Now very rare, as the last-ever 900 Classics
- **Numerous commemorative and dealer anniversary specials** were built round the 900 convertible/cabrio models. Particularly rare was a single car built by Saab to celebrate the 10,000 soft-top 900 when Pierre Olofsson was commissioned to create a uniquely trimmed and coloured special interior for a car with a unique external paint colour
- **A 1983 year development 'mule' for the 9000** was built from a 900 five-door – a car widened like the Saab 96 'Paddan' to test components for a secret new model. Known either as 'Skvader' or 'Project Cecilia', this 900 had axle track extensions and massive external wheel-arch bulges to accommodate the 9000's wider suspension and its drivetrain, for secret testing. Registered as CWN 898 and last seen in the Saab Museum store

- **Two-tone 'flat front' early 900 Turbo** three-door and later four-door cars featuring blue/silver paintwork and some with 'Bridge of Weir' leather trim were on sale in USA and Europe circa 1983–85

Note: **Certain 'one-off' and obscure dealer promotional 'upgrade' specials**, with locally created graphics, or striping kits allied to plastic wheel trim or alloy wheel fitment on injection and base Turbo cars, have been rumoured in France, the Netherlands, Sweden and other European markets including Italy. Similar sales promotion 'specials' have been sighted in the USA and Canada and in Australia. Air-conditioning kits or upgrades known in Asian and Australian markets. 900 injection and Turbo variants on sale in Singapore, Hong Kong and Japan. Four-door shell popular in Asia and Australia. In tropical market cars and Middle East market cars the battery was moved to the boot for lower temperature. In Italy, Automatic Performance Control-equipped cars were labelled with 'EP' – EcoPower – not 'APC' badges.

Note: In 1981 a Saab 900 estate car or wagon model was built as a one-off factory-spec prototype, constructed by Nilssons for Saab.

ABOVE: **Saab 900 pick-up – non-factory!**

LEFT: **The Saab friction tester – a modified 900 used to test rolling resistance and friction on road and runway surfaces using under-car equipment.**

ENVALL'S VEHICLE SHOWCASE: EV1

Experimental Vehicle One, or 'EV1', was first shown to the public in 1985. Based on the Saab 900 T16, the EV1 was redesigned into a two-door 2+2 coupé, which could accommodate four adults and their luggage under a composite plastic/aramid fibre skin in a shell cooled by solar panels and reinforced by a substructure skeleton. The shell was built by Leif Mellberg. Underneath was a 285bhp Turbo engine. But there was more to EV1 than this brief résumé implies.

In EV1, Envall had blended together a stream of Saab themes and his own natural talents. The result was a shape of modernity and timeless elegance – indeed, it still looks fresh, and in the flesh has a presence not communicated by its photograph.

All the lines 'work'. EV1 was a glasshouse-topped concept car built in less than six months. It had an up-swept tail, and forensically effective aerodynamics, especially so at the critical rear end. There, the separation point, wake envelope and lift were all tuned to perfection without any 'stick-on' spoilers. The organic shape of EV1 did its job, and proved that Envall and Saab knew what they were at for the future, and not just the past.

EV1 caused a sensation on the motor show circuit, and was widely admired by other designers. It also created interest in Saab and its talents from other, larger car makers. It did more for Saab than many people realize, as it marked a level of professionalism and engineering and design integrity far beyond that which outsiders could have envisaged. If ever a concept car had true, honest design wrapped up in future vision, then Bjorn Envall's EV1 did.

Envall's 900 T16-based EV1 Saab design sensation. Per Rudh was the former Saab rally service manager who was the EV1's test driver.

THE 9000

Saab 9000 Turbo at launch.

*TROLLHÄTTAN
TO TURIN*

THE 9000 | TROLLHÄTTAN TO TURIN

IN 1978 SAAB'S MANAGEMENT knew it faced a quandary, in that it had left behind its small car roots and moved upmarket. After the 99 EMS, GLE, Turbo and the 900, Saab needed to make more cars and more profit per car. Volume and costs were Saab's perennial problems – and the growing Swedish economic crisis of the time hardly helped.

Saab needed a proper, completely new car, but it could not afford such a prize. Internally, it had started a major new car design project known as 'X29'. But even under Sten Wenlo's great vision, Saab needed to spread its design costs base. It also needed a new big car to ride the 1980s executive car wave, and to make the most of its prestige success in the USA and in its other major market – Great Britain. And what of Germany? Could Saab build a new version of the 900 to take on BMW, and up and coming Audi, as well as others?

Just as in 1963, a Saab-Volvo merger had been on the cards from 1977 to 1978, but as before, it never happened: the psychological differences between the front driven and the rear driven, between the teardrop and the box, were simply too great. But waiting in the wings were friends of Saab, people with whom Saab had had a relationship going back to Sixten Sason and the Saab 92 and 93: the Italians.

Surely for Saab, international polyglot of an aerospace and automotive company, the solution lay in one of the earliest examples of recent global car platform and engineering co-operations – and the Wallenbergs were, once again, pivotal in the outcome for Saab.

TURIN AGAIN?

Saab had had a pre-existing relationship with Lancia by selling Lancias in Swedish Saab dealerships. Through a series of coincidences, meetings and further conversations, Saab's Georg Karnsund began to frame an idea for a stronger link between Saab and Lancia. The Italian with a penchant for Sweden and Saab was Gianmario Rossignolo, the head of Lancia, who was friends with Saab's Sten Wenlo. Through such relationships, Saab and Fiat/Lancia began to talk about a tie-up.

For Saab, Karnsund met with Lancia's Gianmario Rossignolo, and the men sketched out a possible framework for collaboration. With the Saab and Volvo merger dead and buried (again), movement began and a plan was made, but it required sign-off from the top of Saab and Fiat, above the level of Gustafsson, Wenlo, Rossignolo and Fiat's Vittoria Ghidella, who had become involved.

Through a friendship with the Agnelli family, Saab's Marcus Wallenberg, as the main investor, sat down in a room in Geneva in February 1979 with Gianni Agnelli and his team. As Wenlo and all the other players chatted, Agnelli and Wallenberg agreed in fifteen minutes of private talks to proceed, to share the costs of jointly developing a car that each marque would modify into its own piece of branding. As a result of this meeting, Saab, Fiat and its subsidiaries, Lancia and Alfa Romeo, gained a new big car for the 1980s and 1990s. The contract was drawn up, and it allowed any partner a very quick exit option if required – an unusual factor in a deal involving hundreds of millions of bankers' funds and billions of lira.

The early 9000i is a rare car now. This British example has a protective strip along the bonnet's leading edge, but is otherwise standard spec.

This was not Saab's first link with Fiat, Agnelli and Lancia: in the 1970s, the little Autobianchi A112 – a sort of Turinese version of the Mini – had been sold through Saab dealers in Sweden via the Agnelli–Wallenberg relationship. Next, the stylish and very smart, Guigario-penned Lancia Delta was marketed as a Saab–Lancia 600 in Sweden. It was a good car, yet it was horrendously unaerodynamic by any standards, let alone modern ones (Cd 0.46). Neither did the Lancia have a surfeit of safety. Furthermore some of the fixtures and fittings also tended to depart from the vehicle in true Italian style. As a 96 replacement, the Saab-badged Lancia Delta was a disaster, selling no more than a few thousand examples.

For the new big car, Fiat was to undertake much of the steel tooling and engineering design work, and although Saab was involved, the chassis and the styling stemmed from Agnelli's Italian lead. But that did not matter to Saab, nor to its lead engineers on the project, Rolf Sandberg and Gunnar Larson, as well as designer Bjorn Envall – for Saab had been working with the Italian industry and its designers for decades.

Tipo Quattro

The project was entrusted with the title of 'Tipo Quattro' or 'Type Four', some say to reflect the number of marques involved, others to mirror a Fiat internal code. The four cars would eventually emerge as the Saab 9000, Fiat Croma, Lancia Thema ('Tayma') and the less obviously related Alfa Romeo 164.

Much wine may have flowed, but the relationship was not always easy. Saab, obsessed with safety and design details, found itself out on a limb. The costs of making the Saab version of the car were going to be greater than expected. The simple, politically and financially expedient thing to do would have been to re-trim the big Fiat and stick some Saab badges on it. But Saab refused, not least because it reputedly had needs and issues above the required levels of crash safety that the new Fiat/Lancia was achieving in early testing. For Saab, the need to change so much in a collaborative deal could have been an ominous portent of the GM days that were to come in later years.

How Safe was Safe?

The Fiat version was legal and it met the test requirements, but it had not passed all the extra tests that Saab's own safety standards demanded over and above any legislation. At an early stage of prototype development it was suggested that the Fiat car suffered deformation in its windscreen frame and sill area at the vital A-post structures during frontal offset crash testing. Subsequent crash testing in Germany proved the point.

Fiat's idea of a side-impact door beam was not Saab's, either. It was an odd paradox, as Fiat had a large safety centre, and in its 130 and 132 ranges had tested for the difficult offset crash scenario long before it became a key safety issue. Fiat's 1970s big cars had performed well in certain crash tests, but Saab, with its 99 and 900 safety record, was in a different league. The Saab version of the Type Four would be sold in America and had to address expanding legal and consumer crash-test rules and changes; the Fiat/Lancia variants of Type Four would not, so they could be of lighter build. European safety legislation in 1980 still lagged behind the world class standards of private experience such as that at Saab. However safe Fiat's car was, Saab wanted more.

So the Saab version of the car had a unique Saab-engineered front end and an A-pillar zone of greater strength. Special offset crash, impact-absorbing panels and tubes or 'crush cans' were engineered into the front wings of the car, and thicker guages of steel used in the struts, firewall and floorpan. There was even an ultra high-tensile steel cable across the bulkhead to stop the windscreen pillar frame sides separating under heavy impact. An extra cross-beam under the dashboard reduced bulkead intrusion, too. And although the Fiat/Lancia and Saab all looked as though they shared the same doors, they did not, as the Saab's were heavier and had specially designed lateral protection beams engineered into them; it was therefore not possible to swap doors between the cars.

Only the roof was shared as a major panel betwen the Saab and the Fiat/Lancia version. From over 150 potentially shared panel pressings between the cars, Saab adopted fewer than a dozen. This was a far cry from the original cost-saving plan of sharing over 1,000 components. In later years, Saab would redesign its car's rear C pillar to further update its safety to incorporate a massive structural member as a roll-over hoop and rear-impact reinforcement. All 9000s came with an advanced, cellular steering-wheel design that absorbed impact and cushioned the blow.

Intriguingly, Agnelli approved the extra costs of the Alfa Romeo version and its own unique body that used only the Type Four floorpan from its Fiat big brother. Subsequently, a post-9000 large Saab, using a modern, safe platform shared with Alfa Romeo, was planned. This car would have become the new 1990s Saab 9-5, but it was cancelled after GM bought into Saab.

To prove the point of Saab's safety obsession over its partners, Saab's version of the Type Four won numerous safety awards: it achieved a lead in the Swedish Folksam insurance claim-based low injury league, being voted the safest car year after year. In the USA the strength of the 9000 and its revised Mk2 version also gained recognition from leading safety bodies. Of note, even in a heavy crash where some deformation is inevitable, the crucial head, thoracic and leg injury criteria that can be used to quantify the degree of injury, were all commendably low in the 9000. In fact the 9000 was the first front-drive car with front seat-belt pre-tensioners and anti-lock brakes as standard. As with the 92 to 96, the 99 and the original 900, Saab had made its safety mark again, and the awards to prove it rolled in.

Saab 9000 Safety Awards

- USA: Safest In-Production Car, lowest passenger vehicle fatality rates 1994, *Insurance Institute for Highway Safety*
- USA: Substantially Better Than Average for injury losses, 1994 *Highway Loss Data Institute* (HLDI)
- EUROPE: Best Protection from Neck Injuries (Saab 9000, 1985–93) *1996 study of 8,000 rear-end collisions in Sweden*, Folksam Insurance, Karolinska, Institute and Chalmers University of Technology, Sweden
- Safest Car in Sweden 1989–90
- Safest Car in Sweden 1991–92
- Safest Car in Sweden 1993–94

Assessed by Folksam Insurance.

STYLING STUDIES

With a fixed, Guigario design style for the Type Four partners, the Saab version of the car could have looked very similar to the Fiat/Lancia variants, but thanks to Björn Envall and Rolf Jonsson in the Envall-directed Saab design studio, the Guigario Fiat design – a smooth yet bland 1980s shape – was Saabized

as far as costs and tooling could allow. The Saab trademark C-pillar 'hockey stick' design motif and rising side lines may have been missing, constrained by roof, door skin, glass and side panel toolings (as was the clamshell bonnet/trunk), but a new modern, clean, Saab 'look' was achieved. Lights, panels, bumpers, the rear windscreen, all were smoothed, curved, sculpted and blended into a harmonious form of integrity that never looked compromised by its shared origins. Over in America, Bob Sinclair wanted something more distinctive, but Saab and Envall delivered the best that the hand of collaboration had achieved.

The 9000's new style presented a new design graphic at a time when many car makers were still evolving previous themes or simply copying each other. Despite its shared design contraints, the 9000 possessed a rare and unique design achievment – a niche, a sense of occasion amidst a distinct design statement that reeked of modern Scandinavian style. Few product designers could have managed that with a clean sheet, let alone a framework handed down by an alternative design need. Parked next to each other, the 9000, Croma and Lancia all looked different, but only one had a timeless appeal – the Saab. Croma and Thema were soon eclipsed, gone, yet 9000 lived on, in the true spirit of Saab.

Envall and the team also teased out a lower drag coefficient of Cd 0.33 for the 9000 by smoothing off panel joins, closing up panel gap tolerances and fine detailing the mirrors (with vented struts), by streamlining the door handles, headlamps and window trims and by sculpting the sills and undertray. Although the airflow separated atop the rear windscreen, careful attention to shaping, in true Saab technique, reduced the turbulent drag wake, kept the 9000's elegant three-piece rear glass area clean and reduced problems in side winds. Perhaps

Saab styling from 9000 Mk1 to 9-5 Mk1, both controlling the rear wake flow.

the big black rear deck spoiler did work, but it also looked great – yet it cannot have been aerodynamically vital, as it was removed for the later non-Turbo version of the 9000.

Even more impressive was the interior – a real Saab 'cockpit' affair with ergonomically zoned controls and instruments. As well as Saab's best ever orthopaedic seats, there was acres of space from the long wheelbase (big enough to qualify as a 'large car' according to US rules) and fold-down hatchback cargo area to remind Saabists of the 900.

Early 9000s came with expensive and very high quality grades of leather and plastic fittings in the cabin. Interior trim colours were dark grey, a very smart dark maroon, and soon lighter blue and beige trims were offered. Early dashboards were all-black mouldings, but matching coloured mouldings to reflect the overall interior trim colour were very quickly offered. Press and customer reaction to the interior was very positive. Subtle but very smart seemed to be the wordwide verdict, both for the inside and outside of the new Saab. Given the shared origins and constraints of the result, Guigario delivered as requested by Fiat, and Envall's reinterpretation of a set form into a Saabized shape was a massive success in terms of industrial design – yet few have accorded him the credit he deserves for this design achievement in the 9000.

ENGINES – TURBOS AND TORQUE

Saab's decades of engine design expertise had culminated in the variants of the 2.0-litre engine first seen in the 99 and then modified and updated across the 900. A new engine might have been a good idea, but there was very little wrong with Saab's existing engines; turbo technology had seen to that.

For the 9000, Saab turned its engine sideways to fit the car's design parameters – using an in-line configuration would have scared the other design partners away. Transverse front-wheel

ABOVE: **The early, slant-nose 9000 MkI performance variant.**

LEFT: **Sleek, slant-front 9000 5-door.**

This 9000 Carlsson has multi-spoke wheels and a more subtle rear spoiler.

drive had been a must from the first discussions with Fiat. The engine was a 4 valves per head, 16-valve design, which had also been given specially shaped domed combustion chambers and piston heads, allied to symmetric spark patterns from a centrally mounted sparking plug – all to aid 'swirl' of the fuel-air mixture and the combustion pattern and efficiency. There were twin overhead camshafts, a new turbo with efficient intercooling to keep temperatures and wear down, and APC – Saab's automatic performance control, which had developed from the earlier 'anti-knock' ignition technology of the 900. The fuel injection process represented an early attempt at the 'stratified charge' technique where fuel flow patterns as opposed to fuel volume were computer controlled via a microprocessor. For later models there would be 'DI' – a direct ignition system with a coil for each cylinder, which created a spark twenty times faster than the norm and gave a 60 per cent increase in voltage – a very early, pioneering 'multi-spark' technology now widely copied.

These developments, bringing advanced science into an engine block and head design, represented another obsession within Saab, yet one that had less PR than safety. The Saab ethos had spent decades refining engine design and technology. In the later 900 and 9000 engines, Saab took a lead in efficiency, economy and emissions, a lead that resulted in a range of engines offering the sort of performance that, as framed by the 9000 Turbo 16, could see off a Porsche and even a Ferrari. So quick was the 9000 Turbo that it would spin its wheels and torque steer – Saab had to add an early traction control system to manage the power delivery.

Originally launched only as a turbocharged car, the sheer design efficiency of the 9000 Turbo and its speed and Saab handling made it an instant success – but Saab did not sit back, and as usual, started to add to the design.

As yet another example of Saab's inability to stop fiddling with its components, in 1989 a team based at the Finnish Uusikaupunki plant created a V8 engine for the 9000. In a move reminiscent of Mellde's 'Monster' of a 6-cylinder 93, two standard, 4-cylinder engines were mated together to create a 300bhp engine mounted transversely in a 9000 engine bay. No steel changes were needed to make it fit, but the idea came to nothing.

A NON-TURBO VERSION?

Launched in May 1985 as a 'Turbo'-branded car, by the summer of 1986 Saab released a non-turbo version of the car fitted with a straight, detuned, fuel-injected version of the engine, but with the weight (and power) of the turbo and its plumbing removed. Intended as a cheaper, less performance-oriented variant of the

9000, which it was hoped would scoop up sales lower down the price range, the 9000i 16 turned out to be a strong seller in its own right. Across Europe, and particularly in Great Britain, the lighter, less aggressive non-turbo car seemed to offer an easier drive with lower maintenance costs; it became a popular 'company' car for executives.

If anything, although slower than the turbocharged version, the lighter 9000i handled with more sharpness, as less front-end weight meant even better steering response. Driven carefully, this large car was also very economical. With 125bhp versus the 160bhp of the 9000 Turbo, the normally aspirated car was no slowcoach, and in manual transmission guise had the true feel of a 'press-on' drive in typical Saab style. To show just how popular both versions of the 9000 were in their early lives, the sales figures prove the point: in 1985, in the 9000 Turbo's first full year, Saab sold 13,721 of the 9000 Turbo – but in 1987 it sold a total of 49,081 examples of the 9000 Turbo and the 9000 non-turbo injection model. In 1988, Saab sold 52,199 of the combined 9000 model range.

Ever More Models

As normal, Saab's men did not sit still. For the 1989 model year, Saab increased the bhp of both the 9000's engines by 5bhp, and the direct ignition system was fitted to the turbocharged cars. For 1990, Saab pulled out all the stops in the engine department and announced a developed 2.3-litre version of its main engine. This time it had been given twin balancer shafts, another electronic self-monitoring makeover, and a modified direct injection system. With 2229cc, 150bhp in non-turbocharged form, and with its very efficient combustion and fuel-control systems, the engine was not only fast, it was also to prove more economical than its lower-powered ancestor – a true testament to Saab technology.

Saab was still busy. The standard 2.0-litre turbo unit was given a bigger turbocharger chamber, and power went up to 185bhp. Then the new 2.3-litre was turbocharged for a late 1990 launch. Power was up to that benchmark 'performance gateway' – 200bhp, or nearly 150kW. This was the stuff of real performance. The 9000's overtaking abilities and through-the-gears acceleration figures, always impressive, were now into supercar territory.

AERO

'Aero' emerged as a Saab brand/badge exercise which built on the company's aviation – or by now, aerospace – links, and its penchant for aerodynamic styling. Although the 9000 Mk1

The booted 9000 sedan. Saab designed an expensive new rear suspension system for their version for the Type Four car.

had spawned a bodykitted, larger-spoilered Talledega and a Carlsson edition, these were rationalized in 1991 under a Turbo 16S Aero label.

Aero as a sub-brand was expanded by the idea of a sportier, yet more responsible and more aerodynamic revised 9000, and it stemmed from a one-off experiment within Saab in 1991. This led to the CS 'liftback'-type Mk2 bodyshell, and within that framework, saw the creation of an Imola Red 9000 CS or Mk2, known as the 'Ecosport'. This was a smoothed-over 9000 with restyled bodywork, which was then turned into a concept car.

Fittings on the 'Ecosport' included a heat storage device – a thermo accumulator to keep the engine and car warm when left standing in arctic temperatures. There was a solar panel for powered ventilation when the engine was turned off. The car had low-weight alloy brakes, an early version of a Saab electro-mechanically signalled automatic gear change (latterly called the Saab 'Sensonic' system), and a 225bhp full pressure turbo-charged engine.

This one-off prototype sowed the seed at Saab for a revised 9000 Mk2 CS with sporting potential.

Before this, in 1991, the 9000 Turbo 16S with Aero brand was Saab's fastest ever car – yet the Ecosport was based on the late 1991, 1992 model year 9000 CS bodyshell, one that was quickly adapted to become a wider Aero model range with 200bhp, and more if re-mapped. It took the honours as Saab's ultimate early 1990s flyer, and was Saab's fastest car ever.

The first Aero cars were based on the slant-fronted 9000 Mk1 half styling themes of 1991. The 'Talledega' versions and the British Carlsson models also used this car as their base, with the addition of a bodykit and larger rear wing. The Talledega branding originated from Saab taking three 9000s to the Talledega racing circuit in Alabama and running the cars non-stop (except for refuelling) for three weeks at 230km/h (143mph). The average speed was 213.299km (132.54mph).

In the main range, the 9000 CS – or facelifted styling revisions of the 1992 – created the ultimate Aero based on the CS Turbo. Other CS cars were equipped with a low-pressure turbocharger producing 170bhp, while the CSE Turbo had a full-pressure turbocharger with 200bhp. Both cars used the Garrett T25 turbocharger with a base boost pressure of 0.4 bar (6psi) in the lower-boosted LPT; the HPT high-pressure turbo was equipped with a boost control valve manipulated by the ECU. This allows the boost pressure to be increased as the ECU commutes demand from multiple sensors; maximum factory

The 9000 CS Turbo in green, a classic of the British Saab line-up.

setting boost on a full-pressure turbo varies from 0.7 to 1.02 bar (10–15psi). After-market kits greatly increased this figure.

So Aero as a badge brand saw cars that were framed by a definitive Mk1 Aero, firstly as a Talledega model replacement, then as a 'hot' version of the revised Mk2 bodywork 9000 CS range of 1992. CS Aero sales began in the USA using 1993 half-model year cars – a 1994 car. In 1994, 3,850 of the 9000 CS Aero were sold by Saab of America.

Aero cars came with stiffer and lower suspension springs and thicker anti-roll bars; 205/ 55 ZR-rated tyres meant business in anyone's language, and so too did the exquisite alloy wheels that Saab came up with for these models. Torque was up to 258lb ft (350Nm)– higher than the bhp figure, which is always a sign of a great engine. Ultimately, Aeros with well over 225bhp (166kW) and a 250km/h (155mph) top speed came out of the factory.

The 9000 CS Turbo or Aero looked great in solid, glossy Saab black, but they were also available in Imola Red, Silver, Le Mans Blue, Cirrus White and the very popular Eucalyptus Green metallic – a bright yet darker shade of emerald green that suited the car. Saab's advertising for the Aero claimed that it was faster than a Ferrari Testarossa and a Porsche 911 Carrera 4 – which it was, in a straight line.

Towards the end of the 9000's production life, Saab came up with yet another variation on the theme: the 'Anniversary' models, or 'Jubileum' for Sweden. These included certain Aero trim items, new alloy wheels, and specially made leather seats embossed with the old Saab aeroplane label and badge to go with it. For 1997, the anniversary was perhaps eclipsed by the revised Aero models, with even more power and new fittings including a Mitsubishi turbocharger.

Beyond the headlines of the bhp ratings of Saab's engines, there were more subtle indicators of engineering excellence – for example, the torque figures were high, and the torque curves – the point in the engine's power delivery where torque is most useful to the driver – all tell a story of a much deeper engineering ethos. Turbocharging at Saab was not about bolting on a bog turbo blower and accelerating away in a straight line, only to run out of boost and torque: instead it was about tuning the delivery of that boost and the resulting power and torque. Saab's torque graph curves were never peaked, but always had a nice flat band of high torque delivery across a wide, low to mid-range powerband. For men such as Granlund at Saab, it was about knowing the difference between power and thrust – another aviation legacy, perhaps.

For the given bhp range of 150–200bhp of Saab's engines, the levels of torque are class leading, as is the efficiency of the delivery. Getting 240 and 280Nm respectively, in a flattish torque band starting at 1,800rpm out of such capacity engines, is a huge achievement. The 1997 2.3-litre full pressure turbo delivered 330Nm of torque at just 2,000rpm – and no other comparable car could do that.

These facts apply to Saab's recent engines, and in turn stem largely from the work carried out on the engines of the 1985–97 Saab 9000 model ranges, yet have roots in the 1950s and 1960s engine design studies of Saab.

The reliability of the 9000's high torque engines and the cylinder heads that kept the lid on the power was proven by the testing of the 9000 at the American Talladega race circuit, where in 1986 a team of 9000s and Saab drivers drove continuously at high speeds to gain a string of international and world record-breaking performances using standard production cars.

RIGHT: **Saab's Recaro-style racing safety seat for the 9000.**

BELOW: **The airbag-equipped 9000 with wood kit.**

BOTTOM: **Saab 9000 CS Turbo in French fog.**

TRIONIC – MEASURING IONS

For 1993 Saab pressed ahead with a world class, technology-leading engine system: 'Trionic'. This name meant that Saab had created an advanced engine management system, one not dissimilar to those used in aviation, to assess and adjust the fuel–air mix and its combustion at the point of its entering the engine, by regulating the mixture, ignition and turbocharger pressure via a central microprocessor system. Trionic measured three of the engine's main functions: air supply/boost, fuel injection and ignition.

Trionic also developed the use of light pressure turbocharger (LPT) pressure in lower-powered engine variants. Saab's Trionic was a unique, patented innovation, named after the system's ability to measure ions in the combustion gas mix. Ions are electrically charged particles produced during combustion, and by analysing them using a 32-bit processor capable of two million actions per second, the Saab system allowed each cylinder head to have an individually tuned supply. The spark plugs themselves were used as an ionization measurement device, and the measurement voltage between the main spark cycle was initially 80V in comparison to the 40,000V maximum ignition volt charge – later exceeded.

By adding an electronically linked throttle to the system, Saab created a way of reducing excess fuel use, and it was this which led to the 'Trionic' engine being so economical – 'Ecopower' as Saab called it in later years. Saab claimed that the Trionic system gave rise to exhaust gases that could be cleaner than the inner city smog going into the engine from the outside air in certain polluted cities. Saab developed Trionic into 'Trionic 5' – T5 – and then into the more advanced 'Trionic 7' – T7. The difference between the two amounted to the fact that the T5 was a speed density engine management system based upon a direct injection management cassette taking its readings from a main sensor and various pressure sensors. This information was used to determine the fuel injection parameters. T5 was simple to tune and had no critical mass airflow sensor; its activation was based upon the throttle position. T7, used post-2000 by Saab, reacted to a calculated torque request at the throttle. All T7 systems have a mass air sensor, so the car does not boost to a predetermined level in the way that the T5 did.

T7 is more flexible – more reactive to conditions – and can modulate its boost by adjusting the fuelling in relation to air mass and temperature upon compression; thus T7 has a secondary 'thinking' capability beyond the set values that T5 was limited by. However, due to such reactive processes within T7, a blow-off turbo valve cannot be used, whereas in T5 it can. T7's main performance advantage lies in its reactions to temperature and altitude/density changes, making the car faster in more demanding conditions that would normally see a fall-off in performance.

The Trionic system had its roots in Saab's automatic performance control (APC) system first announced in the 1980s, and the man who led these developments was Saab stalwart Olle Granlund. APC was the true beginning of developing the anti-knock self-ignition – or anti-ignition retardation – into a more complex overall engine management system. APC was self-monitoring, and its key development was the ability to make the engine react to differing grades of fuel and local operating conditions. Initially APC was based literally on an audible signal from the engine, but soon switched to ion/air measuring – itself the stepping stone to Trionic T5 via direct ignition sensing systems built into each cylinder head.

Trionic T7 was one of the world's most advanced micro-processor-controlled engine management systems; it also reduced emissions as well as managed performance and fuel efficiency. Perhaps most impressive was the way Trionic could be used to reduce turbo lag and constantly tune the engine. It was another example of the genius of Saab.

Saab's top engineer Olle Granlund proudly said of this engine management system: 'Saab is one of the few, very select car makers in the world to have developed its own engine management system – and succeeded. It (Trionic) boasts several capabilities which I haven't seen elsewhere.'

MODEL MILESTONES

Just over 400 examples of the 9000 T16 were built in late 1984 – these were production cars used for press and company events – and then came the early customer cars. In 1985 over 13,000 were sold, and from 1986 to 1996 peak sales in one year exceeded 50,000; in fact Saab never sold fewer than 30,000 per year of the 9000.

Across that lifespan, Saab made its usual changes and created a complicated and confusing range of models, including a long-

RIGHT: **The C pillar of the revised 9000 was heavily restyled and reinforced beneath its skin.**

BELOW: **The new rear panel and full-width lamps for the 9000.**

tailed saloon, Talledega specials and an array of frontal design facelifts; this created a situation where some of the 9000s had an original 'flat front' grille and headlamp design, whilst at the same time a 'slant-front' revised version in a different body style was available. To cap that, Saab then completely revised the 9000

five-door hatchback and created another new, 'curved front', CS-type design, only latterly applied to the four-door versions.

Customers could order a 9000 in five-door, four-door, hatched, booted and even long-wheelbase limousine forms. They could choose between turbo, no turbo, CDE, CS, CC, Aero, Anniversary, Griffin, Turbo 16S Aero, Carlsson, and a confusing spec sheet of Saab variations. A range of paints, trims and alloy wheel designs, not to mention badging, made the 9000 years some of Saab's busiest ever.

The 9000 could easily have been developed into an estate car to bring Saab back into this lucrative sector. The Lancia Thema had been made into an elegant estate by Pininfarina, and all Saab needed to do was graft that elegant rear on to its own strengthened substructure. Given that the Thema estate was not sold in Saab's main export markets, it is odd that the chance to use its panels was not taken – though by this time, the joint Saab-Fiat Type Four agreement had been dissolved.

Further oddities include a convertible version of the 9000 – this one-off design study was built by Saab's Finnish, Valmet partners. Other ideas included the fitting of a creamy smooth,

SAAB 9000: MODEL HISTORY AND VARIANTS

May 1985 The 9000 was launched in Stockholm.

Autumn 1985 Early 1985 model year 9000 Turbo 16 cars delivered to customers.

1986 The French car magazine *L'Action Automobile* votes the 9000 as the 'Best Prestige Car' of the year for 1985.

1986 Trim changes to the 9000 T included wider tyres and optional driver's computer. In the winter of 1986 the non-turbo 9000i 16 was launched, to critical acclaim.

1987 Anti-lock brakes were added as standard; also water cooling for the turbo unit; and a four-speed autobox was announced. The 9000 SE was launched for the British market, with wood and leather cabin trim kit.

1987 The four-door, door-booted 9000 saloon was announced, as Turbo only with DI fitted as 9000 CD; it was on sale in the spring of 1988. The four-door body features a unique, inclined 'slant front' revised design with new lamp, grille and bumper panel fittings.

1988 Automatic seat-belt tensioners were added across the range. 'Talledega' special edition with sports suspension settings and dark grey leather seat trim.

1989 Exhaust 'cleaning' system was added, and catalyst with Lambda sensor, giving a 5bhp engine-power increase to both engine types and a 10bhp rise to the Talledega edition. Electric front seats were installed. Also in 1989 was the British launch of the non-turbo 9000 CD.

1990 The 2.3-litre B234-type engine was announced. Revised turbo for the 2.0-litre: 185bhp for the Talledega, with new wheel styling and a revised rear-wing spoiler design. The Talledega was marketed in Great Britain with full bodykit, stripes and a 'Carlsson' branding tribute to Erik Carlsson. The four-door CDi was added to the range.

1991 The 2.3-litre engine with full pressure turbo was announced, giving Saab its first 200bhp car. Talledega was dropped, and replaced with 9000 T 16S Mk I 'Aero' using the new 2.3 T engine. It came with a special bodykit similar to the 'Carlsson' kit, with curved sill panels and rear wing. The four-door CD Aero was made available in late 1991. Five-door 9000s were finally given the inclined 'slant front' of the type fitted to the four-door bodyshell.

1992 The new facelifted Mk2 9000 five-door bodyshell was completely re-worked as the CS variant, with a new rear end of higher and larger styling concealing major structural reinforcements. Revised low-line curved frontal styling. CFC-free air con was fitted, a 'world first'. A new base model of the old shape five-door bodyshell was launched as the 9000 CC.

1992 Swedish market special model only, featured the older Mk1 9000 five-door shell, 2.0-litre engine and luxury trim as a re-born Saab GLE-badged car. A 9000 CC using the Mk1 body shape was also sold in Sweden only.

1992 'Griffin' model as a four-door saloon bodyshell only; the US Griffin version as a numbered limited edition. The definitive Saab 9000 CS 'Aero', with high-power turbo, unique trim and Recaro-type seats, was announced as the fastest-ever Saab; the later model uses the Mitsubishi turbocharger instead of the usual Saab spec Garrett B-series unit. 225hp.

1993 The 'Trionic' engine system was announced in 2.3-litre engines. Light-pressure turbo of 150bhp was launched across the CD and CS ranges. Saab attempts to rationalize the confusing model badging nomenclature: thus five-door cars are now all CS and CSE-badged, and four-door cars are now all CD and CDE-badged, but the top-of-the-range model retains its 9000 'Griffin' label without CD badging. The 9000 CST Aero sales begin in the USA.

1994 Balancer shafts were added to the 2.0-litre engine block, and Trionic was extended across the range; light-pressure turbo at 170bhp was announced. Revised gearbox materials. First fitment of the Saab information display (SID) computer and display to 9000s.

1995 General Motors supplied the 3.0-litre V6 B306-type engine, with a claim to 210bhp announced. Traction control was fitted to the V6. Styling changes to the CD/CDE and Griffin.

1995 'Ecopower' brand across the 9000 range is launched for the 1996 model year. Non-turbo 2.3-litre engine is discontinued and replaced by the turbo 2.0-litre.

1997 Saab's 50th anniversary: special 9000 'Anniversary' edition with unique propeller-badged leather seat embossing, Aero wheels, special badges and trim items including a wooden steering wheel and spoiler kit. Four-door V6-engined models were discontinued except in limited markets. The 1997 Aero model with 225bhp is the fastest ever Saab. Manual-only 230bhp cars were offered in 1997.

1998 Late 1997 saw the last of the 9000s being built – less than 4,000 being left with dealers beyond the turn of the year and phased out to make way for the new 9-5 range. In the USA, 1,300 9000s were imported – as the last of the line Aeros and as a special CSE Turbo with the Aero's engine but not its sports suspension package.

Production figures were 503,000.

Yamaha-tuned V6 engine, and further Italian links through the idea of creating a diesel-powered 9000 by using the superb VM motor diesel engine, which had also appeared in the Rover SD1, to great acclaim.

With its advanced engines, the 9000 was ripe for performance enhancement and a number of upgrades. Remapped computer components were made available by after-market specialists such as Maptun of Sweden, whose tuning kits could get over 330bhp out of a 9000, and via Abbot Racing and Neo Brothers in the UK. Some owners fitted massive turbochargers, increased cooling and strut braces. Today, many Saab 9000s soldier on, and it is an enthusiast's favourite. Apart from rust in the doors, 9000s last well and still provide cheap yet unusual transport to those in the know; they can also achieve huge mileages provided they receive regular servicing. The hard-worked automatic gearbox can require a rebuild.

The 9000 in all its guises had many followers, but perhaps the final production cars, the Anniversary model and the ultra-fast 1997 Aero with all its equipment, represent a high point for Saab's last home-grown engineering expertise and design function. Saab's two-millionth car was a 9000, and Sten Wenlo's sixtieth birthday present from Saab was a 9000 Turbo – nice work, if you can get it.

Ultimately the 9000 was a great Saab, yet one underestimated by Saab purists due to its part-Italian roots. Yet the 9000 reflected Saab's early 1930s and 1940s aviation ethos rather well – taking a shared design and Saabizing it. True, the 9000 was not a Saab in the historic sense of the 92–96 or the 99 and 900, and yet it was a brilliant car, as well as being a superb Saab that encompassed all the crucial aspects of the Saab car ethos and the Saab spirit. The men (and women) of Saab deserve more credit for the 9000 than current history delivers. Surely, above all, the manifestation in the Saab 9000 of the industrial design of Bjorn Envall and the engineering of Olle Granlund should be honoured as great achievements. Saab 9000 was stylish, safe and very fast. It was therefore, whatever its origins, a true Saab.

The ultimate Saab of the early 1990s: the fastest ever Saab 9000 Aero.

SPECIFICATIONS — SAAB 9000 T16 MK1

Body
Reinforced steel monocoque with door beams, and offset impact system in front structure. Braced windscreen frame

Engine

Type	4 valves per cylinder. Chain-driven ohc. transverse mounted
Cylinders	4
Cooling	Water-cooled
Bore & stroke	90mm×78mm
Capacity	1985cc
Compression ratio	10:1
Carburettor	Bosch Jetronic fuel injection. Garrett T3 turbocharger
Max. power	175bhp (128kW) at 5,300rpm
Max. torque	201lb ft (273Nm) at 3,000rpm

Transmission
Front-wheel drive via five-speed manual box

Suspension
Front strut with coil springs and dampers. Rear dead axle with Panhard rod and multi-link arms with coil springs and dampers

Brakes
All round discs +ABS (from 1985), dual circuit diagonal split

Dimensions

Wheelbase	2,670mm (105in)
Track	1,520mm (60in) (front), 1,492mm (59in)
Width	1,764mm (69in)
Height	1,420mm (56in)
Weight	1,325kg (2,918lb)

Top speed
222km/h (138mph), 0–60mph in 8.2sec

Some think this was Saab's best-ever interior and seat combination.

RALLYING AND
THE SAAB LEGEND

Rally Monte Carlo. The stuff of Saab.

MELLDE, CARLSSON,
BLOMQVIST, EKLUND
AND THE TEAM

RALLYING AND THE SAAB LEGEND

MELLDE, CARLSSON, BLOMQVIST, EKLUND AND THE TEAM

ERIK CARLSSON DROVE A Saab, as history will always recall. But amid Carlsson's amazing record there have been other occasional vignettes of Saab's magic. One of these came on a day in 1974 in a Finnish rally when Juan Manuel Fangio drove a Saab 96 V4 rally car and was entranced by the feel and response of the Saab. Another highlight was the sight of two Saabs racing in the Le Mans 24 Hours event. Saab's rallying prowess even reached as far as Uruguay.

Carlsson is forever associated with the rallying legend of Saab: he became the star of Saab rallying and his wife, Pat Moss Carlsson (sister of Stirling Moss) also became a successful proponent of Saab rally driving. Carlsson made the legend and, quite rightly, is the revered name and big personality of the story. Yet Saab's interest in rallying began not with Carlsson but with car-mad, DKW rally-driving, ex-army Rolf Mellde who joined Saab in late 1946, and it was Mellde who went on to create the branding and iconography of Saab rallying and its competitions department (latterly under 'Bo' Hellborg). Mellde, Carlsson and a small group of men had the Saab spirit, and they took Saab to the world through their rallying exploits. Saab's name – its brand pillars before it went upmarket in the late 1970s – was its rallying pedigree. Saab's original rally enthusiast had been its late 1940s test and development driver Olle Landby (or Landbü). He and two colleagues died in a non-car-related marine accident in 1948, and Mellde, who had been working closely with Landby, took over his role as the rally and competition enthusiast and driver.

As early as 1950, a Mellde-specified and prepared Saab 92, driven by the man himself and partnered by K. G. Svedburg, won a major rally, the Rikspokalen, a tough off-road rally through ice and snow. Svedburg also took the new 92 to a local rally and won the Ostgotland road race, while Greta Molander took the Ladies Cup in the same rally in her Saab 92. Early that year, Mellde and Svedburg, alongside Greta Molander and Margaretha von Essen, had taken part in the Monte Carlo Rally. Molander finished 55th overall, 8th in class and 2nd in the Ladies class.

In these rally events they were using very early production Saab 92s, and it would not be long before Mellde sought official management sanction and funding for Saab's growing rally preparation needs. Thus the Saab works team was born, and the staff rose from two to six, with David Persson as the first service manager. Always short of funds, the Saab rally team drove to most of its European events, often taking a long ferry crossing to get to their destination. Saab and Carlsson also competed as far afield as the Californian Baja 1000 rally in the 1960s. The origins of the Saab reputation in the early years included a rollcall of major events (see box, *opposite*).

LE MANS AND SAAB?

As an example of just how seriously Rolf Mellde took competition, the tale of the Saab 93B at Le Mans provides the Saabist with a true story of the ultimate in Saabism. Erik Carlsson was at the time test driver for the Saab works team, and tested the Le Mans car before the race.

As so often happened, the entry into a race of a Saab which was 'supported' by Saab was not entirely officially sanctioned. In 1959, Sture Nottorp decided he would race a Saab at Le Mans, and the obvious candidate to ask for some help was Mellde – and help was soon forthcoming. The co-driver to Nottorp in car No. 44 was Gunnar Bengtsson, an experienced Swedish race and rally man. Coincidentally, in the same June 1959 race there was also a privately entered car, No. 43, a British Saab 93 750GT driven by Sydney Hurell and Roy North. Sadly it was to suffer a seized piston and withdraw, but it did provide the brief sight of two Saab 93s racing at Le Mans.

First, Nottorp's car was stripped down to the bare essentials. Next, the engine was internally blueprinted – polished and honed to the closest degree possible. It would run at a 4 per cent fuel/oil ratio. A large 97.7ltr (21.5gal) fuel tank was fitted, with its own quick access refuelling valve. Triple Solex carburettors were fitted, and a Saab four-speed gearbox included in the spec sheet. This little 750cc car managed 65bhp at dynometer measurement. Top speed was 169k/h (105mph) from a two-stroke, 3-cylinder engine.

The Nottorp/Bengtsson Saab raced all day and all night, finishing the Le Mans 24 Hours event in 12th place overall and 2nd in its class, amid fifty-five entrants in total. Apart from greasing, servicing and some attention to the alternator, the Saab performed as intended, covering 232 laps of Le Mans at an average speed of 130km/h (81mph). Amid the Le Mans exotica, the slippery Saab had scored some major profile for Saab and its fledgling competitions department.

Rallying in the 1960s and 1970s

In the 1960s and 1970s, Saab's rallying and rallycross legends were carved using the 93, 96, 96V4 and the 99. From Sweden to America, via Great Britain and Europe, the hard-charging Saabs, all revved up and simply flying along against heavier and more powerful cars, scored victory after victory. With their deft handling, easy revving, and with Carlsson having developed a constant power-on technique for the two-strokes, Saabs were simply invincible. The low power of the Saab meant that it had

THE FOUNDATIONS OF THE SAAB RALLYING LEGEND

1949 K. G. Svedburg wins the Tour of Ostgotland in the new Saab 92's first event.

1950 R. Mellde/K. G. Svedburg and G. Molander/M. von Essen contest the Monte Carlo Rally and Swedish Rikspokalen Rally. Mellde also drives with Bengt Carlqvist.

1952 G. Molander/H. Lundberg win the Ladies Cup in the Monte Carlo Rally, starting from Oslo.

1953 R. Mellde with Pelle Nystrom races Saab 92 'P9101'. Mellde wins the Swedish national rally championship for the year.

1955 Erik Carlsson wins the Rikspokalen Rally. Sten Helm is co-driver on this occasion and at various other events.

1956 B. Wehman/L. Braun win the Great American Mountain Rally. R. Mellde finished 6th and another Saab is placed, securing massive US launch publicity for Saab in the USA.

E. Carlsson and C. M. Skogh win the Midnight Sun Rally.

1957 E. Carlsson/M. Pavoni take 1st place in the Finnish 1000 Lakes.

1959 S. Nottorp/G. Bengtsson finish the Le Mans 24 Hours in 12th place and 2nd in class.

E. Carlsson wins the Midnight Sun Rally with E. Svensson. E. Carlsson is also 2nd in the Adriatic Rally and 5th in the Tulip Rally. He also wins the Swedish and German national rallies, and is 2nd in the rally championship rankings.

1960 E. Carlsson wins the British RAC Rally.

1961 E. Carlsson enters a Saab 95 estate with four-speed gearbox in the Monte Carlo Rally and finishes 4th.

1962 E. Carlsson/G. Haggbom win the Monte Carlo rally overall.

1963 E. Carlsson/G. Palm win the Monte Carlo Rally for the second time and as a rare consecutive winner. Further Saab placings in the Monte Carlo event included in 1963 with driver Arne Ingier, in 1964 with Pat Moss Carlsson and in 1965 with Ove Andersson and Torsten Aman.

Carlsson and co-driver Gunnar Palm were placed 2nd in the Spa-Sofia-Liege road rally, and Carlsson won the Flowers Rally, with P. Moss-Carlsson 2nd. They also had podium placings at the Liege, Monte Carlo and Geneva rallies, and later, top placings in the Safari Rally.

After early events with Sten Helm as co-driver/navigator, Carlsson's two main co-drivers were Torsten Aman and Gunnar Palm. John Sprinzel, Walter Karlsson and Tom Trana were also on the team. Erik Carlsson's British rally navigators were Stuart Turner, John Brown and David Stone.

Saab GB encouraged British club privateers and supporters, but its main official support was to Carlsson in the RAC Rally campaigns. Chris Partington from Saab GB's technical department drove a specially equipped 95 estate as support car.

**More Monte moments as Carlsson
pushes on between banks of snow.**

ERIK CARLSSON – 'MR SAAB'

RIGHT: **Carlsson's Saab
screaming into town.**

BELOW: **That man's on the
roof again...**

BOTTOM: **The 96 rally
car with its distinctly
unaerodynamic extra
lights.**

Erik Carlsson was born close to the Saab factory in
Trolhättan and began developing his feel for driving by riding
high-powered Norton motorcycles on slippery rural Swedish
roads. Here he learned his craft of handling and anticipation.
Carlsson was immersed in speed and Saabs from his formative
years. He became a legend, driven by genius, talent, and a
strong and competitive personality. Rolling the Saab on its
roof earned him the sobriquet of 'Carlsson-on-the-roof',
although this was perhaps a touch unfair – the rally and road
stages were rough, the Saab fast, and he was not the only driver
to have roll-overs. So strong was the little Saab that sometimes
after a roll the roof was undented and no one suspected or
ever knew the car had been rolled over. Ford tried to emulate
the Carlsson 'roll-over and carry-on-regardless' technique with
a Mk1 Cortina in the 1960s, but the results were not pretty.

In his early years, after the end of World War II, Carlsson
worked for Per Nystrom the motorcycle dealer, from whom
he learned the craft of rally car navigation, somewhat ironically
from the spare seat of Nystrom's Volvo!

Through buying a second-hand Saab 92 and competing
as a privateer, Carlsson was soon noticed by Saab, and in
particular by Mellde, who offered the young giant help in
preparing his private entry car; by 1954 Carlsson had won
a series of local and national events. Mellde and Carlsson

ABOVE: **The Boss, and with a range of Saabs bearing his name.**

BELOW: **Carlsson at the wheel of the Saab 94 Super Sonett 1.**

Erik Carlsson and co-driver Stuart Turner remember their Saab days.

constituted a fateful and inevitable meeting and friendship. Saab lent Carlsson a newer car to drive, and from that developed the relationship that led to the 'works' drive and the unique legend of Erik Carlsson. That story entered a second chapter with the 96 V4 cars and Carlsson's co-driver navigators Gunnar Palm and Torsten Aman. The prestigious East African Safari Rally was the only rally the gentle giant never won, despite leading on several occasions.

Even though he missed that trophy, Erik Carlsson was probably the most gifted and the fastest thinking driver, with the most astute blend of mind and technique, that rallying had ever seen. In Britain, where Carlsson has lived for decades, he won the RAC Rally three times, in 1960, 1961 and 1962. Stuart Turner was Carlsson's British co-driver and once recalled how the pair had been reconnoitering for a Scottish rally stage in a borrowed Morris Minor when they had to swerve off the road to avoid a lorry. Carlsson had the foresight to turn the ignition off as they rolled. Erik thought he had broken his ribs, but could not stand the wait at the hospital next morning, so strapped himself up and drove off to win the RAC Rally.[16]

In John Gardiner's James Bond continuation novels, where Bond drives a Saab 900 Turbo, Bond is given driving instruction by Erik Carlsson, who also delivers Bond's Saab to him. Carlsson and his wife Pat also wrote their own book about driving: *The Art and Technique of Driving* (published by Heinemann).

Legend is an over-used term, but Carlsson was just that, and an inspiration to thousands of young people.

to be kept 'on song' and revved up, so deft use of the brakes, steering and gears all came into play; the car had to be kept at speed because it took a long time to accelerate back up to pace.

URUGUAY AND SAAB RALLYING

In Uruguay, Saabs were being locally built by the Automotora company; its director, José Arijon, campaigned a 96 Sport, which he raced in Uruguay and Argentina, while Hector Marcias Fojo became a South American rally legend in a Saab 96 Sport. In 1965, Fojo came 2nd in the Rally Grand Prix of Argentina. First place was taken by Yuyu Lepro in an Alfa Romeo GTA, and 3rd by a certain young local gentleman of the name Carlos Reuteman, who was driving a Fiat 1500. Between them was Fojo in his Saab 96 Sport.

In 1964 the strength of the Saab 96 was well and truly proven when Torres de Oza, driving a 96 Sport in a local Uruguayan rally, without any roll-bar or roll-cage fitted, flipped the car, which rolled over many times at high speed. Although part of the central roof dome was crushed to a degree, the Saab's standard-fit reinforced windscreen pillars remained intact and in place, and the vital 'B' pillars, the main mid-section of the car, remained upright and undamaged, protecting the driver. Despite the massive impact on the roof, the cabin cell remained largely intact and survivable – and that without a roll-cage. José Arijon did the same thing and also walked away.

Saabs were tough, and now the Uruguayans really knew that, too. To this day, South American Saab fans are still rallying their cars in classic car club events.

FORMULA JUNIOR

In 1960, Formula Junior was a passing moment in the history of Saab cars, but one that could have taken a different, longer-lasting course.

This low-cost racing series originated in Italy and France in 1959–60, and was principally a small, lightweight racing car series based on a chassis powered by 1000cc Fiat engines. Soon, other car makers' engines were allowed into the Formula – notably Ford and BMC units. Saab decided to enter the Formula Junior, and created a racing car with the two-stroke front-drive, understeer-as-standard Saab drivetrain. Two Saab Formula Junior cars were built, although Saab's busy PR department issued enough material to make people think a series of the little cars were campaigning on the Formula Junior racing circuits, which they were not.

The yellow and blue-painted Saab Formula Junior cars were raced in 1960 and 1961 by Erik Carlsson, Carl-Magnus Skogh, Gosta Karlsson and a small number of other temporary guest drivers; Tom Trana also contributed.

Despite its poor handling, the little car was fast and allowed Rolf Mellde to test the durability of engine developments in a demanding environment.

A Saab racing car, the Formula Junior car seen in later years.

RALLY, RALLY!

For more than two decades, the 92, 93, 96 and 96 V4 stormed the world rally scene. From Greece to Finland, from Uruguay to East Africa, the speeding Saabs were the rally icon of their era. Victory and placings at the Great American Mountain Rally had provided Saab with massive launch publicity in 1956, and in 1957, at what the Americans called 'Little Le Mans' at the Little Rock Circuit in Connecticut, Saab 93s stormed to class victory – even if they did have to 'borrow' some extra tyres from road-going, privately owned Saabs in the car park! From 1958–62, Saab and Volvo battled it out at the Little Rock Circuit. American Saab driving teams included Mayforth/Thompson and Andang/Rutan.

In 1957, Harald Kronegard with navigator Charlie Lohmander competed in a Saab 93 in the Oasis Rally in Morocco, and won their class in the Mille Miglia. Saab had also taken second place in the Acropolis Rally in 1957, won the Tulip Rally in Sweden in 1953, and also won the 1959 Canadian Rally. Carlsson and Palm triumphed in the Spa- Sofie-Liège rally over several years, just as happened with the British RAC Rally. Winning the Monte Carlo Rally in 1962 and then again in 1963, with a third place in 1964, seemed somehow inevitable.

But it was not just the tough little Saabs that were rallied. Early Sonett outings included a 1969 Monte Carlo Rally third-in-class placing, although this was deflated by a scrutineering row and the organizers' dysfunction, to the Saab's cost. Simo

The Saab rally team under 'Polar' sponsorship with the 99 EMS.

PAT MOSS CARLSSON

Pat Moss was sister to (Sir) Stirling Moss. She learned to drive on the family farm in Land Rovers, and also learned hand, eye and leg co-ordination skills on horseback. Pat Moss had a class victory at the 1950 Horse of the Year Show and in 1953 won the Queen Elizabeth Cup at White City.

Switching from four legs to four wheels, Pat's early drives were in a Triumph TR2, and she won first time out in a regional rally. A Triumph factory drive did not happen, but MG snapped up the young Pat, and she drove an MG TF to a top three Ladies Class place in 1955. Her first drive in the Monte Carlo was in 1956 in an Austin as a crew member, when all on board survived a crash over the barrier on a mountainside hairpin bend.

Various drives in a range of car makes came and went, but it was when she won the 1960 Liège-Rome-Liège rally outright in a big Healey 3000 that she was marked out as something special. Pat might have won the 1961 RAC Rally if she had not stopped to assist a certain Erik Carlsson who needed a spare tyre. The following year she won the Tulip rally in a Mini Cooper. Pat married Erik Carlsson in 1963 during her drive for Ford. Not surprisingly, Pat found herself driving Saabs in very quick order. She finished fifth in that year's Monte Carlo and third the following year, beaten only by a faster Porsche and a lighter Mini Cooper.

Pat then switched to driving for Lancia, with that easy familiarity that the Swedes and English have with the Italians, and drives in the fast but fragile Renault Alpine followed.

'Mrs Carlsson' retired in 1974, after a brief spell driving for Toyota.

Lampinen, the car's driver, was not happy to be demoted for what he thought was the race officials' actions...

RALLYING THE 99

The 99 had a lot to live up to, and it was bigger, heavier and consequently less nimble – and until the advent of the EMS and the Turbo, it was hardly a performance-oriented rally car. The foundations of the 99's rallying career were laid in the late 1960s Saab rallying department led by 'Bo' Hellborg. The Saab rally team evolved into a well staffed department with twenty mechanics and with Mr Hellborg and another 'Bo', by the name of 'Baby Bo' Swaner, as the managers.

The 99 EMS received work on its cylinder head, which eventually led to an early 16-valve head. A claimed 200bhp from this engine was fitted into a two-door EMS shell in 1975. The 99's first competition outing was the Boucles de Spa Rally in Belgium in 1976, with Stig Blomqvist behind the wheel. Development problems occurred, but Saab won the 1977 Swedish Rally. The 99 EMS developed into 'Team Polar' as a result of sponsorship from the Swedish caravan manufacturer Polar.

For 1978, the Saab 99 rally team produced a boosted 240bhp – which may in fact have been too peaky in its power delivery for its own good on muddy and snowy stages, where low-end torque was important. The turbocharger had been boosted from 0.8 to 1.6 bar! However, this issue did not stop Stig Blomqvist winning the World Rally Championship in 1978. The 99 might not have had the subsequent Audi Quattro's 4WD, but it was the first turbocharged car to win the World Rally Championship.

The 99 in EMS guise, charging on with Blomqvist at the helm in snow. Borje Jarl was the Saab rally team manager for twenty RAC rallies. Per Rudh was the service manager.

99 Turbo-spec rally car. The two-door was lighter and more nimble than the combi bodyshell.

A cadre of 99 rally drivers was used by Saab: these included Stig Blomqvist with co-driver Bjorn Cederberg, Per Eklund with co-driver Hans-Eric Sylvan, Simo Lampinen with Taipo Raino, and Ola Stromberg with Carl Orrenius.

The years 1979 to 1982 were the 99 Turbo's most rewarding campaigns. In 1981, Clarion, the car audio company, entered into a sponsorship deal with the Saab rally team, and the Clarion-liveried 99s were seen across the European rally circuit and Group 2 class. But in late 1982, after a series of mechanical failures – which ironically would lead to improvements to production Saab turbos – Saab withdrew from rallying.

Stig Blomqvist, the Original 'Stig'

Stig Blomqvist was actually called Lennart, but the term 'Stig' was a great PR tool and one later picked up by the BBC's *Top Gear* programme. Blomqvist lived in Great Britain for decades, and many wondered if he was indeed the original 'Stig'.

Blomqvist first rallied a Saab 96 in 1964, but his name was perhaps best associated with the 99 EMS and 99 Turbo. His international victories included the Swedish Rally, 1,000 Lakes, RAC Rally, Cyprus Rally, Boucles de Spa, and a long list of major events. On snow or ice, often with Bjorn Cederberg or

Hans-Erik Sylvan as co-drivers, respectively, Blomqvist was a speed sensation, driving around the 99 Turbo's lag and lack of low-speed urge – just as the old two-strokes had had to be kept 'on-song', so too did the turbocharger in the 99. Such was his success that Saab was the major rallying name in the 1970s, long before Audi and Lancia stormed to prominence.

The real Stig: Mr Blomqvist and his 99 T.

SPECIFICATIONS   SAAB 99 T RALLY

Body

Internal roll cage and fire suppression. Bracing to cross-member to carry sump-guard loads

Engine

Type	4-cylinder in-line, base Saab unit
Cylinders	4
Cooling	Water
Bore & stroke	90mm×78mm
Capacity	1985cc
Compression ratio:	6.5:1
Turbocharger	Garrett AirResearch T3 at max boost of 1.6bar
Max. power	225bhp, then raised to 246bhp @ 6,000rpm (275bhp in ultimate spec)
Max. torque	236lb ft @ 8,500rpm rev limit

Transmission

12.4 drive ratio compared to 18.1 (standard spec) mph per 1,000rpm in top. Specially strengthened gearbox with removal of synchromesh rings

Suspension

Independent with front double wishbones/coil springs/shock absorbers. Rear tubular axle with twin links and Panhard rod.

Wheels

'Minilite' type with Dunlop tyres, Bilstein gas dampers

Brakes

Discs all round

Performance

0–60mph: 7sec, 0–100mph: 14.58sec

Top speed

191km/h (119mph)

Dimensions

Fuel tank	74.5ltr (16.4gal) in safety shield, later in boot for two-door variant
Wheelbase	2,473mm (97in)
Length	4,354mm (171in)
Width	1,676mm (66.1in)
Height	1,450mm (58in)
Weight	1,102kg (2,425lb); two-door shell 18kg (40lb) lighter

Privateers

Private entrants continued to run the Saab 99 in rallies in Europe and North America. In Britain, John Harrison with navigator Richard Burdon drove his 99 EMS to fame in many club-level events. From 1979 David and Joan Martin ran a private 99 rally car, with sponsorship from Alexander's, the Saab dealer. The pair used a 99 with seam welding, uprated brakes and suspension, body reinforcements, and a lighter glassfibre bonnet.

Phil Davies of Bolton Saab entered the Welsh rally in 1979, while the Saab Owners Club of GB followed the event in its Saab GB-supplied 99 three-door support vehicle. In 1985 Dave Broadbent and Barry Rowson entered a 99 in a series of British club races. Saab employee Mike Bennion entered a 175bhp 99 Turbo in the 1982–83 Monroe-sponsored production Saloon Car Championship. Jane Neate campaigned both a 96 and a 99. Rob Johnstone was a leading 99 competitor.

In Australia, Saab Automotive of Brisbane, run by John Rues, entered a 99 EMS in Australian club events. Ian Ferguson drove a 99 EMS prepared by Saab Automotive in a series of historic races in Australia. Dave Elund of Saab Automotive built a circuit racer from a carbonfibre Saab 900 that was fitted with a Chevrolet 350cu in engine. Former Formula One ace and World Champion Alan Jones drove his own private Saab 900 and competed in a Saab 900 race series; latterly Damon Hill also drove a 900 in a circuit race.

In the USA, a number of privateers entered Saab 99s in various states of tune and modification in a series of events in the 1980s; Sonetts were also campaigned. In 1976 *Car and Driver* magazine's editorial staff drove a Saab 99 in a magazine 'challenge' at the Little Rock Circuit. The first Saab 99 EMS racer in the USA belonged to a Texas Saab dealer named Glen Seureau. In 1977, Saab America's PR manager Len Lonnegran managed a *de facto* Club series 99 team; the drivers were Don Knowles,

RIGHT: **Privateers in Sweden and Britain used the 99. Rob Johnstone was a leading British competitor.**

BELOW: **Ola Stromberg's restored 99 rally car.**

Jan McKnight, Bill Fishburn and Tom Walker. Saab's first US national championship placing came from a 99 driven by Don Knowles. In 1979 over forty Saab 99s were raced in the SCCA Club series of circuit races.

From the 1980s right up to the present decade a 'Vintage Saab Racing Group' (VSRG) campaigned highly modified Saab Sonetts (and other Saabs) across North America. The lead names in the US Sonett privateer racing teams included Randy Crook, Charles Christ, Steve Church, Ed Diehl, Mary Anne Fieux, William Hardy, Chris Moberg, George Vapaa and his son Stefan, and Bruce Turk. Dr Richard Thomson also raced Saabs, and went on to drive Corvettes in competition. Father and son George and Stefan Vapaa became well known Sonett racers and restorers. Jack Lawrence was the anointed guru of Sonett tuning modification and Club series racing, and his design improvements were the rock upon which Saab privateers based their driving.

Saab 99s continue to be raced and rallied to the present day, notably in Belgium, Holland and Sweden. Polar Caravans, the original sponsors of a Saab 99 rally car in the 1970s, were still

LEFT: **Chris Partington the legendary Saab GB rally expert and tuner seen with his 93 which he has twice taken to Le Mans. A true Saab 'guru'.**

Saabs old and new – the 92 and the 96, brothers in rallying.

sponsoring in 2008 a Malbrad-tuned 99 EMS rally car driven by British privateer Jim Valentine, with John and Caroline Lodge and John Sparks supporting. This car performed in the 2008 Omloop van Vlaanderen rally in Belgium.

ABOVE: **Bjorn Cederberg at speed in the 96. You can almost hear it.**

RIGHT: **Jonsson and Muller drove these two in the Mille Miligia re-run. One got damaged...**

Per Eklund

Per Eklund, nicknamed 'Pekka', was a Saab rally driver who made the crossover into rallycross and continued to win events beyond his sixty-fifth birthday. Eklund was a Saab works driver from 1970 to 1979, and achieved the distinction of being the last Saab factory driver to compete in the World Rally Championship in 1979. He continued rallying a private Saab to 1984 in the world championship classes. He also drove a 900T in British rally events. In 1982 Eklund was placed fifth in the FIA world rally rankings.

In the 1970s, Clarion were the 99T rally car's sponsors, as they would be over twenty years later when Eklund would campaign a 9-3 rallycross car. He would go on to use a 9-3 series two sedan for rallycross and circuit racing.

Eklund had taken to rallycross in the 'chuckable' little 96 V4, but not only did he rallycross the 99, he became a top

Per Eklund was still a rally-cross winner in his sixties, and Clarion were still sponsoring a Saab.

competitor in the 1990s and the early years of the new century. He was FIA European Rallycross Champion in 1999 with a Saab 9-3 T16 4x4, and a consistent 2nd overall in the 1998, 2002 and 2003 FIA European Rallycross Championships. He was 3rd overall in the 2000 and 2001 FIA European Rallycross Championships, and Swedish Rallycross Champion in 2004. In 2000 he achieved the record time of 11:21.58 in his Saab 9-3 Viggen 4x4 in the American, Pikes Peak 'unlimited' class.

RALLYCROSS

The British in particular took the 99 to their rallycross and autocross hearts. A Saab-sponsored 99, festooned with 'Saab Finance' decals, was raced by Will Gollup in the British rallycross series in 1982. The car's mechanic was Tim Skinner. This followed on from a successful late-1970s emergence of the 99 on the rallycross scene. Gollup had used a 16-valve 99 EMS, but switched to the Turbo. Victories included events at Lydden Hill and Snetterton in Group A.

For 1982, with continuing Saab sponsorhip, the rallycross team with Lyndon Fraser used a lightweight 99 with glassfibre body panels: this made it a massive 280kg (616lb) lighter. The Garrett turbocharger was replaced by a Schwitzer unit delivering 265bhp.

In the following decade, 99s were still being used for rallycross. Saab Owners Club members Ian Scott and Ken Bell took over Malcolm Dickinson's two-door 99 and added a water-injected 900 Turbo engine, a quicker steering rack and revised suspension.

The 900 and 9-3 at Pace

The Saab 900 did not achieve such glory as the 99 in rallying or rallycross, but it was successfully campaigned by a number of privateers, and formed the basis of a one-make circuit series named 'Mobil Challenge' in 1988 with Saab sponsorship. Damon Hill drove a Saab 900 Turbo in the series. Dealers and privateers raced in the nationals series, and Chris Day, sponsored by Haymill Saab, was a well known privateer. Charles Tippet, Tony Dron, James Latham, Lionel Abbott, Gerry Marshall, Andy Dawson and John Lewellyn were also the 'names' of the series.

At home in Sweden, the 900 excelled in ice rallying events, driven by Ola Stomberg and Tina Thorner. Back in the UK, Beechcroft Saab Rally Team was set up following success in the Turbo Challenge series. The dealer team from Beechcroft scored several rally placings between 1989 and 1994. RAC rally class placings were achieved. Drivers included Ola Stromberg, Will Gollup, John Wheatley, Dave Wood and Ian Wood. In

Australia a Saab 9-3 wide-bodied Abbott Racing Motorsport specification car, sponsored by the Swedish Prestige tuning and repair company, was campaigned at club circuit level by Dean Randle – who survived a massive shunt in 2008 at the Phillip Island circuit.

In America, the early years of Saab 93-96 and Sonett racing had carved a competitive Saab niche and a 'Team Saab' saw the new 900 go circuit racing. The 900 Turbos of Complete Saab of Woodstock Georgia won numerous events, including an endurance event in 1980. The team's drivers included Bill Fishburne, Don Knowles, John Dinkel and Joe Risz of *Road and Track* magazine.

Also in the USA was the little known use from 1987 to 1991 of Saab 2.0-litre turbocharged engines of 225bhp to power a single-seat entry-level 'Club' racing car for the John Barker Race School. This race series was known as the 'Barker Saab Pro Series'.

JL Racing is one of Canada's premier sports saloon racing teams. In 2006, JL Racing formed a partnership with Saab Canada to race the series two 9-3 as a racing saloon car. JL won its first race and had many podium finishes in the Candian Touring Car Championship. In 2008–09 the JL team went up in bhp to enter the Super Touring Car Class, the JL Saab 9-3 finishing 5th overall in the 2007 championship. The 2008 driver line-up included Diane Dale, John Lockhart and Jason Sharpe.

The new generation of cars, notably the GM-based 900 and 9-3, also found favour as rally cars and club-level circuit racers. The tuning company Nordic Saab built a 550bhp (410kW) 9-3 hatchback in 2005. Using a bored-out Saab 2.0-litre block, Nordic's 'Concept Extreme' was one of the fastest Saabs in the world when it was built, boasting a quarter-mile time of 1.41sec to 220km/h (137mph); it also accelerated from 160km/h (99mph) to 230km/h (143mph) in 3.5sec.

In 2007 SpeedParts built an 802bhp (598kW) 9-3 Turbo X4R based on the 9-3 Mk2 saloon shape. This car was an expensively rebuilt circuit racer, and was also used for promotional purposes. Per-Anders Johansson built the Saab 9-3 X4R. Johansson worked at Saab and knew just how powerful Eklund's earlier 'Pikes Peak' 9-3 racer had been – over 600bhp. Saab's technical department helped design the bodykit. Lowered, widened and with more downforce, the 9-3 X4R was a circuit saloon car racer with a touch of street-hot rod thrown in. A Turbonetics/ITS T76 turbocharger created the warp-speed acceleration.

Slower down the speed scale, in 2010 Saab chairman Victor Muller and acting Saab chief executive Jan Ake Jonsson – 'JAK' – each drove 1957 vintage Saab 93 rally specification cars in the historic Mille Miglia race. A 93 had won its class in the event fifty-three years previously. Said JAK: 'Saab's early success in this event is part of our rich heritage. We enjoyed competing again with the Saab 93, although we didn't drive quite so fast!'

THE SAAB 900 MK2 – 9-3

New generation 900, all Envall in style, but **GM**
underneath. This is an early three-door variant.

GENERAL MOTORS'
GENETICALLY MODIFIED CARS

THE SAAB 900 MK2 – 9-3

GENERAL MOTORS' GENETICALLY MODIFIED CARS

A S THE 900, like all Saabs, aged gracefully and yet began to lose sales, Saab and its new major shareholder knew that the race was on to build a fresh face. General Motors (GM) decided to put the idea of a new small Saab – aimed principally at Europe – on the back burner, and to proceed with the prestige branding it had perceived as Saab's value. Perhaps this was the moment that GM made its major Saab mistake?

Imagine if the first new GM car from Saab had been a modern version of the 92–96, a sort of sporty, Swedish take on the Golf or the old Alfasud? But GM went with the moment instead of looking to a wider perspective, and a bigger car for the 1980s resulted. When a 'new' 900 was first thought about, General Motors (GM) had not yet purchased half of Saab, but by the time the car was launched 'the General' had totally absorbed the Swedish company.

Before he left Saab, Björn Envall had sketched out the shape of the replacement for his essential '900' iconography. The British Saab styling studio man Simon Padian had also been involved in creating the feel of the new car. The new 900 would be a new shape, yet one that reflected Saab's curves. It was not a retro-pastiche in, for example, the mould of the Rover 75 or the Mini, but it was clearly a shape of Saab. When Envall made his first sketches he had no idea what base chassis platform would represent the foundations of the new car.

Saab was soon to find out, as GM told Saab to fit the new car to the underpinnings of the existing Opel/Vauxhall Calibre, itself a part-Cavalier model-derived platform. This was the first full collaboration between the engineers of GM and Saab, and it was a time when both parties had to adapt to each other's way of doing things. Saab learned about economies of scale and sharing components, but GM had to learn about Saab's way of engineering – structural enhancements and forensic aerodynamics, not to mention tweaked engine behaviour. Using the Opel/Vauxhall parts bin and platform meant that the new design had to be shrunk to fit – it was narrower than the Envall studio team had originally drawn, which had been based on a modified version of the wider-tracked 9000. This change caused at least one year's delay to the new 900's birth.

The new car would be a hatchback – in five-door and then three-door style within the first year of production – and an essential convertible was also included.

DESIGN CUES

It was impossible for Saab to repeat the curved windscreen of the original 900, and the long low front and rear overhangs were out of fashion – a longer wheelbase would give more cabin room. But by tuning certain design elements, such as the roof turret and front windscreen profiles, allied to sweeping compound curves and elliptical themes, the new car's shape was made to look like a proper Saab and not an ersatz piece of design trickery. From the rear, the curved tail and rear windscreen architecture was pure Envall-for-Saab in its graphics.

The basic new model 900 had an excellent drag coefficient for its size, Cd 0.30, but that would rise with the fitment of bigger bumpers, spoilers and wider wheels.

The elegance of the Envall-penned GM 900 is captured here in the five-door model. All the Saab styling elements are present except the clamshell bonnet.

Suspension would be by a conventional McPherson front strut and a multi-linked rear axle. Saab took the GM Opel components and subjected them to the Saab process: this meant that metal gauges were increased, extra struts and supports built into the floorpan, and stronger sills and door panels created. Across the top of the rear seat a special steel box-beam would lock into the C pillars, providing extra strength and safety in the rear of the hatchback – an idea first tried out in the 99 three-door. The car would also have a reinforced windscreen frame to resist the danger of crushing from elk and deer – a major road traffic safety hazard in Scandinavia.

The car's engines were to come from Saab's pre-existing range, although a GM 2.5-litre, 54 degree-angled V6 with smooth power characteristics would appeal to Saab's American customer base; this was the first V6 to be used in a Saab. Top-of-the-range variants of the new 900 would of course be turbocharged – a continuation of the essential branding. The base model was a 2.0-litre non-turbo, and the Saab 'Trionic' system, first developed for the 9000, would also be used to create a cleaner breathing and less polluting engine. Saab devised a special support frame for the engine to reduce noise vibration and harshness – or 'NVH' to the engineers.

The new car also saw the early launch of an electro-mechanical semi-automatic gearbox. Saab called it 'Sensonic', and it stemmed from Saab's early investigations into 'fly-by-wire' self-steering, self-driving, computer-controlled cars. Sensonic pre-dated the fashion for semi-automatic gearboxes and was not without its problems; Saab fans did not take to it.

As with the 9000, Saab went to its usual measures for the interior. Under the lead of designer Aina Nilsson, an ergonomic cockpit 'zone', blackout or 'black panel' instrument panel function, to reduce unwanted night-time instrument glow, reflected aviation practice. The new seats were, as usual, orthopaedic masterpieces with safety-enhancing head rests and neck protectors.

The interior was thickly padded and moulded in high quality synthetic materials. Leather and cloth seat trims were chosen in upmarket colours, and the whole cabin ambience was of a level to match that of Germany's finest.

Although based on more 'normal' Opel underpinnings, a great deal of design thought and testing went into the new 900. Erik Carlsson drove an early development car and suggested some changes to the 'feel' of the brakes and steering.

SAFETY QUESTIONS

Safety was a major issue for Saab, and the new 900 had to be safe. Saab subjected the car to the current regulatory requirements and it passed them with room to spare. Saab also tested the car to its own higher requirements in side, roll-over and offset frontal impacts – nineteen extra crash-test criteria.

Crucially, Saab had re-engineered the GM floorpan-based car to pass a 50km/h (35mph) offset frontal impact; it had even patented its own design of wheel arch and sill reinforcement panel to reduce intrusion into the front footwells, thus lessening the risk of leg injuries. With its careful addition of thicker steel, fillets, extra load paths and stronger front wings and doors, Saab had done all it could to make its new car Saab-safe. It subjected the car to offset frontal crash testing at 35mph – just on 56km/h, a speed in excess of the 50km/h (30mph) test norms. The car passed with minimal A-pillar and firewall deformation, and with low injury readings for the occupants. The doors also opened easily and the survival cell was sufficiently undamaged at the test speed to indicate that at higher speeds it would still perform well.

It therefore came as a major shock when during subsequent 1997 EURONCAP crash testing, after being subjected to a 63km/h (39mph) offset frontal crash test into a barrier, the new 900 was found to have suffered a major collapse of the A post and sill, and that the door had failed. Inside Saab, in the hearts of its safety obsessives, there wasn't just genuine shock, there was real concern. How could EURONCAP's barrier tests produce such a different result? The poor performance of the car was a deeply felt shock to Swedish pride and its safety ethos, and Saab was criticized in the Swedish media.

Although it was a PR disaster, Saab moved swiftly. It wondered if there was an issue with the differences between the crash test barriers used by it and EURONCAP. Saab designed for real-world car-to-car impacts, not laboratory tests into simulated concrete and aluminium walls. Saab also noted that whatever the deformation issues, the EURONCAP car had protected its occupants by subjecting them to low impact forces in the vital head and leg regions. Damage to the cabin there may have been, but unlike certain other cars, occupant injury forces were low. In real-world crashes, the car had not signalled a problem.

The Saab was not alone in suffering excessive A-pillar movement, and even the Mercedes C Class had encountered such an issue in its own EURONCAP test. The 900 still performed well in comparison to its base vehicle platform, but Saab's first GM-based car had, despite all Saab's efforts, failed in one of its prime Saab clauses. To say that there was consternation at Saab was to underestimate the event. How had GM and Saab missed the fact that the base platform, even when Saabized, failed with only a small increase in crash energy over the norm? GM, having funded and tolerated the Saab obsession, could perhaps justifiably question the turn of events. But had not Saab *strengthened* the GM base plate? Something strange had gone on, but the scars still run deep.

The 900 became 9-3 in 1998. This one has the **Airflow** bodykit. Lead engineer on the 9-3 development and notably the 9-3 Viggen was John-Gustav Gudmundsson.

SPECIFICATIONS — SAAB 900 NEW GENERATION (GM) 1994–1998

Manufactured at Trollhättan, Sweden and Uusikaupunki, Finland.

Body

Based on GM Vectra/Calibra/Cavalier-derived platforms with Saab body and mechanical upgrades, notably to safety cell and rear suspension. Available as 3- and 5-door hatchbacks and 2-door convertible

Engine

Note: 900 'B' series engines (B204/206) were shortened derivatives of the B234 type engine used in the 9000. B206 engine at 2.0 litres non-turbocharged dispensed with balancer shafts

2.0 litre 16V

2.0 litre 16V Turbo

2.3 litre 16V Turbo

(Saab B series 204 /234) with APC: DI: Trionic 2.5 litre V6 (GM) 54 degree vee 6.

Typical power outputs 130bhp (99kW); 185bhp (136kW); 150bhp (110kW); 170bhp (130kW)

Transmission

Front-engined, front-wheel drive via five-speed manual and 'Sensonic' electro-mechanical until replaced with four-speed auto

Dimensions

Wheelbase	2,601mm (102.4in)
Length	4,638mm (182.6in)
Width	1,712mm (67.4 in)
Height	1,435mm (56.5 in)

For Saab, however, there was only one answer: changes had to be made. Thus the 900 received stronger sill and A-pillar panels, more welding, and a change to the roof rails. All these changes were worked into cars produced after September 1998, on the cusp of the car's relaunch as the Saab 9-3. Subsequent EURONCAP testing showed that an improvement to the cabin's resistance to deformation and intrusion was achieved, with less A-pillar movement and a higher safety rating. Injury forces were still low.

DEVELOPING THE RANGE

First presented to the press in the summer of 1993, the first GM/Saab car was launched as a 1994 model in 900 S and SE variants as the new five-door 900: it became known as the 'New Generation' 900. Reaction was positive, despite a few qualms about a loss of Saab soul in the feel of the car and how it drove. The styling received much praise.

With ABS brakes, airbags, alloy wheels, smart cabins and fantastic seats, the car ticked many Swedish boxes. British sales began in 1994, and later that year came the American debut and that of the three-door car – an even cleaner design that looked closer to the original, classic 900.

Saab's No. 1 Alloy, called ALU 36.

The car could be had in 2.0-litre, 2.3-litre Turbo, and 2.5-litre V6-powered models. This included the twin balancer shaft engine from the 9000, which still remained in production. The cloth-trimmed, base 900 S 2-litre with 133bhp/99kW power rating proved to be an excellent lead-in model for the range.

From 1996 to 1997, the 900 was subjected to the normal Saab improvement process; this included the fitting of computerized electronic 'EBD' brake force assistance. By late 1996, the convertible or cabrio model had sold 14,200 examples, and demand was rising. Sales of the 170bhp 2.5-litre V6 were also surprisingly strong in Europe. Engine designation badges – and notably that of the V6 – were removed from the front grilles at this time.

In 1997, the 900 received new wheel trims, minor styling changes and for the 1997 model year, another Saab 'Talledega' branded car was born – the 900 Talledega reflected yet another visit to the US raceway to perform long-distance record-breaking runs. The fastest car racked up a distance of 40,000 kilometres (24,850 miles) at an average speed of 226.450km/h (140.716mph) – in other words, flat out. Saab celebrated by fitting a rear lamp décor panel, smart new alloys and special badges. A new bumper design – soon to be seen on the revised 900, the 9-3 – made its debut on the Talledega. 900 Talledegas were often seen in Cayenne metallic, and looked very smart indeed.

A one-off, bright yellow, three-door 'Turbo Sport' 900, with added performance and a unique bodykit, did the round of the motor shows and signalled that Saab was toying with creating a performance badge. This would soon be manifested as the 'Viggen' branding based on the revised 900 – the 9-3.

THE 9-3 AND A SECOND BITE AT THE APPLE

The Swedes might have been somewhat partisan at the launch of the new generation 900, but the truth was that although it had a depth of design it did not feel totally convincing in the manner of a 'real' Saab. To prove this assertion, a 900 Mk2 was evolved that was given a new number – that of 9-3, itself continuing the Saab '9' theme. Over 1,000 detailed changes were made to the 900: these included structural reinforcements and a real attempt to make the car feel and steer like a true Saab.

Thus the steering was quickened, front struts were strengthened, and there were longer spring travel rates allied to recalibrated dampers. Crucially a strut brace under the bonnet reduced flex, as did a stronger steering-rack mounting, although it was still mounted to the front bulkhead rather than a subframe. This was strange, as GM had let Saab create a special engine cradle subframe for the 900, on which 9-3 was based.

Engine options included the use of sixteen valves, distributor-less ignition, a light-pressure turbo and a high compression 2.0-litre engine to replace the 2.3 in some models. The Saab 'Ecopower' 2.0-litre engine was to offer a blend of power and economy that proved just how good Saab's engine designers were. The motoring media and the 9-3 owners soon came to love the sweet, seamless, instantly responsive 4-cylinder: 0–60mph in 8sec and 50km/h (35mph) in the cruise was achieved long before expensive, variable valve-timing trickery was credited with achieving such gains by other manufacturers.

With its revised steering, better suspension and taut front-end structure, 9-3 now felt as much like a Saab as it could. Only the Opel-inherited road/tyre roar coming up through the front wings and bulkhead hinted at more humble origins. But despite that, the 9-3 was a driver's car that could clearly handle more power, even if torque steer and the consequent creation of the Abbot Motorsport 'Rescue Kit' – a device to tame the wayward front steering and driveshaft response under full power – proved the point about the car's origins.

ABOVE: **The 9-3 with the amazing Toppola bolt-on camping house!**

RIGHT: **Monte Carlo Yellow 900 convertibles.**

BELOW: **Giallo Fly part two! Convertibles from the rear at a Swiss Saab meeting.**

Classic setting for a Saab soft-top – the Bristol gliding club.

The 9-3 was marketed with the revised version B204 engine of 154bhp (115kW), which was low. In America, 9-3s were sold only with the 185hp 138kW turbo engine. European markets saw a GM-sourced 2.2 diesel engine across the markets, later replaced with the GM-Fiat 1.9 diesel in the 9-3 second series.

Viggen and Lightning Blue

The name 'Viggen' or in English 'Thunderbolt', was taken from the Saab fighter jet of the same name: Saab Type 37 Viggen.

Established as a sub-brand using bold blue and yellow brand colours, in fact a specially created Lightning Blue, the 9-3 Viggen started out as a three-door bodyshell, but soon became available in other forms – notably as a convertible. The cars had 239bhp (173kW) and 1.4bar turbo boost from a Mitsubishi turbocharger. The vital 0–60mph speed was a tyre-eating 6.3sec in a straight line. The electronically limited top speed was 259km/h (155mph).

Development work was entrusted to TWR in the UK. Apart from the bodykit, major work went on under the skin of the 9-3. A stronger gearbox from the 9-5 was used, with stiffer casing, a heavier output shaft and a stronger clutch. The drive-shafts were also upgraded.

However, despite other engineering changes – including recalibrated shock absorbers, revised and lowered springs and rates, stronger CV joints, and increased stiffness in the steering box and rack – Viggen still suffered from bad torque steer. A 'rescue kit' that braced the steering rack was an after-market must for Viggen owners – although little could alter the effects of massive power going through front-wheel drive and unequal length driveshafts.

The 9-3 Viggen was a manual-only car, and had an electronically limited torque-sensing unit to prevent overload of the gearbox.

Special Viggen trim items installed between 1999 and 2002 included heated sports bolstered seats that could be ordered with a range of contrasting colours to the seat panels, also

This SVO 'Sport' concept was a 900, but led to the 9-3 and the Viggen.

Viggen badges and leather embossing. A larger rear spoiler increased downforce at the expense of drag, but this increase was ameliorated by smoothed side panels at sill height. Up to 2001 Viggen had a carbonfibre facia insert, but this was deleted for the last year of production. It also had unique alloy wheels, although these turned out to be soft and easily kinked by kerbing, so many owners substituted other Saab wheels. Inside,

the two-tone leather seats had the Viggen logo embossed into them. The compression ration of 9.3:1 was high for a turbocharged car, but resulted in better burn efficiency and mpg.

Just 4,600 9-3 Viggens were manufactured, many in blue, black and silver-grey. A few dozen were produced in Saab's famous Monte Carlo yellow. The 9-3 Viggen is now one of the rarest of all Saab models.

Typical Saab aerodynamics work – a revised spoiler design.

Saab Viggen branding badge for the 1990s.

SPECIFICATIONS — ABBOTT ARMT 16 AND VIGGEN

Abbott Racing created an ARMT 16 car in late 1994 based on the 3-door new 900. This 235bhp, 2.0 litre Turbo had traction control, sports suspension, with limited slip differential and 215×45 ZR 17 tyres. This was effectively the first performance version of the 900 NG and was studied by Saab. Consequently Saab created the 'Viggen' performance branding based on the Saab Special Vehicle Operation (SVO) department and the one-off, 230bhp 900 3-door SVO. Saab's team headed by Peter Leonard, worked with TWR to develop the Viggen range. Lead development engineer on the project was Saab veteran John-Gustav Gudmundsson.

Engine
Saab B235R with larger Mitsubishi TD04 turbocharger, Trionic & engine management system, revised intercooler, nimonic alloy exhaust valves and revised final drive ratios

Power	230bhp (168kW)
Torque	149.34Nm (258lbft) torque

Wheels and Tyres

Wheels	7.5 × 17 alloys
Tyres	215/45 ZR 17 Dunlop SP

Dimensions (Viggen 3-door)

Wheelbase	2,605mm (102.6in)
Length	4,639mm (180.9in)
Width	1,711mm (55.7in)

Top Speed
155 mph (249km/h)

RIGHT: **Saab 9-3 Viggen at the Saab UK Owners Club national meet.**

BELOW: **Viggen Blue. Enough said.**

9-3 Second Series

Introduced in 2002, the 9-3 Mk2, or second series, was still a car based on GM parts but it was more heavily 'Saabised', and at cost of time and money. Although a hatchback version was designed and planned for, it was dropped, and the 'new' 9-3 emerged as a three-box business-class saloon somewhat in the manner of the BMW 3 series, although different in character.

Early cars of 2002 and 2003, although equipped with many Saab features and a definite character, suffered from some quality issues, notably in electrics and plastic trim items; however, build quality definitely improved thereafter, although the use of a cheap grade of leather for the seats meant that the driver's seat outer bolster suffered heavy wear in just a few thousand miles.

In 2005, an estate car or combi wagon version was launched, and the convertible arrived soon afterwards from Austria; it was built in this country by Steyr under contract for some time before returning to Sweden. The 9-3 was launched with trim names as sub-brands similar to those used on the 9-5 – thus Linear, Arc and Vector indicated varying sports and comfort trims. These were eventually dropped, but the Aero branding remained, notably in the USA.

Several engines have been available on the car, and although European markets have latterly focused on the Tid and TTID diesel variants, the smooth, sweet-revving and economical Saab 2.0-litre and 1.8-litre petrol engines, especially in 'Ecopower' tune, suited the car and earned many admirers who could see beyond the diesel fad.

Engines included a rare non-turbo 1.8-litre. The more common 1.8- and 2.0-litre Turbos were 'Ecopower' LPT variants, but the 2.0-litre Turbo with 175bhp (130kW) became available as a high pressure, full-bore turbo. From 2003 to 2004 a GM-sourced 2.2-litre diesel was fitted, but this was changed to a GM-Fiat 120bhp 8-valve, and then 150bhp 16-valve Tid unit from 2005. Latterly a 2.8 Turbo V6 was launched; this also evolved into the tweaked Turbo X unit. A 210bhp 2.0T was available in both the Arc and Vector trims and as an Aero in the UK. Automatic transmission was available, though in the Vector, paddle shifters mounted on the steering wheel were added to the Saab electronic shift system.

In 2007, the 9-3 was updated and given a new interior with better quality mouldings, and a revised external badging and

A late model 9-3 interior: simple yet stylish, in true Swedish design.

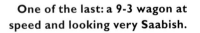

One of the last: a 9-3 wagon at speed and looking very Saabish.

Saab finally made a soft-roader version of the 93, here in its intended element.

trim. For 2008 the car was subjected to a major redesign in appearance, overseen by Simon Padian: it was given new metal and an upgraded clamshell bonnet/hood design, with an aggressive new Saab frontal treatment that reflected the three elements of the old Saab grille design, inspired by the Aero X concept cars.

In 2009 and launched at the Geneva Motor show in March, the 9-3X was a 4WD 'soft roader' version of the 9-3 Sport-Combi, designed to tap into the market of the Volvo XC70 and Audi All-Road. Regretfully the 9-3X only had 4WD in its petrol-engined form – the diesel versions could only accommodate FWD, and this cost the car many conquest sales in a competitive European market place.

SPECIFICATIONS SAAB 9-3 SERIES 2 2002–2012

Made in Nykoping, and Trollhättan Sweden, convertibles made for some time by Magna-Steyr, Austria

Body

Based on GM Vectra platform as revised by Saab design and components. Available as 4-door saloon, 5-door estate/wagon and 2-door convertible. Front-engined, front-wheel drive; four-wheel drive available

Engine

Note: engines included GM Ecotec series

1.8 litre 16V + Turbo and Biopower fuel variants

2.0 litre 16V + Turbo and Biopower fuel variants

2.0 litre Turbo

2.8 litre V6 Turbo

2.2 litre Turbo Diesel 2002–2004

1.9 litre turbo Diesel 118/148bhp 2004 onwards: 1.9 TTiD variants

Power

(with low-high boost pressures) 4-cylinders 210bhp (160kW); 6-cylinders 250bhp (190kW); TX 280bhp (210kW) with optional Saab boost kit to 300bhp; diesel range from 118–177bhp (88–132kW)

Transmission

Five/six-speed manuals; six-speed automatic with paddle shift and 'Sentronic' electro-mechanical actuation. Haldex 4WD system on TX

Top speeds

2.0 T XWD 146mph; 1.9 TTiD 140mph; 1.8T 131mph

Dimensions (base series 1)

Wheelbase	2,675mm (105.2in)
Length	4,635mm (182.5in)/4,648mm (183.5in)
Width	1,753mm (69.0in)/1,781mm (70.8in)
Height	1,443mm (56.8in)/1,540mm (60.6in)

RIGHT: **Turbo X and XWD branding underneath the elliptical rear lip spoiler.**

BELOW: **Black Turbo. The 9-3 AeroX launch photography from Saab.**

BOTTOM: **Special wheels and aerodynamic kit and shades of the old 900 T.**

The Turbo X

Saab made over 2,000 changes to the 2008 cars. The 2008 range was first presented at the Saab Festival in June 2007 at Trollhättan. A V6-powered all-wheel-drive variant was somewhat obscured by the launch of the all-black 'Turbo X' variant of the new car. Turbo X was a limited-edition car designed to evoke memories or emotions of the old 99 and 900 Turbo ranges. It had a 280bhp (211kW) 2.8-litre Turbo V6, with a massive 400Nm of torque. It also had twin exhausts, very special Saab-designed alloy wheels, and a vast array of kit and trim enhancements as standard. Of note, a 'take off' management program pre-empted the engagement of rear-wheel drive without the need to detect 'slip' in the front driven wheels beforehand. This put down the power faster, and improved grip, and was an aspect of the Saab-Haldex XWD application that was unique to Saab. An elliptical rear deck spoiler tunes the separation of airflow and reduces lift over the rear end at higher speeds. The twin exhausts were rhomboid in tailpipe shape and matched the re-styled rear valance. In the cabin, the dashboard featured a turbo boost gauge identical to that fitted to the original Saab Turbo.

Announced in late 2007 for the 2008 model year, the Turbo X had a Haldex all-wheel-drive system, which included an electronic limited slip differential. A six-speed manual or automatic gearbox was offered. Carbonfibre trim panels and a range of aerodynamic trim items were added to the car, which, like the 9-3 Viggen, is one of the rarest of the recent Saabs.

ABOVE: **Raven beauty, Turbo X at home in the forests of Scandinavia. Note the front bumper styling, seen on subsequent Saabs.**

BELOW: **Subtle but meaningful 9-3 interior, with 'cockpit' design carry-over.**

ANOTHER REVAMP FOR 2012

As Saab-Spyker became Swedish Auto, or 'SWAN', the new owners rushed through a range of superficial and in-depth engineering changes to the by now decade-old base plate of the 9-3. Significantly the engine CO_2 ratings were reduced, and the TTID got to below the magic 120g figure. Externally, a more aggressive use of alloys, air vents and bumper and spoiler shapes brought significant visual updates for minimal metal tooling changes. Suddenly the 9-3 felt even more like a 'real' Saab. A limited 'Independence Edition' convertible was announced in 2011 to mark Spyker-Saab's own independence. These lavishly equipped cars are now highly sought after.

ABOVE: **Saab safety – not a barrier test, but car-to-car offset at high speed. Note how the driver's survival space remains intact.**

LEFT: **A Saab 9-3, with Hirsch bits and smart alloys as options.**

Reinforcing structure of the 9-3 convertible.

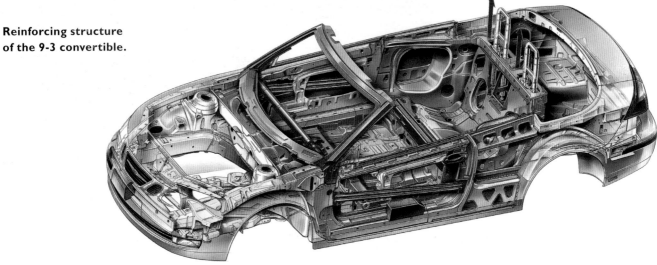

ABOVE: **One of Saab's best shades of blue seen on a 9-3 convertible.**

RIGHT: **A 9-3 with the hood down, showing off leather and style.**

THE JOHANSSON BOYS AND A FOUR-WHEEL-DRIVE CLUTCH

Peter Johansson was a Saab chassis engineer who followed his father, Sigge, into Saab. Siggevard had worked for the Saab competitons department and, notably, had worked on both the fuel-injected and turbocharged V4 projects. Peter's maternal line grandfather was Tage Flodén, one of the original team of fifteen who built the first Saab 92.001, or 'UrSaab'. Tage had then worked on the 92 production series and engine tooling.

Sigge Johansson had invented the electronically controlled, limited slip differential (LSD) using a multi-plate clutch system, which he patented, and which was later developed by Haldex into a 4WD transmission management device. Peter Johansson tested the system: he had grown up rallying and racing karts (at one stage as a youth beating Ayrton Senna in a kart race). 'My father took out the original patent on this new transmission system back in 1980,' recalls Peter.

In fact the 4WD device, which seems such a natural for a Saab to be equipped with, given Scandinavia's icy roads, lay dormant at Saab for many years until GM sanctioned its use on the later 9-3 second series range and the new 9-5 of 2010. The system works by taking the drive off the front differential and into a propshaft mated to an electronic rear diff via a set of Haldex electronic clutches mounted within the rear axle, instead of waiting for wheelspin to activate the limited slip differential.

Electronic software with locally sited sensors detects the vehicle, engine and relative wheel speeds, lateral acceleration, steering angle, throttle position and yaw rates, and the system apportions torque between axles for maximum grip and roadholding, effectively balancing or re-balancing the car. It was a sort of road-going equivalent to vectored thrust, and was used effectively on Turbo X and was destined for the subsequent 9-5 and later hoped-for Saabs.

Last of the lineage: the 2010, 9-3 Independence model – fast work from Saab and more Saabish than ever.

THE 9-5 AND
THE NEW 9⁵

Original 9-5 in white, with full Aero styling and
classic Saab alloys – a French owner's pride and joy.

HIGH HOPES AND A
LAST CHANCE SALOON

THE 9-5 AND THE NEW 9⁵

HIGH HOPES AND A LAST CHANCE SALOON

S AAB'S NEW CAR – a supposedly completely new car – was badged as the 9⁵, or 9-5. Saab advertises it as the 9-5, pronounced 'nine five', not 'ninety-five'. Based on a General Motors Opel/ Vauxhall Vectra floorpan, the new Saab was more thoroughly developed, more Saabized, than the new generation 900 and 93 had been. For all its GM underpinnings, the new big Saab was heavily reworked and contained a number of styling and engineering features that stood the test of time. For the 9-5 was to stay in production for a very long period, far too long in hard commercial terms. However, for a car that was not a 'real' Saab – according to the purists – the 9-5 made many friends.

The new 9-5 was in fact not that new, for Saab had talked to Fiat about creating an updated version of the 9000 but basing it on a development of the Alfa Romeo 164 version of the Type Four car platform. This came to nothing, and then GM bought into Saab, effectively ending any potential Saab link with Fiat for good. But in a strange coincidence, GM created a tie-up with Fiat in the mid-1990s. This led to a suggestion of a shared, GM-Fiat large European car platform that could be engineered into a new, large Saab, thus fulfilling GM's 'prestige' desire for Saab, notably in America. Much work was done in planning such a car, but then the idea was terminated. So Saab's new 9-5, based on GM underpinnings, had nearly been a reverse-engineered Fiat-Saab. Perhaps in the loss of this bespoke and tailored car,

Saab lost its last chance to create its 'own' car rather than the GM-based 9-5 that eventually resulted.

The new GM Vectra-based 9-5, designed and engineered in 1996–97 as a 9000 replacement and known as 'Project 640', took a basic GM Vectra floorpan and added essential Saab ingredients – safety, aerodynamics and performance. The styling was directed by the Norwegian Einar Hareide. Also cited was the clever thinking of Tony Catignani as a lead designer, the aerodynamics were by Haken Danielsson, the safety by Mats Fägerhag, and the chassis handling by Leif Larsson. Project manager and lead engineer of the 9-5 was Saab veteran Olle Granlund. Ingrid Karlsson was a lead interior stylist and colourist, giving the 9-5 its subtle yet secure interior ambience. Arne Näbo was a Saab aeronautical engineer who played a role in the ergonomic design of the 9-5's cockpit zone. And of Simon Padian's influence, time would tell.

A NEW STYLE

Einar Hareide said of the 9-5:

> My personal view is that Saab's identity lies first and foremost on a state of mind. Designing a car is a matter of balance; this applies equally to form and function.

Early version of the 9-5 wagon, Saab's first estate for decades.

However, its design must not be so harmonious that it loses its identity – like subdued background music. We must offer the eye pleasing contrasts, unexpected transitions from soft to hard lines, from concave to convex surfaces... Then it becomes exciting and dynamic, a product with true personality. [17]

Those words frame the true ethos of recent Saab design in visual, sculptural terms, and draw upon older Saab themes for their context. So the key styling ingredients of this new car included a Saab 'face' at the front, and at the rear a very strong C-pillar shape – an emotive hark back to the upswept curves of the Saab 99 and 900 four door. The overlapping clamshell bonnet/hood design that started life on the 99 was included, as were some very clean panel lines and junctions at the base of the A-pillar and windscreen-to-roof turret joints.

At the rear, although the car was a 'three-box' saloon with a boot shape tacked on, the aerodynamics were very carefully managed to reduce to an absolute minimum the separated airflow drag from the rear windscreen. This was an old Saab trick – tuning the airflow off the back of the car. With a booted saloon shape, the airflow normally breaks or separates at the top of the rear windscreen and creates a large wake off the boot/trunk lid. Most spoilers that are added to the trailing edge of such boot/trunk lids usually perform no other real aerodynamic function and are solely marketing devices. Given that such rear deck spoilers sit in a wash of separated airflow, their effect upon that airflow is often pointless, other than being a marketing con.

However, on some saloons, such as the pioneering NSU Ro80, careful design can create a high boot/trunk lid that works in conjunction with the C pillars and rear windscreen angles to tune and even reattach airflow in this vital 'wake' region of base drag. With sharp-edged blades to the C pillars, and with correct curves on the rear flanks and windscreen angle, the airflow can be controlled and set to perform at known parameters – it does not wander about and move its separation point as it might on an ill-defined curved bulb of a rear-end shape. The two vital ingredients of such tuning are side-wind stability and rear-wake pressure, and Saab excelled at tuning their effects.

In the 9-5, Saab's design team, notably under the direction of senior aerodynamicist Haken Danielsson, employed all it had known for decades and created a three-box shape that actually preserved airflow down its rump, and made an integral rear lip spoiler fitted to the 9-5 that was aerodynamically effective. Danielsson explained:

One of the car designer's most difficult tasks is to minimize dirt accumulations on the car body. The sides are most vulnerable owing to wheel spatter, and the rear panel owing to air turbulence. Dirt accumulation is not just a matter of aesthetics – clean windows and lights are vital to safety.

A fast-moving car leaves a 'hole' in the air behind it. The trick is to fill this hole with clean air from above, instead of dirty air from below. Everything interacts to minimize drag. [18]

With a claimed Cd of 0.29 for the fully trimmed production car on standard wheels, the curved front, domed roof, clean-sided teardrop rear, and Kamm-theory cutlines of the 9-5 reflected the same knowledge that had gone into the 92 and 99 all those years previously. The proof was in the driving, for the 9-5 saloon and estate had clean, low drag aerodynamics, excellent pressure control and expertly tuned airflow separation and side-wind stability qualities. Even the door handles were low drag, and the window seals were thin and the glass as flush as possible, thereby lowering cabin noise levels as well as total drag. So efficient was the rear-end styling of the 9-5 saloon that in a reversal of normal rules, the estate had a slightly higher drag figure of Cd 0.31. Later sports versions with larger alloy wheels and bodykits increased the figure to Cd 0.33.

The styling of the later 9-5 estate/wagon was particularly handsome and did not look as though the estate rear had been tacked on to a saloon shape. The new glasshouse rear swooped stylishly off the C pillars and created a very strong visual graphic statement: it looked as though it had been inspired by the long-forgotten Saab 99 'Multikaross' styling study from two decades before.

The 9-5 went through two 'facelifts', or styling 'refreshes', as PR men might say. The first, in 2002, saw a new, sleeker frontal treatment and revised trims and rear lamp motifs; the second revision, in 2006, was more controversial. In a bold move, Saab added shiny 'chrome'-effect grille and headlamp trims to a new frontal architecture. In light colours like silver, the new front trim looked stylish, but set against a darker body colour, especially black, the shiny headlamp trims at the front looked odd – perhaps echoing old-fashioned spectacles as worn by a certain famous Australian impresario. This led to the 'Dame Edna' nickname, which was not exactly flattering for a car, however talented Barry Humphries of Dame Edna fame was.

At the rear of the revised 9-5 there were new light shapes, but no shiny trim to match the front. Some Saab fans were revolted, others grew to like the individuality of the front. Hirsch, the Saab performance and trim accessory makers, produced a special trim kit to reduce the bright and shiny effect of the frontal trims. Some owners painted the shiny trims body colour, which proved very successful.

As usual with Saab, the 9-5 came with an array of wonderful alloy wheel designs throughout its life, and a wide choice of stylish interior colours and trims, ranging from old-fashioned

2002 saw a revision to the 9-5's frontal styling, with a one-piece grille and bumper unit.

walnut wood through to carbonfibre. Fantastic alloy wheel design had always been a Saab trait, but on the 9-5 Saab's wheel designers really went to town and there were over twenty different alloy wheels that could be fitted – all Saab designs.

The 9-5 was produced in a wide range of colours: some owners insisted on having a black one, when the car perhaps had the feel of the old Turbo classics; others loved silver, grey or red, and the 9-5 looked very large in white. Saab came up with a wide palette of grey shades, which caught the light on the car beautifully; and in its later days, it came in great range of blue, from slate blue to sapphire hues. Three blue colours in the life of the 9-5 stand out – 'Cosmic', 'Nocturne' and 'Fusion'. These

blues seemed really to make the most of the facets of the 9-5 styling and the alloy wheel combinations, the wheels known as ALU 36 or ALU 60 series often being favoured.

A rare, midlife 9-5 colour was 'Hazelnut', which made the 9-5 look less sporty and more Lexoid – fit for the golf club perhaps? A spoiler – notably a rear 'bridge' spoiler – was a common fitment for the sports-minded 9-5 enthusiast, as were a vast catalogue of tuning parts and body trims from Maptun, Abbott, Hirsch and a host of tuners. The 9-5 looked very businesslike in the various shades of grey in which it was available.

Throughout its life, the 9-5 also came with a diversity of interior seat trims – notably full leather, ventilated leather (with

**Saab-safe structure of the 9-5 wagon.
The shell has multiple deformation zones.**

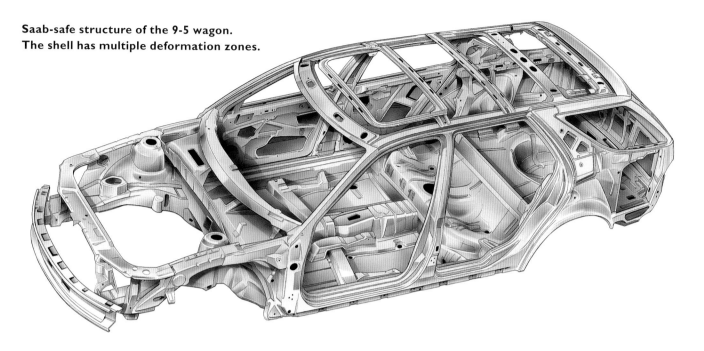

cooling fans under the seats) and a sporty part cloth, part leather combination. Later 9-5s also dispensed with the somewhat boring, original four-spoke steering wheel, and were given a more sporty, three-spoke helm. A range of wood, fake brushed alloy and carbonfibre inserts were used on the facia panel. With a long production run, no one can argue that Saab did not constantly tweak the car and offer the loyal fans and owners a stunning array of trims, changes, colours, shapes and identity for their cars.

An oil breather and sludge transferral problem became apparent with the 1997–2004 engines, and Saab instigated a remedy for engines post-2004. A warranty claim programme was launched for owners of earlier cars who had experienced problems in cars with the correct servicing history.

SERIOUS SAFETY

On the safety front, the 9-5 had to re-establish Saab's safety credentials after the new-generation 900 suffered its EURON-CAP debacle. Under the front end were massive, wide, flat-topped, impact-absorbing panels running down the front wings – broad 'steel bellows' that could suck up impact forces as the wheel-arch housings did likewise, especially in angled or offset impacts. The soft front was designed to crumple and reduce energy being transmitted to the cabin and its occupants. Special members transmitted impact forces downwards into the lower bulkhead and floor.

To capture impacts from varying angles, not just head-on, the 9-5 was given three major load paths in its front end, and

The 9-5 was top of the class for safety, and this car-to-car crash test shows why: the cabin cell has only minimal deformation, and loadings on the occupants are low.

a five-zone deformation area that featured steels of differing strengths. This engineering effectively bought extra time for managing the crash forces – channelling and absorbing them so that their effects on the central safety cage and its occupants were lessened.

A special sill reinforcement fillet stopped the front wheels buckling the sills, while each door also had several reinforcement beams to channel lateral compression forces. The rear end also had multiple impact-carrying load paths and structural members. Of particular note, the Saab 9-5 had a 'pendulum' design B pillar. This meant that the central or middle pillar in the cabin was designed to buckle in a planned manner, at its base: by swinging inwards and downwards at an unbraced floor point, lethal side-impact forces were directed away from crucial areas of human vulnerability – the head, chest and thoracic regions. An angled upper-level roof fillet to the B pillar reduced head-level intrusion. These design innovations reduced injury forces in the vital mid- and upper body region, assisted by a full height side airbag system deploying from the seat.

Building on the 99 and classic 900 experience, the 9-5 had very strong A pillars and a network of reinforcements around the windscreen aperture. Roll-over strength and roof strength

The early 9-5 interior was soon transformed from wood-lined lounge to sports-trimmed cockpit.

The same mouldings, but revised trims and motifs took the cabin into a new era.

to elk-test standards were built in. The 9-5 passed the basic, legislated crash tests, but it also exceeded their requirements by up to 60 per cent in some areas. Crash-barrier tests were one thing, but real-life car-to-car crash testing across a wide range of potential impact scenarios was the 9-5's safety development forte. This was not just the safest Saab ever, it turned out to be the safest car in the world at its launch. Numerous safety awards – often based on real-life survival stories – came the 9-5's way, including top ratings in EURONCAP and Insurance Institute and Highway Loss Data Institute crash tests in America.

Even the head-restraints – known as the 'Saab Active Head Restraint' or 'SAHR' – were rated the safest on the market, drastically reducing the risk of neck injury in a rear crash. The 9-5 also had the 'Saab-Safeseat' system for all its seats, with reinforcing bars and impact-absorbing ratchets. Of note, the two front seats had an 'active' head protection system that moved the head-rest upwards to 'catch' the occupant's head and reduce rear impact whiplash.

The 9-5 was fitted with the fashionable plethora of airbags, but all the airbags in the world are worthless if the structure to which they are attached is not properly designed to resist structural intrusion. The 9-5 team made sure that the car was thoroughly engineered from a safety standpoint and resisted intrusion to a very high degree. Other cars of the late 1990s were also safely designed, but it was the Saab 9-5 that scored the highest marks for occupant protection in the EURONCAP and US crash tests. The proof of the Saab safety engineering was in the crashing, and the Saab 9-5 stayed a top crash-test performer even a decade after its launch. This was true testimony to Saab's safety commitment. By being so far in advance of basic safety requirements and the basic safety specifications of certain other car makers, the 9-5 saved lives and retained that ability for twelve years, despite the 'catch-up' of other car makers in safety engineering.

This was true testimony to the ethos of the men and women of the Saab safety centre.

SPECIFICATIONS

SAAB 9-5 4-DOOR SALOON 1997–2009; 5-DOOR ESTATE/WAGON 1997–2010

Manufactured Trollhättan, Sweden.

Body

Base on GM Vectra platform with Saab revisions; front engined, front-wheel drive.

Engine

Note: Petrol engines were Saab 'H' type derived from Saab 'B' type

2.0 litre with Biopower E85 variants

2.3 litre APC/DIN Trionic derived systems

3.0 litre V6 Asymmetric Turbo

2.2 litre Turbo Diesel

3.0 litre Turbo Diesel

1.9 litre Turbo Diesel

Power	2.3 litre 178bhp (132kW); 3.0 litre 168bhp (125kW); Aero 4 cylinder 256bhp (191kW)
	Hirsch Performance tuning options deliver 20–60bhp more and 45–80Nm increases; Hirsch spec gives 2.3ltr Aero 300bhp/400Nm and 1.9 Tid 175bhp/350Nm

Transmissions

Five-speed manual, four-speed auto and five-speed auto

Top speed

2.0 T 134mph; 2.3T (220bhp) 146mph; 2.3 HOT 155mph; 2.2 TiD 124mph

Dimensions

Wheelbase	2,703mm (106.4in)
Length	4,805mm (189.2in), 4,825mm series 2
Width	1,793mm (70.6in), 1,790mm (70.4in)
Height	1,448mm (57in) 1,496mm (58.9in) wagon

MODEL DEVELOPMENT

As usual for Saab, the 9-5 was kept on far beyond the industry's normal model cycle. But Saab did not let it wither on the vine: instead they threw money at the 9-5 across a twelve-year lifespan.

The 9-5's life can be divided into three phases – calling the different variants merely 'facelifts' would be to underestimate Saab's thoroughness. The 9-5 gained between 2.5 and 6.5cm (1 and 2.5in) in overall length due to revised front and rear bumper mouldings over the course of the three styling changes.

Across its life the car had a range of engines that offered ever more power. Early engines were the heavily modified 2.0-litre and 2.3-litre Saab units. GM provided a 3.0-litre diesel engine that made the 9-5 a great towing car, but it had an appetite for automatic gearboxes. Then came the GM 2.2-litre diesel engine, which was superseded by the GM-Fiat 1.9 diesel engine of 150bhp, though this had to work hard to pull the heavy 9-5 around. The 9-5 GM-V6 was unusual in its asymmetric turbocharging, a Saab application that worked well. At the top of the later 9-5 range came the Aero 'Hot' (manual gearbox) versions, which featured an overboost function giving 20sec of extra power that turned the 9-5 into a temporary 270bhp supercar performer.

The most numerous 9-5 was the popular estate car version that stayed on in production after the saloon variant died in July 2009. The estate was removed prematurely from the market in February 2010, and the new 9-5 combi wagon was not ready, thus leaving Saab with no estate car in its line-up; however, the old and venerable and still excellent 9-5 was. Over its lifespan, from 1997 to 2010, the 9-5 range had 252,236 saloons and 231,357 wagons built, total production being 483,593 units. So Saab made nearly half a million 9-5s, almost the same number of cars as the 9000, its predecessor.

The 9-5 might have been an Opel Vectra-based car of decidedly mediocre – by Saab standards – underpinnings, but two facts stand out: first and foremost, it was developed into a characterful Saab, and contained a degree of 'Saabness' that gave it a feel of occasion akin to that old special Saab feel. The interior and the engines were a particular highlight of Saab design, as were the passive safety features. The turbocharged performance, in a straight line at least, was stunning – no wonder police forces used 9-5 Aero H versions as motorway patrol and pursuit cars as far afield as Yorkshire and Poland.

ABOVE: **Original Saab 9-5 rear with 'bridge' spoiler.**

LEFT: **The revised 2006 9-5 rear lamp and bumper treatment.**

SAAB 9-5 MODEL DEVELOPMENT AND VARIANTS

1997 Launched in the summer of 1997 as a 9000 replacement. Introduces SAHR – Saab Active Head Restraint, the award-winning system that drastically reduces neck injuries. Launch engines included the 2.0-litre and 2.3-litre Saab engines, Cd 0.29.

1998 First full model year of 1997 cars. Sales launched in the USA in late 1997 for the 1998 model year. The GM-sourced V6 engine with asymmetric turbocharger of Saab design is announced for the 9-5 range.

1999 Estate car or wagon version launched as 'Sport-Combi' variant with Cd 0.31. The Estate has the innovative cargo-track luggage system taken from the aviation industry.

2000 9-5 'Aero' sub-brand launched, with 230bhp, 2.3 Turbo engine with lowered and stiffened suspension.

2001 Five-speed auto replaces four-speed autobox. The 3.0-litre, 176bhp, Isuzu-sourced GM V6 diesel engine mated to an autobox is launched.

2002 Refreshed frontal styling. The 247bhp engine is used for Aero models. The 2.2-litre, 218bhp, Opel-sourced GM diesel engine makes its debut. Linear, Vector, Vector Sport and Aero model brandings are introduced. Increased steel gauges in certain components, and reinforcements to sills and A posts help retain world-leading crash-test performances and ratings with EURONCAP and the IIHS/IHLDI.

2003 New colour schemes, revised alloy wheel designs.

2004 For late 2004, new positive crankcase ventilation system and revised internal flow solve a sludge problem in the early 9-5 engine breathing and oil pipes. A warranty claims mitigation programme is announced for 1997–2004 engines with this design issue.

2005 Controversial, chrome-style frontal redesign complemented by new interior trims and colour choices. Revised rear lamps and bumpers on the saloon and estate. 2.0-litre, 178bhp, Biopower engine runs on a blend of fuels. Revised Aero gets 256bhp with over-boost function to 270bhp on manual cars only.

2006 2.3-litre, 207bhp, Biopower launched. 2.2- and 3.0-litre diesels discontinued. Fiat-sourced 1.9-litre, 150bhp TiD diesel launched.

2007 Interior trim revisions. New range of alloy wheel designs. Anniversary models announced for the UK. 'Turbo Sport' editions with twin exhausts and Hirsch options launched.

2008 Specification and trim revisions. TiD 150bhp Sport variant launched.

2009 Last year of 9-5 saloon production. Estate car body continues into 2010.

Production figures Saab 9-5: 483,593

Note: Abbott, Hirsch Performance, MapTun Performance, Nordic Uhr and BSR are after-market tuners who can remap and rebuild 9-5 engines to produce 330–470bhp.

Police specification 9-5s were used by police forces in Sweden, Norway, Denmark, the Netherlands, Great Britain and in Aspen and Vail, Colorado USA. British police forces, notably Hampshire and Yorkshire constabularies, used unmarked, Aero-spec 9-5s for high speed pursuit, while the Scottish police at the Lothian and Borders constabulary used police-branded 9-5 patrol cars to 2.3 Aero spec.

Controversial re-style for mid-decade created the 'Dame Edna'-tagged frontal aspect.

Hard at work in the snow, a late model 9-5 estate shows off the controversial chrome frontal treatment. This one has the Hirsch satin finish kit applied to its face.

SIMON PADIAN, THE BRIT WHO BECAME A SAABIST

Simon Padian was born in Britain in 1965; his wife is Swedish. He attended Coventry University's transportation design course and gained a BA Hons degree in Industrial Design, and found his way to Saab in early 1989. Bjorn Envall was still in charge then, and Padian, despite a later brief period working in the USA for Cadillac, became a Saabist, immersed in the lore of Saab design.

Padian achieved design headlines building Saab-concept cars under GM. He held numerous designer, lead designer and concept car design roles within the ethos of Saab, and notably guided the shape of the 9-3 Second Series. From 2005, in conjunction with GM's German-based European design unit headed by Mark Adams, he directed the Saab design function at the Saab Design Centre near Gothenburg.

Padian worked on the new 900 with Bjorn Envall, a car originally based on a modified Saab 9000 platform but which was changed to a GM-sourced platform late in the design stage. Padian also said in an interview with Steven Wade that Saab had been working on a 4x4-type vehicle long before the Chevrolet-based 97x was born. Such thinking would be manifested in the excellent, albeit late to the market, 93X Combi concept.

A hatchback version of the 9-3 Series 2 was also drawn up inside Saab, but never made it to production, therefore denying Saab a buyer base of its former hatchback followers.

Padian, as a Swedish convert with nearly two decades of experience at Saab, knew what Scandinavian design meant. He knew how to sculpt Saabs, and in the new 2010 9-5 Mk 2 presented a memorable piece of moving sculpture – but perhaps his greatest Saab design legacy was the stunning 'cockpit' interiors that he created.

Secondly, the 9-5 sold well and brought to Saab ownership a new generation of owners who had no experience or knowledge of the previous incarnations of Saab. Some 'old Saab' owners bought 9-5s, but the 9-5's success as a business saloon meant that legions of company car drivers who normally would not have gone near a Saab, got to experience the Saab product, however diluted some might suggest the GM-Saab 9-5 was. Others, private owners with families, soon discovered the comfort, safety and sense of security that Saab 9-5 ownership offered.

Saab owners love to modify their cars, and this 9-5 has gone all the way.

DCA Saab's 9-5 panel van and behind it their 9-5 limo.

The Swedish police loved the 9-5, as did the law enforcers in Great Britain and the USA.

LAST CHANCE SALOON: THE 9-5 MK 2, 2009–11

Overseen by a dedicated team of Saabists, notably design chief Simon Padian, yet also under the wing of Mark Ward as head of GM's European design centre, the new Mark 2 version of the 9-5 was perhaps the most 'Saabized' vesion of any GM-based platform used by Saab.

Using the GM 'Epsilon' platform, and based round the Opel Insignia's framework, this 9-5 was a lengthened and deepened car compared to the Insignia. It had a long, sweeping tail that echoed the original 900 body style. There was also a turret roof and visually curved and smoothed A-pillar treatment. The Saab 'hockey stick' design motif of a rising window line running up into a reverse-angle C pillar made a strong design statement in graphical terms. A single chrome-effect trim strip added to the

effect. Like most modern cars, the nose was deep and high with a large impact-absorbing front valance panel, created to meet legislation concerning pedestrian impact.

At the very rear, an 'ice-effect' rear lamp treatment gave the new car a defining graphic that separated it from the mainstream executive-class herd. According to model variants, the new car had differing under-bumper styling and air vent treatments.

The interior was a Saab sensation, a true 'cockpit' or 'flight-deck' design that included an optional head-up display. Sadly, the wonderful traditional Saab seat design was ditched in favour of a more GM-based seat pan and headrest. The new 9-5 came with many options, including the Haldex-based 4WD system, not to mention a plethora of trims, engines and the usual array of sensational Saab alloy wheels.

ABOVE: **Early 2010 and the last of the 9-5s at the factory.**

LEFT: **New 9-5 on the production line at last.**

The new 9-5 was a car with a massive job on its hands: it had to share certain elements with a corporate parts bin, and above all had to rebuild a brand and a model line that, however good, had become aged. In the new 9-5, in an instant Saab had a car of such design integrity and purity that it looked as if it could have been honed by a master of Turinese sculpture. The 9-5 simply oozed the elements, the smell, the stance and spirit of Saab, yet did so genuinely and not with retro gimmicks or false promises. This was design that would last, design that will be seen to be genuine and thoughtful. It is design that is Scandinavian in a marketable manner.

So the new 9-5 was a timeless piece of Saabism, a true auto sculpture in the sense of honest design: it had no gimmickry. This was a car that, outside and inside, looked, felt and drove like a Saab. There was probably only 20 per cent of Opel left in it! Launched at the Frankfurt Motor Show in late 2009, Saab waited until March 2011 at the Geneva Motor Show to introduce the estate or 'Combi' version and its stylish new rear end.

The car was safer than any Saab: it had a massive impact-absorbing steel 'bellows' up front, and expertly tuned load paths to steer impact and energy away from the occupants. Behind the dashboard was a network of reinforcing beams that ensured the engine did not intrude into the cabin. Side-impact and roll-over protection were also of the best possible design. Top scores in crash testing for EURONCAP and the US IIHS/HLDI were achieved.

TRIMMED UP

The new 9-5 came in a range of trims and badge-engineered variants according to the global marketplace: Turbo4, Turbo4x, Premium, Turbo6 XWD, Linear Vector, Sport and Aero were the key badges.

Engine choice was a major selling point, and just two months after its debut, Saab added two extra engines to the 'new' 9-5. The line-up included a 1.6-litre, 180bhp (134kW)-base petrol model, which was ideal for restricted European business user markets – but the mainstays of the range, according to market place, were the light and sweet-revving, 2.0-litre 220bhp (164 kW) turbo petrol, or the 1.9TiD diesel – an engine that had to be worked hard to haul the heavy body around.

For the new 9-5, Hirsch – the performance-parts people – went to town, adding power, special alloy wheels and a subtle range of body-enhancement addenda – less bodykit and more sports-style additions. 2011 models benefited from a tiny aerodynamic tweak: a thin, elliptically formed lip spoiler, expertly blended on to the rear trailing edge of the car, which enhanced the airflow separation point.

Saab launched the 9-5 in a sober shade of metallic grey that did the car no favours, and soon bright silver, red and blue cars featured in the publicity and advertising shots. The new 9-5 looked great in red, and all-white versions with an optional black-painted roof gave the car a distinct image. In the dark hues

New 9-5 interior cockpit design and head-up display.

of a deep bronzed metallic 'Java' brown, on black-painted alloys, the 9-5 was a massive design statement. But some say that never was a car so affected by paint colour choice: in pale colours the 9-5 looked rather heavy-nosed and deep-sided, yet in Fjord Blue or Laser Red it looked lithe. All that was really needed was a pair of 'Inca' alloys.

The early cars had an all-black coloured interior, but for 2011 production, a two-tone colour scheme with pale beige or mid-grey for the seats, door cards and lower facia panels made the interior look and feel larger and more relaxing. 2011 models were equipped with the correct centre console moulding, which made a big difference, though problems with the supply of this plastic-moulded trim panel caused the media to criticize its fit and finish. But it was the detailing that was exquisite – from steering wheel to gearstick, Padian and the team had worked wonders.

A popular new 9-5 choice in 2010 was the twin-turbo TTID 190bhp (142kW) engine mated to either a manual or automatic six-speed gearbox. The range-topping 2.8T had 300bhp (224kW), the all-wheel-drive system and every conceivable extra. The TTID could be ordered with either front-wheel drive or all-wheel drive, as could selected other models.

Saab in Switzerland. A Fjord Blue new 9-5 in action.

SAAB PEOPLE

Saab engineers and production/marketing leaders assoicated with new 9-5 and 97x, and 94x during the final years of Saab production:

Mats Ahunlund: engineer
Kjell Bergström: lead engineer 94x
Henrik Bjerkelund: production engineer
Gunnar Brunius: production director
Peter Dörrich: chief engineer
Per Jansson: chassis engineer
Ingrid Sjunnesson: emissions engineer 9-3/9-5
Knut Simonsson: VP marketing

The new 9-5 looks great in Laser Red. This is the top-spec Aero model with differing vents in the lower bumper.

The 9-5 also came with 'DriveSense', a Saab melange of electronic settings for the suspension, steering, transmission and XWD all-wheel-drive torque settings. There was a special handling kit that provided constantly adjustable damping as an intelligent mode driver's aid. But the highlight of the car's abilities had to be the Haldex-based, XWD-branded, all-wheel-drive system that, integrated with the electronic stability system (ESP) and a rear limited slip differential, gave the 9-5 advanced handling traits, just as a Saab should have. Equipment also included the Saab active head restraint, a lane departure sensor warning, and curtain airbags.

This rare 9-5 is the Saabs United car equipped with retro-style Saab stripes in the Swedish national colours – last seen on a 99 T rally car!

SPECIFICATIONS   SAAB 9-5 NEW MODEL 2010–2011

Built Trollhättan. 4-door fastback saloon: 5-door estate/wagon not mass produced, approx 110 constructed.

Body

Based on GM Epsilon 2 platform as modified Opel Insignia base. Front engined, front drive/four-wheel drive

Engine

1.6 litre Turbo (Eco)

2.0 litre Turbo + Biopower variant

2.8 litre Turbo

2.0 litre Tid Turbo Diesel

2.0 litre TTid

Transmission

Six-speed manual; six-speed automatic; 4XWD; 2WD; 'Drive Sense' management system of adjustable suspension and engine/transmission settings automatically adapts performance to conditions and usage.

Power

1.6 Eco 180bhp (134kW); 2.8 Litre 300bhp (224kW); TTid 190bhp (142kW). Full Hirsch performance and styling upgrades available

Dimensions

Wheelbase	2,837mm (111.8in)
Length	Saloon 5,008mm (197.1in); Wagon/SportCombi 5,010mm (197.2in)
Width	1,868mm (73.2in)
Height	Saloon 1,466mm (57.7in); Wagon/SportCombi 1,466mm (57.7in)

AN IGNOMINIOUS END

The precarious nature of Saab's existence between 2008 and 2012 meant that the new 9-5 was almost stillborn. Yet in the end it arrived, entered the showrooms, and sold well. Just over 10,000 were produced before the production lines stopped in April 2011. The final insult was that the 9-5 Combi, the beautiful wagon version, never made it to the buyers. Worse, in February 2012, GM instructed British Car Auctions (BCA) to sell the remaining completed new cars that had lain in the factory for months. BCA auctioned the cars online from Germany, and buyers had to go to Hamburg to pick up the last Saabs ever made as Saabs, by Saab's men and women. It was an ignominious end for a great car. Rumours of 9-5 Combi wagons being spirited away under a 'non-Europe sale' clause abounded, as did tales of complete showroom-ready cars being crushed in secret at Trollhättan. In America, brand new 9-5s sat in storage on docksides and began to fade as legal wrangles as to their ownership began.

LEFT: **9-5 Combi-Sport. The car that never was, and perhaps the car that might have saved Saab.**

BELOW: **So smart, so Saab and such a shame. A surefire 'car of the year', and GM-Saab's best car was stillborn. What a waste of millions of dollars...**

THE GM YEARS

Under **GM**, Saab made more concept cars than it did
new production models. The 2001, 9-X designed to redefine
Saab imagery – neither retro nor cliché, but a bit 'hot rod'
perhaps. The grille motif was an essential **Saab** element.

NEW CARS AND
OLD TROUBLES

THE GM YEARS

NEW CARS AND OLD TROUBLES

'THE GENERAL' – OR GM – is big, and always has been. GM is part of America's very structure: it epitomizes the American way, or it did. But the American way changed, and the over-stuffed US auto industry was perhaps the perfect example of the smoke and mirrors games that giant corporations began to play with their money and their products from the late 1980s onwards. But GM seemed to forget that a brand is defined by its product, and not the other way around.

The GM of old, the company that gave America the cars it wanted through the decades from the 1930s up to the 1960s, had known all about design, brands and niche marketing, and about producing wonderful cars with distinct characters that reflected the desires of loyal bands of followers. GM did not used to be in the mess it found itself in during the first decade of the new millennium.

Recently it has been fashionable to lampoon GM, but it is all too easy to forget its past – a past that was an essential part of American social history, and which shaped society. GM and its products were important to America and its Americans – and the GM effect blew across the Atlantic as well, influencing design and car buying across Europe.

GM may have been a century old, but it was not like some old colonel sat by the fire in its dotage. GM had been lithe, lean and fast-moving, and above all had inspired industrial and social design across several decades. Yes, GM needed rescuing in 2008 and 2009, but the GM of this time was not the fault of the GM of the past – a fact some commentators inexplicably forget. The irony is that GM is now recovering as a result of the methods that once made it great – design, independence and creating brand loyalty from its customers.

In its golden decades, GM was made up of a squadron, or maybe a circus of brands that competed with each other, yet all under the GM tent. Of particular note in social science terms, GM's brands evoked a tribal following amongst the American car-buying public. You could be a Ford man or woman, or a Chrysler fanatic, or a GM follower. The 'big three' all had brands within their badges, but it was perhaps GM who, above all, shaped and developed car design and car marketing as part of the American way of life from about 1955 to 1970: Chevrolet, Buick, Pontiac, Oldsmobile, Cadillac – these were all GM brands that were the very stuff of Americana. Through its designed-in diversity, GM could sell you anything you wanted, so why on earth would you shop elsewhere?

GM's secret was its management structure, where the strong and independent brand or tribal chiefs were given free rein to create what they wanted using generic GM-created parts from a central hub of co-operation. Then the engineers and designers worked their magic.

Contrary to recent fashionable attacks on GM and its management, the truth is that GM, prior to its malaise, was a creative, reactive, fast-moving, tuned-in and switched-on company run by people who knew about cars and their buyers. GM's dealers were allowed to tell its designers what the customers had said they wanted. GM was so influential that the brand of GM car you owned defined your position in society your class and your tastes.

Under the ethos of its founder William Durant, GM owned Cadillac, Buick, Chevrolet and Oldsmobile by the time Europe was finishing World War I. In the 1920s and 1930s, GM's president, Alfred P. Sloan, encouraged the brand camps under the GM umbrella. There they achieved a closeness, a contact with their customers in a manner that lasted for decades and built the GM we came to know. GM's Alfred Sloan is often quoted, but his most telling phrase was: 'We learned to react quickly.'

In the 1950s Harlow Curtice continued this thinking as GM's president. Under him, as under Sloan, GM did what it did, quickly and well: it did not submit itself to a politically correct, scientific process of evaluation by committee, it just got on with the job. When Ford and Chrysler hit back, GM reacted with new products and a non-stop stream of ideas. GM was, then, perhaps the company notable for ultimate ideas, and was at the leading edge of car design for over two decades. It produced cars that reflected what people said they wanted, and that society had embraced.

But somewhere along the line, GM replaced its design and brand-led thinking with a pared-down, focus-grouped plan that put committees of accountants and corporate strategists in control. Under its new head, finance man Frederic Donner, GM's tribes of the 1970s, its core brands, were reined in and forced to build cars that were centrally designed and centrally sourced from shared bodywork. The brands were no longer semi-autonomous states within GM – they became regiments in a bean-counters army. GM, some of its people and its cars became boring and predictable. Most of GM's cars in the USA and in Europe began to look the same, as they were often based on the same parts of cloned cars. Only GM Holden in Australia were really allowed to experiment for their local market conditions.

In Britain, once-proud Vauxhall was reduced to sticking its badge on GM's Opel cars, designed in Germany and lightly revised for the British market. Some of these cars were good, others were boring, and Opel and Vauxhall both declined in image. Both companies had once enjoyed strong and respected branding: Vauxhall had once been 'posh', and Opel had not always been as second tier as some like to suggest, since Fritz von Opel had also had aviation design links. The 1970s to 1980s concept cars or design specials of GM Europe were stunning examples of their genre.

By the early 1980s, men trained in finance took over at GM – but what did they know of design? Economies of design and

9-X had a typical Saab windscreen emotion and a 'wagon'-type rear.

Michael Mauer was Saab design leader circa 2001.

build were forced upon GM's divisions. The shining brands, the essence of a generation of Americans, began to die, with Oldsmobile succumbing in a long, painful dance with death. By 1990 it seemed GM had forgotten what its brand foundations, its brand pillars, were, and this malaise, this deep-seated change in GM's character, is perhaps the underlying cause of its own near-demise. As such, it mirrored the decline of an industry in an era that led to the self-inflicted crisis that came upon it.

The world of corporate jets and corporate language, the veneer of the suits and their faux military hierarchy, the 'expense account' brain-set of lowering operating costs by killing identity, and a desire for regurgitated designs, had usurped the world of actually producing products that people wanted to own. It was as if someone had forgotten that real design was what sold things – and good design cost no more than bad design and usually involved smaller committees and fewer meetings. It

seemed as though the customer could not possibly be expected to know anything – at least that was the impression.

GM also created Saturn, a stand-alone sub-brand that seemed to work well. Then GM bought Swedish car-maker Saab, in two tranches from 1990 onwards. Quite what GM's bean counters thought they were doing, spending all this money on foreign escapades when they had just spent a decade trimming their own US brands, designs and images to the point of likely self-destruction, was a paradox that GM's management seem to have quietly chosen to overlook. And would Saab stand alone like GM's Saturn brand?

Saab's troubles did not start with GM, however, and that is an undeniable fact, however uncomfortable for Saabists. The on-off Saab–Volvo mergers had come and gone in 1963 and 1977. Saab had worked with Fiat, and even talked of a merger. By the launch of the 1990 model year in September 1989, Saab, maker of large prestige cars only, had racked up losses of 800 million Skr, heading towards 100 million dollars at the exchange rates then current – and that was a half-year figure!

Saab had survived a sales crisis in the mid-1960s by creating the 96 V4, and it had entered the 1970s with the 99. It had escaped the late 1970s economic crisis by inventing the 'Turbo' brand and perfecting its mass marketing. And then in the 1980s, it had moved away from its roots to reinvent itself as a premium brand reliant on US sales and European executive car markets. These moves had saved Saab on each occasion – yet in turn they created flaws in the foundations of the brand and the structure of Saab as a car maker. In one decade Saab made small, sporty cars, and in the next it made family cars that it turned into turbocharged cars, and beyond that it created prestige cars – and *only* prestige cars in the form of the 900 and 9000.

Paradoxically Saab had followed fashion, not in design terms but in market terms, and by 1988 it would feel the full force of its own economic exposure. The engineering ethos, the internal ways and thinking of the Saab club and the Aeroplan men, struggled to survive the rush of more normal industrial thinking in a global market place. The true, harsh facts were that Saab, for all its fabulous engineering and wonderful moments, had ignored change in the world car market, and naively, or maybe even arrogantly, continued steering towards oblivion. Thus once a maker of a small sporty car, then a maker only of big expensive cars as fashion moved back towards the smaller car, Saab was swamped by a fashion it refused to adopt.

Amid what was, in 1989, a global corporate rush to secure assets and brands, GM, sneaking under Fiat's bumper, bought into Saab very quickly. Discussions took place in neutral Zurich during late November 1989, and by early 1990 GM owned 50 per cent of the Saab-Scania entity. GM rapidly injected its directors, planners and engineers into residence at Saab; many found a good fit with the team at Saab, others had to readjust. For some, a suggested Swedish arrogance was perceived; for others it was the start of an adventure with some of the world's greatest engineers.

DREAMS UNFULFILLED

Saab's first GM chief was David Herman in early 1990; he faced declining sales, notably in Saab's American profit centre, where for 1989 sales were down nearly 27 per cent compared to 1988. Saab had managed a very small operating profit of just over a million US dollars, or SKr11 million in 1987, but had made a SKr2.13 billion loss on 1989 – a figure that would balloon to hundreds of millions of US dollars in 1990. A round of staffing cuts and plant closures was soon to follow. Getting the operating costs down was vital, and their high pre-GM level shows just how insular the thinking of Saab had become. Pre-GM, Saab took 110 man-hours to build a 900, post-GM, the new 900 took thirty man-hours to build. Was this proof that the Swedes had grown a touch complacent on planet Saab?

A total of 2,000 dedicated Saab employees were made redundant. Amazingly, Saab's brand new production plant in Malmo, one that had cost millions to build and could have built cars for any part of GM, was closed. It was a move that would, paradoxically, lessen Saab's ability to build more cars and reduce its costs. Three years into GM's full tenure, Saab employed only 11,500 people.

With financial losses and sales of assets devaluing the company, GM and Saab-Scania had to inject large amounts of money into Saab to keep it going. The losses would have been even bigger, perhaps fatally so, if GM had not trimmed Saab's operating costs from 1990 onwards. For 1993, a new name took over the running of Saab: Keith Butler-Wheelhouse arrived from GM's global division. Butler-Wheelhouse oversaw the difficult days when old-model 900 production stopped in early 1993 before the new GM generation 900 model was announced in July 1993 – yet it only came into full production for the 1994 model year starting in September 1993. Further trimming of the workforce took place – down to below 10,000 staff.

Saab's rather quaint internal functions were trimmed on a supply and demand, 'just in time' supply basis. GM's global rationalization programme, a computerized ordering and manufacturing system, drastically reduced Saab's operating costs. Stock control ordering, build time and even worker absenteeism were all addressed. These important changes were managed by Saab's Stig-Goran Larsson and GM's David West, and they played a major part in returning Saab to profit in 1995. The new 900, and the new factory operating regime, achieved this turnaround. Saab was producing nearly 50,000 cars a year – a strong output, but less than half the number the accountants said was both possible and needed for survival.

1996 was a poor year for Saab – the 9000 was by now ageing and the new 9-5 was yet to make its debut. Sales figures slipped by 12 per cent. But the mid-decade years saw a new GM figure placed into the control of Saab when Robert Hendry arrived as the new CEO. For by the late 1990s, Saab was no longer owned by the old firm of Scania, with Scania removing itself from its historic partnership with Saab. An investment arm of the Wallenburg empire assumed the Scania share of Saab, and Saab as the car maker was now no longer linked to Saab aircraft production. Before long, GM would swallow even that last link to the past.

The new 9-5 of 1997 provided some respite for Saab under the GM umbrella, and a heavily revised, second series 9-3, based on more GM parts, kept sales running in Saab's fiftieth anniversary year. But there was no new small Saab, not even

BERGSTRÖM, BIOPOWER AND MORE

Kjell ac Bergström rose to be one of the stars of Saab's engine or 'power train department' in the GM years. Bergstrom and his team of engineers continued Saab's work on combustion efficiency, engine design and technology. Of note, Saab under Bergström's IQ pioneered the 'Biopower' plant-derived fuelled 'E85' engine and brought it to commercial reality. E85 has different combustion qualities and normal 'knock' sensors within automatic performance control cannot keep up with E85's 'burn'. Bergstrom and his team worked on solving this issue with such success that GM adopted the technology.

Another Bergrström area of focus was on reducing diesel emissions via lower compression ratios and on creating turbo charging, APC and driveline control systems. The new 9-5 was packed with such innovations, including adaptive ride and both petrol V6 and twin-turbo TTID diesel technology.

The Phoenix platform – an intended base for future Saabs – featured many novel possibilities including an electrically powered all-wheel-drive rear axle known as 'EXWD'.

Within the power train and engineering departments at Saab was also Saab Project Centre Director and lead engineer Peter Dörrich – another time-served Saab thinker. Men like Dorrich, team players Mats Fagerhag, Stefan Rundquist, Tommi Lindholm, Bengt Persson, Ola Granlund, Per Jansson and Mikael Jacobsson, all contributed to the 92x, 97x, 94X, new 9-5, and Phoenix platform. Hybrid technology, aerodynamics and drive train were all 'hidden' Saab contributions – as were advanced handling and steering dynamics.

Although patented under a GM branding, much of the technology within GM started life as Saab research. From Opel Insignia to Cadillac SUV, Saab contributed much to GM's patent applications.

This 2006 concept clearly influenced the new 9-5's frontal styling and graphics.

one based on a quick re-skin of a GM car. By 2005 the losses were horrendous, and the idea of a prestige Saab among the GM stable, one perhaps to tackle Lexus and Acura, never mind Audi, was a dying dream.

By 2008, a floundering Saab under GM was approaching death's door, with the GM paymasters ready to throw in the towel. Tinkering with the trim, and turning out Saab-badged Subaru Imprezzas and the 4x4 Chevrolet Blazer-based Saab 97x, had only fogged the landscape of Saab.

As 2008 ran into 2009, with the world economy in crisis and the banks failing, the story of GM, its rescue and its Swedish sojourn was set for an unknown end. But at least GM would be rid of Saab, and if Saab subsequently died at the hands of a new

owner, would the American tax payer or Barack Obama care? For President Obama *did* have to deal with the GM crisis and the issues of Saab, Opel/Vauxhall, and the plan he created at the White House was to manage the problem via his direct appointee, a man named Ed Whitacre, as GM's new boss.

Several thousand miles away from Barack Obama's $18 billion GM crisis talks of 2009 the temperature was colder, but there was still enough strength in the sun to cause reflections from the shiny new metal that lined the tarmac at the Saab factory in Trollhättan, Sweden. Trollhättan was a proud place, and the very thought of it closing after over sixty years of making cars was something none of the workers or the management could envisage. Saab and its factory *was* Trollhättan.

A RUSH TO RESCUE?

The selling and buying of Saab all sounded very simple, but it was not. For the Saab saga has never been simple, and this time no one really knew if Saab could be saved. What was worse was that in General Motors' new boss Mr Ed Whitacre, President Obama had appointed a man with a wonderful business record, yet someone who, by his own admission, had no knowledge of the motor industry. The same had happened at the death of GM's Oldsmobile brand, when its last new boss had previously run a dog food company before trying to sell cars.

But this was different, in that Whitacre was acting under the Obama imperative, and what Whitacre said was law: anyone who wanted to argue could answer to the President. And the presidential edict was simple: sell off what you can, recoup some cash, and dump Saab and the other brands from GM's portfolio, fast. Sentiment and emotion were to have no place – and about time too, reckoned many.

The reality of life and death in the real world of globalization and corporate relations was a hard lesson for Saab to have to learn. And anyway, who cared? Car companies had failed before, and they would fail again – and this was hardly the De Lorean fiasco. Such were some sentiments expressed at the time by those who will remain unnamed. So long as General Motors, Ford, Chrysler, Boeing, Airbus, VW Audi and their ilk could survive, then all would be well. The victims of the cull, just like the banks, would soon be forgotten, and resistance, to coin a phrase, was futile.

But just what was all this about? How could a small Swedish car company be causing Barack Obama, GM and the echelons of corporate warriors so much trouble? Saab was becoming not just a political issue, but a diplomatic problem. Worse, the European governments were beginning to speak out about Saab and Opel, and the EU and the British were getting in on the politics of the act: Saab in Britain was a big brand, and Saab GB was another jewel in Saab's crown. With directors such as Jonathan Nash and Charles Toomey and men such as David Pugh, Saab GB had built on its history and flourished, and the threat of it being adversely affected by the fall-out had to be steered around. Meanwhile GM's British Vauxhall was making political headline news at prime ministerial level.

Saabists allege that the truth about GM was that in classic GM 'accountant's' fashion, GM, it is claimed, starved Saab of new model investment, and failed to appreciate Saab's buyer base, its brand niche and the incredible collection of dealers across the globe. But that claim ignores just how much money GM *did* put into Saab – it ran into billions of US dollars.

The story of the Saab dealers should not go untold. Many of the dealers had become part of the Saab family, and had provided a level of customer service and brand loyalty rarely seen, except perhaps in the 1960s days of GM's own dealer network. The Saab dealers, notably the American ones, had created their own strand of Saabness: they were the unsung heroes in a plot that was not going to reward them. GM's accountants seemingly cared little for this kind of heritage, yet did they ignore its inherent value?

Under GM's European design chief Anthony Lo, Saab went 'Aero-emotional' with the flip-topped Aero X with this aircraft-style canopy, and shades of Sonett III.

**AeroX was voted 'Concept Car of the Year' by *Autocar* magazine.
Principal designers were Alex Daniels (exterior) and Erik Rokke (interior) under
Anthony Lo's design management. They had every reason to be proud of its brilliance.**

In the end, many long-standing, loyal Saab dealers across the globe – and in America, too – had to seek insolvency protection as the Saab brand and Saab USA collapsed. There were even new, unsold, unregistered Saabs owned by dealers, but with no one to supply a warranty other than the dealers themselves, sales were likely to be limited to the brave. For the true Saabist, it was a great time to pick up a GM-based bargain and use GM/Opel/Fiat parts to service it if Saab parts ever became unobtainable – which in the main was unlikely.

Before that epilogue happened, could GM not have done what VW–Skoda–Seat did, and share car 'platforms', and reskin outer bodies around shared components, to save costs, yet at the same time create properly branded and perfectly acceptable cars? If VW could turn a Polo into a Skoda Fabia and a Seat Ibiza, or a Golf into an Audi, why did GM not do this with the Opel Astra or Corsa and create a new small or mid-sector Saab? It would have been quick, easy and cheap to do, and would have diluted the 'prestige' angle of the brand far less than other ideas, such as Saab–Subarus. Yet just as Saab died in 2012, GM Opel launched the stunning Astra GTC coupé, a car that looked for all the world like a Saab 96 reinvented. The irony was not lost inside Saab.

If Lexus could make a small car, and BMW create the 1 Series, why could GM not take an Opel Astra and Saabize it into something more acceptable than a 'Saabaru'? Such were the unanswered questions that lay at GM's door – after all, Saab's concept cars, the 'designer specials' of 2000 to 2008, used the GM Opel Astra as their base. Saab's AeroX was even based on an Opel Omega platform and engine. Would Saab have resisted? How could it?

But GM did let Saab spend huge sums turning the second version of the 9-3 and the Epsilon platform-based 9-5 into more of a Saab. Saab was also allowed to create a development of the 9-3 and the Turbo X, so it would be wrong to frame Saab's men as being totally starved of opportunity or funding, even if there were fundamental structural problems within the relationship.

But there was worse, much worse, for GM even sold those re-badged Japanese Subaru cars, with Saab's name liberally splattered across their flanks and interior. GM made the most of its own sub-brand in America, Saturn, and kept it separate from GM at large in terms of brand perception, so why did it not do the same for Saab, its prestige brand? Such were the essential questions of GM's stewardship of Saab.

The Reality of Lutz

Although decent enough cars in their own right, the 'Saabarus' were created at the edict of GM and under the aegis of the new vice chairman Bob Lutz, the US motor industry's veteran luminary-upon-high. But why was GM bastardizing the Saab brand with ersatz Subaru–Saabs? And it wasn't doing Subaru any favours, either. The last planned 'Saabaru' was based on the Subaru Tribeca four-wheel-drive wagon, though luckily it never made it to production, and the remaining prototype was sent to the Saab museum where its 1950s Saab 93 'Italian front' styling rip-off can be seen.

In 2005 the Subaru Imprezza estate became a Saab 92x, and GM's ancient cast-iron lump that was the Chevrolet Blazer 4x4 off-roader gained a Saab nip-and-tuck facelift and a Saab '97' badge. All this was framed in PR terms by GM's then head of development, Bob Lutz, a classic car enthusiast and aviation fanatic who had worked for BMW, Ford and Chrysler – a legend in his own time who perhaps ought to have known better.

Lutz maintained that this diversification was just a stop-gap measure. He said in 2005 that the 'brand dilution' was 'short-term', and the justification behind it was that it gave the dealers more cars to sell – as they might 'abandon their franchise otherwise. We have to sacrifice brand purity for a while, until the next generation,' said Mr Lutz to the US media.[19] But surely the paradox was that some dealers were more likely to abandon the franchise as a result of being told to sell Saab-badged Subarus, than having no new real Saabs to sell after a decade of waiting for GM to create them.

Commentators were forced to ask whose fault was this situation – surely not the dealers, they sell cars, they don't design nor make them... and did GM not remember what sacrificing brand purity had already done to GM's brands? But Lutz was a brilliant and decisive car (and aviation) man, he knew his stuff and had the record to prove it, notably in a European perspective while working for Ford in the 1970s, at BMW under Eberhard von Kuenheim and again with Ford for the launch of the

Sierra, not to mention the turnaround at Chrysler. The most charitable interpretation of the Lutz–Saab story was that Lutz, late to the party, ex-Chrysler, seems to have overseen an inherited 'between a rock and a hard place' scenario. Lutz knew his stuff – he had steered BMW's 1970s sales and marketing, had framed the 1980s Ford Sierra as something far more than it was, and at Chrysler his ideas had saved the day.

A true 'petrol-head' he was, but Lutz was also a sharp commercial operator. In his book *Guts* he makes it clear that there are seven laws of business that he used to steer Chrysler. Amid those laws, design quality beyond the norm, and reflecting the customers' brand sentiment, seem somewhat obscured.

Could it be that Saab's GM ethos – one of step-by-step development, and now, of taking GM parts and enhancing them to a new level – was in fact far beyond the theories of GM and of Lutz after he joined the company? Engineers of the Saab ilk wanted to do better than better, but accountants did not, and corporate warriors who seemingly wanted to avoid too much expense would not share the Saab mindset.

Perhaps therein lies the core of the lack of connection between GM and Saab?

Without doubt the Saab–Subaru experiment was a desperate measure in desperate times. By 2008, GM's treatment of Saab had wrought the whirlwind that it sowed so many years before. And for Robert Lutz there was an enigma, a riddle in the ruins of Saab, because on 14 February 1980, Lutz, then chairman of Ford in Europe, had written to Marcus Wallenberg of Saab as the two companies ended their joint agreement for the supply

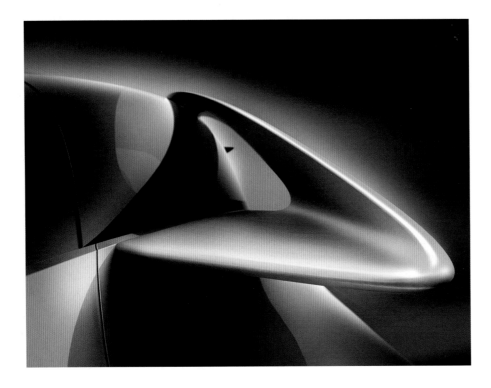

Brought in by Muller, Jason Castriota created a strong sculpture in PhoeniX. It had elements of UrSaab and visions of the future. These vestigial rear wings were an elliptical aerodynamic tweak par excellence.

of Ford V4 engines for Saab's 96. Lutz expressed admiration for Saab, and the hope that there might be an opportunity in the future to work together again. Events were surely to add irony to that wish.

Pre-GM ownership, Saab had done its best going along its own road, and had been beaten by a different world order to the one that Saab and its Swedish socio-economic model and ethos had known. The whole Saab story – in location, thinking, design and action – was perhaps micro-cosmically emblematic of a uniqueness unlikely to survive the new world order of globalization. Clearly under GM a different behavioural psychology was apparent, and there was no place in GM's world for a low-volume car producer making fewer than 100,000 cars a year. Saab was surely swamped by a fashion for smaller cars that it refused to adopt, and yet paradoxically had been born from.

Many Saabists should ask themselves a vital commercial question: if GM had not bought Saab, would some other car maker have allowed Saab to continue doing its own sweet thing (even as the supertanker of globalization and industrial efficiency bore down upon it)? The answer in cold hard business terms is, of course not. Could Saab have become a Lexus? It didn't for GM, but maybe that *had* been the idea. And if it was, why did GM not make it happen?

However hard it is for Saab purists to read or accept, the Saab way of doing things, once framed in a book entitled *The Saab Way*, was over: it was unsustainable, and whoever purchased Saab would have had to have changed things. So Saab, as the old purists knew it, probably died in 1989. But as a brand and as a mystique, it survived until the early days of 2012. It may have been the longest death in automotive history. The months of what could be, what should be, what was not to be and whose fault it was, surely felt like a slow-motion death for Saabists. In the end, that painful tortured death, drawn out for all the right reasons of hope, was a decidedly unseemly chapter for a noble brand and a proud people.

GM would argue that it poured hundreds of millions of dollars into Saab and the return was slow in coming back amidst a mindset and a product that frustrated many in its outcomes. Some have suggested that the men of Saab were reluctant to play a wider game, cocooned as they had been for so long from the common realities of basic, down-to-a-cost engineering. But the Saabists would quite correctly point out that GM tethered Saab to a thinking that restricted it from doing what it was good at, and for which GM had purchased it in the first place. For example, Saab's engineers even went as far as rejecting GM's door handles from its parts bin, and spent hours creating a new Saab-designed door handle. From light switches to seat belts, the feel, the action of everything was deemed as in need of Saabification. Was this taking Saabism too far in a new order of existence?

Did GM see Saab as a small, prestige brand that could react quickly – much as the 'old' GM brands had done? If so, it did not happen, and GM kept Saab from a small car renaissance or a Sonett reincarnation. They had nearly two decades – twenty years – to think about all this, yet the outcome seems to have been sticking Saab badges on a Subaru or a Chevrolet alongside creating 'new' Saabs from revamped, pre-existing GM cars. And of the later GM Saabs? It can hardly be argued that the 9-3/2 Turbo X was a car that would save Saab and GM's investment, no matter how good it was. And it took the men of Saab to create the 9-3/2 'Independence' models and the latest 9-5 circa 2010–12. Was turning the Saab 9-3 into the Cadillac BLS likely to benefit Saab?

These then, were the landscapes and questions that surrounded Saab in the years from 2000 to 2009. But the question that remained for GM and for the Swedes was, what *was* Saab, and did it have a future? From 2006 to 2008 Saab staggered on, racking up losses and ill-will with some. By late 2008, as the world recession took hold, GM put Saab 'on notice', and by 2009 the writing, for Saab – after much delay and many personal reputations stained – was finally on the wall.

SAAB FOR SALE

Having paid US $600 million for its first portion of Saab in January 1990, GM went on in mid-decade to formalize its full ownership of Saab. By 1999 it had purchased another US $125 million of shares options, and Saab was a fully owned GM brand. Yet by the early 2000s, with the desperate Saab–Subaru experiment, and the Saab-badged Chevrolet 4x4 failing to make a mark, and having cancelled the original 9000 replacement and delayed the 9-5, GM's tenure of Saab was unravelling. The threat of Swedish jobs moving to Opel plants in Germany did not help. And GM had closed a brand new Saab factory that had only just been built in order to add capacity – Saab's crucial need. And then came that Obama imperative to Ed Whitacre: save GM, and sell what you have to sell to do it.

Bidders for Saab circled like vultures over a wounded lion. Over twenty interested parties, ranging from other car makers to financial institutions, were sniffing around Saab: BMW, Fiat and Tata were reputed to have expressed some interest. But by 2009 there were only bids from Koenigsegg, the supercar maker, and two financial outfits – Merbanco and the Renco Group. Merbanco's Christopher Johnston was a Saab fan and seemed keen to debate Saab with the Saabists, but he also knew enough to know that time and money were of the essence. GM decided to side-step Merbanco's interest.

Talks with other parties slowly evolved, but Saab was soon under a European or Swedish version of 'Chapter 11' Bank-

SAAB – THE INNOVATIONS

1947 Aerodynamic, transverse-engined, front-wheel-drive car with flat floor and Cd 0.35 in safety body with unique reinforcements. Created by aeronautical engineers on wing shape and structural theories. Launched in 1949.

1953 Factory-fitted seatbelts.

1955 Saab 93 3-cylinder, two-stroke engine mounted longitudinally.

1956 Plastic/glassfibre and aluminum composite two-seater construction Saab 94 Sonett 1.

1960 Airflow-tuned cabin-air system.

1960 Saab 95 seven-seater family estate.

1961 Air wiper rear aerofoil on 95 estate car.

1963 Diagonal split braking system Saab 96.

1967 Saab 99 with advanced safety body with 2.5mm steel sandwich A pillars and crush-resistant roof. Key between seats to reduce injuries from facia panel. A-frame headrests.

1969 Self-repairing cellular bumpers to meet new legislation in USA.

1969 Headlamp wipers and washers fitted.

1972 Integrated side-impact beams with lateral compression paths built into doors. Protective roof lining. Impact-absorbing interior door panels. Steel reinforcing bar across rear seat of hatchback 99 Combi.

1971 Heated seats.

1977 Successful application of turbocharging across mid-performance band in mass-market car Saab 99.

1979 Cabin air ventilation filtration system Saab 900. Ergonomic dashboard design. Knee-roll impact pads in lower facia.

1981 Anti-knock APC-type engine control in turbocharged cars.

1982 Asbestos-free brake pads.

1983 16-valve turbocharged engine with tuned chambers for efficient combustion.

1984 Full automatic performance control technology in engine/fuel management.

1985 Direct ignition system. Automatic seatbelt tensioners.

1986 ABS used front-wheel-drive car for first time in Saab 9000.

1990 Light pressure turbo design and application across Saab 900 range. Electrostatic cabin air filter developed from earlier Saab 900 system.

1991 Trionic 'ion' engine control/emissions management system Saab 9000. CFC-free aircon system.

1993 Electro-mechanical semi-automatic gearbox 'Sensonic' pioneers semi-auto systems.

1994 Night panel system for facia in Saab 900.

1995 Saab Ecopower engine designs.

1997 Saab 9-5 with active headrest system to reduce injuries. Ventilated seats with seat pan fan system. Pendulum-design B pillar to reduce side-impact injuries. Assymetric V6 turbocharging.

2005 Saab Biopower concept and production.

2008 Saab XWD all-wheel-drive system with E-LSD via Haldex unit.

2011 Sub-120g CO_2 rating for TTiD engine. Top scores for all Saab range in US and Euro crash tests.

---

ruptcy Protection. By June 2009, Koenigsegg announced a bid for its troubled Swedish compatriot. Intriguingly, part of Koenigsegg's bid was co-financed by the Chinese car concern Beijing Automotive Industry Holding Company (BAIC) – to whom GM would subsequently sell off a selection of previous-model Saab rights and toolings once the Koenigsegg bid was stopped by the firm's voluntary withdrawal in November 2009.

Koenigsegg and an Aftertaste

No matter how clever and how talented Koenigsegg was under its owner Christian von Koenigsegg and director Bard Eker,

observers, customers and auto-industry pundits could not help but wonder how a tiny prawn like the Koenigsegg company could steer a whale (and a beached one at that) like GM's Saab. But then again, GM had failed to do it, so why doubt the Swedes at Koenigsegg? So ran the not illogical argument of the pundits.

Koenigsegg created a plan for Saab, investing real money into the planned acquisition. The firm applied for a European Investment Bank loan based on a business plan for Saab. But ultimately, Koenigsegg walked away from the chance to buy Saab. Many wondered why, but time would reveal that Saab *may* have had its hands tied behind its back by a GM clause relating to its technology. There was likely to be little value and little return on a deal so hamstrung, surely? This book's

PhoeniX, seen from above, 'worked' in all its integrated elements.

author wrote an article stating that any buyer of Saab would need money, real money, about $500 million US dollars, in working, available, titled hard cash, to rescue and run Saab and help it to new-model profitability – and that was without addressing the rules of sale and the sleeping speed hump of GM's hold on Saab's GM-related, internal product intelligence.

The Swedish government seemed to want to keep Saab and its problems at a distance. The fact that the unemployment rate would jump and that Trollhättan and its economy would collapse, invoking massive social benefit and health bills, seemed to be of curiously low-key concern to the politicians. The parliamentarian with the choice job of handling the Saab situation was Maud Olofsson, Sweden's industry minister. When Koenigsegg walked away, she stated the obvious facts about time, money and security – a move that did little to endear her to Saabists or the Swedish media.

What was it about Saab and its fate that engendered such a distancing, as seen from the Swedish government? Could the grand 'EU' European social science experiment have anything to do with it? After all, if GM were possibly going to cut 9,000 German jobs at Opel, and if Vauxhall were needing British taxpayer support, with GM's Nick Reilly having to make statements in the UK, what were the chances of the European Investment Bank offering a massive loan to Saab ex-GM, to keep a few thousand people in work, while Germans and Brits of GM were made redundant? Maybe this was the unspoken political pustule that was brewing up under the Swedish government?

Any potential Saab buyer would need secure long-term financing to get Saab over its short-term problems, the deal would have to be done quickly, and any application to the European Investment Bank for a loan would have to be a fresh (time-consuming) application, structured around a new business strategic plan. By November 2009, Saab was drowning and no lifebelt was in sight.

2009, END OF THE AFFAIR?

All looked lost, and in late 2009 GM actually appointed a 'wind down' administrator for Saab. Koenigsegg had walked away, other possible investors had sniffed at the edges of GM's Saab, but nobody had got as far as due diligence and real discussions with GM. Bankers, financiers and what the motor trade would call 'tyre-kickers' had come and viewed the carcass of Saab. The announcement of the new model 9-5 actually going on sale in dealerships also hung in the balance. And what of the Saab 94x, a compact 4x4 of a Saab? Incredibly GM got it into production in Mexico, but Saab dealerships, and particularly the American ones (often family owned for decades) were going down with appalling regularity.

Early on in the Saab crisis, in the autumn of 2009, Victor Muller and Spyker Cars had looked at Saab but had not been successful in getting into GM's mindset. But previous bidders Merbanco and Spyker were soon back at the table, as was Genii

Capital, a Luxembourg-based group with a reputed interest from Formula One rights owner Bernie Eccelstone.

But then came weeks of silence and hope. Christmas came and went, and a 7 January close-down process start date by GM also passed. Behind the scenes a tall Dutchman with a liking for Lancias and an ability to borrow money (as akin to most financiers) had been busy. It looked as though there might be a deal, but time was running out. Suddenly the public, the Saab owners and enthusiasts, started to protest: if GM were going to kill Saab, they would not be allowed to get away with it quietly. The PR for GM would be an internet-led time bomb.

Save Saab

The Saab enthusiasts of the world swung into action; first moves had in fact come earlier in the year from a Dresden-based Saab dealer who started a 'Rescue Saab' campaign. An independent worldwide consciousness soon developed in late 2009, mobilized via Steven Wade's SaabsUnited.com website and a host of supporters, Saab owners clubs and Saabists the world over, including the author.

From TV and radio to newspapers and local pubs, Saab was in the news and on people's minds. BBC news in Britain and on the international BBC news channel debated Saab. Saabists (including the author) appeared on late night media discussion programmes explaining the allure of Saab – that elusive quality of 'Saabness'. It was clear that Saab had a place in people's hearts. The aim of 'Save Saab' was to protest, to try to help Saab, and to make GM feel very uncomfortable about its plan to kill the

Control of the wake separation points and lift were all considered here at the rear of PhoeniX.

Saab brand. Ultimately, over the weekend of 17 January 2010, on the cusp of GM's formal threat to start the ordered close-down of Saab, an estimated 50,000-plus Saab enthusiasts held their global vigil, and 1.5 million Saab owners worldwide supported them. The sight of a 'Save Saab' convoy in Times Square, Manhattan, New York, brought tears to the eyes of many.

'Save Saab' was the first online organized automotive brand protest. In major cities of the world, across dozens of countries, Saab owners took their Saabs on to the streets in convoys, to support and to try to save Saab. Media coverage was global and the viability of Saab as a brand with expectant customers was proven. The proof of Saab and its following was placed upon the world's stage.

LEASE–LEND

But by this time Victor R. Muller was fully in the frame. By late October 2009 he had decided to bid for Saab and had begun negotiations. Muller was the last and final bidder, but it took weeks to thrash out the details with GM. By now, following GM's *de facto* devaluation of Saab through announcing its closure, a reduction in Saab's value and price may have been logically expected. But GM still wanted a very large amount of money for Saab – USD$440 million. Somehow, Muller secured a price in cash allied to a schedule of deferred payments and options that also left GM as a dormant small shareholder in what would still be Saab the car maker.

It seemed that Saab and its intellectual property rights, its new models and the on-going supply of GM parts to make and service them, was the real deal. But there was more to it than that, and the deal was as complex as the history of Saab and the finances of the men involved.

So who was Victor R. Muller and his Spyker Cars of Zeewolde in the Netherlands? 'Spyker' was the reinvention of an ancient name, and as a new company first built cars from 1900 to 1925. The Spijker, or as the branded 'Spyker' brothers, built a 2-cylinder car, and in 1903 created a 4WD, 6-cylinder performance car. The brothers Spyker also created an aerodynamic undertray for a car in 1905 to reduce dust and dirt spray under the car and its tendency to rise up into the early unsealed, coach-built cabins of cars – it was touted as a 'dustless' car. Before World War I London taxis were made by Spyker, and the firm's Dutch/Belgian origins and designs seemed to appeal to the British. A Spyker had also won the 1907 Peking to Paris race, achieving massive international brand recognition for the little Netherlands-based company.

Perhaps Spyker's most glorious moment was the design and construction of the original Spyker C4. This was a 5,471cc, German Maybach-engined car with a French chassis and a body

Anthony Lo at the Saab studio with team members.

The build team hard at work on the 9-x Bio concept study in Saab's design centre.

designed by Fritz Koolhaven. Spyker also created an 'aero-coupé' – a teardrop-shaped, 1920s streamliner. Spyker had been a serious name in early car design, and its story was bound to appeal to a brave and adventurous personality such as Victor Muller, even if he did have to borrow the money to reinvent Spyker and return it to glory. And if he could do it for Spyker, why not for Saab.

But in 1990 Spyker consisted of the remains of a tiny company intent on selling exquisite super or hyper cars by the handful. It would take a decade and the parting of Muller and his Spyker engineer/designer Maarten de Bruijn for Spyker to reach the headlines. Muller wanted to make Spyker bigger, and to enter wider ownership – perhaps he had to keep it solvent,

too? After all, design costs money, and Muller was very good at keeping that flowing.

There were questions, however. Was Spyker a rich man's plaything or a real car company? Both opinions were easy to find. And Spyker was hardly profitable – it had made 205 cars in a decade, consumed vast development and design costs, and earned 54 million euros before posting a loss of 120 million euros over the same period. Spyker's backers included Mubdala, an Arabic investment fund, and Vladimir Antonov from Russia. Other silent or invisible partners of Spyker existed and may have also been invisible backers of Spyker's Saab bid. And did Muller have a Saab link to explain his sudden interest in the Swedish icon? Muller was a positive and encouraging character who could make things happen. But to some, was he a maverick?

GM's asking price for Saab was US $440 million. Muller did not have it, but he arranged US $74 million in cash and US $326 million in preferred stock options. Muller refused to detail all his investors, but the trail ran to a company called Tenaci Capital BV, and a structure of supporting bodies via numerous entities. US $25 million came from this Dutch company with links to Muller-Tenaci BV, and another US $25 million was reputedly loaned from Epcote, an investment business run by Peter Heerma, a former employer of Muller's. Muller also soon arranged back-up financing from GEM Global Yield Fund to the tune of 150 million euros, and through this agreement, Saab-Spyker could issue shares to an agreed convertible percentage and term.

During his first look at the 'for sale' Saab, he had had Russian investor backing, but this had been deemed unacceptable by GM and the Swedish government; the name of Vladimir Antonov had been linked to Muller's bid for Saab. In fact negotiations by Muller for Saab had been questioned in December 2009 by the Swedish government. Even the FBI were alleged to have had an opinion. Whatever the unstated and unproven allegations against a backer who had had no fair hearing, if Muller wanted Saab, Antonov and Russian finance had to be replaced, and fast. If not, GM would enact a wind-down of Saab – and they named their chosen agent, who was about to do it. Only Christmas intervened, with great timing.

Antonov was a Spyker backer, but in a complex shuffling of the deck that would apply once the deal for Saab had been enacted with GM, Muller would buy Antonov out of Spyker, purchasing 4.6 million shares. As agreed when Antonov bought into Spyker in 2007, the priority share would revert back to Spyker. Three men – N. Stacikas, M. Bondars and Mr V. Antonov – would retire from Spyker upon the sale of Saab to Spyker by GM. The Tenaci company would then not only loan the money to pay GM for the first US $25 million for Saab, but Tenaci would also make a second loan to clear Spyker's outstanding 57 million euros of loans to banks and other investors.

Through this amazingly complex web of transactions between owners, part owners, bankers, financiers and investors, Spyker's bid, or rather Victor Muller's bid for Saab, became acceptable to the Swedish and American legislators, the EIB and to GM.

In an intriguing twist to the plot, the new company would be called Saab Spyker Automobiles, but Spyker was soon announced as having moved, to be part of a company with Swiss and British roots named CPP Manufacturing, based in Whitley, near Coventry in England. This location would be the new manufacturing base of Spyker. To add spice to the tale, CPP were latterly announced in 2011 as being associated with

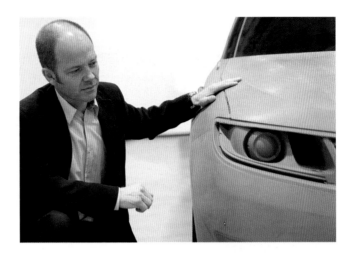

Simon Padian, Saab's design brand chief and a time-served Saabist works on the new 9-5 for the 2010 launch.

the revival of the Jensen brand. But who owned CPP? A connection to Antonov ownership has been claimed, and when in 2011 Saab Spyker became Swedish Automobile NV, or SWAN, Spyker was moved off to a group reputedly linked to an affiliate in a complex deal where no 'payment' in cash terms took place.

Before that happened in 2011, there was the 2010 deal to buy Saab from GM, where Saab-Spyker would have to make payments to GM in February and July 2010. GM would retain redeemable preference shares of US $326 million, representing less than 1 per cent of the voting shares. A sliding scale of dividends and non-payment penalties was part of a deal with key dates for payment of 2012 and 2016. GM, it seemed, could not lose. Spyker also purchased the British Saab GB and the dealerships it owned as part of the Saab deal.

The deal was announced on 26 January 2010, and the first instalment paid on 15 February. In Muller's statement as the new owner of Saab, he praised the 1.5 million Saab owners and the thousands who had protested to save Saab. After signing the contract for Saab, Muller's first telephone call was to SaabsUnited.com's Steven Wade, and Wade then went online to the world. Saab was saved! Muller also added:

> Spyker Cars will provide Saab with the backing required to compete as a competitive global brand along with an entrepreneurial leadership team sensitive to the uniqueness, heritage and individuality of the Saab brand. I would like to extend my sincere gratitude to Vladimir Antonov for his formidable support during the last two years. His contribution has allowed Spyker to get to the point that this transaction was made possible.

9-2X Air – a super redefining of the Saab convertible theme. Note the strong rear buttresses. Renault's later Wind model aped such themeology.

Clearly Muller respected Saab, but the wheeler-dealing within his complex set-up was obvious. Antonov's subsequent arrest in England and his facing (as yet unproven) financial allegations only served to heighten the palates of the detractors of Muller. Yet one of Muller's friends in high places was Dutch Prime Minister Jan Peter Balkenende, who praised the takeover deal and Muller's success at pulling it off. Muller may have suffered adverse media headlines, but the true details will await the outcome of history. Like many, Muller may be judged more kindly by history than the perceptions of the present. But there was one vital question: did Muller have the money to run Saab?

For Saab, its 8,000 employees and for Saab's Jan Ake Jonsson, the acting CEO of Saab who had steered the foundering company towards survival in around 2008, it looked like time to finally relax. Trollhättan's shopkeepers, hotel owners, taxi drivers and citizens could also relax: Saab's city was safe. GM's European boss, Nick Reilly, played the corporate citizen and wished Saab well – after all, as he implied, GM had always wanted a positive outcome for Saab.

STOP-START, BUT NOT WITH TECHNOLOGY

In the first heady months, employees hailed their heroes, and they hailed the new captain – Muller, a reluctant chairman who wanted to appoint a top auto-industry man to be Saab's boss. In the meantime, Muller made regular factory visits and pushed through a rapid pace of revision to models, including the Saab 'Independence' variations of the 9-3, the launch of the new 9-5 saloon and work on a new, smaller, sportier car – the new 9-3 – and a sort of Mini rival, at last that small Saab that would sell so well. But all this would take three or four years, surely? How could Muller promise so much by 2012 – as he did? Was there enough cash flow in the accounts to keep Saab going? Could Saab sell the vital 100,000+ cars a year, and break even by 2012 from a sales figure of 31,696 in 2010 when 50,000 and then 120,000 had been cited as targets?

This was Muller's incredible claim. He made it to the leading Dutch newspaper, *NRC*, on 2 February 2010. It was an astounding claim, one that relied on getting the new 9-5 in saloon and wagon form into the dealerships, selling the 94x in huge numbers, and readying the refreshed 9-3. A more experienced automotive industry man – whom Muller was always looking for, having always admitted his shortcomings and that he was an unwilling boss – would have known that this schedule was inappropriate. According to I.H.S. Global Insight, an automotive research body in the USA, and also a host of industry observers, that 2012 date was an impossible aim: four years would be needed, not two.

HEADY DAYS OF HIGH HOPES

In a few short months from early 2010 to early 2011, Muller and the team got a lot done. Saab's existing 'TTID' twin-turbo diesel engine was redesigned to produce less than 120g of carbon – a vital pollution tax-related number. The critics said it could not be done, but Saab did it. Styling changes were made to the 9-3, and to celebrate Saab's new independence, 'Independence'-badged 9-3s were produced. Revised engines for the new 9-5 were announced, and the 9-5's suspension settings were changed as a result of media feedback. A deal was signed with BMW for the production of a new 1.6-litre engine for the new small Saab, and Muller teased the media and Saabists with a sketch for a new, iconic small Saab to rival the BMW Mini genre, a reinvented Saab 92. A revised 9-3 with a hatchback was designed and rushed forwards into early development.

Then came PhoeniX, the concept car that reeked of a Saab past and a Saab future, yet which must have cost a very large chunk of money to create at a time when cash-earning oppor-

**Saab's Subaru-derived 92x,
made for the US market only.**

tunities such as the new 9-5 Combi Sport wagon should have been a resource priority to be forced into production.

But the obvious question was, what was all this doing to cash flow and Saab's ability to service its suppliers' invoices? The rush to reinvent Saab and convince the markets that Saab had a future was obvious, but how could all this expenditure be sustained? 'Show me the money' was an all-too-obvious statement.

The 9-4x

Included in the sale deal was the GM-built, Mexican-produced, 9-4x 'soft-roader'. Late to the market it might have been, but it was still handsome, capable, and felt like a Saab should. Re-skinned over Cadillac basics, the 9-4x was also safe, and achieved top marks in the US (IIHS) crash tests and a 'Top Pick' rating. Yet there was no diesel option, and the 3.0-litre V6 or 2.8T-optioned car was produced in less than 1,000 examples in 2011.

Wagon Woes

Crucially, the 9-5 Combi Sport – Saab's big, new, world-class wagon – never made it to the showrooms across Europe. In its late development days, it had previously been taken back under the GM umbrella and kitted out with GM and American market fittings, including GM intellectual copyright. Whatever it was that went into the back of the 9-5 Combi, nobody else ever saw it. Saab's biggest failure was not getting this car into the showrooms. Perhaps less time and money spent on PhoeniX and more spent on the 9-5 Combi might, with admitted hindsight, have been a good idea.

By late March 2011, events were overtaking Saab, and the rapture of survival was unravelling: Muller presided over a moment that was, by his own admission, a 'mistake', and one that he vowed would not be repeated: a Saab component supplier's bill went unpaid. That bill *was* paid, but it unleashed a classic 'domino' effect, a tidal wave of 'no confidence' in Saab. By the first week of April 2011 the production lines had stopped, other suppliers were demanding cash up front, and Saab faced a short-term crisis. But it was just that, a short-term crisis for a company with a great legacy inheritance and a huge future, one packed with already planned design and development. In under eighteen months, Saab had gone from no hope to every hope.

The tragedy was, that for the summer of 2011, in an unseemly slow-motion car crash, Saab lurched from crisis to crisis and hope to hope, only to be overcome by factors, many of which were beyond either its control or its agenda. Saab had a long-term solution, if only it could get over its short-term problems. Over at Saab's new corporate web-blog *Inside*

In the metal, the brilliant but stillborn 9-5 Combi Sport wagon.

Saab.com, ex-SaabsUnited.com man Steven Wade found himself stuck between a PR rock and a product that was not being made. The immediacy of the electronic news age would be difficult to handle for a dedicated Saabist, but he was an inexperienced non-PR man with no story to tell. And then the company became the story, leaving Wade gagged. He voiced the frustrations of Saab's paradoxical position.

CHINESE SPRING, A SILENT SUMMER

Enter the 'Chinese spring' of 2011, where Saab failed to pay its staff their wages on time on several occasions, but a variety of suitors ranging from Hawati Motors, Great Wall Motor, and Pang Da to Youngman – all Chinese automotive specialists if not all actual car makers – vied to grab a share of Saab.

Due to the supplier issue and the cash flow problems allied to a lack of confidence, Saab had to stop production on 5 April. On 3 May 2011, Spyker Cars reached an agreement with Hawati to obtain emergency funding for Saab, aiming to restart production within a week. This rescue deal collapsed in May, when it failed to get the necessary Chinese government approvals. A further Chinese automotive entity, named Great Wall, was also rumoured to be in talks with Spyker about investing.

By mid-May, Saab announced that they had signed a Memorandum of Understanding with Pang Da Automobile Trade Company. This deal would give Saab the financing needed to restart production, and give Pang Da an equity stake in Saab. Pang Da insisted that if they gave their money, production must restart within two weeks. This took place and the production lines fired up again – but for less than fourteen days. A lack of parts supply was then blamed

By 26 July Saab announced that they were unable to pay July salaries to over 1,500 white collar staff; the company was also unable to confirm when the salaries would be finally paid. Yet the workers were paid on 25 July. At the end of July, the main Swedish trade union announced that if Saab did not pay the white-collar workers within two weeks then the union (Unionen) would force the company into bankruptcy.

On the same day, the EIB announced that they rejected the request from Vladimir Antonov to become part-owner of Saab. In response to that decision, the director general of the Swedish National Debt Office, a Mr Bo Lundgren, criticized the EIB for their handling of Antonov's involvement. On 5 August, Saab paid the white-collar workers' salaries through an equity issue – Gemini Fund bought five million shares in Saab.

Saab had said that production would re-start in July, but then it did not; but apparently production would re-start in August – which it could not have done, as this was Swedish national holiday month. September and October came and went, and still production did not re-start. By this time, China Youngman Automobile Group were the keen, sole bidders for Saab, and they would inject cash to pay later monthly wage bills for Saab.

To the Chinese, throwing money at Saab on a monthly basis did not matter, because the rewards would be huge: if China got Saab not only would it be a vital leap forwards in terms of car design, engineering, aerodynamics and safety, it would also gain a portal to a global network. Through the summer of 2011, vital infusions of Chinese cash, down payments on promise, and even an order for 10,000 cars (which could not at the time actually be built) kept Saab from death, and paid the blue-collar wages bill as well as executive salaries. Muller raced around the world trying to save Saab. But key directors and board members resigned, and the dream was turning into a nightmare – yet the unpaid bills were small by auto-industry standards: millions of dollars, yes, and which sounded even more when multiplied by more than a factor of ten into Swedish kronor. Saab – or SWAN – hived off its real estate and assets in various complex deals. Ultimately, in early 2012 it was revealed that the total accumulation of Saab debt was 23bn Swedish krona – or over 1bn in euros, pounds sterling or US dollars. This figure came as a surprise to many and must have had an impact upon the bidding for the remains of Saab in April 2012 when Saab's 'value' was estimated at 3.4bn Swedish krona: time was revealing the size of the Saab iceberg.

From April to November, Saab had stalled and lurched its way into an oblivion of hope, over the reality of a silent factory. The Saabists of the internet refused to face this reality. Anyone who said that time was up was shouted down and criticized for being negative. The dawning of the death of Saab was a slow, emotional and painful process, and many simply refused to believe or accept it, even when it was upon them.

But in December 2011, Saab *had* to file for bankruptcy. Before that, it had initially filed for Court protection from its creditors and potential asset strippers. This would buy time to sell Saab, ran the argument. Yet it also left the workers with a see-saw situation regarding whether Swedish Government rules ensured that the state and the unions would pay their wages if Saab could not. Evidently only if certain criteria were met would state support step in for the workers and their lives and bills.

The end of Saab was delayed because it was protected by law – but there was still a twist in the tale.

COULD HAVE, SHOULD HAVE...

It did look as if the Chinese might buy Saab. But then there was the curious role of the Swedish-appointed administrator, a Mr Guy Lofalk. He was appointed to administer the orderly and successful realization of any potential value left in Saab. It meant he had a role in the continuing negotiations that Muller, GM and the Chinese were still thrashing through in a last desperate bid to save what Muller called 'this beautiful little company'.

Then suddenly, between 5 and 15 December 2011, it was claimed that at a critical stage in talks over sales prices and assets, Lofalk had been conducting his own conversations with potential bidders and by-passing the Saab team. Was this allegation true? A war of words ensued, culminating in a letter of complaint from Saab to the Varnersborg District Court overseeing the Saab proceedings. That letter cited three specific instances of events framed as 'interference outside his role' by Lofalk. Saab called for Lofalk to be replaced, and the letter was also sent to the Swedish National Debt Office. And in the next death throes, a new bankruptcy administrator replaced the originally

The Mexican-built 94x soft-roader. Although based on **GM** underpinnings, it was a good design and a competitive vehicle in its class.

contracted company as Lofalk stepped down. Soon the unions complained about the level of information and detail being used or cited by the administrators. From November 2011 to January 2012, Saab, SWAN and Muller fought like a drowning man, but in the end Saab really did have to stop.

Anne Maire Pouteaux and Hans Bergqvist were the new administrators, and Bergqvist's words echoed around Trollhättan: 'Saab is a patient who has long been bleeding to death, and the brutal truth is that the patient is dead.'

Whatever the actual details, claims and counter claims, and unpaid bills, Muller's Chinese deal collapsed when GM curtly announced that it would not sell its intellectual property rights as still held within Saab, nor the licences to build GM-based Saabs to a potential rival – meaning the Chinese! GM claimed that to sell its knowledge 'Would be detrimental to General Motors and its shareholders'.

GM's final position was that it would not allow the sale of any of its current technology to China as part of a sale of Saab as it was constituted in 2012. Yet there were amazing paradoxes to this GM position: first, all that anyone who was interested had to do was to do what most major car makers have always done, and that was purchase one of your rival's cars through a dealership using a third party, and then tear the car apart back at the factory to discover its secrets. Thus all the Chinese needed to do was buy a new 9-5 and a new 94x and cut them apart to see GM's intellectual property within the cars – as opposed to within the factories that built them.

Second it was GM itself that had in late 2009 sold off the tooling of the previous Saab 9-5 and the recent 9-3 to the Chinese car maker BAIC. Saab's very last-but-one cars and all the knowledge that they contained had already been sold by GM to China before Muller bought Saab. Wasn't it odd that old-but-recent GM–Saab technology had been sold by GM to China already, but now, the new technology could not be? Perhaps it wasn't, but didn't this last-minute claim make a mockery of the Chinese summer of 2011 and the angst that went with it?

After the GM statement, Muller had nowhere to go, saying: 'After having received the recent position of General Motors on the transaction with Saab Automobile, Youngman informed Saab that the funding to continue and complete the reorganization of Saab could not be concluded.'

Total bankruptcy was declared on 19 December 2011, and Trollhättan was silent that night. In the following days, the allegations, the blame, the lies and the truths all flew about. Some blamed GM, some blamed Muller, some blamed Lofalk, many blamed the Swedish government. Others even noted the passivity of the unions. Perhaps the only obvious truth was that after the longest unintended suicide note in history, Saab was gone, not with a violent impact, but with a long, heart-rending skid.

Muller was applauded by the Saab factory workforce. He said 'I have done everything for the company, but it was not enough.'

Time and history may reveal uncomfortable details of the death of Saab, but the fight for the remains of Saab, either in sections or as whole, raged on into the spring of 2012: but the fact was, Saabism – in the metal, if not the ethereal – was dead.

COMPLETION OF SALE — REINCARNATION AS …

Saab did not die quietly upon declaring bankruptcy. In 2012, Saab struggled on. The unfinished cars left on the factory lines were secured by that old Saab stalwart ANA whose CEO, Joachim Lind, led the emotional final moment of Saabness as the garage chain secured enough parts to complete the unfinished Saabs. Over at SaabsUnited.com, the web-based Saabists raised enough money via internet subscription to buy the very last (ANA) manufactured Saab – a 9-3 in 'Griffin' specification – and donated it to the Saab Museum. Saabists David Ross and Mark Marcon drove the white 9-3 to the museum, with the media in tow.

Saabists carried on rallying and racing. Linus Ohlsson, aged 21, of Team Tido/PWR Racing claimed victory in the Swedish TTA racing Elite League 2012 in a heavily modified Saab 9-3.

In the USA, Charles River Saab of Watertown, near Boston, closed as a Saab dealer after fifty-five years selling Saabs to Americans. Many other dedicated Saab dealers of decades of Saab enthusiasm also closed down across America.

The bidding process for Saab's remains was slow, yet by May 2012 only Mahindra and Youngman survived as final, chosen bidders and in mid-May 2012, Youngman formally withdrew itself from the bid process – only to bounce back with a 'new' bid. Meanwhile in the Saab factory storage facility, 6,000 pallets of Saab parts, from wheels and engines to seats and trims, taking up over 10,000sq/m remained in limbo.

At the end of May, National Electric Vehicles, a Swedish-based, Chinese-backed electric vehicle/hybrid manufacturing consortium, were suddenly cited as last-minute new bidders for the carcass of Saab's assets. Also in May 2012 the Swedish industry minister during the Saab saga, Maud Olofsson, found her actions criticised by the Swedish National Committee of the Constitution, who reportedly alleged that she failed to adequately share information about the Antonov story with other government departments, which may have led to unnecessary delays for Saab.

By the summer of 2012, the agonising battle to reinvent Saab went on. In the end, a curious stalemate, an adversity of hope, prevailed.

SAAB – SAFETY FAST, STYLISH TO THE LAST

So concludes for the moment the always alternative history of the Saab car. The ethos of Saab and the men and women who created and built the brand should never be forgotten. Few annals of engineering and industrial design history can contain such a blend of art, design, IQ, and rally-driven thinking.

In 2012 as this book went to print, the claim that Saab had been sold was made. Could Saab have a new 'green' future as maker of electric or hybrid cars under the National Electric Vehicles consortium as claimed? Or was a different outcome for Saab hidden in the wings?

Every country has its identity and its traits, which are often manifested in its products, notably in cars, but there can be no doubt that while many cars may just be cars, Saabs are Saabs – those wonderfully curved, ellipsoid sculptures with magical handling and advanced engines amid an aura of being a Saab. There is a sense of occasion at every drive in a Saab, an alchemy of themes, the Saab DNA or spirit of a car. Some people thought the cars of Saab were a bit odd, but many more were in love with that elusive yet elemental Saabness of things.

On 13 June 2012, as this book was going to press, a new, different, Saab story began when NEVS did indeed succeed in buying Saab.

End game. As the sky weeps, a blue Saab departs, leaving a ruffle in its wake and a legend behind.

REFERENCES

1. Schilperoord, Paul, *The Extraordinary Life of Josef Ganz*, RVP, New York 2012.
2. Dymock, Eric, *Saab: Half a Century of Achievement*, Dove/Haynes Publishing, 1997.
3. Cole, Lance, *Secrets of the Spitfire*, Pen and Sword, 2012.
4. Saab Veterarerna Arkiv.
5. Saab Veterarerna Arkiv and personal communications, P. Johansson, 2010.
6. Saab Veterarerna Arkiv, Vi Minns Rolf Mellde Sammanstallt av Josef Eklund.
7. Saab Club of Argentina archive.
8. Saab Veterarerna Arkiv, Hemlighteta, Arne Frick.
9. Personal interviews Saab veterans and Saab Veterarerna Arkiv.
10. Stefan Vaapa, personal correspondence, 2011.
11. Saab GB Records and personal communications, C. Partington, 2010.
12. Personal communications B. Envall cited by Cole, Lance, in *Saab 99 & 900 The Complete Story*, The Crowood Press, 2000.
13. Mel Nichols *CAR* magazine FF Publishing 1975 and personal communication.
14. *Motor* magazine Saab 99 road test November 1969.
15. 'Gudmund's Glory', by Mark McCourt in *Sports and Exotic Car* 1 Jan 2010, Hemmings Publishers. Saab feature via arrangement with Mark J. McCourt.
16. *Saab Driver* magazine of Saab Owners Club GB, October 2010.
17. 'Form and Function', Saab AB 1997.
18. 'Form and Function', Saab AB 1997.
19. R. Lutz media statement, New York Auto Show, 2005.

BIBLIOGRAPHY

Car Styling. Numerous volumes 1981–2010

Cole, Lance, *Saab 99 & 900, The Complete Story,* The Crowood Press, 2000.

Cole, Lance, *Secrets of the Spitfire*, Pen and Sword, 2012.

Cole, Lance, 'Sixten Sason, Sweden's Secret Genius', *Classic Cars Magazine*, October 1997.

Cole, Lance. 'Saab's Secret Fighter', *Aeroplane Monthly*, August 1997.

Cole, Lance, 'The Death of Saab', *The Daily Telegraph,* 7 January 2012.

Cole, Lance, Numerous articles Trollhattan Saab.com/ SaabsUnited.com 2007–12

Cole, Lance, 'The Smell of Saab, Inside Saab', Saab.com 2011.

Cole, Lance, PhD thesis 'Essential details and developments in critical separation point design and wake vortex control as road vehicle aerodynamics design techniques for car designers'.

Dymock, Eric, *Saab: Half a Century of Achievement*, Dove/Haynes Publishing, 1997.

Elg, Per-Borje, *50 years of Saabs: All the Cars 1947–97*, Motorhistorika Sallskapet Sverge, Stockholm 1997.

Hansen, Sven, *Hur jag far ut mest av min Saab*, Saab, 1956.

O'Connor, Robin, 'The Saab Report P4', *Saab Driver*, March 2010.

Scibor-Rylski, A. J., *Road Vehicle Aerodynamics*, Pentech Press, London 1975.

Schilperoord, Paul, *The Extraordinary Life of Josef Ganz*, RVP, New York, 2012.

Shenstone, Beverley, personal notes and archive 1930–79.

Sjorgen, Gunnar, A., *The Saab Way*, Gust Osterbergs Tryckeri AB, Nyokoping 1984.

Streiffert & Co, *The Saab-Scania Story*, Bokforlag AB Stockholm 1986.

Turnberg, Anders, *Saab-Ana de forsta 50 aren*, 1987.

Wenlo, Sten, *Mitt Liv Med Saab*, 1989.

Translations from Saab Veterarerna Arkiv:

Några personliga minnen från tillverkningen av första bilen, by Sigvard Lenngren in Bakrutan April 2006.

En katt bland hermelinerna eller Hurledes grunden lades till SAABs bilproduktion vid. flygmaskinfabriken, by Hans Osquar Gustavsson and Sigvard Lenngren in Bakrutan 4-2006.

Minnen fran tillkomsten av 'Monstret', Sammanstallt ac Josef Eklund.

Minnesanteckningar fran inforandet av fytaktsmotorn i Saab 95/96 1966 Olle Ganlund, Injenjor pas Saab motorlaboratorium.

Huruledes Grunden lades till Saabs bilproduktion vid flugmaskins-fabriken. Hans Osquar Gustavsson and Siggvard Lenngren.

Hemlighteta Arne Frick.

Saab Veterarerna Arkiv.

Grattis Saan 60 Ar! Hans O. Gustavvsson, Corren, Ostergotlands storsta 8 June 2007.

Personal interviews, correspondence and conversations with E. Carlsson, B. Envall, D. Bedelph, P.-B. Elg, P. Johansson/T. Floden, R. Morely, C. Partington, A. Rosset, A. Sutcliffe, S. Wade, Saab Owners Club UK, Saab Owners Club France, Saab Veterans Club.

Brochures and advertisements from Saab AB 1950–2012.